S A L I N A S

SALINAS

a HISTORY *of* RACE *and* RESILIENCE
in an AGRICULTURAL CITY

CAROL LYNN McKIBBEN

STANFORD UNIVERSITY PRESS
Stanford, California

STANFORD UNIVERSITY PRESS
Stanford, California

Printed in the United States of America on acid-free, archival-quality paper

Library of Congress Cataloging-in-Publication Data
Names: McKibben, Carol Lynn, author.
Title: Salinas : a history of race and resilience in an agricultural city / Carol Lynn McKibben.
Description: Stanford, California : Stanford University Press, 2022. | Includes bibliographical references and index. |
Identifiers: LCCN 2021021372 (print) | LCCN 2021021373 (ebook) | ISBN 9781503629455 (cloth) | ISBN 9781503629912 (paperback) | ISBN 9781503629929 (ebook)
Subjects: LCSH: Agricultural laborers—California—Salinas—History. | Agriculture—California—Salinas—History. | Salinas (Calif.)—Race relations—History. | Salinas (Calif.)—Social conditions. | Salinas (Calif.)—Economic conditions.
Classification: LCC F869.S17 M34 2022 (print) | LCC F869.S17 (ebook) | DDC 979.4/76—dc23
LC record available at https://lccn.loc.gov/2021021372
LC ebook record available at https://lccn.loc.gov/2021021373

Cover photos: (top) Main Street, Salinas. Courtesy of the Salinas Public Library. (bottom) Cesar Chavez, UFW Farmworker's Rally in Salinas Valley, ca 1970. Courtesy Monterey Herald Photo Archive.

Cover design: Rob Ehle

Text design: Kevin Barrett Kane

Typeset at Stanford University Press in 11.5/14 Centaur MT Pro

For my beloved granddaughter,
MADELEINE ROSE BRUSCA

Table of Contents

Acknowledgments

Every book is a lonely enterprise but completing a book project is never accomplished alone. Rather, it is always a collaborative effort, and this one is no exception. I am deeply and forever grateful for so many people. I received generous institutional assistance from Stanford University's Bill Lane Center for the American West, the Urban Studies program, and the History Department. I thank Bruce Cain, Michael Kahan, Zephyr Frank, Richard White, and my Stanford colleagues and friends. Kris Kasianovitz, head of the Social Sciences Resource Group at Stanford Library, was incredible, as always—helping me understand and navigate government documents and census data and I thank her.

I am enormously grateful to my editor, Margo Irvin, at Stanford University Press, whose steady guidance, patience, and enthusiasm gave me the strength to persevere and to see this project to completion, and to Cindy Lim, who gave me much needed help as the project came to an end. Most importantly, I thank Jennifer Gordon, whose meticulous copyediting made this a much better narrative throughout, and Emily Smith who guided us all.

Ray Corpuz inspired me to take on this challenging history and ensured that I received the support to do so, freeing me to follow the research trail wherever it led. He exemplifies the best about being a city manager in a racially diverse place with a complicated history and an even more complex present. He remains calm in every storm. I learned so much from his example. Along with the debt of gratitude I owe Ray for the opportunity and privilege of writing about Salinas, I am thankful for the Salinas City Councils, 2017–2021, and the city staff, especially everyone at the John Steinbeck Library and Monterey County Historical Society. I especially thank Cary Ann Siegfried, Kristan Lundquist, Mila Rianto, Eric Howard, James Perry, and Sean Briscoe for their guidance and help with sources. I also thank Eric Sandoval for helping me understand how infrastructure really works in cities.

Ruth Andresen guided me and supported me from the inception of this project to its completion. She opened doors to research, introduced me to important narrators from every community in Salinas, and provided insights, stories, and memories that helped me understand Salinas's history through the lens of one of its most critical actors. Her keen powers of observation, sharp wit, amazing resilience, and great sense of humor kept me going even when I struggled. I will never be able to repay her for her love and kindness. Her example will guide me for the rest of my life.

Thom Taft traveled the path of history with me, sharing his insights, memories, and experiences. His amazing organizational ability and help in navigating archives in Salinas were invaluable. Without his support, this book could not have been written.

Robert and Peter Kasavan were great advocates for this project from the outset and provided much needed insight and help in research. Jackie Cruz gave me vital assistance in creating partnerships with students at Hartnell Community College.

Claudia Meléndez has been a guiding light, a true collaborator in writing, a sharp and honest critic. I am enormously grateful for her expertise and her friendship. I also thank Royal Calkins for his timely critique and *Voices of Monterey Bay* for exemplifying good history and great journalism.

Asian experiences became central to this book. I thank Susan Aremas, Ron Cacas, Linda Gin, Mas and Marcia Hashimoto, Jean Vengua, and members of the Asian Cultural Experience who shared insights and experiences, past and present. They all provided guidance on the important roles that the multiple Asian communities played throughout Salinas's history.

Everett Alvarez Jr. spent hours making the history of Alisal come alive for me. He is a war hero and an enormously generous soul. I thank him.

Diego Ruiz inspired me to focus this book on race relations in Salinas from the very beginning. He and so many other students at California State University, Monterey Bay, and Hartnell Community College entrusted me with powerful narrative experiences. I am humbled by their collective sense of hope and optimism in an almost overwhelming environment, especially in the wake of a pandemic that debilitated Salinas and so many other minority-majority communities in California and the nation.

Bill Ramsey showed me boundless grace and generosity throughout this entire process. His clear insights about life in Salinas and the agricultural industry and his vivid memories are everywhere in this book. I thank him. I also thank Tom Nunes and the Nunes family, Lorri Koster, Abby Taylor-Silva, Terry O'Connor, Margaret D'Arrigo, Pam Young, and the hundreds of narrators from the Grower-Shipper Association and the agricultural community who generously shared stories about agriculture in Salinas. Jim Bogart became a trusted narrator and graciously gave me access to the enormous amount of material located in the archives at the GSA. I thank you all.

Lucy Pizarro provided an important window into Mexican American life in Salinas, and the Chicano/a civil rights movement in particular. Through her I met hundreds of other activists and participants from the UFW who showed me the lasting impact of the farmworker movement on city life. I thank the entire Pizarro family, and especially Mariela Pizarro, my Stanford student and research assistant par excellence, who brought me into the fold of her incredible family and community.

Anna Caballero, Dennis Donahue, Phyllis Meurer, Dave Mora, Simón Salinas, and so many others in public service in Salinas provided me with critical insights into city politics especially during its most challenging and contentious period. I thank them for their generosity in time and their honesty in sharing stories about the politics of the past (and present).

The National Steinbeck Center generously aided in this project. I thank Director Michele Speich and her amazing staff, and Jim and Jeri Gattis, Anne Leach, and Colleen Bailey who all helped me understand this institution in the history of Salinas.

Roland De Wolk, Michael Magliari, Mary Ryan, David Vaught, and Richard White all read and provided much needed (and appreciated) feedback on the nineteenth and early twentieth centuries. I thank them. Michelle Anderson, Mark Brilliant, Matt Garcia, Mary Ann Irwin, Paul Nauert, Becky Nicolaides, Vicki Ruiz, Andrew Sandoval-Strausz, and Josh Sides generously read all or parts of this manuscript, shared insights and critiques, and guided me to make this a better book. Vicki challenged me to think deeply about race relations and racism. This book is better for their critique and contributions. Thank you.

I owe my biggest intellectual debt to Lori Flores and David Wrobel, both of whom helped me transform a rough manuscript into a polished, organized, and deeper analysis. Lori pushed me to write much more critically, especially about race relations. David gave the entire manuscript the overhaul that it sorely needed. I thank you both with my whole heart.

Raul Alcantar, Waj Chaudhry, Angie Gomez, and Matt Jacquez did the hard work of helping me prepare this manuscript for publication. I am deeply grateful for their wondrous patience, creativity, energy, and technical support.

Students from my Stanford classes on race and ethnicity in urban California, 2017–2020, constantly invigorated me. Their enthusiastic research carried me through. In particular, Azucena Marquez, my dearest student and now dearest friend—I am grateful beyond measure for your presence in my life.

I most appreciate those friends who shared this journey and gave me much needed respite from the work of research and writing. I give thanks and love to Diane Belanger, Corliss Kelly, Siobhan Greene, Rachel Holz, Ann Jealous, Charlie Keeley, Rita Patterson, Cindy Riebe, Susan Rogers, and Mary Wilcomb for all the long walks, good distractions, and talks that kept me going and made me feel energized and enriched.

My most profound thanks go to my family. I thank my dearest cousins—Janet Frazier, Susan Caliri, Terry Wheeler, Annette Luchetti, and Betty and Freddy Zambataro and all the Caliris—who gave me my understanding and love of all things agricultural. I thank my brother Howard and his family, sister Debbie, brother David, and all Copelans. I thank my extended family of Ereksons, Manwills, and McKibbens, and everyone in the Brusca clan.

My sister Laurie has been my enduring tower of strength and support throughout my life. I thank her with my whole heart.

Scott—my husband, partner, best friend, and true love—knows how much he means to me and how complete I am with him at my side.

My son Andrew is my dearest love—I will always hold you and Henry close in my heart.

I am enormously grateful for my precious son-in-law, Sam Brusca, whom I love dearly. His wit and joy and loving presence made us all a better, happier family.

My most wonderful Becky, daughter and best friend, is my model of how to be in this world, wise beyond her years, loving, kind, brilliant, and the best daughter anyone could wish for.

Finally, and most importantly, Madeleine Rose Brusca, to whom I dedicate this book. You are my hilarious bundle of love and joy. I appreciate your spirit every moment of my life. Your Nonna adores you, as you well know.

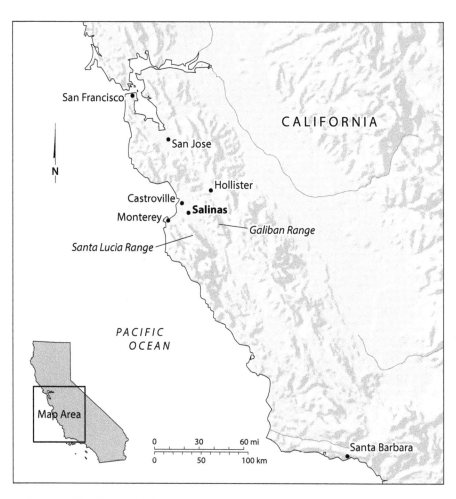

Map of Northern California

SALINAS

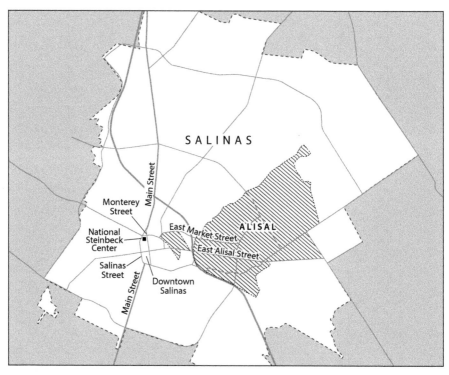

FIGURE 1.1   Map of Salinas with Alisal

INTRODUCTION

IN THE SUMMER OF 2016, Diego Ruiz gave me a tour of Alisal (also called east Salinas), a subdivision of Salinas. He showed me warrens of apartment buildings that gave way to single-family homes. We ended the tour with a stop at his home where his mother had prepared lunch for us. He lived with his parents, an older brother and sister-in-law, a toddler niece, and an adult sister. It was clear that the Ruiz family pooled resources to sustain their place as homeowners in Salinas and that they loved this city.

The Ruizes, like so many residents of Alisal in 2016, were a family of multigenerational co-residents living in a home that they owned. Diego's parents were immigrants from Mexico, and grandfathers on both sides of his family had been part of the Bracero program, also known as the Mexican National Program. The family not only felt an allegiance to Salinas but also expressed a faith in the promise of the American Dream in all its associations with property and business ownership, educational attainment, and social mobility. They wanted their subdivision to be clean, safe, and as developed as the rest of the city with modern infrastructure, housing, parks, and recreational facilities. They lamented the lack of these things but expected action from city government and believed in the possibility for improvement. They considered Alisal their permanent home: a Mexican American cultural space in everything from the people who mostly spoke Spanish, to business enterprises catering to Mexican immigrant people, to the festivals and events that brought the entire Salinas community together as an identifiable Latino/a city. I marveled at their faith—in the American Dream and in the ameliorative power of government—despite evidence all around them of persistent inequality for people of color.

Fast-forward a few months into 2016. Bill Ramsey—a long ago Alisal resident—took me on an Alisal tour too. But his feelings about this subdivision were quite different from those of the Ruizes. To Bill, Alisal represented a liminal space in Salinas, a place one might begin living as a member of the working class but would aim to escape as soon as possible. The Ramsey family arrived in Alisal from Texas at about the same time as the Ruiz family did—amid the Great Depression—and as agricultural fieldworkers, but they came as white American citizen migrants rather than noncitizen workers who would be sent back to Mexico by the U.S. government after the harvest. The Ramseys came as a family, rather than as single men as the Ruiz grandfathers had done. Although they lived in Alisal throughout the years of World War II and the postwar, moving frequently within the subdivision as their collective family economic state rose and fell, the Ramseys left Alisal permanently just a decade after first arriving when their fortunes improved enough to afford better housing in Salinas itself, as most of their white Depression era contemporaries did. Most importantly, unlike Diego's grandparents—who were forced to return to Mexico once their labor was no longer required in the fields—the Ramseys were never forced to return to Texas.

Bill Ramsey and his family became some of the most prominent Salinas residents, a position that many American migrants who hailed from the Dust Bowl region of the country also achieved within one generation.[1] The American Dream of property ownership and educational attainment came true for the Ruizes too, but they did not achieve the great wealth or standing in the community that former Dust Bowlers (as they referred to themselves) enjoyed. By the 1970s, Bill had served as president of the school board and in various capacities as a community activist and had received multiple honors for his good works and community support. In 2016, he was disturbed by the prevalence of criminal gangs in a place he loved and, like the Ruizes, by the lack of infrastructure, new housing, and recreational facilities in the subdivision of Alisal. It was difficult for Bill Ramsey and for so many of his contemporaries not to conflate the influx of Mexican American people and Mexican immigrants with the more disturbing aspects of life in Alisal in the present day. Unlike Diego and his family, who believed that government existed to help them and improve their community, Bill Ramsey's life's experience and that of his cohort was evidence to him that America afforded economic and social opportunity to anyone who worked for it, and government intervention should be kept to a bare minimum. This view of equal opportunity overlooked such government-funded subsidies as federally insured mortgages given almost exclusively to white families, and policies and practices in employment, education, and social networking awarded historically on the basis of a white racial identity.

The story of Salinas is not a simple narrative of Anglo Americans and Latinos/as, however. Salinas's multiple Asian communities—which include the Filipino/a community with both its Hispanic and Asian origins—add complexity to the politics and social order of the city (historically and in the present). The Cacas family, for example, arrived in Salinas as immigrants from the Philippines in the 1920s but acquired wealth more quickly than the Ruizes, although considerably less than the Ramseys. Originally from Alisal, the Cacas family moved into the wealthier and whiter sections of Salinas by the 1950s and shared a politics closer to the Ramseys than the Ruizes. Another example, Linda Wong Gin, traced her origins to Chinese American parents who left Monterey in the 1930s for the more welcoming environment of Salinas where they established a successful grocery store and raised four children. Linda married into a prominent, long-established Chinese American family in Salinas and became a successful banker, achieving a similar socioeconomic success as Bill Ramsey and so many other Anglo American Salinas residents. Unlike Bill Ramsey, she expressed support for the farmworker movement. But, like Ramsey, Linda Wong Gin is a philanthropist and strong advocate for the local community college's efforts to offer opportunities to all of Salinas's children.

When one looks at the city of Salinas, one sees a community divided along class and racial lines that sometimes intersect. One sees tension and struggle rather than progress or decline. Middle- and upper-class Asian, Mexican, and Anglo Americans continue to live mostly in the neighborhoods surrounding the central city, and poor and working classes of all backgrounds live in Alisal, just as they did from the late nineteenth century onward. As recent scholarship on minority-majority cities shows, the nineteenth-century origins of city-building are as important as the complex history of class and race relations for an understanding of these racially and socioeconomically diverse communities.

Andrew Sandoval-Strausz's excellent analysis of urbanization in Dallas and Chicago argued that the influx of Mexican Americans to cities throughout the country (not just the Southwest) created an urban renaissance, despite the marginalization of people of color and their exclusions in housing, education, and development. Along the same lines, Llana Barber showed how Latino/a immigrants arrived in Lawrence, Massachusetts, in the mid-twentieth century and reinvigorated a deteriorating manufacturing town. In both examples and in most scholarship on American cities that have become minority-majority Latino/a entities, Asian people are left out of the story altogether, however. Although this study also emphasizes Latino/a contributions to urban revival in Salinas (despite serious discrimination) in the twentieth and twenty-first centuries, along the lines of Sandoval-Strausz and Barber, it also shows how complicated city-building became when multiple Asian groups and Anglo Americans came together with Latinos/as to create a community based on the production of agriculture.

I begin with Indigenous People and their use of the area that became Salinas as a place for gathering food and hunting rather than settlement. I move into the nineteenth century to show the persistence of all communities in the Salinas Valley, even in the wake of Anglo American immigration. I analyze city-building that included multiple groups of Asians and women, which came about in various states of tension complicated by class divisions and events such as war, economic crisis, and sweeping demographic shifts brought on by fluctuations in immigration policy on the receiving U.S. end. Salinas fought hard to become the county seat and urban center for Monterey County and for the Central Coast region in the nineteenth century. This came with unexpected problems but also great opportunities to cope with the most profound challenges of any given year (or century).

In the first hundred years of its life as a city, Salinas built up and out—dominating the county and the region politically as the county seat and economically as an innovative agricultural center. Salinas also became the focal point for some of the most virulent labor conflicts in America, notably in 1936 and then in 1970. By the 1980s and 1990s, Salinas was beset with the same economic, social, and political catastrophes that afflicted every other city in California (and the nation) in transition from mostly white to minority-majority. The influx of poor immigrant populations in a time of national (and statewide) fiscal austerity and social and political upheaval added a level of crisis to urban America and urban California, also shared in Salinas. However, Salinas (unlike so many other minority-majority towns and cities in California and the nation) did not become either paralyzed or polarized, nor did it descend into a permanent state of economic distress. Instead, pragmatists carried the day, and the city coped fairly successfully, improving safety, education, access to public health, and greater political representation, even in the midst of economic crisis and a pandemic. This was largely because its agricultural economy sustained the city regardless of the fiscal, political, or social pressures. The transition to a Latino/a majority did not happen seamlessly, but it did happen relatively peacefully and in concert with replenished Asian and white communities that did not flee the city but continued to reside, support, and invest in it, identifying all the while as part of a greater agricultural whole.

Between 2014 and 2020, the city of Salinas became a change agent that brought its Latino/a majority into the center of its economic, political, and cultural identity, but within the complex context of Filipino/a, Japanese, Chinese, and Anglo American life. It revitalized its downtown and its outskirts. It built a new public library and broadened educational opportunities for the most vulnerable—and in so doing, provided real alternatives to the gang membership that had dominated headlines in the 1990s and early 2000s. It revamped both its police and fire departments, including women and Asian and Latino/a people in positions of authority. It no longer made the front pages of the national or local media for its high crime, violence, or racial and economic injustice as had been the case during the 1980s and 1990s. It did so not *despite* its nineteenth or early twentieth-century history, but *because* of it.

This story shows just how this version of urban life was accomplished, not by one group alone, especially not by white men only, but by a multiracial, gendered community with a shared belief in American ideals of democracy and equality, even when that belief system proved naïve or misplaced. Salinas people are pragmatists, first and foremost. Salinas is a kind of imperfect model for America in the twenty-first century—multiracial, usually respectful, and attempting to be inclusive in everything from neighborhoods to political representation but often falling short, dependent as it was (and is) on a moderate politics that accepted inequality.

This book contributes to the scholarship on California in multiple ways. It adds to our understanding of city life in the context of rural regions and agricultural economies. It shows us how city-building happened not as a linear process but in a continual and fluctuating state of struggle and tension. In this way, this narrative of Salinas adds to our understanding of race relations and racism in California cities that are in the throes of demographic change.[2]

Salinas, with a population in 2021 of nearly 160,000 (out of a total county population of over 437,000) is the most important urban center in Monterey County; it is a majority Latino/a but racially diverse city and the county seat for Monterey. It is situated at the head of the rich agricultural region known as the Salinas Valley, some 17 miles inland from Monterey Bay, 106 miles south of San Francisco, and 325 miles north of Los Angeles in the Central Coast region that stretches north to Santa Cruz and south to Santa Barbara. This region encompasses both the wealthiest places in California and the nation (Carmel, Pebble Beach, Santa Barbara) and the poorest (Seaside, Marina, small towns in the Salinas Valley). The region is defined by and identified as a place of great agricultural production and wealth and also by the poverty of immigrant Latino/a people who work in agriculture. Yet, with the exception of Lori Flores, whose analysis of Mexican immigrants and Mexican Americans in Salinas figures prominently here, Salinas and the entire Central Coast has been overlooked by scholars.[3] The complexity of race relations in urban life, but in a rural agricultural context, is told here.

Salinas was the site of some of the fiercest labor battles in American history—home to multiple racial and ethnic communities that lived side by side in a kind of complex tension, coexisting, accommodating a normative American white racial hierarchy yet nipping at its heels. Salinas shows us how a typical American city, located in a rural, agricultural setting, managed to sustain a complex social order without breaking down into violence. This is a story of struggle to get America right—socially, politically, culturally, and economically—all the while facing some of the most difficult challenges and biggest crises of American life in the twentieth and twenty-first centuries. To make sense of Salinas history and to understand its significance in the context of urban California, we need to return to its roots, even before the nineteenth-century founding of the city, in order to expose the tremendous changes over the next one hundred and fifty years that created a city known almost entirely for its twentieth-century conflicts over labor rights and race (as portrayed by John Steinbeck and Carey McWilliams and embodied in César Chávez) but not really known at all.

This story is the culmination of a thirty-year love affair with urban history as it played out on the Monterey Peninsula. My first book, *Beyond Cannery Row: Sicilian Women, Immigration, and Community in Monterey, California, 1915–99*, focused on ethnicity and gender as transformative in the development of Monterey from Steinbeck's sleepy *Cannery Row* to a full-fledged, industrialized city. My second book, *Racial Beachhead: Diversity and Democracy in a Military Town*, analyzed race relations in the development of the military town of Seaside, California—a place that became a model of socioeconomic opportunity and political inclusion for African Americans and Asian people at mid-century. This book analyses how Salinas—an agricultural and majority Latino/a city with a significant population of multiple Asian groups and Anglo Americans—evolved to confront some of the most profound challenges of the last three centuries.

The questions driving all my work (and especially this one) are all about city-building. What is a city, who creates it, and why do they do so in a particular geographic environment and at a particular moment in time? Who gets credit for its existence and its subsequent development? How is city culture invented, and why do diverse groups of people choose to join the process of city-building and identity formation? How inclusive and fluid is the process of city-building and city identity as demographics change, or as international, national, regional, and local events occur to disrupt (or accelerate) transformations in the city's economy, in its politics, and in its cultural and social life? What does it mean for a city to be marked for success or for failure, and how do its residents cope with such designations?

I was inspired to research and write about Salinas by my friend and colleague Ray Corpuz, city manager par excellence, who hailed originally from the Philippines and came to Salinas by way of city manager positions in Tacoma, Washington, and Seaside, California. Ray wanted to rectify what he believed was a grossly unfair narrative about Salinas as a place that had failed—a center of violence, poverty, and crime in which the majority of Latino/a residents faced oppression and disdain from whites and in which the Filipino/a, Chinese, and Japanese American communities no longer played any role of significance in the life of the city. Instead, he saw Salinas as a place that was thriving economically, culturally diverse in a mostly congenial political context dependent as it was on a multibillion-dollar agricultural industry that was at the forefront of technological innovation and international reach. He personified inclusion as a Filipino American head of city government. He installed women and minorities at the top of every city agency and worked with a multiracial, majority Latino/a city council that was the poster child for the political incorporation of ethnically diverse groups of people. He emphasized the multicultural aspects of the city in which every community was represented on the city's calendar of events and celebrations. We agreed that the story of Salinas was both complicated and important, and its history needed to be investigated.

I was not so sure Ray was correct about the myths concerning Salinas. It appeared to me that there was truth to those narratives of class and racial oppression, high crime and widespread violence, and also that the apparent inclusiveness might be more façade than reality. As I dug into the sources, however, I discovered more than just oppression or inclusion. I found a rich and complex history about a very diverse group of pragmatic visionaries who were Asian, Mexican, immigrant European, and southern white, women as well as men. They sometimes came together (and often came apart) over the course of two and a half centuries to create a relatively compatible community defined by their connection to agriculture and their version of an American city that they believed (often naïvely) offered the same opportunity to everyone to move up the socioeconomic ladder. They were often wrong about how fair America was either politically or economically, but their steadfast belief in the possibility of socioeconomic mobility for all kept the majority of Salinas's residents from directly challenging the racism in city life.[4]

SOURCES

I had full access to materials previously unavailable to historians and other scholars, and this book benefited enormously as a result. The Monterey County Historical Society, the Grower-Shipper Association (sometimes called the Salinas-Watsonville Lettuce Men's Association or the Grower-Shipper Vegetable Association; I use GSA throughout the book for consistency), the John Steinbeck Library, Salinas families from every ethnic and racial group, the chamber of commerce, nonprofit organizations, and the city of Salinas itself provided me with more evidence than I could possibly include here; they gave me special insight into the history of Salinas as it evolved over the course of the late nineteenth, twentieth, and twenty-first centuries. Over the course of three years, I was able to leisurely pour over manuscripts, newspapers available only in hard copy, minutes of meetings at the city council dating back to the mid-1800s, minutes from the Grower-Shipper Association meetings dating from 1930, and miscellaneous documents located in the basement of the Grower-Shipper Association and the chamber of commerce. Some of the reason that these sources remained hidden away and unavailable to scholars for so many years was simply due to disorder. Local archives lacked both funding and interest in organizing them, much less making them available for scholarly review. As well, there was always concern about what scholars might do with materials taken when no one really knew much about what was in the archive, as was the case with the Grower-Shipper Association.

Two sources in particular gave me invaluable insight. First, the minutes from the Grower-Shipper Association meetings from the 1930s until the 1936 strike were remarkably complete and unvarnished records of what was going on behind closed doors with this important organization. Before the La Follette congressional hearings (1936–1940), association members clearly believed their meetings were confidential affairs, and they spoke freely. Their views, values, and numerous disputes showed chaos within and how strategies and goals were considered and achieved. Second, the *Salinas Independent*, a self-described union newspaper, written for and by working-class residents, offered a window into perceptions, goals, and views of working-class members of Salinas of any ethnicity. They expressed a vision of the city that was surprisingly in line with the business community, but it also revealed important fissures.

Salinas is currently and clearly a Latino/a (I defer to narrators who preferred "Latino/a" to "Latinx") majority city. However, this work made Asian Americans' (Chinese, Japanese, and Filipino/a) experiences central. Asian groups lived in Salinas from its founding in the 1870s and never left. They increased in numbers over time and played an important and active role in the development of the city. Their story is as much Salinas's story as that of Anglo Americans and Mexican Americans. The narrative accounts from Salinas's Chinese American, Japanese American, and Filipino/a American residents, past and present, made a significant contribution to this story.

Memory is tricky, but perspectives matter. That is why, although so many residents and former residents were called upon to contribute their insights, comments, and revisions to this work at every stage of the research and writing, I made sure to compare and check narratives against other quantitative evidence such as census data and used contemporary newspapers

and government documents extensively throughout. I organized community events to share evidence and analysis, eliciting critiques and sometimes
surprising accounts of labor strikes and other important events in the city's
history.

The John Steinbeck Library contained a rich collection of interviews,
particularly from the 1930s, that helped enormously in piecing together
the complicated story of city-building. Meticulous analysis of city council
meetings and city documents available to me through the cooperation of
city agencies and library staff filled out the picture of urban development
and redevelopment, controversies past and present, and the struggles city
government staff and elected officials experienced as they attempted to solve
complex problems within a particular political, economic, and social context.
I tried to understand their decisions and choices on their own terms as they
grappled with some of the most pressing problems of their day.

This work benefited enormously from the expertise and generosity of
staff from Stanford University's Department of Special Collections and
especially from the expertise of Kris Kasianovitz and the Social Sciences
Resource Group. I utilized materials from the National Archives branch
in San Bruno; the University of California, Davis, Department of Special
Collections; the University of California, Berkeley, Bancroft Library; and
the California State Archives in Sacramento to add breadth and depth to
the local history collections that I drew on for this book.

A range of secondary sources helped me understand and place Salinas's
story in broader national perspective. The work of scholars in ethnic studies,
Chicano/a history, urban history, agricultural and labor history, and the history of California and the West also gave me important, broad understandings of Salinas in American historical context. Lori Flores's seminal work
on Mexican and Mexican American experience in Salinas was my starting
point and a godsend of research and analysis. This book also builds on ter-
rific new scholarship that expands the scope of analysis of urban California
from large metropolitan areas like Oakland, San Francisco, San José and the
Silicon Valley, and the Los Angeles region to look for new understandings
of past and present demographic, political, social, and economic change
in smaller towns and on the important Central Coast. Some of this new
scholarship complicates our understanding of how and why towns and cities in regional context developed as they did, for good and for ill. Some of
this important work is an indictment of past policies that gave us a new and

stubborn inequality despite a progressive political climate and investment both by government agencies and more recently by tech giants.

ORGANIZATION AND STRUCTURE

This book is divided into three parts. The three chapters of the first part—"Beginnings: Search for Order, 1850–1930"—show purpose and planning for the region from the outset—and not only by Anglo American conquest but also by Chinese settlers from nearby Monterey and San Francisco, all of whom had a vested interest in displacing former Mexican citizens and establishing an urban center connected to the financial center of San Francisco.

The first chapter, "Claiming Space, Imagining Community," explores how and why Salinas was constructed in its entirety and quickly rather than organically as a long-settled place in California. As such, it was typical of the towns and cities in California that emerged at mid-century. Building on David Wrobel's *Promised Lands,* this chapter also reveals how Anglo American boosters used newspapers and other advertisements to attract nineteenth-century white migrants and assuage their concerns about California's racially diverse population; while they were encouraging this white settlement, these promoters importantly gave minority groups just enough space for whites to take advantage of their labor in creating the city. I show here how Chinese immigrants and Chinese Americans believed that they too were accepted members of this emergent city through cultural inclusions; but power imbalances gave Anglo Americans predominance from the outset, even as other groups did their best to overcome inequality and Anglo American power structures, already in place by 1880. Building on scholarship by Peggy Pascoe, Beth Lew-Williams, Nayan Shah, and Cecilia Tsu, the chapter shows that proximity led to normative intermarriage and sex across racial lines, especially in California's agricultural regions.

Chapter 2, "Racial Crossroads," examines both the urgent city-building in Salinas and the breathtaking pace of agricultural development that funded it as the twentieth century dawned. Building on the work of Stephen Pitti, Cecilia Tsu, Erika Lee, Elliott Barkan, Dawn Mabalon, and Rick Baldoz—other scholars of immigration in California in the early twentieth century—this chapter focuses on new migrations of Asian people (Filipino/a and Japanese) but also Anglo American people, many of whom came from other areas of California (rather than abroad), as was the case in so many towns that formed a hinterland for San Francisco. This chapter also tells the story of agriculture through the Spreckels Sugar conglomerate and just how profit-able agriculture became for elites between 1880 and 1930; this wealth was built on the backs of the mostly Asian groups of different origins who did not just labor in the fields but also invented methods that created new markets for berries and lettuce (both of which surpassed sugar beets in profitability, which had, in turn, displaced wheat production). The wealth generated by new crops built Salinas, benefited whites far more than Asians, and made Salinas the undisputed urban center for the Central Coast region by 1930—a crossroads for business and commerce, state government, and even tourism. And yet, I argue here that marginalized racial groups (particularly Asians) managed to achieve some wealth through property ownership and as middle-men labor contractors; they did so in just enough numbers so as to create a sense of possibility that circumvented their challenging the structure of white supremacy that dominated California and the nation.

Salinas, from its inception, was a place that was created and sustained by people who believed in the possibility of the American Dream. As Chinese Americans, Mexican Americans, and Anglo Americans were joined by immigrants from Japan, the Philippines, southern and eastern Europe, and Anglo Americans escaping poverty elsewhere, they formed a city identity built around agricultural enterprise and claimed prominence as the urban center of the entire Central Coast region.

Chapter 3, "A Lettuce Metropolis," closes out Part I by tracing the begin-nings of lettuce production and the wealth that it generated for the city. By 1925, Salinas had the highest per capita income in the nation. It also became the backdrop for one of the most renowned and prolific American writers of the twentieth century: John Steinbeck. Winner of both the Pulitzer and Nobel Prizes in literature, Steinbeck—whose roots were in Salinas—considered this city a microcosm of America: a true reflection, warts and all, of American people and American life in the earliest decades of the twentieth century.

The three chapters of the second part of the book—"Transitions: Con-flicts and Opportunities, 1930–1965"—take the reader through the tumultu-ous mid-twentieth century of the Depression, world war, and new migrations that transformed urban California politically, socially, and economically. Chapter 4, "The Ins and Outs of Race Relations," explores complex inter-group and intragroup relationships during a period in California (and in American history) when massive new migrations of people from the southern states, Europe, Asia, and Latin America impacted cities and rural areas in new ways. Radical labor organizing and backlash against immigration made front-page news and led to new policies, including the harsh 1924 Immigration Act that eliminated all immigration from Asia and severely restricted it from other parts. At the same time, minority groups adapted in strategic ways to counter the hostility directed against them. Social class always mattered. This chapter focuses on the Filipino/a community, particularly middle-class women, and the ways they claimed space in city culture, but it also analyzes communities of Japanese and southern Europeans to show the contradictions in race relations that defined Salinas and the rest of California in the first three decades of the twentieth century.

Chapter 5 focuses on labor and the specific strike of 1936 that first brought national attention to Salinas. Although narrators who exemplified this strike commonly referred to themselves as Dust Bowlers, most were not escaping the Dust Bowl but the impact of the Depression. Most of them were not even farmers; they were laborers or small shopkeepers before migrating to California. This new population of white Dust Bowl and Depression era refugees— made famous through Steinbeck in *Harvest Gypsies*, *Of Mice and Men*, *In Dubious Battle*, and *Grapes of Wrath*—showed class conflict to be alive and well in 1930s Salinas, but I also describe here how and why class identities intersected with race and gender to make the story of labor so much more complicated than Steinbeck depicted. Steinbeck and Carey McWilliams needn't have feared that a permanent caste system would develop based on class alone as whites would quickly move up the class ladder in the aftermath of that strike, even papering over their own mistreatment by elites in the agricultural industry. I also explain in this chapter how class divisions within Japanese and Filipino/a American communities thwarted any nascent effort to challenge white supremacy by their members. Middle-class Asian American labor contractors sided with growers here as they did elsewhere, linking this history more clearly to Cecilia Tsu's work on the Central Valley. Thus, in the 1930s the general population of Anglo Americans allowed non-white groups of mostly Asian and Mexican descent just enough space in city life to keep the peace; the power structure that was, first and foremost, built on racial exclusion made room for enterprising whites (even from the Dust Bowl regions), and it allowed just enough space to appease Japanese, Chinese, Latino/a, and Filipino/a American aspirants to the middle class. This strategy became the basis for the city's organization and development going forward and precluded a more radical politics from taking root in Salinas. This is what happened in the rest of America too.

Chapter 6 zeroes in on World War II and its impact on Salinas, and it also brings the postwar into the story. First, the war drew poor whites, Filipino/a Americans, Chinese Americans, Mexican Americans, and Anglo Americans into the mainstream of Salinas almost overnight, as soldiers and Americans united—against the Japanese. In this chapter, I tell that story of incarceration and how Japanese Americans felt about it and responded, both during and after the war. I make clear in this chapter that the trauma had long-term implications for the city. Asian communities in Salinas paid attention to what happened to the Japanese during the war years, which affected their collective decisions to refrain from political activism both during and following World War II.

This chapter includes the story of labor and the Mexican Farm Labor Program, also known as the Bracero program. Through the material from the Grower-Shipper Association, we see here how concepts of immigrant labor change from Salinas resident-in-the-making to commodity. I analyze how and why everyone in agriculture (growers, shippers, marketing people, and even residents only tangentially associated with food production) thought of Braceros as merely temporary (hence the term "guest worker"), not people who might join their ranks someday (as white southern migrants did) or at least become integral to Salinas's diverse demographic landscape, as Asian and earlier Mexican American migrant groups had been. By contrast, Braceros were considered disposable and interchangeable, as painfully clear accounts from GSA records and correspondence showed. Many Braceros, like the Ruiz family, returned to Salinas and raised families. Their descendants have not forgotten how their grandfathers were treated and bear scars from that today, as narrators poignantly told me. I weave their stories into this section.

I end this chapter with an analysis of immigration policy in the postwar that lifted quotas on Asians by 1965, both replenishing and splitting Filipino/a, Chinese, and Japanese American communities within Salinas between those who arrived in the first half of the century, some tracing their family roots to the late nineteenth century, and those who arrived in the postwar era, during a more liberal immigration policy and better relations with Asia at the national level. I argue here that these new, better educated, and wealthier immigrants challenged long-established minority communities in Salinas in ways that shook up the assumption of homogeneity. It was not just a façade of harmony between groups, especially between whites and minorities, that needs exposure and analysis; it was also a papering over of fissures within communities, especially over class divides, that requires explanation. Inclusion was based on an acceptance of cultural difference at the expense of real social, political, economic equality. The façade held because enough members of a given group acquired status in Salinas's middle class to create the sense of possibility, a myth reinforced with new immigration of well-educated Asian professionals who succeeded economically into the wealthy class, lived in white neighborhoods, and associated socially with other elites.

Part III focuses on the transformative postwar to the present. Chapter 7, "Expansion, Activism, and Civil Rights," analyzes the impact of the annexation of Alisal in 1963, which doubled both the city's population and boundaries; the annexation was based on Salinas residents' new appreciation of Alisal's population as majority white and economically stable. The idea that Alisal (or east Salinas, as it was also commonly referred to) was only a destination for migrant laborers had ended by the postwar period. Salinas's leadership and the bulk of its population engaged in a concerted effort to annex the area in order to profit from its people and its growing economy.

This chapter also shows how Salinas's business class sought to do more than just add to the city's geography and population base. They invited large corporations and industries into the city, utilizing Salinas's unique geography (an urban center without contiguous borders connecting it to any other municipality) to add tax revenue to the city's coffers and ensure year-round, long-term employment. However, the dark side to their plan was industrial pollution, which generated a vigorous response from Salinas's middle class—mostly women environmental activists. Theirs was part of a larger national movement that forced new regulation on oil and gas companies, as well as on industries generally by the 1970s.

Finally, and most importantly, Chapter 7 examines the United Farm Workers (UFW) movement in Salinas and in the context of these other developments and activism. The farmworker movement was one of the most important civil rights struggles of our time. As with the 1930s labor rights struggles, César Chávez and the UFW made Salinas (along with Delano, California) infamous in the same way it had been in 1936—for its mistreatment of working classes. The UFW sought the support of Asian groups in the city, but these groups, at least collectively, refrained from doing so (individuals from all groups were vocal supporters of the UFW). I show here how the entire city became involved in the UFW, for and against, and the impact this movement had on Salinas.

Chapter 8, "Politics and Empowerment in a New Era," concentrates on the period following legislative successes made possible by UFW activism, when agriculture became highly industrialized and even more profitable; it also became truly global in its reach, marking Salinas as a critical food producer in the world. The new political players who came out of the UFW Chicano/a civil rights movement disrupted city government—not by knocking out the old political elite but by accommodation, persuasion, and moderation, still making incremental (yet important) changes in governance and representation. Cultural demonstrations of inclusion and access to economic mobility through property ownership and the establishment of small businesses continued to be the hallmark of Salinas's response to racial tensions. The history and development of the National Steinbeck Center is included in this chapter as the city coped with the severe challenges of fiscal belt-tightening, environmental crisis, and tax revolts by investing in a reinvigorated Main Street, with the National Steinbeck Center as anchor.

Chapter 9, "Agricultural and Urban: Salinas in the Twenty-First Century," explores Salinas's battles over the rise in gang violence and high crime rates, similar to that of other minority-majority cities in the 1990s. The willingness to make changes at both micro and macro levels, while not always successful, did much to assuage even the harshest critics of policing as we entered the twenty-first century. The city's focus on educational opportunity became the centerpiece of its strategy to confront and confound gang activity and to peacefully transition to a Latino/a majority city. The emergence of tremendous philanthropic support for the local community college (Hartnell) and the new California state college (California State University, Monterey Bay) located nearby provided youth in Salinas access to socioeconomic mobility through educational attainment. Farmworkers still suffer enormously in Salinas, but young people benefit from the investment in education that allows them to leave the fields for better employment, both in and out of agriculture.

That said, the largesse of the philanthropists is still largesse. It is based on a concept of white supremacy and tolerance of others, rather than genuine equality. The new Latino/a majority became the face of Salinas through political representation, but there remains a glaring lack of representation of nonwhite groups (other than a very few Asians) in the elite echelon of agriculture, now referred to as AgTech (to highlight its connections to Silicon Valley), which can be seen as a darker side of Salinas's historical pattern of inclusion without actual challenge to structural, pervasive racism. Salinas, in a nutshell, is an example of how and why racism proved to be so persistent in American life.

The COVID-19 pandemic exposed the fissures in Salinas's strategy of cultural and limited economic inclusion that kept minority populations, especially farmworkers, living on shaky and tenuous ground—aspirants to middle-class life but also dependent on service economies that evaporated with the pandemic. Yet, nonprofits once again stepped up to play an important role in coping with this new public health crisis, and formerly white-dominated organizations such as the Grower-Shipper Association became more representative, including selecting a Mexican American president.

Salinas remains the urban mosaic it always was, making space culturally, politically, and even economically for a diverse, stable, and conservative middle class. Salinas never erupted in the racial and class conflict that disrupted other municipalities in the country in 2020, which may not necessarily be either a model going forward or a good thing. In Salinas, agriculture was the glue that held everyone and everything together: a compelling economic driver that allowed younger generations access to jobs and mobility and blurred the dichotomy between what was rural and what was urban in American life.

We know a great deal about urban/suburban and exurban spaces in this country. Much scholarship has been devoted to manufacturing cities and the high tech regions that command attention today. However, we tend to caricature (and ignore) places that are rural, particularly in agricultural zones outside of major municipalities. The myth that people living in rural communities are backward in their thinking, fearful, and resistant to change is misleading, simplistic, and offensive. This unfortunate view of rural Americans prevents us from fully understanding the deep complexities of whatever we define as the American character and hinders our efforts to create good policy and more equitable and sustainable communities as a result. However, forward-thinking agriculturalists in the Central Coast region, with Salinas as the urban center, offer both new ways of understanding the rural past, not as separate from what was and is urban, but as integral to it.

Salinas became the epicenter of regional agricultural achievement with a global reach. This book is an effort to explain why that matters in understanding California and America, past and present. Beginning in the mid-nineteenth century and extending into the present day, the city of Salinas became one of the most critical centers of agricultural innovation in California and the nation, and as such it offers us a lens with which to understand California's (and the nation's) story in all of its wonderful complexity, weaving the wide variety of ethnic group histories into a comprehensive account of city-building. Like Steinbeck's novels, this story is an effort to show how Salinas became America in a teardrop and how an understanding of its history offers a way forward in the tumultuous present that is riven by racial strife, political polarization, environmental catastrophe, and rampant inequality.

PART I

Beginnings

Search for Order, 1850–1930

FIGURE 1.1   Main Street in Salinas, north of Gabilan Street, 1900
COURTESY MONTEREY COUNTY HISTORICAL SOCIETY.

CHAPTER 1

Claiming Space, Imagining Community

[The entire Salinas Valley] is a long narrow swale between two ranges
of mountains, and the Salinas River winds and twists up the center
until it falls at last into Monterey Bay. . . . [T]he Gabilan Mountains
to the east of the valley were light gay mountains full of sun and
loveliness. . . . The Santa Lucias stood up against the sky to the west
and kept the valley from the open sea . . . unfriendly and dangerous.

John Steinbeck, *East of Eden*, p. 3.

PERHAPS NO ONE DESCRIBED the geography of Salinas better than
John Steinbeck in those opening lines of his 1952 novel *East of Eden*. Steinbeck described Salinas circa the 1930s and 1940s as a slice of rural, agricultural California that included Yankee settlers, Indigenous People, former
citizens of Mexico, Chinese immigrants, and Chinese Americans. Steinbeck did not mention Filipinos/as or Japanese settlers in his work, but
they were present in early twentieth-century Salinas too. The story of Salinas is a story of all the complex relationships between groups who built
a city, beginning with Ohlone people and the mixed-race Mexican citizens
known as Californios.

THE FOUNDING OF SALINAS

Juan Bautista Castro (1835–1915, founder of Castroville) came from a Californio padrone culture. He presided over a contingent of dependents who looked to him for everything from employment to housing to serving as the final arbiter of disputes. However, by the end of the 1870s, he symbolized a way of life that was fast becoming obsolete. Yankee mores predominated, which disregarded so many of the traditions that Juan Castro exemplified and held dear. Newcomers from the eastern United States seeking riches in the gold fields and in agriculture overwhelmed Californios like Castro. New Anglo American settlers eager to seize control after the Mexican-American War ended in 1848 disdained Californio cultural customs and wantonly seized Californio property up and down the state, casually (and often illegally) appropriating even the commons, or pueblo lands, for their own use and profit, marginalizing Mexican people both politically and economically and in short order. Indigenous People, who had been exploited and oppressed by Mexican settlers like Castro in earlier decades, remained in these places too and often claimed Mexican heritage to escape attacks from whites, which were common occurrences in nineteenth-century California, leading to enormous population decline.[1]

Nonetheless, Castro ignored Anglo Americans' disrespect. Like so many other Californios, he shared their big dreams of wealth, lobbying the Southern Pacific Railroad giants to make his land a railroad stopping point, which would bring him both prestige and riches. Elected to the Monterey County Board of Supervisors in 1872, Castro used county funds to build homes for anyone who agreed to settle in his newly named town of Castroville so that "the railroad people would see" Castroville as a viable community that deserved their attention and investment.[2] However, he lost the battle for supremacy over other developing towns in the region. Bypassed by railroad giants, Castroville never achieved any significant status, investment, or population growth.

Salinas, on the other hand, came together fully formed and predominated as the political and economic power center for the region by the 1880s. It was the embodiment of the collective effort of ambitious entrepreneurs who were laser focused on acquiring both economic and political dominance. Located in a literal swamp, Salinas (Spanish for salt marsh), encapsulated all that defined western urban development in the nineteenth and twentieth centuries. In this new world, city-building was hard work that needed luck and shared purpose so that it could potentially overcome harsh barriers of class, race, cultural differences, and stark gender roles. It needed commitment, determination, and resolve often in the face of considerable geographic challenges, as Steinbeck's passage from *East of Eden* suggests. This place was one of awesome beauty and majesty but hardly inviting as a place for settlement. Still, like other places in California and the West, Salinas was meant to be both a "central and centralizing" point in the region.[3]

Salinas, not Castroville, became the poster child for nineteenth century city-building on the Central Coast of California. Ambitious settler colonialists worked in collaborative enterprise to make Salinas into an incorporated city, the county seat, and the urban center for one of the most agriculturally productive regions in California, all in the space of eight years, from 1866 to 1874. They were women and men, whites, Mexicans, and Asians, immigrants and migrants from all over California and the nation, some well connected and others penniless, all bent on claiming space and creating a city. African Americans came to California and the West during this period too, both in rural and urban regions and to what would become Monterey County. However, they largely settled in the city of Monterey and its subdivisions instead of Salinas in order to work in the developing fishing industry rather than in agriculture. This is not to say that no African Americans lived and worked in Salinas, but that they did not settle in large enough numbers to establish a significant community.[4]

White settlers, arriving in the 1860s, described the area that would become the incorporated City of Salinas as an "uninhabited valley floor." It was hardly that. Ohlone peoples occupied the region for millennia and utilized it for crucial hunting, fishing, and the gathering of an incredible diversity of plants for food and medicine, at least until the Spanish arrived to disrupt their communities and force them into service as laborers for the missions.[5] The new Mexican government (1821–1848), which Juan Castro represented, divided this and most of California into vast rancheros that created a profitable cattle industry connected to global markets, absorbing Indigenous People into their communities mostly as laborers and often as little more than slaves.[6] Multiple mixed-race people contributed to the demographic pool that made up the entire region in the nineteenth century.[7] However, in the eyes of the mostly Anglo American colonialists who arrived in the wake of the end of the Mexican-American War and the California Gold Rush, the entire area looked empty: It lacked white American settlement and did not resemble the towns and cities emerging either in the East at that time or on the coast of California, such as San Francisco, Monterey, Los Angeles, Santa Barbara, and San Diego.[8]

As Steinbeck describes, the location that would become Salinas was an area situated in between two mountain ridges, the inviting Gabilan range to the east and the more forbidding Santa Lucia mountains to the west. The Santa Lucias blocked the way to the ocean and to Monterey: one of California's most prominent towns, the county seat and the capital of Mexican California from 1776 to 1846. It was also the site of the 1850 California Constitutional Convention. Salinas, "the largest of the inter-mountain valleys of the coast regions, being about one hundred miles long by from six to ten miles wide," showed great promise as productive farm land: "A great body of bottom land lies below and northward from the Salinas hills extending up to the extreme end of the county, an area of approximately five hundred square miles, broad and level, and so fertile that it has been spoken of as The Valley of the Nile."[9] Nineteenth-century horticulturalists looking to farm and settle found the Salinas Valley enormously attractive.

However, the location of the city itself was more of a mystery. Salinas was described as "a fine place for ducks and mosquitos but not for homes."[10] By contrast, the area known as Alisal located in the uplands on high, dry ground was much more hospitable as a potential township. Alisal had a long history of human settlement reaching back thousands of years. Like other Mexican land grants, Alisal, once property of the Catholic Church, was given to R. M. F. Soto by the newly independent state of Mexico sometime in the 1830s. Soto "owned the town of Santa Rita or New Republic as he called it," within this territory.[11] The Mexican government's Secularization Act of 1833 had removed control of approximately one-sixth of what is now the state of California from mission priests and transferred that property to private citizens in hopes that the colonialist enterprise would cement Mexican claims and protect the territory from incursions by Americans and Europeans. Newly arrived Anglo Americans appropriated these areas in the years following the 1848 Mexican-American War, claimed and divided them, and established towns and cities out of pueblos and ranchos up and down the state of California.

After California's statehood in 1850, Monterey County—like every other region in Northern California—was organized into American-style towns, one of which was Alisal. By 1858, Alisal had a school with 242 students, and by 1866 it had a post office.[12] It might have made sense to build Salinas on this already-established township as so many other Anglo American municipalities did. For example, Yankee settler colonialists supplanted Mexican missions-presidios-pueblos in Monterey, San José, San Francisco, Santa Barbara, Los Angeles, and countless other California towns and cities. And at first, this is exactly what happened.

Some Monterey settlers aimed to create an American town in the Salinas Valley in Alisal.[13] Together—W. S. Johnson: "one of our ablest citizens who drew up the incorporation papers for Alisal and worked as an appraiser and a clerk for the Salinas city bank"; M. C. Ireland: "one of the large ranch owners, and former assembly member and supervisor who eventually lost everything and wound up working for David Jacks poisoning squirrels"; Samuel Irvine: one of the first storekeepers in the Salinas Valley; George Pomeroy: known as a prankster but also a rancher who once owned Bardin and Anderson family land; S. B. Gordon: also a large property owner from Monterey; and Henry Mead: a storekeeper from Castroville who refused to support Juan Castro in his bid to wrest the county seat for Castroville—all teamed up to appropriate the former Mexican land and "build the town on the high, well-drained ground" of Alisal. They incorporated as The Alisal Homestead Association and began to build homes and businesses in the vicinity of Natividad "which had long been a hamlet before any other town was thought of in the Salinas Valley."[14]

They raised the necessary funds. "The capital stock was $100,000, divided into 10,000 shares of $10 each." Moreover, besides the goal of town building, these immigrant entrepreneurs stated in their incorporation records that they also meant to "take all lawful means to take the county seat of Monterey for Alisal." They had a plan to make that happen:

> To donate of said land as much as would be necessary for the erection of all public buildings in case the county seat was changed; also to donate to the Southern Pacific Railway or any other railroad, all the lands required for depots, buildings, and secure free rights of way to and from said town of Alisal. Finally to immediately make contingent contracts for acquiring a large section of land on the Alisal Rancho.[15]

However, their collective ambition to make Alisal the urban center for the region ultimately failed, just as Castro's had, undermined by the original owner, R. M. F. Soto. Soto, who still controlled much of the Alisal rancho in the 1860s, intervened with Southern Pacific to undercut the efforts of these Anglo Americans in order to secure the profit for himself: "The reason Alisal is not a large thriving city now [rather than Salinas] is because fate stepped in. The Southern Pacific Company wanted to run its line from Castroville along the high land [to miss the swamps and sloughs of Salinas Valley] until Soledad was reached." But, "Soto tried to make the S.P. company pay for the rights of way over his property and some of the other land that he controlled."[16] It was not "fate that stepped in," however, but Soto's apparent overreach. Still, Soto's effort showed that Californio landowners from the Mexican state did not just quietly acquiesce to the Yankees but worked as hard as their contemporary Anglo American counterparts to maintain power in a rapidly changing political environment. They fought for exactly the kind of economic control that white settlers demanded and resisted efforts to become sidelined by the new arrivals from either Monterey or San Francisco.

However, in this case, instead of Alisal or Castroville as a regional center and site for a Southern Pacific Railroad stop, Salinas City, located in a swamp, became the urban center for the entire area. Mostly Anglo American migrants from San Francisco overpowered the Spanish, Mexican, and Indigenous People and also brought in new immigrants from Asia and Europe to claim Indigenous- and Mexican-owned land, although not without sustained resistance.[17] According to the *Salinas City Index* under the headline "Commendable," "settlers [from all over the region arrived in the new town of Salinas] . . . which . . . will effect a desireable [sic] increase in population . . . which will add to the value of the land and the wealth of the country."[18] One can only imagine how overwhelming these new migrations must have been to the people who traced their family roots in the Salinas Valley back for centuries.[19]

Those new settlers were not all white or of European origin, however, even though the term "desireable" meant exactly that.[20] Chinese people became the single largest group of foreign-born Californians by 1852, making up 10 percent of the total non-Indigenous population; they came to Salinas by way of both San Francisco and Monterey in large enough numbers to form a conspicuous community all their own by the 1880s. After being driven out of the mines in the 1850s, railroad companies hired Chinese contract laborers to construct a system of complex railroad lines that would link

California to the rest of the country in the 1860s and 1870s. Like their Anglo American counterparts, Chinese migrants remained in place after the railroad systems were completed, participating in the settler colonial project of taking over land owned by Mexican nationals, albeit as a despised minority group that frequently faced dispossession and violence from white settlers, including in Monterey County.[21]

In Southern California, Anglo American immigrants coerced both Mexican and Indigenous People (Californios) into barrios and Chinese people into Chinatowns when they transformed Mexican pueblos into American towns and cities by the 1880s.[22] Segregation practices targeting Mexicans and Chinese people forced both groups into the poorest neighborhoods in cities throughout California over the course of the twentieth century, strengthened by increasingly rigid zoning laws that located environmentally damaging industries in these places too. In Northern California towns and cities, the distance from Mexico kept the Mexican population low so the influx of Anglo Americans and other groups after the Gold Rush meant that until new migrations of Mexicans in the 1930s, the population of Mexican people diminished considerably and quickly.[23] In the new agricultural town of Salinas, whites established boundaries between both Mexican and Asian groups; nonetheless, both Asians (Chinese) and Mexicans participated fully in the enterprise of city-building, even though the Anglo Americans who documented the city's history did not acknowledge their contributions.[24]

Nineteenth-century San Franciscans (and new arrivals to Monterey County) also realized the advantages of establishing an independent municipality in the Salinas Valley as an important strategy for developing a regional outpost that at once reinforced the growth of San Francisco, which had become the preeminent financial and marketing center of the West by the 1860s, and also gave resourceful Americans opportunities to prosper as landowning horticulturalists.[25] However, these landowning horticulturalists would not live in isolation from one another on distant family farms but together in towns and cities, and they would collaborate in the city-building enterprises that the *San Francisco Chronicle* breathlessly applauded as a central feature of Anglo American cultural hegemony in California. Mayors, city councils, commissions, women's and men's civic organizations all combined to create downtowns and establish businesses, construct streets and sidewalks, build schools and infrastructure—and collect taxes that might fund everything.[26] Ambitious women and men of diverse ethnic and racial groups competed with other emerging towns for precedence and prestige.

For their part, political and business elites in San Francisco understood that their rapidly growing city needed two things to achieve genuine prosperity in the 1860s. First, San Francisco required critical links in transportation to connect to markets by land (San Francisco was already connected by sea). Second, substantial regional resources (water and food) were essential to sustain its population, which was expanding exponentially in the late nineteenth century.[27] Therefore, in the aftermath of the war with Mexico (1846–1848), the Gold Rush (1849), and the Civil War (1861–1865), the Salinas Valley became an important area that drew the attention and investment of people connected to San Francisco. San Franciscans hoped that the establishment of sustainable urban centers such as Salinas might lead to their own enrichment as well as supporting the regional development that would benefit San Francisco's rapid population growth.[28]

The first settlers of Salinas needed as many people as possible to drain the swamps and create a town. A diverse collection of individuals acquired land and thrived economically. Among the first to arrive were Chinese immigrants and Chinese Americans who began reclaiming swampland and carving out a city. The land reclamation undertaken by Chinese laborers to clear and drain the swamps, including Carr Lake that surrounded the town, became a major contribution to the agricultural and subsequent financial success of the city of Salinas during the 1870s and 1880s. Chinese immigrants to the Salinas Valley negotiated five-year leases that allowed them to cultivate the land in exchange for their labor in clearing it for city-building; these agreements demonstrate how the immigrants navigated the discriminatory landowner-ship policies imposed on them and achieved a measure of economic gain.

Arduous labor was required to build Salinas. Initially, the immigrants had to clear the forest—including removing tree roots with primitive spades and breaking apart peat soil in the process. And draining the swamps also involved exterminating the rodent populations that proliferated there. It was only after two or three years of hard work that they could plant potatoes, yams, and sugar beets to further break up the soil and make a profit that would allow them some return on their labor. The land was ultimately returned to the white landowner, but by the time the Chinese laborers had completed their work, its value had increased considerably from approximately $28 an acre in 1875 to $100 an acre two years later; and the Chinese workers found a way to accumulate some wealth for themselves.[29] In the face of consistent and outrageous limits on their freedom and severe racial discrimination on the part of whites, Chinese people nonetheless prospered economically through creative use of the land they were allowed to cultivate. They made it profitable, despite the odds, which gave them opportunities in Salinas for further investment.

Although Salinas's non-Chinese residents never considered Chinese people equal partners in the enterprise of city-building, they were. Salinas's non-Chinese residents shared the xenophobia and racism of their day even as they acknowledged the need for many hands to create their city. William Henry Leach, one of Salinas's earliest settlers and the father of Dr. Edmund J. Leach (who served on the Salinas City Council and two terms as Salinas's mayor), gave a speech in 1888 conflating support for tariffs on wheat and wool (that he believed would protect California's farmers and ranchers from unfair competition from Australia and Europe) with the elimination of any further Chinese immigration. "The Chinese must go," he argued, like so many of his contemporaries in that era. He and so many other policymakers and Americans generally (led by Californians) believed that economic disaster would result if "the free trade policy of England be adopted in the U.S.," which included importing foreign labor, particularly Chinese immigrant workers who were willing to work for lower wages. "American labor and American industries [should] be protected," he proclaimed in his unsuccessful bid for Congress.[30]

Although the 1868 Burlingame-Seward treaty ensured protections for Chinese immigrants, political and labor unions combined to support stringent racially based restrictions for Chinese workers, who were often described at the time as a "degraded race." When prominent Salinas landowner C. D. Abbott was criticized for hiring Chinese workers on his ranch and accused by anti-immigration agitators of being a "Chinaman-lover," he angrily responded by saying, "I have no choice, white men refuse to work up to their knees in the water, slime, and filth of the sloughs,"[31] which was hardly a ringing endorsement for the Chinese people who had done so much to make settlement in Salinas possible; yet Abbott's comment revealed that on ranches and farms, workers of various racial groups lived in close proximity with one another creating a world far different than the one evolving in towns and cities outside of agricultural regions. Although Chinese people were forced into racially restricted spaces in Salinas (like every other town and city in California), they could not be segregated into Chinatowns on the ranches and farms adjacent to the city—those ranches and farms that supported Salinas's growth and development and shaped the city's identity, first and foremost, as an urban center for an agricultural area with racially diverse populations.

Thus, as a consequence of deliberate planning, happenstance, and some maneuvering from a variety of competitive actors, Salinas sprang up almost overnight as a fully formed township, rather than emerging organically over many decades or building on prior Indigenous, Spanish, and Mexican settlements—like Castroville, Alisal, Monterey, San José, Santa Barbara, San Juan Bautista, and other pre–Gold Rush communities that were first founded as missions and presidios in the seventeenth century. However, just like the towns emerging in Contra Costa County to the north and so many spaces circling San Francisco, new settlements comprised of diverse ethnic and racial groups dotted the entire area that became the Central Coast region by the late nineteenth century. Like other agriculturally dependent towns, Salinas merged what was defined as rural and what was defined as urban, becoming both.

Salinas's population growth reflected the suddenness of its founding. Fifteen people lived there in 1868, but 700 did so by 1874 when it was incorporated, recognized as the county seat, and an established stop on the Southern Pacific Railroad. Although the population increased significantly to 1,854 by 1880, demographic growth remained relatively slow and steady through the 1920s. Just like other regions in Northern California, Salinas was defined by the diversity of its population. Almost from its incorporation, it was interwoven with San Francisco in everything affecting its settlement to subsequent development, yet it was rural in its feel and identity.[32] It was a farm town formulated as part of a regional and national settlement plan for Northern California with a predominantly white, native-born population that included both people newly arriving from Europe and those coming from all over California.[33] It also included populations of Californians of Mexican, Chinese, Filipino/a, and Japanese descent who arrived in the first decades of the twentieth century and who defined themselves as part of an agricultural world just as Anglo Americans did.

All these settlers were determined to remain in place—to build Salinas into a permanent community rather than allow it to become an obsolete ghost town as so many small western settlements did by the early twentieth century.[34] The flow of residents from San Francisco to Salinas sustained the connections between the cities and throughout the farming and ranching region during this period. By 1880, Salinas's population was comprised of 973 white men, 782 white women, 97 Chinese men, 5 Chinese women, and 8 "colored persons."[35] It was a white space, surely, but white included people of Mexican origin. As well, a visible and significant minority of Chinese people lived in Salinas. They had arrived both from San Francisco, just like their non-Chinese counterparts, and also from nearby Monterey, an increasingly hostile environment for them. They all made up Salinas and all created the town as a multiracial agricultural city.[36]

GRAIN

The economy of the Salinas Valley depended on ranching throughout the nineteenth century, just as was the case throughout California and much of the West during the period of Mexican settlement. "The ranchers or large landholders were cattlemen. Cattle thrived here with little or no attention. Practically the whole unfenced expanse of the Salinas Valley . . . was grazed by herds which had resulted from . . . the original stock driven up from Mexico in the days of the missions."[37] That all changed with the influx of Anglo American settlers and competition from superior breeds of cattle from the East, coupled with disastrous droughts in 1862–1864 that decimated herds and left rancho owners impoverished and indebted to American bankers and developers: "Two successive years of drought have almost swept the county clean of cattle, horses, and sheep. Out of 70,000 head of stock cattle [in Monterey County] . . . only 12,724 [were] left by 1865."[38]

At the same time, wheat and barley production in California increased dramatically as it did throughout the West. California went from exporting 74,087 hundredweights of wheat and 46,841 barrels of flour in 1855 to 4,864,590 hundredweights of wheat and 354,106 barrels of flour by 1870.[39] As rainfall increased after 1865 and agricultural production rose, California became one of the most important producers of wheat in the West, most famously engaging in international trade with Great Britain.[40]

At first, it did not appear that the Salinas Valley would join in that grain production.

No one believed that this territory would produce grain and no one wanted to run the risk of trying [until] the Campbell brothers made the attempt at growing grain, having found water and plenty of flat country. In the first year they made enough out of the venture to pay their seven years' lease on two hundred and thirty acres. This fact established the fertility of the valley.[41]

As a result of that success, although only 570 acres were devoted to wheat farming in 1857 in Monterey County, this increased to 100,450 acres by 1881. Combined with the main line of the Southern Pacific running through the town, Salinas "became the center for the shipping of a vast amount of Salinas Valley grain [by the 1880s]."[42]

Improvements in harvesting grain largely made increased production possible. According to numerous local histories of agriculture in the Salinas Valley, technology led to ever-increasing yields: "The Great Western harvester enters a field of twenty-five acres in the morning and at night the grain lies in neat bags—mowed, thrashed, cleaned and stacked."[43] Steam power replaced horsepower during this era, making grain production even more profitable and extensive. By the 1880s, wheat grown in the Salinas Valley no longer had to be transported to San Francisco for processing. "In 1883 a flour mill with a daily capacity of 35 barrels was built in the new town of Salinas," and upgraded in 1885 "to give a capacity of 500 barrels, making it the largest mill in the state south of San Francisco" at that time.[44] Although very little of the grain that Salinas Valley farmers produced in the 1860s through the 1880s was meant for local consumption, Salinas Valley agriculturalists sustained the ever-growing market in nearby San Francisco, which gave them the economic security that wheat farmers in the Midwest lacked. To accomplish that, they needed the railroad: "The stimulus which the connection of Monterey County with San Francisco by rail gave to the production of grain, especially wheat, was clearly evident."[45] It also made possible the development of the town itself.

In addition to defining itself as a farming community, Salinas's founders aimed for regional dominance as the county seat, as did so many other small towns in Northern California in their respective regions.[46] As the most significant center in the county, Salinas hoped for pride of place, but most importantly for revenue from official (and unofficial) government business, from business elites looking to gather for conferences and meetings, and from visitors and tourists who might see Salinas as the major urban cultural center for Monterey County and the Central Coast region. This is why the city founders intensely lobbied the Southern Pacific Railroad for a stopover in Salinas. It is also why they devoted much time and energy into creating cultural events such as Big Week (the Salinas Rodeo) that might draw crowds who would, in turn, bring needed revenue, settlement, and recognition to their developing town. These events were first and foremost inclusive of the town's population, and as such, they served the dual purpose of tourist attraction and reinforcement of a group identity as farm and ranch folk, blurring both racial boundaries and definitions of urban and rural.

These founders' collective strategy was in keeping with nineteenth-century boosters all over California and the West who utilized the work of travel writers to encourage both white tourism and white settlement in racially diverse rural places. Rather than note racial difference, these writers treated minorities as harmless and deliberately minimized or ignored any suggestion of racial conflict, brought on by Mexican Americans and Asian groups' efforts to challenge white mistreatment and white hegemony, co-opting minorities by means of cultural inclusion (without social, economic, and political inclusion). As well, these boosters portrayed western town life nostalgically, based on cowboys, missions, and ranching culture.[47]

RAILROADS

The increasing wealth generated by agricultural development and mining in the West created an urgent need for railroads—the connective transportation thread that, in turn, made town-building and settlement possible.[48] William Cronon famously wrote in his analysis of late nineteenth-century city-building in Chicago that much of Chicago's greatness could be understood by looking at the development of the railroads that allowed surrounding environs to connect directly to markets in urban areas without relying on bodies of water, as they had for centuries. According to Cronon, "The train did not create the city by itself . . . [instead] the chief task [of the railroad] was to remake the boundary between city and country . . . opening a corridor between two worlds."[49] His view of Chicago and its surroundings applied to California generally and explained how and why its towns and cities fought so hard for inclusion into railroad systems. Salinas was one of them.

America generally experienced massive new industrialization, urbanization, and immigration in the late nineteenth century. Eastern cities like New York, Philadelphia, and Baltimore and midwestern cities like Chicago were overflowing with southern and eastern European immigrants and native-born whites and African Americans from the South and other parts of rural America. As Cronon and other scholars showed, railroads played a critical role in producing and reinforcing these drastic changes in American urban life. Similarly, railroads had a dramatic impact on rural places as well, making it possible for increases in farm acreage by 44 percent in the 1870s alone as farmers and ranchers suddenly had access to markets far away from waterways. Farmers no longer had to rely on steamships or riverboats to get their beef or grain to processing plants and markets in industrializing urban centers, but could do so from interior places, opening the Great Plains and inland California to new settlement and agricultural production.[50]

Yet, this apparent window of opportunity came at an enormous price not at all obvious at the time. As Salinas's agricultural production exploded decades later in the 1930s, Chicago controlled prices for everything from wheat to lettuce, leaving growers and shippers in the Salinas Valley vulnerable to their decisions. They had little flexibility to determine price or profit except by controlling wages for workers, which led to some of the most violent and long-standing labor disputes of the century.

The pattern of development along railroad lines led to the creation of towns based on agricultural production that fed into larger cities and market centers. In the aftermath of the Civil War, we see a gradual pattern of interconnection emerging that created farm towns that were dependent on faraway urban centers for their economic stability. American life sped up in the postbellum years and was transformed dramatically as cities and towns vied with one another for pride of place, fusing rural farmlands and farming towns with urban hubs and processing and market centers. The railroads did not create just one central city, like a Chicago, San Francisco, or even Denver or St. Louis. Rather, places designated as railroad stops rapidly grew into critical new municipalities, as smaller cities and towns within rural and agricultural zones linked with metropolitan urban centers to create an interlocking web of agricultural production, processing centers, and market hubs for the nation and, eventually, the world. None of the populations of these smaller farming and ranching towns like Salinas fully appreciated the dark side of this dependency. Boosters saw only a positive outcome in such a link. However, eventually many of the railroad towns dried up and blew away. Survival of any given municipality depended upon settlement, and towns could not sustain themselves without a critical mass of people. This national pattern played out in California as well and in Salinas in particular.[51]

FIGURE 1.2   Southern Pacific Railroad lines in California, 1915

COURTESY MONTEREY COUNTY HISTORICAL SOCIETY.

To the Anglo American settlers who arrived in the context of late nineteenth-century railroad building, California had potential as both a rural and an urban place, a land that was as ripe for city-building as it was for agricultural development and one that would be connected to major marketplaces. Migrants from the East (and from abroad) envisioned a land of cities surrounded by productive farms and ranches to support them, with each vying for precedence, without concern that interconnectivity was not created equally or that market centers might wield unlimited power over the economic viability of these smaller centers of agricultural production. No one anticipated the fallout that such interconnectivity and dependency might bring.

Like Fresno, Stockton, Visalia, and many other agriculturally based towns founded in late nineteenth-century California, Salinas was a city deliberately constructed in the immediate aftermath of the Civil War as part of an integrated regional development strategy, and as a direct result of railroad building by people, working collaboratively, who aspired to be part of a new interconnected economy and American political structure. Salinas's residents seized on the popularity and momentum of railroad building to displace Monterey as the agricultural market center for the Central Coast region. Rail, not ocean, would be the modern method of transport to carry grain and other goods to markets in San Francisco and in the East. Salinas, not Monterey, would be the epicenter. It was an ambitious strategy.

Salinas residents shared a value system based on family farm ownership, with small businesses tied to a ranching and farming economy and a stable community structure with whites at the top of the racial hierarchy. They were keenly aware of resources and how to go about increasing their wealth with ties to San Francisco, Chicago, and New York. Salinas's founders, like their counterparts elsewhere in the state, "firmly believed they were cultivating not only . . . crops, but California itself. Their mission was to promote small, virtuous communities *and* economic development,"[52] which also required acceptance by whites of the presence of diverse racial groups to ensure a relatively stable and peaceable community, nonetheless firmly entrenched in an ideology of white privilege. After all, farming and ranching needed labor, and that labor was usually provided by immigrant Asians, native-born and immigrant Mexican-origin people, and whites from southern and eastern European countries.[53]

There was little sense that there might be a downside to the combination of small market centers connected to big ones, nor was there a sense that social and racial diversity might lead to serious conflict as long as everyone believed that socioeconomic mobility was possible and cultural inclusions were maintained. Salinas's early residents expected to be part of a regional, urban world linked by the Central Pacific and Southern Pacific Railroads, which they viewed collectively as only positive. The first train from San Francisco officially arrived in Salinas in 1873.

Up and down the new state of California, each region's residents felt the same way. Connections to centers of commerce like San Francisco allowed access to regional, national, and international markets for grain, specialty crops, and livestock; there, products were processed and prices were set, sometimes to the detriment of the growers and ranchers. In fact, railroad executives themselves created towns, speculating that their success would lead to even higher profits than the railroads themselves promised.[54] Ranchos and settlements turned into towns and cities that might become important places—locales in which prospective new settlers might choose to build a home, invest in a business, establish a ranch or farm—thereby increasing population and adding both economic and political clout to areas that had only been sparsely settled by the end of the nineteenth century. The possibilities seemed endless and the stakes high, so much so that townships were established seemingly overnight as focal points on the road to financial and marketing centers.[55] But the risks were apparent from the start when prices fell for cattle or grain and when frequent fluctuations in the economy hurt everyone. Many of these places disappeared overnight as economic volatility and settlement patterns diverted populations and investment elsewhere.[56]

It was in this context that settlers of Salinas gambled on the fact that it was already a regional crossroads of sorts, on the road where mid-nineteenth-century stagecoach drivers raced to reach the halfway mark between San Juan Bautista and Monterey.[57] Together with their Anglo American counterparts, Chinese people from nearby fishing villages in Monterey County, such as Pacific Grove and the city of Monterey, stayed in the emerging town after the initial development phase; they created an ethnic network over the course of the next decades that encouraged more Chinese people to migrate out of the increasingly hostile environment of San Francisco and into the relatively peaceful (and apparently accepting) smaller milieu in the farming and ranching towns in regions outside of the city.[58] Salinas was no exception. Those who followed in the path of the original laborers were just as entrepreneurial as their Anglo American counterparts and also just as well connected to their own ethnic businesses and financial sources of support in Monterey or in San Francisco.[59] They ignored the racist attitudes of Salinas's white townspeople because they believed that there was room for them to prosper economically and to find space socially and culturally within the city.

BUILDING A CITY

Salinas's founders proceeded with urgency and determination to make Salinas into the county's regional center despite the geographic limitations of their proposed city. Eugene Sherwood—together with San Francisco merchants Alanson Riker, Elias Howe, and William Jackson—served as Salinas's first agents for Wells Fargo and Company, which opened a branch in Salinas in 1868, another demonstration of interest from San Francisco's financial community in the city's regional development.

Sherwood was a large landowner, unlike most immigrants to California in these decades, most of whom were poor squatters on Mexican-owned land. However, the fluctuations Sherwood experienced in his personal and financial life were typical for nineteenth-century Anglo Americans who were vulnerable to extreme weather patterns, rigged market forces, and political turmoil; but this did not deter him from pursuing his dream of city-building. The late nineteenth century was an era of drama and catastrophe marked by two devastating economic depressions, in 1873 and again in 1893, sending multitudes of farmers and urban workers alike into bankruptcy and poverty.[60]

In 1860, Sherwood, who was the father of seven young children, owned a 24,000-acre sheep ranch near King City. The years of floods (1861–1862) and droughts (1862–1864) that destroyed 90 percent of the Salinas Valley's cattle also ruined Sherwood's adobe home and killed off most of his sheep.[61] We see these patterns playing out throughout the West as Anglo American settlers flooded into previously undeveloped areas—cutting down trees, plowing up native grasses, and planting grain—triggering environmental catastrophes such as droughts and floods on a massive scale.[62] But instead of succumbing to misfortune, Sherwood saw a different outcome. He may not have had the same success as his contemporary Leland Stanford, but he shared a similar expansive worldview based on a sense of superiority as a white man in a diverse racially mixed milieu.[63] Salinas, in a nutshell, is what happened in California in the nineteenth century.

Sherwood and his colleagues purposefully attracted the attention of the railroad barons in a determined enterprise to recoup their losses by creating a town to serve as a major stop on the Southern Pacific's planned route to Los Angeles. They laid out a town at the Halfway House Inn, which was first owned and operated by "Deacon" Elias Howe, then, after 1865, by tinsmith and entrepreneur Alberto Trescony of Monterey. Their "town" was a half-mile square, and Sherwood named it Salinas City. Others shared Sherwood's vision and zeal for Salinas City: to collectively develop an enterprise dependent on agricultural production that would drive the area's economy—a dicey proposition at a time when the Chicago markets kept wheat farmers and cattle ranchers off balance with wild, unpredictable fluctuations in pricing.

Samuel Conklin, William Vanderhurst, and Newman Day Sanborn, along with the other first residents of Salinas, were just as driven, entrepreneurial, and prescient as Sherwood. Although oriented toward San Francisco, they ventured to Salinas with big dreams of wealth and stature. They established businesses that catered to the needs of the stagecoach drivers and passengers stopping in Salinas City for repair and refreshment. Michael Hughes set up a saddlery and harness shop in 1866. On what is now Market Street, Joseph V. Lackey founded a blacksmith and wheelwright shop. Jesse B. Iverson, James Henry McDougall, and John B. Scott started a blacksmith shop two years later. Henry Johnson opened a barbershop, and John H. Menke created the first brewery in town. The Abbott family constructed a hotel, Abbott House, later called the Hotel Cominos, and Michael Tynan built three hotels: the Diamond Hotel, the Salinas Hotel, and the Commercial Hotel—near the site of what is now Bataan Memorial Park across the street from the National Steinbeck Center: All these important markers of Salinas as a destination for business and tourism happened within the space of less than a decade. The flurry of building showed that these entrepreneurs envisioned something bigger than just another farm town; but overreaching, they wanted to become a new San Francisco or Los Angeles.

They aimed to make Salinas both an urban center and tourist destination with an identity firmly established in ranching and farming. Their hotels were designed to accommodate what they hoped would be waves of visitors, guaranteeing that in the future organizations and government entities might decide to plan events and important meetings in Salinas rather than in Monterey or in any of the other emerging towns in the Salinas Valley or on the Central Coast. Business entrepreneurs intended Salinas to be not merely a stagecoach stop nor a market center for the valley's wheat production, but also a county seat and railroad junction: Salinas City might become a critical center for commerce, agricultural production, and settlement, a major player in a larger regional economic tourist and political network. The railroad arrived officially in 1872, seemingly making all their dreams come true. It was a big reach and a big vision. Still, these founders carefully crafted the city's identity as western and rural, nostalgically connected to cowboy culture with its independence, risk taking, and ambition.

These businessmen became involved in local politics and city government while at the same time maintaining connections at the county, regional, and even national level. They encouraged population growth and city-building by supporting the development of infrastructure that proceeded at a frenetic pace between 1866 and 1880 when the railroad made development of the city imperative. They advertised statewide, encouraging settlement in Salinas based on the opportunity of rich farmland in the valley surrounding the town rather than business enterprise, identifying as a rural community always. Sherwood, writing for the *Petaluma Weekly Argus* in September 1868, encouraged potential settlers to come to Salinas City with promises of cheap, available, and fertile farmland. He envisioned a town supported economically by farming and ranching and defined its identity as an urban agricultural center. Sherwood described Salinas as a "well established farming district" with "first class farming land" to be had at "ruling rates," suggesting that this was not only a great place to establish a farm or ranch, but it was also affordable: He added that "Cheap Residential Building Lots" were available in town as well on the outskirts, all the while implying that this brand-new instant city was established enough to offer residents "good school facilities" and "easy" access to markets through "warehouse and landing facilities."[64] This is what an urban center in a rural landscape looked like.

Population growth was slow but steady, making it possible for city leaders to stay on top of needs for clean water and other infrastructure such as streets, sidewalks, power, and lights—all essential in creating a municipality that compared favorably with other developing cities and towns in the state and in the nation at that time. By 1873, one year after the railroad made Salinas into a regional center, a correspondent for the *San Francisco Chronicle* described Salinas City as a "pretty place" that had developed with "remarkable" speed, noting that only three years earlier 50- by 100-foot lots were available for $100 but now sold for $100 per foot, making clear that the Southern Pacific and Central Pacific's choice of Salinas City as a point that "ties up" the railroad added great value to the place, just as Sherwood and the other founders intended.[65] By the end of 1873, the *Santa Cruz Weekly Sentinel* reported in a humorous note "Salinas was lighted with gas for the first time on Saturday night. The rejoicings of the inhabitants will only be checked by the presentation of exorbitant monthly gas bills."[66] These and other reports on the incipient town indicated that it was no isolated entity but part of a web of regional city-building that continued at an accelerated rate by the end of the century. The language was in keeping with other booster literature in California and the West that aimed to encourage white settlement and tourism but also interwove the awareness that rural converged with urban to create an identity firmly entrenched in agricultural production and ranching culture.[67]

The California state legislature granted Salinas City incorporation in 1874, along with San Rafael, Visalia, and Wheatland, all similarly founded in agricultural regions. Forty-seven other California towns were granted the same status (including nearby Santa Cruz and Watsonville) between statehood (1850) and 1874. By 1898 sixty-five more towns (including Monterey and Pacific Grove) were added to the list of incorporated cities.[68] However, within the Salinas Valley, Salinas City remained the only incorporated body. King City was not incorporated until 1911, Soledad not until 1921, and Greenfield not until 1947. Nonetheless, the spate of incorporations made clear that it was not enough to create settlements in agricultural regions, but that urbanization and incorporation were central to the process of claiming California by Anglo Americans.

The strategy of incorporation was part and parcel of a national movement to create areas of local control while also establishing critical interconnections within and across regions and states. These municipalities, large and small, developed parallel to one another throughout the West as American colonizers of Mexican territory methodically established infrastructure, schools, churches, and cultural and social centers resembling those in the towns and cities of the East, Midwest, and South.[69] The difference in California was the diversity of population and the persistent rural character of these new cities. As these cities and towns emerged seemingly overnight, they included multiple communities of Asian and European immigrants, Asian Americans, African Americans, people from Central and South America, and Mexican Americans, many of whom depended on agriculture for their living. These were spaces of mixed races.[70]

In 1879, California amended its constitution to allow communities the right to home rule through incorporation to establish their own infrastructure, to create zoning laws, and to regulate public and private spaces. Salinas and other rural California towns used incorporation to reflect their shared values for landownership and business enterprise as well as to gain independence from too much federal or state control, even as they depended heavily on state and federal investment, attention, and connection to sustain their communities. Salinas joined other emerging California towns in this era as an integral part of a regional western and national enterprise in city-building, but also as a critical urban center in an agricultural landscape rather than in an industrializing or manufacturing one.[71] This meant that even residents whose livelihoods were not connected directly to agriculture depended upon it and identified as farming and ranching people, with all of its ebbs and flows, its vulnerability to weather conditions and markets, and, most importantly, its dependency on a large, migrant labor force. They needed a stable city government to maintain order within this sometimes chaotic environment.

Salinas's Anglo American founders sought prominence as much as incorporation, however. They wanted to ensure their municipality became a permanent feature of California and also the predominant one in the region. The county seat had been located in Monterey since 1850, but Salinas's founders managed to convince the California state legislature to establish Salinas, rather than Monterey, as the county seat in 1874.

Historically, Monterey had been the Spanish capital of Alta and Baja California in 1776, and after Mexican independence in 1821, it was one of the most important ports for trade in the region. After the war with Mexico and during the Gold Rush in 1849, the first California State Constitutional Convention convened in Monterey, adding to its historical significance in the region. It made political sense to locate the county seat there. Nonetheless, advocates for Salinas as the county seat succeeded in 1874 in large part because Monterey appeared to be in decline as a significant urban center in California. Salinas's American residents were determined to take advantage of being seen as the up-and-coming political and economic center in the region, blurring the distinction between their collective identity as a rural agricultural settlement and as a city.[72] It was a tension that emerging municipalities such as Santa Barbara, Los Angeles, or even nearby San José, for example, did not face. For those places, agriculture was only one of the economic drivers and community identifiers, not the only one. As a result, these other places restricted residential space for nonwhites effectively by the 1880s; Salinas, on the other hand, struggled in its identity: It needed multiple (and diverse) groups of people living in proximity as farmers and ranchers, but it also aimed to emulate the urban centers spatially divided by both race and class.

"A treacherous and tortuous roadway"[73] separated Salinas from Monterey and prevented residents from Hollister and other towns and communities in Monterey County from ease of access to courts and administrative offices needed to conduct county business. The stated reason for moving the county seat out of Monterey, with its ocean access, and into Salinas, with its railroad stop, was that county residents disliked making the arduous trek to Monterey over the Santa Lucia Mountains or, if they lived as far away as Gilroy, over the Gabilan Mountains, just to file a claim in court. This might have been true, but it was more likely a good excuse to seize power and control for Salinas from Monterey. These ambitious settler colonialists knew full well what a county seat meant in terms of prestige and profit. As well, residents of Hollister (incorporated in 1872) aimed for predominance in the area. The new Anglo American residents of these emerging settlements had obvious practical reasons to support Salinas in its effort to wrest the county seat from Monterey, and in return Salinas's residents backed them in creating a separate county (San Benito) with Hollister as the county seat, which they succeeded in doing by 1872 as well.[74] The power struggles that created counties and county seats out of instant cities in the nineteenth century happened throughout California. The entire state was a place of urbanization within an agricultural expanse that defied easy definition or identity, as Salinas exemplified.[75]

JESSE CARR: ESTABLISHING SALINAS'S REGIONAL PROMINENCE

Many of the families who arrived in Salinas in the late nineteenth century came by way of the rural, postbellum Confederate South and Midwest in pursuit of dreams of landownership and new beginnings in the aftermath of the defeat of the Confederacy. They were agricultural people creating an urban space, like so many other migrants to California in the late nineteenth century.[76] Many of their descendants remained in Salinas through the next century.[77] They often began their California odyssey in San Francisco, some of them well connected financially and socially to San Francisco's business and political elites.[78] Eager to accommodate the needs of the railroad giants for retail shops, hotels, and restaurants, as well as repair shops such as blacksmiths, they built up their emerging town at a frenetic pace. Minutes of Salinas City Council meetings going back to the 1860s attest to the founders' vision of city-building as a strategy for creating prosperity and predominance in this rural region with clear connections to state and federal governments. Jesse Carr, an entrepreneur from the South who came to Salinas first by way of San Francisco, became one of the key figures in Salinas's late nineteenth-century strategy of making itself into a regional center.

Like his Salinas and California cohort, Jesse Carr was one of those ambitious visionaries who epitomized late nineteenth-century city-builders deeply dependent on farming and ranching. People motivated by dreams of wealth in a turbulent economic and political world sought reflected glory through the creation of urban space in the new state of California, but they were farmers first and city dwellers second. Just like his contemporaries in Salinas and other striving immigrants with grand dreams, such as Leland Stanford, Carr aimed for more than a home: He wanted a showplace and a notable landmark as a marker of his own accomplishments.[79]

Carr epitomized exactly the kind of determined striver that defined immigrants to Salinas and to California in the late nineteenth century. His was something of a rags-to-riches story, with racial privilege and unabashed opportunism attached to it. Carr not only attained great wealth from agriculture in the Salinas Valley, he also invested in the city itself; and like so many of the most successful entrepreneurs of the twentieth century, he founded a community bank to ensure that this newfound wealth remained in Salinas. That pivotal role—as both an agricultural and business entrepreneur and as a forward-thinking city leader who initiated development in his adopted city—was a common denominator in the emergence of urban settlements throughout rural California. The histories of Visalia, Merced, Stockton, Fresno, and many other communities in San Francisco's agricultural hinterland all showed evidence of similar strategies by former San Franciscans seeking to make their communities predominant (and ensure their own investments and historical relevance); their visions of city-building included constructing grandiose opera houses, hotels, and conference centers in the first years of the new century.[80]

Like so many of his counterparts, Carr was born poor in 1814, a farmer's son from rural Tennessee. At age sixteen, he left home to work as a store clerk, first in the small town of Cairo and then in Nashville. With $1,000 in savings, he opened his own store in Memphis in 1834. At that time, Carr's business partner "lost his mind" and incurred a $20,000 debt, for which Carr took responsibility and paid off over a two-year period. By 1840 Carr had made a $40,000 profit in part because Memphis had, by that time, become an important trading center for enslaved people and merchandise as a result of the Indian wars in that area. Southern cotton growers hoped to expand the institution of slavery into new states in the South and the West, and Tennessee was one of their targets.[81] Carr benefited from a world that profited from enslavement.

Carr married and built the first brick house in the city of Memphis in 1842. Like so many other young southern men of his generation, Jesse Carr traveled widely in search of fortune, engaging in multiple new businesses along the way, including owning and trading in human beings. He moved to New Orleans in 1843 and became a cotton commissioner, in the collective effort to expand the cotton kingdom, but when cotton prices plummeted, he once again lost his fortune.

When Americans instigated war with Mexico in 1846, Carr quickly turned his fortunes around again by becoming a supplier for American troops stationed in the Southwest. However, shortly thereafter, 3,000 Mexican soldiers under General José de Urrea captured the railroad train carrying Carr's supplies to U.S. troops in Mexico. Summoned to explain to a livid General Zachary Taylor, Carr bonded with the general, who, luckily for Carr, would become the twelfth president of the United States in 1849. Carr stayed in Mexico for the duration of the war, engaging in trade and recovering some of the investment that he had lost in the train robbery. Returning to New Orleans in 1849, he contracted cholera (for the second time) but recovered from his illness in time to attend Taylor's inauguration ceremony in Washington, DC. Taylor did not support the expansion of slavery into the territories and advocated (in a bitter battle with Henry Clay) for California's admission to the Union as a free state, which contrasted with Carr's own views. But Carr was far more interested in power and profit than he was in ethical principles. He took full advantage of the fact that Taylor wanted to have allies in positions of power in California.

Carr utilized his friendship with the U.S. president to seize the opportunity of government service. He was appointed deputy collector of the Port of San Francisco and arrived in California August 18, 1849, right amid the Gold Rush—an event that would bring over 300,000 people to the state over the next seven years. Carr leveraged his political connections to run successfully for the California State Assembly as a Whig in 1851, representing San Francisco where he served as chairman of both the Committee on Commerce and Navigation and the Committee on Ways and Means. He became involved in mining and real estate development but also bought a ranch in the Pajaro Valley in 1853. He was elected to the Santa Cruz Board of Supervisors in 1859 and engaged in grain farming and cattle ranching before moving to Salinas that year. Carr acquired massive amounts of land and benefited from the flourishing wheat production made possible by the ever-increasing railroad lines that linked remote areas of California to San Francisco and markets in the East and Midwest. He may not have achieved the dominance that Charles Crocker, Collis Huntington, Leland Stanford, or Mark Hopkins did, but it was not because he wasn't trying.

It was from the vantage point of a wealthy San Franciscan that Carr set his sights on the Salinas Valley as an ideal place to establish himself, a big fish in the small pond of Salinas that might become a real center of California life if he could help it along. He went into the stagecoach business in the 1860s and became the largest stage contractor on the Pacific Coast from 1866 to 1870. He bought 20,000 acres of land in Modoc County and controlled the water rights for over 150,000 acres. He had acquired 5,000 cattle and 500 horses by the time he moved to Salinas in 1866.

At this point, Carr focused on building up the city of Salinas and gave up residency in San Francisco, making Salinas his permanent home. According to the *Salinas Daily Index,* "There is no stately or pretentious private dwelling like the residence of the Honorable J. D. Carr being the nearest approach to this class of home."[82] In 1883 Carr "sank a well on the bank of the [Salinas] slough," built a windmill and 14,000 gallon water tank, and his very own gas works to supply power and water to his newly built "cabin," as the *Daily Index* termed it, somewhat tongue in cheek. It was a mansion compared to other homes of the day. Carr also purchased Central Hall in Salinas for $16,000 and established offices there, which included the Salinas Post Office. Besides building his mansion in the heart of Salinas, Carr built an opera house (in 1901), and he endowed the first library in Salinas with a

$5,000 donation ($100,000 in today's currency). By 1890 Carr was described by historian Hubert Howe Bancroft as successful and well established: "In the Salinas Valley one of the largest agriculturalists is Jesse D. Carr!"[83]All of this was meant to enhance both himself and his chosen place of residence, to cement his place in the history of the city and in the history of California. His investment in the town showed that urban development became just as important to Salinas's population as agricultural production. This is what building a farm town looked like in late nineteenth-century California.

Carr became an increasingly influential figure in California Democratic politics even as he focused on the well-being and growth of his adopted city. He assisted in getting the town marshal, Christian Franks, appointed to the position of U.S. marshal for Northern California. "A strong and often successful contender for control of patronage by the conservative forces in central and northern California," Carr was instrumental in selecting the site for the San Francisco Post Office and Federal Court Building at 7th and Mission Streets. According to a reporter for the *California Wasp* writing in 1888, Carr was a prominent San Francisco figure even though he had relocated to Salinas some years before: "It may not be generally known in San Francisco, yet it is a peculiar fact that Jesse D. Carr of Salinas is the colossus that constantly bestrides the Pacific Coast Postal Service . . . while administrations come and go, Jesse D. Carr 'goes on forever.'"[84] Carr became an important conservative leader in the state and nationally. He attended both of Grover Cleveland's inaugurations (in 1885 and 1893) and was a prominent enough figure in California political circles that when President William McKinley visited the state in 1901, Carr made sure he stopped in Salinas. Carr was often mentioned as a candidate for U.S. senator and governor and served as president of the California State Board of Agriculture. Thus, he succeeded at many levels in making both himself and Salinas emblematic of an expansive vision of California as a place of wealth and prominence in late nineteenth-century America, based on a concept of the rural that included towns and cities, rather than in opposition to them.

Carr aimed to enrich himself and gain power, but he also worked to benefit Salinas, helping to propel the city into the orbit of San Francisco's business elites and make it a permanent and prosperous urban center in its own right. An ambitious man with a San Franciscan viewpoint, Carr saw enormous opportunity in Salinas that included elevating Salinas's stature as a city of note in California. He was the personification of elite Progressives who were, above all else, city-builders with the value system of agricultural-ists.[85] As a new century promised new opportunities, these women and men envisioned themselves as leaders of a modern and, above all, urban California based on a population of white, citizen landowners engaged in farming, ranching, and the business enterprise that supported a farming culture.[86]

Arguably, Jesse Carr's most important and lasting accomplishment was in organizing the Salinas City Bank in 1873 and serving as its president for the next two decades. The Monterey County Bank (1890), the Salinas Mutual Building and Loan Association (1897), and the Salinas City Bank (1873) formed the backbone of the county's financial sources and maintained critical ties to San Francisco's financiers in the process. These were impor-tant building blocks in firmly establishing Salinas as a regional center in the Salinas Valley and in Monterey County.

Salinas thus became an important destination for ambitious people in the aftermath of the Civil War and well into the twentieth century. San Francisco overflowed with farming and ranching entrepreneurs who wanted to establish towns and cities throughout the region's agricultural expanse and who self-identified as rural people, consummate westerners. Salinas and the Salinas Valley were rich in land that promised (and delivered) enormous economic opportunity based on a particular combination of innovative agri-cultural production and business enterprise; and Salinas City, as the county seat, could draw tourists and government officials alike.

RACE AND ETHNICITY

The 1870s through 1900 is known as the Gilded Age in America. These years are also part of a long era of urbanization throughout California and the nation as a whole as cities began to fill up with new populations of im-migrants, mainly from Ireland but also from all over Europe. Formerly en-slaved African Americans from rural areas in the South also began to move north and west, especially with the end of Reconstruction and the beginning of Jim Crow terrorism. In California, those populations included Mexican people and other immigrants from Latin America as well as various Asian (Chinese and later Japanese, Sikh, Korean, and Filipino/a) communities.

Although Asian immigrants presented a "problem" for native-born white Californians, the racially mixed Mexican population in the state was also dis-turbing to the Anglo American immigrants from the South and Midwest.[87] John C. Miller, a delegate to the 1879 California Constitutional Convention, proclaimed that "[only the] lowest most vile and degraded [of the white race were most likely to] amalgamate . . . resulting in a "hybrid of the most despicable [people], a mongrel of the most detestable [kind] that has ever afflicted the earth," reflecting the increasingly rigid notions of racial hierarchy that began in slavery and would grow into the early twentieth-century eugenics movement. According to California's 1853 Anti-Miscegenation Act, "All marriages of white persons with negroes or mulattoes are declared to be illegal and void." By 1880 the act was amended to prohibit marriages between "Mongolians" and "white persons." The fact that these laws existed suggest that both intermarriage and sex between racial groups were commonplace in the West and California—otherwise there would have been no need for legislation prohibiting them.[88] This was particularly the case in agricultural communities such as Salinas where groups lived in close and intimate proximity to one another.

In Salinas we see this revealed in the emergence of a white-dominated city made up largely of immigrants from northern Europe and native-born Americans from the South and Midwest, who shared their nineteenth-century cohorts' concerns over racial mixing and intermarriage; these fears were expressed in statutes governing morality and public health and the city's zoning regulations meant to manage population growth and urban development.[89] The city planners depended on increasing federal and state legislation to support their efforts.[90] But, however much the city planners denied the full humanity of their Asian and Mexican American cohorts, these nonwhite groups were also engaged in the project of city-building in Salinas and shared the same goals and strategies as the Anglo Americans: to prosper by establishing homes, farms, businesses, and to create a politically and economically stable city. Although these minority groups aimed to create such an inclusive city, they faced insurmountable odds, because like every other incipient municipality in California in the late nineteenth century, Asian people and Mexican Americans were systematically excluded from city politics and representation, setting the stage for exclusions in the decades to come.[91]

With the selection of Salinas as the county seat came a coterie of professionals, including lawyers and judges, journalists, and physicians as well as a host of entrepreneurs. Among the extensive biographies of male elites of Salinas printed by a booster publication in 1889, Dr. May P. W. Gydison was featured as a prominent physician "of Danish extraction" who attended Omaha Medical College and trained in Germany and Denmark before graduating from Women's Medical College in Chicago. She came to Salinas City in 1884 with her parents, who founded the Danish Lutheran Church to support the increasingly large population of Danish immigrant horticulturalists and dairy farmers who arrived in the Salinas Valley in the late nineteenth century. Dr. Gydison was described as a "lady of fine intellectual capacity and womanly sympathy, and thoroughly enthused with her profession." Dr. Gydison was a widow when she arrived in Salinas but later remarried and returned to Denmark. Her parents remained as leaders in the quickly expanding Danish immigrant farming community of the Salinas Valley.[92] Like her male contemporaries, she played a critical role in the formation of Salinas in the late nineteenth century. She did not merely practice medicine but also founded a "ladies hospital . . . paying particular attention to the diseases of women . . . the only institution of its kind in the county . . . it supplies a great necessity."[93] She was just as ambitious as Salinas's male founders were in making the city the regional center for medicine, the first of its kind on the Central Coast. Decades later, her hospital (renamed Natividad Medical Center) remained a major regional teaching hospital directly affiliated with the residency training programs of the University of California, San Francisco.

Dr. Gydison's life and experience exemplified important aspects of Salinas's early history. First and foremost, Salinas residents prided themselves on being a community that needed immigrants, even groups who were considered out of the mainstream in the nineteenth century because of language and religious differences such as the Danish (or Swiss Italians and Portuguese who also settled in the area). In Salinas and California generally, Danes and other European-origin immigrant groups were accepted and absorbed as whites and equal members of Salinas's society in contrast to the multiple Asian and Mexican American populations that made this one of the most multiracial regions of the country. Like other groups who arrived in the area, Danes and Swiss Italians were farmers, dairymen, and ranchers, and so they shared the agricultural sensibility that connected Salinas's other residents. Dr. Gydison also epitomized the significant role women generally played in city-building in late nineteenth-century America, especially in the West.[94] There was room in the professions at that time for women doctors, teachers, librarians, and community activists who may not have been able to vote but enthusiastically became involved in city politics and city life. They had enormous influence in every aspect in defining the character of their respective communities including Salinas. Most importantly, Dr. Gydison exemplified the striver, the dreamer, the visionary—not content to practice medicine only but determined to build a hospital that would be preeminent in California and particularly in the Central Coast region. Her effort was part of the larger one to purposefully make this municipality the urban center for the Salinas Valley at a time when this designation was challenged by every newly incorporated town in the valley.

Like other booster publications, local writing about the growing metropolis in the *San Francisco Bulletin* referred to Salinas in 1870 as "a rising place" and "a bustling agricultural town" in an effort to showcase the city's attributes and agricultural identity; promotional materials always downplayed the racial composition of the population in a concerted effort to quiet white fears of racial diversity and the intermixing of people, which were also features of rural California.[95] By the 1880s, Salinas was described as "the largest and most flourishing town in the county," according to an assessment in the newly founded local newspaper, the *Salinas Standard*.[96]

Promotional literature in 1880 described Main Street as "admirably macadamized [paved] built up on both sides in fine city fashion" and claimed that the entire town had adequate supplies of both power (gas) and fresh water. Moreover, Salinas already had such "facilities for arts and culture" that might be available only in a more established city:

> Its county buildings, churches, schools, hotels, stores, shops, and residences cause it to rank among the first of its size in the State. The town is embowered in trees and adorned with pleasant gardens and lovely flowers. The aspect of the whole is that of a true, enterprising, progressive, permanent American city.[97]

A Salinas baseball club soon appeared in this period, further reinforcing Yankee American culture as well as a rural sensibility within an urban context.[98] It was clear from this glowing account of the city that the Anglo American founders were on a fast track to create a space that might attract capital investment as well as increased white settlement by showing Salinas City to be a thoroughly "American" urban environment dominated by white citizens and therefore politically and socially stable, culturally attractive to

Anglo Americans and economically viable without the taint of racial conflict. Yet, racism was alive and well in Salinas in the nineteenth century.

Minutes of the Salinas City Council meetings show the city's political leadership to be preoccupied with both growth and racial control. They developed a vigorous policy establishing public works and paying for them by means of local taxation and borrowing funds from financiers in San Francisco. They not only established schools, issued business licenses, built streets and sidewalks, and provided water and both electrical and gas power for the growing population but also established committees made up of the city's elite property owners to create police, fire, and sanitation departments within city government as a way of instituting order and marking off residential space—sectioning off a portion of the city for Chinese, Mexican, and African American residents. They created ordinances for everything from the laying of pipes of very specific size and depth, to providing "pure fresh water for the accommodation of the people," to building sidewalks of specific size and placement, all measures of local control over municipal space. These improvements were meant to convey a sense of a city under control.[99]

Salinas's residents expeditiously created a municipality that might withstand the social and economic turmoil of the nation in the 1870s and the increasing anxiety Americans generally experienced over a new massive population of freed African Americans, people of mixed-race, and the increasing immigration of multiple Asian communities; these populations seemed equally threatening to native-born whites and to European-origin immigrants in California, especially as the native-born children of marginalized groups laid claim to American citizenship. And yet, intermarriage and sexual interaction between people of different racial groups were not uncommon, especially in communities like Salinas that based their economies on agriculture, which necessarily required close and intimate living spaces.[100]Although there is little evidence in newspapers, city records, or archives of intermarriages between whites and Chinese people or other people deemed nonwhite, the restrictive legislation belied the general concern of white politicians and residents that this was a possibility. Clues abounded in literature too. As the century wore on and we see Salinas through the eyes of its most famous novelist, John Steinbeck, we see many examples of close, intimate living among people of various racial backgrounds and ethnic groups, driven by the necessities of farming and ranching.[101]

City council meetings focused on elections and the establishment of poll taxes, which were another way for the city to raise money from citizen residents who directly benefited from city services and infrastructure; but they were also a way to exclude those unable to pay for the right to vote, which had become a common method to enforce the disenfranchisement of freed African Americans in the South after the end of Reconstruction. City expenditures were mainly dedicated to engineers surveying the town ($33 was the biggest expense in 1872 to pay for the work of a surveyor, Francis Logan Ripley).[102] By July of that year, Salinas had raised funds for a bowling alley[103] and spent $175 for paving and grading a street near the railroad.[104]

Liquor license taxes, road taxes, and dog taxes (wandering dogs seemed to be a big problem brought up repeatedly at council meetings) provided revenue for the city's General Fund. Salinas's council members advocated new taxes frequently, justified by the need for both infrastructure and the establishment of a school system to accommodate an ever-growing population. On April 20, 1874, the city council voted to tax residents a total of $1,485 to fund a public school.[105] Schools were built and supported early on in Salinas's history, evidence of valuing an educated citizenry literate in English that might transform populations of non–English-speaking immigrants into patriotic Americans and at the same time make unassimilable Asian people less threatening, even as they were excluded from citizenship and neighborhoods.

The Panic of 1873 that led to global depression and economic collapse lasting until 1879 did not make much of an impact on the booming agricultural city, although a series of city council meetings in the 1870s focused both on assessment of property and the unpaid property taxes that might have been related to the economic downturn.[106] Still, the local impact of the twin economic catastrophes that severely hurt homesteader farmers in the Midwest did not cause havoc in the more diversified farming and ranching environment of Salinas. Agriculture in the Salinas Valley included dairy farming, the production of vineyards, vegetables, and berries as well as large-scale wheat and grain. Salinas also depended on tourism from its role as regional political and social center defined by ranching and farming and a mythology of the West that merged Mexican ranching culture into a vaguely Anglo American version of cowboy culture.[107]

The city council commissioned a map of the town costing the city $200 and completed by February 1874.[108] Upon incorporation in 1874, Salinas council members initiated a flurry of road building, annexations, and infrastructure development.[109] The council supported numerous local newspapers besides the *Salinas Standard,* including the *Salinas Index* in 1873, which became the main daily publication from the 1910s throughout the 1930s.[110] City council meetings in July and August of 1874 were almost wholly dedicated to street paving and sidewalk construction.[111] On August 10, a bond was issued by the California state legislature to support the "build[ing of] a School House and to provide for a Fire Department."[112] However, it was also clear from city council minutes that Salinas's leaders could not fund their city's development entirely on their own. There are mentions throughout the minutes of bonds issued through San Francisco's banks to help the city support its need for infrastructure and schools.[113]

In a relatively short span of time (six years), Salinas City residents fulfilled their vision for a full-fledged city within the rural. They were planners and organizers—predominantly white, Protestant, and adherents of Progressive era moral and racial codes. They formed a sanitation committee to report on problems with waste and sewage, targeting a newly established Chinatown, which was informally rather than officially segregated spatially in the city. Yet, they still made room for Chinese people in city life. The increasing population of Salinas always included new immigrant groups who often did not speak English or hold American citizenship. Agricultural communities might have shared American ideas of racial hierarchy but they knew they needed the population to survive. So, alongside their white space, a vibrant Asian community formed and contributed to a city that was notable for its multiracial and multicultural identity in the next century.

Salinas emulated San Francisco. As the first city in the nation to impose racial segregation by law, San Francisco modeled excluding Chinese people with an 1890 city ordinance that segregated them into a very tightly controlled portion of the city. Although nullified two days later by the U.S. district court, whites in San Francisco and California disdained and abused Chinese people even as they employed Chinese residents for much needed work as laborers, skilled and unskilled. At the federal level, Chinese people would officially be barred from further immigration in 1882, thanks in large part to California lobbyists. This first exclusion law prohibited the immigration of Chinese laborers (though not merchants or anyone of obvious wealth) for ten years. It also denied Chinese eligibility for naturalization and citizenship. The law was reenacted and extended in 1888, 1892, and finally as a permanent measure in 1902. It was not repealed until 1943.

Throughout the early years of Salinas's development, Chinese people of all socioeconomic classes shared space in Chinatown, just as they did in every other town and city in late nineteenth-century California. As the century came to an end, legislation at both federal and state levels increasingly targeted Chinese people, reflecting venomous, pervasive anti-Chinese views, which were increasingly pronounced in California and throughout the Pacific Northwest. Between 1849 and 1906 mobs of angry whites in "over two hundred towns . . . had [completely] driven out their Chinese residents" and committed acts of violence against them (usually ignored by law enforcement) because white Californians (and westerners generally) were afraid that Chinese workers might replace them in a tenuous and competitive labor market, believed the Chinese were so culturally and racially distinct as to be unassimilable, and thought that Chinese prostitution and opium dens constituted threats to city-building and American values.[114] In San Francisco, for example, the Queue Ordinance of 1873 allowed police to forcibly cut off Chinese men's queues (traditional long braids), and another statute prohibited Chinese people from carrying laundry or food on shoulder poles on sidewalks. In 1871, a mob made up of over a thousand Mexican Americans and whites attacked Los Angeles Chinese residents at random, killing nineteen men and boys, including a prominent Chinese doctor.[115] Throughout California and the western United States, in almost every municipality and settlement, whites viciously attacked Chinese people and blamed them for everything from epidemics that were common in the nineteenth century (including bubonic plague, smallpox, influenza, and cholera) to economic downturns.[116] The very existence of a Chinatown in Salinas suggested a community set apart from other residents of the city based on perceptions of racial difference and inferiority.

Both citizenship and property ownership in this period were also directly linked to ideas of race. The 1870 Naturalization Act, for example, expressly limited American citizenship to "white persons and persons of African descent." It effectively barred Asian people from U.S. citizenship, although the 1868 Fourteenth Amendment provided a critical exception with the birthright clause in Section 1. Further, the Chinese Exclusion Act of 1882 still allowed merchants and other persons with wealth to immigrate (although this did not allow them to naturalize or become citizens), indicating the act was as much about population control as exclusion, favoring those with means.

It was in the interest of the residents of emerging towns like Salinas to be wary of new populations of immigrants deemed unassimilable that might develop a stake in city government through citizenship and business enterprise. As a result of their fears of native-born Asian Americans and other minority groups who claimed citizenship, white residents maintained control of city affairs through strategies of spatial segregation and outright exclusion of those deemed inferior racially such as the Chinese people who claimed space in Salinas from its earliest settlement, even denying their collective contributions to city-building in promotional literature.

Anglo Californians expressed their fear and hatred of Chinese through concerns over contagious diseases such as leprosy, tuberculosis, smallpox, and cholera, which were described in newspapers of the time as "inherited and in some countries national;" by defining these illnesses in this way, entire populations from Asia, Africa, the Middle East, and southern Europe were condemned to marginalization. After describing elephantiasis and leprosy in graphic terms in an interview in the *San Francisco Examiner* in 1882, one doctor attributed cases in Northern California to "Chinatowns." Although the doctor claimed "an entire immunity" from "ordinary contact," he went on to warn that sexual relationships and "intermarriage with Chinese people" posed "a great danger to our people." Arguing that this possibility was not just fantasy but reality, he claimed evidence of "quite a number of marriages between Chinese to American girls." The doctor went on to argue that disease transmission happened with or without marriage: "nor is marriage absolutely necessary," insinuating sexual relationships between Chinese men and white women outside of marriage were both dangerous for the community as a whole and not uncommon. It was not always possible to know who carried disease and who did not, the doctor explained, arguing that "If a Chinaman [carrying disease] married a white woman," their "half-breed" children would carry the disease too and spread it, even unknowingly, among the general population. Therefore, using the language and logic of eugenics, this doctor advocated "the necessity of stopping the reproduction of such animals."[117]

As early as 1873, the segregation of Chinese people in Salinas was justified on the grounds of public health to minimize possibilities for sexual relationships and intermarriage, especially between white women and Chinese men.

The Chinese community of Salinas was located in the least desirable part of town, four blocks north of the Southern Pacific tracks between North Main and East Lake Street and by 1880 consisted not only of homes, but also retail shops, laundries, restaurants, gambling houses, and various forms of illicit entertainment, serving both Chinese people and other non-Chinese Salinas residents of color.[118] By 1877, Chinese settler farmers began irrigation projects and experimented with a variety of new labor-intensive crops such as sugar beets and mustard. By 1880, Chinese people leased over 1,000 acres of Salinas Valley land for agriculture. However, the unique aspects of agricultural life precluded the kind of isolation or hierarchy based on concepts of racial difference that town life afforded. In her analysis of Chinese male–white female relations in a rural California community, Beth Lew-Williams turned conventional understanding of power and place on its head.[119] A Chinese male landowner employed young white female workers and subsequently formed an intimate relationship with one of them, which landed him in jail. Although the Chinese man faced grave consequences for the upside-down power and sexual relationship, nonetheless Lew-Williams provides a clear picture of how agricultural life demanded intimacy in ways that urban life did not.

The fact that Salinas, an urban enclave, was situated in the middle of a rural area meant that both marginalization and close contact between disparate racial groups, particularly between Chinese people and whites but over time with other groups deemed nonwhite as well, became commonplace. This meant that race relations existed in tension, at best. The barriers so evident in cities located outside of agricultural zones could not be sustained here.

Control over space included restrictions on gambling and the selling of liquor licenses. Just as in every other Progressive era municipality, the Salinas City Council passed numerous laws throughout the decade of the 1910s that penalized Chinese (and other) businesses for illicit activity, restricted the availability and location gambling houses, and limited the sale of liquor licenses in Chinatown. The city prohibited tobacco sales to minors and circumscribed both the establishment of saloons in the area for the hours of operation.[120] Yet, the fact that these places existed showed how Chinese people responded to restrictions over landownership by developing businesses that allowed them to prosper and resist.

Taken together, all these ordinances were efforts to control city space by enforcing racial hierarchies.[121] The Salinas City Council was presented with a petition to remove Chinatown—in its entirety—from the city altogether following a suspicious fire there in 1892:

> Chinatown has had its share of fires. The first leveled "old town" near Main Street and all the buildings a block around. . . . Water was brought by the fire department from the corner of Sausal and Pajaro Streets but in the midst of it all the hoses burst. During the excitement firemen rescued a lame Chinese gentleman from the hospital [nearby].[122]

Indeed, fire was routine in Salinas in this era of highly flammable wooden buildings, an all-volunteer fire department, and disputes over funding and equipment.[123] Nonetheless, in the aftermath of the fire, "A petition asking for the removal of Chinatown beyond the city limits was received [at a June 1893 city council meeting]. . . . It was then moved and carried that the Sanitary Committee be instructed to investigate the matter of a nuisance now in houses of Chinese within the City Limits and report on same at the next regular meeting."[124]

> The Sanitary Committee reported back to the city council . . . that "they have examined the premises occupied by the Chinese on Soledad Street and the same are a nuisance and a great menace to the health of the people in that locality." . . . it was then moved and carried that the City Attorney be instructed to commence proceedings against the proper parties to abate said nuisance.[125]

The investigation concluded that problematic businesses should be penalized for violations deemed "nuisance" rather than removing or punishing all Chinese people in Salinas or all Chinese enterprises as was the case when mobs randomly targeted Chinese neighborhoods in Monterey, Los Angeles, and San Francisco in this period.[126]

Although many of the city council minutes have gone missing, other accounts of the era demonstrated that Chinese people persisted in creating community and resisted marginalization despite racism directed at them and the implications of that suspicious episode in 1893. Chinatown was not moved out of the city limits after all. Yet, the ordinance on "nuisance" focused on public health was a veiled attack on Salinas's Chinese residents based solely on their race and is an example of typical Progressive era efforts to blame pandemics on people deemed nonwhite.[127] Although the Chinese community was quickly rebuilt and the fire attributed to carelessness rather than racially motivated action based on fear of disease, the impact was felt by Salinas's Chinese's residents for generations after.[128]

White women were at the forefront of lobbying efforts that marginalized Salinas's Chinese population. Without the vote, women could not be elected to any office. But women in Salinas, as elsewhere, were activists nonetheless, and not always in the same positive way as Dr. May Gydison. They were often featured on the front pages of Salinas's newspapers for their efforts at city-building through community works projects that usually reflected animosity over the very presence of Chinese people.[129] As they did elsewhere in California and the nation, middle-class white Salinas women appropriated the language of public health, public safety, and the search for order to justify their collective racist views. In 1874, the *San Francisco Chronicle* noted that the Women's Christian Temperance Union was active in shaping the city of Salinas into a city that controlled morality, which meant controlling Chinese residents and limiting the bars, gambling operations, and houses of prostitution located in Chinatown:

> Miss Cassie S. Ritchie addressed the Common Council of Salinas City recently in favor of raising the license of saloons from $60 per month to $150. This was a strategic move of the Prohibitionists "who [sought] to circumscribe so far, at least, as our young and growing city is concerned the baneful influence of this desolating evil by compelling those who are engaged in the sale of intoxicating liquors to pay at least a molety [sic] of the expense entailed upon the community in consequence of their business."[130]

White women also served on committees that were formed to deal with the urgent need for fresh water:

> [The] Committee on Water Works was directed to write a contract between James Hagan & Enright and Salinas City for supplying the city with water to introduce within three months of this date into Salinas City from wells capable of supplying at least three hundred thousand gallons of water per day a supply of good, pure, fresh, water for the use of Salinas City for public city purposes . . . [furthermore this firm was legally responsible for] to build, erect and construct upon some convenient

site of their own within the limits of Salinas city a suitable, substantial reservoir of sufficient capacity to contain not less than one hundred thousand gallons of water . . . specs included here . . . to be used in case of fire in the city.[131]

By November 1874, women lobbied for ordinances to create sewers, to construct streetlights, and to clean up the remaining sloughs in town. They demanded parks and recreation areas too, which was all in keeping with what women in newly formed towns and cities in California and the nation were doing toward the nineteenth-century enterprise of city-building.[132] On November 16, 1874, Eugene Sherwood donated "sixty acres of land for a park and city clerk was ordered to notify Mr. Sherwood of said acceptance." By December 7, 1874, thanks in large part to the lobbying efforts of women's organizations, the mayor and city council authorized the purchase of a "suitable lot" for a fire department and authorized the purchase of a hook and ladder truck. By May 1875 Salinas had a jail and employed both a police officer and a marshal.[133] Hiring a police officer and establishing a jail to control a wayward population merged seamlessly into efforts to build sidewalks and establish infrastructure. Salinas's residents may have had farming and ranching sensibilities, but they conformed to all the Progressive ideals associated with city building too.

With public urging from organized groups of white women at city council meetings, the mayor and city council tasked the city marshal and night watchman to "arrest Boys under eighteen years of age that were found on the Streets or Alleys between the hours of Eight o'clock P.M. and Five o'clock A.M. without a reasonable excuse, or are with their parents or proper guardians."[134] The collective efforts of women in Salinas to legislate morality was in line with efforts at national, state, and local levels to contain and control a growing urban population that included immigrants from what was believed were racially inferior cultures.[135] In California, however, this effort was directed at Mexican people and Asian groups and less at African Americans (still very small in number) or anyone of European origin (always a desired population in California). By contrast, in eastern and midwestern cities and in larger municipalities in California such as Los Angeles, containment and control applied in equal measure to southern and eastern Europeans, African Americans, and in the case of Los Angeles, to Mexican Americans and Asians from all national origin groups.[136] Salinas women focused on Chinese people almost exclusively in addressing concerns over class and race by supporting coercive legislation on morality.[137] City council members acknowledged the political power of these women by routinely making formal presentations to the Salinas Civic Women's Club to request support for various initiatives they intended to put forward to the board of supervisors that they believed would enhance Salinas's standing in the region.[138]

The sanitary committee (composed of both women and men) investigated Salinas's Chinatown as a real and present danger to the city's public health.[139] They suggested removal of all Chinese residents from city limits but subsequently reported to the Salinas City Council: "The petition . . . to have the Chinese removed from the city be indefinitely postponed."[140] The sanitary commission also reported on conditions of the remaining sloughs in the city; they recommended assessments of city land and taxation to provide revenue to fund schools, sewers, drainage systems, and to sustain the fire department, conflating such problems as improper sewage systems with the mere presence of Chinese people.[141] Residents, women and men, worked constantly in the early years of city-building to utilize local taxes to create clean, ordered city spaces under local (rather than state or federal) control and fused ideas about the ideal city with racism directed at Chinese people to justify both marginalization and control; the very real contributions Chinese settlers made to city-building were ignored. Instead, Salinas's founders focused only on Chinese people as troublesome and threatening, even though these immigrants had little choice in occupations within a segregated economy that did not allow them to own land and a social and political world that excluded them.[142]

By April 1887, Salinas had formed committees on gas and water, schools, police, fire, licenses, and ordinances. The city council supported a petition that year for a special election to issue bonds for "public improvements" signed by 123 resident voters that was overwhelmingly approved.[143] In August 1888 a franchise was granted to Salinas City Gas and Water Company for the furnishing of electric lights, and the city fixed the rates for the service.[144]

As the minutes of the Salinas City Council meetings and newspaper accounts of the era made clear, just twenty years after its initial founding, Salinas showed every sign of being a full-fledged municipality comparable to many other towns emerging in California at the time. It was a city infused by a Progressive spirit largely represented by women activists. It was a population of Anglo American immigrants that segregated Chinese residents and reduced Californios and Indigenous People to the shadows. It was a place of streets, lights, schools, and even glamour, exemplified by the opera house (constructed in 1901 thanks to investment by Jesse Carr).

By March 1902, the city's newspaper reported triumphantly the following:

> A narrow gauge railroad connects Salinas with Watsonville by way of Moss Landing on Monterey Bay. The Southern Pacific coastline is now completed and through trains are now running between San Francisco and Los Angeles, placing Salinas on a direct overland route. This line runs within full view of the Pacific ocean for over one hundred miles, and is one of the most beautiful and picturesque in the world. With such transportation facilities and surrounded by rich agricultural lands of the great Salinas Valley, the resources of the Gabilan range on one side and those of the Santa Lucia on the other, Salinas City cannot fail to become a very important trade center, and one of the best business localities in the State.[145]

Salinas was perceived by Californians (both new immigrants and native-born arrivals) as an up-and-coming place with the promise of becoming a centerpiece of an increasingly urban California—a state that included many other places made up of postbellum horticulturalists building towns and cities based on communal spirit, farming and landownership, and orderly growth. Salinas was nostalgically identified with cowboy culture and featured the rodeo as the biggest event on the city's calendar.[146] A confluence of forces determined Salinas's twentieth-century identity as a market center for the rich agricultural region surrounding it and, as the county seat, as the political and social center for the region too.

After California's entry into the Union in 1850, a wave of incorporation took place throughout the state that created Anglo American instant towns and cities in agricultural regions, fusing urbanization with the rural. Like Salinas, many of these places developed under the auspices of the Southern Pacific and Central Pacific Railroad Companies, but Salinas also now had the distinction of being the market center for a rich agricultural region. Its settler colonialist founders were comprised of Anglo American women and men, immigrants and migrants from other parts of California, and Chinese immigrants and Chinese Americans, who purposefully and callously

appropriated space from Indigenous People, Mexican settlers, and prominent Californios, such as Juan Castro and R. M. F. Soto, with considerable
resistance. Wheat remained the significant crop, but new developments in
irrigation and technology would change that in the next decades, marking
Salinas as one of the most productive, wealthiest, and most diverse places
in California and a microcosm of California's late nineteenth-century urban
landscape.

FIGURE 2.1   Salinas Rodeo parade float, circa 1920s
COURTESY MONTEREY COUNTY HISTORICAL SOCIETY.

CHAPTER 2

Racial Crossroads

All through my six years at Lincoln Grammar School, classes
numbered thirty pupils or more. In most of my classes, there were a
couple of Japanese children. Our principal was a Caucasian woman
and her secretary was a young Japanese woman whose younger sister
was in my class. We all respected our administrators and teachers
and followed the rules. Many children were offspring of immigrants.
There was no discrimination or bullying. In those days, we were all
there to be educated.

Blanche Chin Ah Tye, *Full of Gold: Growing Up in Salinas*
Chinatown, Living in Post War America, p. 20.

BLANCHE CHIN AH TYE was a daughter of Salinas whose family story
illustrated, in part, what urban life in a rural environment meant for Chinese Americans. She was born on June 20, 1919 in Salinas's Chinatown (on
Soledad Street) to a family that included her parents and three brothers,
all of whom were born in the United States and were thus, by virtue of the
Fourteenth Amendment, American citizens. Her Chinese-born noncitizen
grandfather (a merchant originally from San Francisco) also lived with
the family.[1] Her earliest memory of Salinas was of concrete being poured

for sidewalks in Chinatown, which she described as a "big event" for the community, an indication of the increasing infrastructural development happening throughout the city that included Chinatown. The fact that Salinas had a Chinatown at all characterized California urban life during the late nineteenth and early twentieth centuries. However, and in contrast to cities such as San José, Los Angeles, and San Francisco, where barrios and Chinatowns notably lacked basic infrastructure and families lived in tents and ramshackle housing, in Salinas and other towns in rural, agricultural California, Chinatown was part of the central city; it had permanent housing and the basics of infrastructure such as paved streets, lighting, and sidewalks.[2] Yet, Ah Tye was quite aware that she lived on "the other side of the tracks" as she described it. She was a sharp and perceptive observer, commenting on both distinctions and similarities between her Chinese family and friends and "the Caucasians" in everyday life in 1920s Salinas.

INCLUSION AND EXCLUSION

The Chinese community Ah Tye described of merchants and retailers (including her family who were herbalists) was closely connected to San Francisco's Chinese community. Her father purchased supplies from "Yen Ning Tong," of San Francisco and, Ah Tye noted, "a Chinese truck driver delivered to Salinas once a week," making the critical connection to San Francisco commonplace and suggesting ongoing business relationships.

Chinese residents established an insular mutually supportive community in Salinas as they did in other places within a context of marginalization and racism. "We Chinese trusted one another," she noted. Her mother frequently "took in" single Chinese men down on their luck from gambling or smoking too much opium, also a habit of her grandfather. Ah Tye's mother embraced Chinese residents and newcomers who just felt alone in a new American environment that was uniformly hostile to them: "Our door was always open," she remembered, describing her mother as "very kind-hearted." Ah Tye's mother could see how isolating the experience of immigration could be, especially in the harsh racist environment of America. Ah Tye remembered a flow of people coming and going through her household as evidence of communal intimacy and support that helped mitigate the racism all around them. "Some Chinese men . . . wanted a little family atmosphere . . . Whenever my mother made anything, it would be an all-day affair because people would come and eat and leave as more friends came," she recalled.[3]

Yet, her reflections also showed connection to Salinas's non-Chinese community. The tiny population and its identity as a farming community required a certain intimacy, and that meant that schools were less likely to be segregated by race, as they were in nonfarming environments or larger municipalities.[4] Ah Tye described a public school environment that felt free and fair, at least to her, reinforcing the way that small communities in rural areas allowed for an informality and closeness absent in urban centers. Ah Tye believed that neither gender nor race kept her from active participation in school or recreational activities, but as an older woman remembering childhood nostalgically, she may have forgotten (or overlooked) the myriad ways that Chinese American children were not treated as well as whites within the school system, a situation that was documented in the 1970s. She recalled playing sports: "In baseball I always played shortstop, and in soccer, I played wing position."[5]

Ah Tye attended both Chinese school and American public school. Her mother made apple pies and doung, which she called "Chinese tamales." Her family celebrated American holidays such as Christmas as well as Chinese ones and participated fully in citywide events and celebrations, notably the Salinas Rodeo in July, just as much as others in the city. They also craved home ownership, the definition of American middle-class values. She explained that "for most Chinese families it was important to own your own home . . . no matter how poor you are, at least you have a roof over your head."[6] This was true for non-Chinese families too. She expressed her sense of cultural difference from non-Chinese people in Salinas in the same ways other Americans of various ethnicities did—through culture and food—and also shared with non-Chinese immigrant children the desire to conform to a perceived Anglo American custom, suggesting a clear sense that the normative model was distinctively anti-Asian: "For lunches we children didn't have sandwiches like our Caucasian classmates. My mother made rice balls filled with ham or Chinese sausage. . . . Since we didn't like to seem different, we'd go to the baseball field to eat in privacy. . . . As time went by, we learned about bread, mayonnaise and lunch meat and started bringing sandwiches to school."[7]

In Salinas as in most other rural places, race and ethnic diversity were a normal part of the social fabric, yet not everyone's incorporation into town life was on an equal footing.[8] Nowhere was this more apparent than in Salinas's celebration of the rodeo, which became the very definition of identity for the city. The Salinas Rodeo was part of the effort of city boosters to lure tourists and to define Salinas in rural, cowboy cultural terms. Ah Tye described "Rodeo Week" as "full of fun" that included not just the usual roping events, but also a "carnival . . . set up by the train depot." As a child, she expressed the wonder and delight of being in the mix of people and activity of this huge and defining event for Salinas: "Just to be in the crowd with bright night lights was exciting. . . . My family looked forward to the Saturday night rodeo parade down Main Street." Besides tourists, Salinas families invited kin from all over California to share in the event. For Ah Tye, this meant her cousins from nearby San José, "Mae and Ada Chan, who came to stay with us for a few days."[9] In the context of a cultural celebration at least, the racial boundaries may have been less apparent than in day-to-day life.

Ah Tye was elderly when she recollected these happy memories and may have blocked out the negative events or hostility that she had encountered due to her Chinese origin. Nonetheless, her views suggested a context in contrast to what most Chinese people experienced in large municipalities in California in the first two decades of the century, but one that was shared by Chinese people and other Asian groups in Silicon Valley and Pajaro Valley as well as throughout the Central Coast region. Like Salinas, multiple agricultural communities included increasing populations of diverse groups of Asian immigrants by the early twentieth century, including both horticulturalists aiming to own land and property and city-builders aspiring to be permanent stakeholders rather than migrant workers in agricultural fields.[10]

Ah Tye even explained neighborhood segregation of Chinese people in Salinas in positive terms: "The old days in Chinatown were called 'segregation,' but the Chinese were like one, big happy family and lasting bonds of love and affection were formed."[11] This suggested, once again, a nostalgic view that may have softened over time, but it also reflected her sense of belonging. This was in contrast to the ostracization that most Chinese people felt in the bigger urban environments of Los Angeles and San Francisco; those who lived in more intimate settings in agricultural regions—not just in Salinas but also in Pajaro, Contra Costa, and Santa Clara—seemed to find a more solid socioeconomic place.[12] It is human nature to put a positive spin on what was clearly racially based exclusion and inferior treatment; it is a common response among African Americans, southern and eastern Europeans living in the eastern cities, other Asian communities, and Mexican Americans. Human beings find ways to survive and even thrive despite difficult, painful, and harsh circumstances.

Ah Tye's perspective is valuable also for her focus on the women in her life and her awareness of gender. Women activists in Salinas were not all white people nor all members of the Women's Christian Temperance Union or the Women's Civic Club. The Chinese women she knew and remembered—her mother, teachers, and friends—were involved, active in community life, and played as significant a role in creating community as their Anglo American counterparts, even as Chinese women clearly were not part of the social world of white women nor were they accepted as equals. Ah Tye's mother nonetheless persevered. She performed the important role of community support person for people in the neighborhood made desperate by economic circumstance. Her memory of her mother cooking for all and utilizing a barter system to supplement the family's food supply point to the innovative ways families came together to support one another and to their collective strength and resilience. It is a tribute to her mother's fortitude that Ah Tye was protected, insulated from the harsher consequences of life in a neighborhood marginalized both by class and race, albeit a gentler one than those that existed in either San Francisco or Los Angeles. Women of every ethnic and racial group played powerful and important roles in every aspect of society in America, particularly in towns and cities. But if they were nonwhite, they had to do so on the margins.[13]

As mentioned in Chapter 1, the Chinese Exclusion Acts did not allow permanent immigration by people of Chinese origin to the United States with exceptions made for elites, mostly merchants, and their immediate families. The acts were clear evidence of the deep hostility of Americans and particularly Californians and other westerners toward Chinese people generally, who were viewed as unassimilable citizens and unwelcome residents. As a result of this legislation, immigration from China to California and the West halted in the early years of the twentieth century. Most large agriculturalists, railroad barons, and industrialists had depended on contract labor from China to cultivate crops, build infrastructure, and toil in emerging industries.[14] Moreover, the Chinese Exclusion Acts did not allow Chinese immigrants of any class the right to naturalize and become American citizens (as immigrants of European or Mexican origin were able to do after a short period of residency in the United States). Despite the Burlingame-Seward Treaty of 1868, which had required equal treatment of Chinese people in America, by 1902 Chinese immigration was made permanently illegal. Restrictions on entry and citizenship were subsequently extended to all people from the continent of Asia in 1917, culminating in the restrictive Johnson-Reed Act of 1924 that based entry on national origin (race) with an eye to replicating the majority white population of the United States as of 1890.

Due to the popular sentiment and new policies of exclusion, Asian people were barred from neighborhoods, from certain employment and educational opportunities, and most importantly from access to American citizenship regardless of class or qualifications. Beyond this, municipalities such as San Francisco and Los Angeles, but also smaller entities throughout the West, exploded with anti-Chinese violence throughout the late nineteenth century, which persisted into the early decades of the twentieth.[15]

By contrast, Salinas (along with other towns in California located in the remote outskirts of populous San Francisco) appeared to have functioned as one of the safety valves for Chinese residents of San Francisco seeking new prospects and an escape from the virulent anti-Chinese violence, which marked the big cities (San Francisco and Los Angeles) in this period.[16] In the much smaller setting of Salinas and in other agricultural communities, Chinese people did not make up a critical mass, and so they found a reprieve from the worst assaults and discrimination they had experienced from San Francisco's white, mostly immigrant working classes. And in Salinas, the Chinese people were integral (and valuable) to the diverse regional economy. Chinese residents also found opportunity in employment and property ownership, just as they did in other emerging towns in the region surrounding San Francisco.[17] Like other smaller towns, Salinas's residents not only needed Chinese labor but also came to know Chinese people as individuals rather than as merely a threat based on the color of their skin and physical appearance—although, as William Leach showed in Chapter 1, there was certainly open hostility toward the Chinese population, with recurring fires destroying Chinatown as evidence.

CLASS AND THE URBAN-RURAL DIVIDE

Despite Ah Tye's rosy view, the animosity most Californians expressed for Chinese people was very real and present in Salinas too.[18] Still, white immigrant workers had little interest in replacing Chinese workers in draining sloughs although there were some notable exceptions.[19]

Chinese people appropriated land to yield labor-intensive crops such as strawberries and produce in this period, which supported the local farm economy.[20] The Chinese who arrived in Salinas in the first two decades of the 1900s gradually built a strong community in Salinas, layered by class and modeled on the society they remembered in San Francisco, which included establishing a network of tongs or extralegal gangs.[21] Ah Tye and her descendants remained in Salinas through the twentieth century. Her family were founders and integral to the social history of the city, but they were never acknowledged in newspaper articles or local histories as central to any history of Salinas. Instead, local journalists and historians consistently portrayed Salinas's Chinese residents as having a distinct history, apart from the main narrative; they were dependent on whites for employment and without purpose of their own—along the lines of Steinbeck's portrayal of Lee in *East of Eden*. As one critic pointed out, "Lee's character is framed around the concept that he is safer as a servant and doesn't actually want freedom. While this may be true for Lee as an individual character, it implies that Chinese Americans are incapable of following their own dreams and need to be led by rich white families."[22]

Thus, it is only small consolation that Salinas's residents did not attack Chinese people in eruptions of mob violence like they did in San Francisco or in other western cities or in nearby Monterey and Pacific Grove.[23] Like so many other western communities, Salinas's residents generally expressed their anti-Chinese sentiments through ordinances controlling space and behavior rather than violent actions. Salinas's white residents may have shared the anti-Chinese sentiments of their time, but they did not want Chinese immigrants to disappear. Population mattered to sustain the city, and Chinese people were needed and wanted as workers, retailers, and horticulturalists.

The restriction of residency for the Chinese residents of Salinas came in the context of a wave of racial segregation in the post-Reconstruction era, which gained authority from the highest level of the federal government with the 1896 *Plessy v. Ferguson* Supreme Court ruling legitimizing racial separation in neighborhoods, towns, and cities throughout the country.[24] These Chinatowns and barrios in California were the first of their kind in the United States, predating twentieth-century African American ghettoes in the East and Midwest and the increasingly rigidly segregated spaces in the South.[25] In cities and towns throughout America after the turn of the last century, African Americans were increasingly relegated to these spaces along with poorer populations of new immigrants from southern and eastern Europe, and in California, from the Philippines, Korea, Japan, South Asia, and all over Central and South America. When European Americans left the worst areas of cities as they gained wealth, middle-class and professional Mexicans who identified as Spanish joined them. But even middle-class Chinese, African American, and Japanese people could not do so until well after the 1940s. Even after the 1960s, spatial boundaries were apparent for groups considered people of color in Salinas as was true elsewhere in the state and the nation. In Monterey County beginning in the early years of the twentieth century, African Americans joined working-class southern European immigrants, Japanese and Chinese immigrants, and Mexican immigrants in creating mixed-race neighborhoods along the waterfront to support the emerging fishing industry. Gradually, African Americans were forced into the subdivision of Monterey known as Seaside, while most Mexican Americans moved into Salinas, joined by an increasing number of Filipino/a immigrants.[26]

Yet, just as in many other agricultural communities in regions across California, the lines were softened in Salinas because there was room on ranches, farms, and in the unincorporated spaces to the east and the north of the city in which people lived in multiracial, multicultural settings.[27] Salinas's residents made no effort to annex these spaces until they became more desirable socially and economically in the 1960s when white settlement from the Dust Bowl migrations matured.[28] By then, it appeared that places like Alisal might make a significant economic contribution to the city as a subdivision. However, long before the annexation of Alisal, we see the complexity of Chinese settlement in Salinas, revealing the fuzzy urban-rural divide in the city's development. Chinese agriculturalists developed farming, including new methods and new crops in Salinas, but they also came from an urban world of businesspeople like Ah Tye's family. When we examine the life of another prominent Chinese resident and his family in Salinas, we see how migration from San Francisco and patterns of settlement played out in Salinas, which set the stage for the treatment of other racially marginalized groups arriving over the course of the twentieth century.

Like so many other Chinese youths with roots in Guangdong Province in China, Lee Yin (later known as Shorty Lee) arrived in San Francisco in 1897 at age nine to "learn the mercantile trade" in a store owned by his uncle, Lee Kwok Doon.[29] Lee Yin's upper-class merchant family was able to move back and forth between China and the United States with relative ease compared to their contemporaries because of their class status as merchant elites. Unlike so many thousands of poorer Chinese people, the family did not face detention (sometimes for years) at Angel Island Immigration Station or experience the extreme hardship of being refused entry altogether and forced into imprisonment at Angel Island or returned to China.[30]

Lee Yin arrived in the United States relatively unscathed. Collective family memories of San Francisco in particular, with its substantial Chinese population, showed routine violence that erupted in rioting, lynching, and ordinances designed to keep Chinese people impoverished and locked into an inescapable and overcrowded ghetto in one area of the city designated as Chinatown; the ghetto lacked basic sanitation or infrastructure and was purposefully mired in disease and filth due to lack of city intervention.[31]

Lee Yin returned to China twice and then managed to reenter the United States two times with little difficulty based on his class status, even in this hostile climate. He married in 1902 and escaped the violence and overcrowding of San Francisco's Chinatown to settle in Salinas in 1908, arriving shortly after the 1906 earthquake devastated both cities. He found employment in the Quong Chong Yuen general store on Soledad Street that was owned by an uncle. Lee Yin thrived economically and socially. Besides managing small retail establishments, which were legal, he also engaged in gambling and other illegal enterprises. Many Chinese people, including Lee Yin, were forced to get involved in illegal activities just to survive, giving Chinatown a notorious reputation as a center for crime and violence by the early decades of the new century.[32]

By 1908 when Lee Yin settled in Salinas, the Chinese community was clearly marked by class. He described the class hierarchy as "Merchants, the Servants/cooks/vegetable peddlers/laundrymen, the Laborers, and the Lost Souls (mentally retarded, vagabonds, hobos, homeless in those days) in that order from top to bottom."[33] Thus, in contrast to accounts from white chroniclers of Salinas history who only described Chinese laborers, the population of Salinas's Chinese community was diverse: some rural and some agricultural, some city dwellers, some accumulating considerable wealth and property. According to Lee Yin, important merchants like Blanche Ah Tye's father "provided products and services to the laborers and were able to maintain families and better living conditions than the camps and group housing that the laborers had."[34] Lee Yin was wealthy enough to house and support an extended family of three generations. To be sure, the Chinese neighborhoods in Salinas included "gambling and opium joints" connected to tongs in San Francisco that drew the ire of Salinas's white, mostly women activists in this Progressive era.[35] Chinatown became home to non-Chinese immigrant groups by the turn of the century—most importantly Japanese people—and by the 1920s, Filipino/a people and Mexican Americans who were also denied access to neighborhoods designated as white spaces in Salinas. All these groups settled in Chinatown around Soledad Street and in the unincorporated adjacent area of Alisal, in neighborhoods to the north and east sides of Salinas.

Because Salinas remained rural, it had a built-in safety valve in the subdivisions and unincorporated areas of the city that were both agricultural and multiracial enclaves. These included working-class Anglo Americans. In addition, multiple and diverse racial groups settled onto the farms and ranches adjacent to the city and throughout the Salinas Valley. As a result, the increasing numbers of people of Japanese, Mexican American, and Filipino/a origin lived among whites rather than being isolated in certain city blocks within the city of Salinas itself, just like in so many other agricultural regions in California.[36] Like Chinese people, Japanese and Filipino/a immigrant groups did not make up a critical mass in city space in smaller agricultural towns; perhaps because of their smaller numbers and the nature of farming, these minority groups comprised more intimate work and living environments.[37]

By the beginning of the new century, Salinas contained a rapidly expanding population that resembled other, longer established California communities such as Monterey, San José, or Santa Barbara, yet it also diverged from them. Like those places, Salinas included many native-born Anglo Americans and Asian people (almost all Chinese) who were somewhat segregated from white neighborhoods but also lived among whites in the unincorporated spaces of north and east Salinas and in surrounding farms and ranches. We see in Salinas a population of whites (many native born but also recent immigrants from northern European countries) who formed a business and governing class that remained in place until the 1980s, a population of Mexican Americans and Indigenous People from the Spanish and Mexican eras, and a scattered smaller population of Asian people (mostly Chinese but also Japanese and Filipinos/as) and working-class whites both in the area designated as Chinatown and scattered in the north Salinas subdivision and throughout Alisal. City boundaries did not change drastically, but city wealth increased noticeably in these years as agricultural growth intermeshed with business development. In Salinas the two became inseparable.

By the turn of the new century, Salinas's residents had settled in fully to the area they now claimed as an American space: a town that now resembled any other municipality in America in its homes, paved streets, sidewalks, power and light, schools and libraries. But Salinas's city leaders imagined something more than just another township. They wanted to create an "industrial garden"[38] and collectively pursued a strategy of town develop-ment economically dependent on agricultural productivity, tourism based on Salinas's status as county seat, and investments by finance and industry that would provide a solid tax base and offer employment for residents within the city and in its outlying areas. Most importantly, city identity was tied to a self-image as a rustic, cowboy town expressed in the annual Salinas Rodeo.

TOURISM AND CITY-BUILDING

Salinas's city-builders believed that industrial growth and tourism together with agricultural production might support the development of the town itself—its schools, parks, recreation centers, and transportation systems—rather than relying solely on taxes from residents to do so. They had every reason to be optimistic. Agriculture thrived and new crops such as row crops (lettuce) and sugar beets promised great possibilities. The expanding population—3,304 by 1900, 3,736 in 1910, and 4,308 by 1920—would more than double to 10,263 by 1930 when the production of lettuce pulled in new populations and made Salinas one of the most promising and wealthi-est cities in the United States. Population increases verified Salinas's place as the economic, social, and political focal point for the county and the entire region. The high-end hotels and restaurants in Salinas's downtown could (and did) accommodate thousands of visitors from throughout the state attending important agricultural and political meetings and social and cultural events regularly happening throughout the first two decades of the new century. City leaders encouraged the development of elegant hotels on Main Street with just such a purpose in mind.

In the first twenty years of the new century, Salinas's strategy of enticing tourists and organizations to meet in their town, coupled with collectively encouraging both industrial investment and agricultural production, worked successfully to build the city into a regional agricultural center. We see evidence of this in the local newspaper accounts of the era and the continuous efforts of the city council and the chamber of commerce to create regional transportation systems (with county funding) that went beyond the railroad, focusing mainly on road building but also on constructing an airport. City leaders became actively involved in any effort to connect Salinas to the smaller agricultural and ranching communities in the region by sharing identity as rural places, but also to the larger municipalities north and south, through a regional transportation network and a shared identity as county sets and urban centers. Salinas's city leaders vehemently resisted any effort to build roads linking San Francisco to Los Angeles that might bypass Salinas.

The establishment of multiple community banks—and the development of the lettuce industry with its multiplicity of small farms interconnected with packing plants and shipping facilities—all combined to encourage development and population growth throughout the 1920s. Some of the most committed city-builders in this time joined forces in 1924 to form the Salinas Women's Civic Club. This group would champion everything from the building of the library and public school systems at the turn of the century to passage of ordinances such as the 1921 "Little Wright Act," which made liquor sales illegal in the city. By 1926, Salinas had an active chamber of commerce and a city manager to bring the city into a more business-oriented model of governance.

The city planners succeeded, as the minutes of chamber of commerce in the 1920s attest. For example, in 1926, one "Mr. Lawton of the Pacific Highway Association" presented a plan to the Salinas Chamber of Commerce urging them to help him raise money to build roads under the auspices of the Pacific Highway Association. As a way of generating support, this booster produced "one hundred thousand new folders in which they were featuring Salinas." In addition, the advertising committee sought visitors from eastern and midwestern states, encouraging them to make Salinas a stopover on any road trip. One such example "reported that [the chamber] purchase one page in the Michigan Tour pamphlet for $50.00," which the members voted to approve. It was a typical suggestion usually met with approval in meetings throughout the 1920s.[39] This note from the minutes showed both active involvement in soliciting funds to support transportation systems through Salinas and efforts to advertise the town to prospective businesspeople and organizations seeking meeting venues. It was also meant to showcase Salinas as a desirable town for white settlement in keeping with efforts by boosters throughout the West and California to make their towns and cities important by attracting population and business investment as well as tourism.[40] They did not see any contradiction between an identity as a modern city and a rural, agricultural community. For them, the two were part and parcel of a city identity, not in conflict.

The large Victorians that these early twentieth-century settlers built in downtown Salinas and the infrastructure that they created to support their prosperous lives were displays of economic power and more evidence that this was a bona fide city, not a fly-by-night settlement that might blow away with the first drought or flood. It was also evidence of the stability, prosperity, and aspiration of residents who wanted to ensure Salinas a significant place in the rapidly developing urban environment typical of California at the turn of the century. Economic development was a critical component to achieve this planned urban growth based on ideologies of corporate business and farm ownership.[41] It all required financing and credit that could only be obtained through the networks of community banks linked to San Francisco financial centers, which proliferated during this period and throughout the early years of the twentieth century, marking Salinas as the wealthiest city per capita in the United States by 1924.[42]

The farmland surrounding the city was some of the richest in the entire country and therefore a valuable lure for Americans who believed deeply in farmland ownership as a cornerstone of American values.[43] Salinas's leaders pursued a strategy of growing their city through increased population, identifying as a prosperous agricultural and ranching community with room and opportunity for all. They encouraged settlement for newcomers in the surrounding unincorporated areas and focused on developing the city within its late nineteenth-century limits. They also wanted to professionalize governance and management of the city. At a meeting of the chamber of commerce on March 23, 1926, Exchange Club President Ralph Hughes reported that there were a series of discussions between his group and the Salinas Rotary Club about hiring a city manager. In keeping with efforts to keep Salinas connected with the rest of the towns and emerging cities around San Francisco, "several speakers [including] City Manager Eddy of Berkeley, City Manager Dorton of Monterey, Mayor Hudson of Monterey, and Mayor Clark of Salinas" were all invited to discuss "if a city manager was practical and needed for Salinas." It was decided to invite the city managers from Monterey and Berkeley to visit Salinas and "make a survey" paid for by the chamber of commerce to decide the matter. Ultimately, they chose to hire a city manager as one more effort to bring Salinas into the community of cities run by professionals and city planners rather than by resident politicians.[44]

SALINAS IN NATIONAL AND INTERNATIONAL CONTEXT

The 1890s had marked a critical turning point for the city of Salinas, as it did for Californians generally. The Spanish-American War (1898) and industrialization in cities and in agriculture brought new working-class populations into the region and the state, which included multiple Asian groups. The radical labor activism and anti-immigration, anti-Asian climate of the country in the 1910s, and the U.S. involvement in World War I, created a sense that the country might be moving toward chaos and anarchy. These sentiments affected the development of the country, the state, and the city of Salinas in profound and important ways as well, altering settlement patterns and adding political, social, and cultural stresses. But there were also new opportunities for growth. Salinas's agricultural development diversified significantly, which allowed residents of the entire area to avoid the most severe consequences of the depressions of 1873 and 1893 that hit grain farmers in the Midwest hardest and gave rise to an increasingly ardent populist movement.[45] It was this innovative approach to agricultural development made possible by the rich farmland of the Salinas Valley that contributed to Salinas becoming an orderly, protected space in contrast to the more chaotic and virulently nativist environments of larger municipalities such as San Francisco, Los Angeles, and Oakland in the early years of the century. According to one historian writing about agricultural towns in this era, "In agricultural communities, traditions of nativism confronted . . . stability [so that] interdependence . . . tempered overt hostility [against immigrants]."[46]

That fundamental difference in intergroup relations between large urban centers in California and smaller, diversified, agricultural communities showed in the local reporting of a bombing in San Francisco on the eve of World War I. The San Francisco Chamber of Commerce organized a Preparedness Day Parade on July 22, 1916 to show support for the war raging in Europe. During the parade, anarchists against American involvement in the conflict in Europe exploded a bomb hidden in a suitcase in the middle of the parade route killing ten people and wounding forty. It was the worst terrorist attack in San Francisco's history. That attack was part of a widespread, increasingly radical politics in California in the first decades of the twentieth century, especially in cities undergoing rapid industrialization, economic volatility, and dramatic demographic change. It was designed to sow doubt and discord over the U.S. entry into World War I and create chaos and terror as well. Salinas's residents barely shrugged.

The Salinas newspapers minimized the bombing. It was sandwiched between headlines featuring Allied progress in the war with Germany and laudatory articles about the parade in San Francisco as a reflection of the patriotism of San Franciscans and all Californians:

> With bands playing national airs, fife and drum corps rendering martial numbers that never fail to make the blood tingle, and with thousands of flags floating in the breeze, San Francisco went on record in favor of adequate preparedness in one of the biggest processions the West has ever held . . . represent[ing] every city and town [in the] entire bay section.[47]

The article documented that a delegation from Monterey County participated in the event, coming on "special train" and that they were "wildly cheered."[48] In agriculturally based Salinas, immigrants were welcomed as valued workers who added to the population numbers, not feared as labor organizers, even when incidents like this one might have led to backlash.

Although news about the perpetrators of the bombing regularly made the front pages, there was no indication in subsequent issues about a growing labor movement or radical activism as a widespread threat to order. Instead, editorials waxed eloquently about the need for preparedness for the European war on the horizon and generally focused on the more mundane aspects of city life such as deaths of prominent citizens, sporting events, and new developments in transportation systems or agricultural news. Chinese people, especially leaders and wealthier residents, featured prominently in the local newspapers alongside non-Chinese political and social elites.

In the 1910s through the 1920s, California was a state teeming with new migrations, both internally and externally.[49] Cities and towns in California became destinations for hundreds of thousands of Americans from southern and eastern states. Within the state people were constantly on the move too.[50] Millions of new immigrants from southern and eastern Europe (fleeing poverty and political repression), from many parts of Asia (suffering from widespread war and famine), and refugees from revolutionary Mexico (also undergoing political and economic turmoil) sought new lives in California. As a result of the new migrations, population in regions throughout the state markedly increased and diversified.[51] The cities themselves became congested as needs for housing and infrastructure could not keep pace with demand. As a result, we see a worrying context of poverty, disease, and waves of unemployment due to an unstable, unpredictable economy and increasing pressure on politicians to restrict immigration.

The anarchist politics behind the San Francisco bombing were intertwined with a new international labor movement, which focused its organizing efforts on these immigrant groups in the United States who labored in factories under dangerous conditions for subsistence wages, leaving them impoverished and exploited. As a result, union activity became entwined with violence and radical politics in the minds of many Americans. That conflated thinking fueled a backlash against immigrants generally that, in turn, led to the passage of the most restrictive immigration legislation in American history, the National Origins Act, also known as the Johnson-Reed Act of 1924. This piece of legislation combined with the 1917 Barred Zone Act effectively eliminated new immigration from the entire continent of Asia and severely limited immigration from southern and eastern Europe. Filipino/a and Mexican immigrant workers (mostly men) arrived in California in this period (1910s and 1920s) to fill the labor shortages that occurred in the wake of this restrictive legislation that removed Japanese, Chinese, and most European immigrant groups from the labor pool. As a result, Filipinos/as, both immigrants and native born, and Mexican immigrants and Mexican Americans became new targets of the backlash against immigrants in California. They were victimized in towns throughout the region surrounding San Francisco including the cities of Watsonville and Monterey, both next door to Salinas.

Salinas, on the other hand, diverged. It became less an example of this typical California city fraught with conflict and more of an outlier, a position it would solidify in the ensuing century. Even with the notoriety of labor strikes, Salinas's dramatic agricultural growth and the wealth it generated needed workers of all kinds—business and marketing people, professionals and retailers. It required diverse peoples to get along somewhat peaceably in the common effort of growing, harvesting, and marketing crops and maintaining its place as the urban hub of an entire region.

Salinas experienced less of the violence and turmoil that large municipalities felt in these decades. Like other regions based on agriculture rather than manufacturing, those who arrived in the 1910s, 1920s, and even into the 1930s—immigrants, first generations, and native Californians—supported the new development patterns in agriculture begun in the late nineteenth century when new arrivals might start out as laborers but aspire to become managers and landowners too, even with the constraining legislation that prohibited Asians from landownership.[52]

Although residents of Salinas in the 1910s and 1920s remained predominantly white and native born, the population included Chinese Americans, Mexican Americans, and newly arrived Japanese and Filipino/a immigrants, all of whom took their places as integral members of the community. Like their Progressive era counterparts in other regions, Salinas's builders represented by all ethnic and racial groups, including a handful of African Americans and South Asians, created new schools and built libraries in order to speed assimilation of immigrants and their children and to encourage a responsible, patriotic, and educated citizenry. They continued to build infrastructure too, not just in white neighborhoods, but also all over the city, paving streets and ensuring the availability of safe drinking water and access to power supplies. They built sewer systems throughout the city. They paid attention to cultural needs, including building that opera house financed by Jesse Carr, and organizing cultural and educational events that were routinely advertised in the city's multiple local newspapers. They perceived themselves as a vital part of the mosaic of cities that made up a network surrounding San Francisco but also as an integral rural center for one of the most productive agricultural regions in the United States.

SUGAR BEETS

As part of their strategy for city-building and industrial development, Jesse Carr, J. B. Iverson, William Vanderhurst, and several other local business leaders organized the first Monterey District Agricultural Fair Association in 1890 to bring Claus Spreckels to Salinas and to cement Salinas's place as a centerpiece for the region. They might have been better off had they considered the old saying, "Be careful what you wish for." Spreckels was a ruthless, self-centered industrialist, who—unlike the visionary Lee Yin or the Ah Tye family, or Jesse Carr or Dr. May Gydison—had little interest in Salinas much less giving back to the community, as was clear from all extant records. Spreckels ignored Salinas. Instead, he decided to build his own town, named after himself, adjacent to his fields and factory.

Claus Spreckels was born in Lamstedt, Germany, in 1828. He arrived in the United States as a teenager fleeing military service and worked as a grocery clerk first in South Carolina, then New York City, before finally settling in San Francisco in 1863. There, he and his brother Peter co-owned and operated the Bay Sugar Refining Company, utilizing cane sugar from Hawaii for production. Ebenezer Herrick Dyer was one of California's first and most successful growers and producers of beet sugar, but his efforts soon paled in comparison to the success of Claus Spreckels and the Spreckels family.

Spreckels had observed a beet sugar plant in the California town of Soquel owned by Dyer and became interested enough to return to Germany to learn firsthand about the closely guarded secrets of beet sugar processing. It had been a flourishing industry in Europe throughout the early nineteenth century that only increased at mid-century with innovations in agriculture. In Europe, factory owners and farmers were one and the same, so that growing beets and processing them into sugar were all one enterprise under single ownership, expediting the entire process. Moreover, the leftover beet pulp fed cattle so that every part of the beet was utilized completely by these farmer-processors. Returning to Germany in 1867 and pretending to be a common laborer working at a beet sugar processing plant in Magdeburg, Spreckels gained enough knowledge about sugar production to create his own processing plant when he returned to San Francisco.

Between 1888 and 1913, processing beets into sugar became a successful industry in the United States. Over the course of the 1890s, the sugar beet was improved for quality and quantity, and production methods were upgraded dramatically:

> The diffusion process of manufacture was introduced. Originally, the beets were ground or sliced and the juice was extracted by pressing, or by centrifugal force. By the diffusion process . . . sliced beets or "cossettes" were submerged in hot water so that the sugar (and certain other substances) passed through the cell walls, leaving behind the exhausted cossettes or pulp. The new process was not only more efficient, but extracted a far higher quantity of sugar.[53]

The Civil War (and with it the end of slavery as a labor force) cut off importation of cane sugar and molasses from the South. The U.S. government under the auspices of the Department of Agriculture intervened, providing new supports for growing beets for sugar through protective tariffs and for developing processing plants based on the European model.[54] As a result of federal subsidies, American entrepreneurs (including Mormons in Utah) were able to grow beets for sugar and build new processing plants, counting on limited competition from European producers. In the United States, beets grown for processing into sugar became big business, and like other corporate enterprises at the turn of the century, this quickly became a fiercely competitive industry. The Sugar Trust was a monopoly that controlled price and production by organizing producers in Utah, Idaho, and throughout the Midwest and Hawaii to control prices, utilizing the railroads as part of a powerful conglomerate. Spreckels challenged the Sugar Trust and the railroad giants. He built his own factory in Philadelphia and then another in San Francisco. He then built the Pajaro Valley Consolidated Railroad and subsequently became president of the San Francisco and San Joaquin Valley Railroad (sold to the Santa Fe Railway by 1901) that paralleled the route of the Southern Pacific to markets in Los Angeles and allowed him to undercut the Southern Pacific in getting his sugar to market. Spreckels had created the Western Beet Sugar Company and bought land in Watsonville in 1888. He brought in "experienced beet growers, builders, operators, and machinery from Germany, and erected a $400,000 factory [there]."[55]

It was in this context that Spreckels negotiated with Carr and other Salinas Valley business leaders to abandon his Watsonville plant to build a factory near Salinas, with the critical provision that Salinas's farmers would sign contracts at guaranteed prices to provide Spreckels with sufficient product in sugar beets to make the enterprise profitable for all. In 1896, the city of Salinas pledged the requisite number of local farmers to commit to Spreckels to grow the beets near the Spreckels plant, guaranteeing Spreckels a steady flow of produce to supply his plant.

Known as the "sugar king" for his success in processing Hawaiian sugar cane for market, Carr and his partners wanted Spreckels to build a beet sugar manufacturing plant in the Salinas Valley with the idea of bringing greater wealth and employment to the city, which they believed would solidify Salinas as a metropolitan center of significance in California and ensure their stature as leaders of an important urban center.[56] They wanted personal gain to be sure, but they were also looking for opportunities to create the kind of ideal community that exemplified American Progressive values. A beet sugar factory not only meant more revenue to build schools, parks, and infrastructure for Salinas, but might also create new opportunities for long-term employment for residents both in and around the city. A beet sugar factory also might bring in a new population of farmers to grow the beets for processing, thus expanding a city population founded on the ideal of landowning small farmers.

Carr and the others had little understanding of the kinds of farmers that Spreckels would bring, however; nor did they appreciate that Spreckels did not share their collective (and visionary) goals for city-building and city progress. Unlike Carr and his late nineteenth-century contemporaries, Spreckels, an immigrant himself, had a background as a Hawaiian sugar plantation owner who supported importing contract laborers (many of whom were diverse groups of Asian workers) as a strategy for the creation of a malleable labor force restrained from collective action due to language and cultural differences among them. Most importantly, these workers could not be on a path to citizenship because they were Asian; so rather than contributing to Salinas's permanent population base, Spreckels exploited labor in the same callous way that his contemporaries such as Leland Stanford did. He was not the first (or hardly the only one) who imposed a racial hierarchy to exploit workers, but the sheer size of his manufacturing and agricultural enterprise and its prominence in the small, rural environment of Salinas made his racism both more obvious and certainly more impactful.[57]

The result was that the establishment of his factory in 1898 did not so much provide employment for residents of Salinas as it complicated Salinas's racial picture by bringing in a new labor force of Japanese, Mexican, and Filipino/a immigrants without guarantees that the new workers might become integrated in city life or even permanent residents.[58] However, in the end, only about 10 percent of farmers who grew the beets for processing were ineligible for citizenship based on race and national origin. Most of them, 90 percent, "were either American citizens" or eligible for naturalization and citizenship as whites, according to the *Pacific Rural Press*.[59] Nonetheless, the press indicated that "Orientals do most of the hand labor" and proceeded to identify them by race linked to specific task: "The color of one's skin relegated the Chinese, Japanese, Hindu, Mexican, and Filipino to the difficult work of stooping at the end of a short handled hoe."[60]

Salinas's population rose from 3,304 in 1900 (3,500 by 1902)[61] to 10,263 by 1930, but the city itself remained mostly white and Anglo American in racial and ethnic identity and kept its small footprint. Groups who arrived to work for Spreckels generally lived in north Salinas neighborhoods or in multiracial spaces in east Salinas and in surrounding farms and ranches, yet they gradually found residences in the city itself as they found ways to circumvent racial restrictions placed on them. The Cacas family exemplified this pattern within the Filipino/a immigrant community in the early twentieth century.

Born in Salinas in 1938, Ron Cacas spent most of his childhood in the labor camp that his father owned and operated. According to Ron, Filipino/a Americans "were able to become independent businessmen because Filipino American contractors prospered. . . . Those farm labor contractors were the root of the Filipino American middle class," he explained.[62] Ron Cacas described his family's journey from the Philippines to Salinas by way of Hawaii in 1919 or 1920 as part of the Filipino/a American labor force Spreckels was known to employ: "My Dad [John Cacas] came across on a ship, got off in Hawaii, worked on a sugar plantation. . . . My Dad was about eighteen or nineteen years old at the time. He was there [in Hawaii] for a year or two then [decided] to try the mainland. He arrived in San Francisco in the 1920s."[63] Ron described his father's shame and horror at the way Filipino/a immigrants were treated on board the ship to San Francisco— forced because of their poverty into the worst conditions in steerage:

The Filipino workers in steerage would go up on top of the deck on the back of the boat and they would be wearing their underwear, and the first class passengers would look down at them like [they] were in the zoo. They were laughing and pointing.[64]

Internalizing the harsh Anglo Americans' view of his compatriots, John Cacas apparently "jumped up and shouted to his fellow Filipino workers, 'Look at them [the first class passengers]. [T]hey are looking at us like we are animals. Put on your shirts and shoes. Look decent.'" His action attracted the attention of the officer in charge who offered this eighteen-year-old a position as representative for the rest of the workers on board: "'You seem to control these men,' he is said to have told John Cacas. 'If you can control them we'll give you your own room.'"[65] John Cacas apparently accepted the offer; that pivotal moment became an opportunity to assume a leadership role among his fellow workers thenceforward.

After landing in San Francisco, Ron Cacas explained how his father found his way to Salinas and assumed the leadership position that would allow the family to escape from the poverty and racial discrimination that kept so many of their fellow compatriots marginalized and poor in California. Growers, including representatives from Spreckels, approached the Filipino immigrants as their ship from Hawaii landed in San Francisco and asked John Cacas if these were his men.

My Dad asked them, "Are you guys with me?" They said "Yes Manong," which was the Ilicano term for older brother, an honorific title. That's how Dad got [to Salinas]. He didn't even know what a contractor was. He apparently spoke English better so they [the other workers] looked to him. That's how he started. He was a natural born leader. He only had a fourth grade education. His whole life was like that.[66]

Ron's father John Cacas advanced at the expense of his fellow immigrant compatriots whom he now employed as fieldworkers while he developed his labor contracting business. John Cacas was ambitious and eager to separate himself off, to find a bit of wiggle room at least for himself and his family in the racially oppressive and competitive world of California agriculture.[67] Most importantly, by doing so, he modeled possibility. Most Filipino/a immigrants would not be able to achieve even a modicum of mobility during this period. The deep, sustained racism ingrained in California's system of agriculture prevented them from ever rising above the level of fieldworker, which shamed them and made it impossible for many to return to homelands with even the minimal amount of wealth that they had hoped for when they started their journeys. Many just disappeared into American cities and towns, ending all contact with family and friends in the Philippines and living out their lives as single men in Salinas's worst neighborhoods over the decades of the twentieth century.[68]

Nonetheless, residents of Salinas ignored the inequality that was attached to Spreckels and generally were proud of the impact Claus Spreckels had on the city in the 1920s. The proximity of this factory, located less than 5 miles from Salinas city center, not only drove up the population of whites but also contributed to the establishment of new business enterprises in the city in support of the increased working class and farming population.

Spreckels had long used his political connections to advocate for tariffs to fight competition from sugar producers in Europe; this plan succeeded most notably with the passage of the Dingley Tariff in 1898. In this, Spreckels was supported by many other growers in Salinas, including William Henry Leach, who argued passionately in favor of tariff protections. Even though Spreckels had little interest in Salinas, the city enthusiastically embraced him and his factory. The *Salinas Daily Index* enthused in 1898 that the Spreckels plant "[was] the largest in the world," claiming reflected glory for the city.[69] The report then gave dimensions of all the buildings with the comment that the main office (not yet constructed) promised to be a "magnificent structure" that would produce 450 tons of sugar daily from 3,000 tons of processed beets. An entire issue of the *Salinas Daily Index* in September 1899 was devoted to details about the Spreckels's factory including an entire page of drawings of equipment and the step-by-step process of "how sugar is made from beets."[70]

Even though his intention was to enrich himself, not benefit Salinas, Spreckels provided employment opportunities for residents, migrants, and immigrants alike and also was a promoter of new technologies that would transform agriculture in the Salinas Valley: "You can imagine the small population of Salinas at the time [1900], the factory itself employed 1,300 people, that's just within the grounds of the factory, not including all the agricultural operations,"[71] one former employee explained. Furthermore,

Spreckels inadvertently paved the way for the real wealth producer in Salinas: "It [sugar beet production] brought the technology and skills. With agriculture it brought irrigation. That opened the way for green gold: lettuce."[72]

Like Jesse Carr, Claus Spreckels personified entrepreneurial capitalism at the turn of the last century. But unlike Carr, Spreckels was not a civic-minded city-builder. He was interested in building an economic empire to benefit himself and his family rather than in promoting or supporting Salinas in any purposeful way. The distinction was important because latter-day historians and journalists (beginning with Carey McWilliams) used industrial agriculturalists such as Spreckels to define the nature of corporate agriculture in twentieth-century California. According to Mc-Williams and the historians who followed in his path, growers were people who owned vast tracts of land, which they leased to smaller farmers; they disdained workers and had little or no connections to the communities associated with their farms and ranches. These elite corporate agriculturalists attained great wealth at the expense of both the people and the environment rather than in conjunction with them.

This characterization applied to Spreckels, but other growers, packers, and shippers in Salinas and the Salinas Valley demonstrated the opposite: a deep, passionate connection to the city and the community of Salinas itself. Salinas's horticulturalists and businesspeople had a stake in Salinas where they and their descendants remained throughout the next decades. It was a striking persistence that was notable in other rural towns and cities in California too. Farmers in Salinas and the Salinas Valley also came from a diverse array of racial groups who created a hierarchy of their own. Like the founders, they were not all white people. Members of Asian communities, even when they could not own the property, found ways to circumvent harsh racial restrictions and stayed in Salinas for generations as upwardly mobile middle classes.[73] Salinas defined a new model of urban life in farm country that was based, first and foremost, on multiracialism. Yet, it disguised the growing racial inequality that kept a hierarchy in place that privileged Anglo Americans. The mobility that immigrants like the Cacas family achieved was built on the immobility of the Filipino/a immigrants employed in the fields.

By 1911, it seemed that dreams of Salinas's residents for a thriving city based on agricultural production had more than been fulfilled. The local newspaper, the *Salinas Daily Index*, reported enthusiastically on its front page, under the headline "More Big Ranches Being Cut up into Small Farms":

> Things are coming our way. . . . The time for cutting up some of the large tracts in this valley . . . has arrived. . . . With small farms well tilled taking the place of large land holdings . . . Salinas will experience a growth as phenomenal as that which has marked the progress of cities of southern California . . . sustaining in comfort a population of many thousands where hundreds are now existing. . . . If this liberal policy continues the trading populations tributary to Salinas will be increased tenfold in as many years.[74]

Beyond sugar beet production, Chinese and Japanese immigrant tenant farmers developed new innovative methods of irrigation and planting in farming berries, and following that, lettuce and other row crops in the 1920s. The local newspapers encouraged these new practices and highlighted increasing yields for those who irrigated rather than depended on natural methods. On November 25, 1903, the *Salinas Daily Index* promoted irrigation: "The results shown in irrigation should convince farmers and those who have lands suitable for beet raising that irrigation is the one thing necessary . . . to insure good yields." The editorial gave examples of those who irrigated with stunning results.[75] The deep wells dug to supply water also made the production of row crops possible. Beans, corn, tomatoes, celery, asparagus, carrots, and most importantly for the local economy, lettuce, came to dominate agricultural production throughout the Salinas Valley, which thrived throughout the 1920s. The newspaper reported with enthusiasm that "great things for Salinas and its suburbs."[76]

However, there were a few bumps along the way because farmers (especially new arrivals) were not able or willing to fulfill the obligations for farming sugar beets promised by city leaders to Spreckels. This led to the Salvation Army buying up hundreds of acres of land to sell on easy terms to families from San Francisco as a way of alleviating poverty in the city and circumventing the radical politics that they feared was growing among increasing populations of unemployed working classes. Named Fort Romie, this "colony" of former city dwellers acquired between 10 and 20 acres of land apiece. At first, they succeeded somewhat in their efforts at farming, but they were city people, not used to the hardships and volatility of a farming life, and most sold off their land by the 1920s when land values increased significantly as a result the boom in lettuce production and other valuable row crops.

Demand for beets increased during World War I, but blight (which diminished the amount of sugar in the beets) severely damaged the sugar beet harvest in the 1920s, forcing Spreckels to sell off much of the 66,000 acres he had acquired to grow beets in favor of "contracting for beets [for his factory] and providing farmers with the most up-to-date technical information."[77] With wild fluctuations in sugar prices and tariff reforms that eliminated Spreckels's competitive edge both domestically and in the world market, the sugar beet industry appeared to have failed by the time the stock market crashed in 1929: 16,222 acres of sugar beets had been planted in the Salinas Valley in 1925, but only 197 acres were planted four years later.[78]

New Deal legislation in the form of farm subsidies saved sugar beets. By 1934, Spreckels had recouped his losses and become the fifth largest producer of sugar beets in the United States.[79] The Smoot-Hawley Tariff helped stimulate beet production, but because consumer prices continued to drop significantly in the 1930s, tariffs were roundly condemned as wrongheaded approaches to the problem farmers faced in the Depression era. Low prices for lettuce and beans in 1931 and 1932 incentivized farmers to return to beet growing, but the selling price of sugar did not increase.[80]

Claus Spreckels died in 1908, but his family retained control of his operations in the region and profited handsomely from its extensive sugar beet operation. Along with Spreckels family investments and landholdings in California, the Spreckels family became important philanthropists—but not in the Salinas Valley where they acquired much of their wealth. Unlike May Gydison, Jesse Carr, William Vanderhurst, and the others who moved from San Francisco to Salinas—and who not only established businesses (and in Gydison's case, a first-rate hospital) but also homes, as they invested their own fortunes in the city—Spreckels focused on turning his company into an international economic force that would challenge the hegemony of the monopolists of his day, from the sugar conglomerates in Hawaii to the Southern Pacific Railroad. Salinas's residents benefited from Spreckels decision to locate his biggest sugar processing plant nearby in terms of employment opportunities for its citizens and incoming immigrant groups, but Spreckels did not make any attempt to improve the lives of the city's residents through public service or public works. Instead, Spreckels built his own town to serve the needs of his workers in terms of food, housing, recreation, and infrastructure.[81] Thus, there was a clear difference between the women and men who formed Salinas's leadership in the first decades of the twentieth century and agricultural capitalists like Spreckels who became the model of the brutal corporate agriculturalist for journalists and historians such as Carey McWilliams.

The separate and sometimes conflicting goals of Salinas's city leaders and that of agricultural and railroad corporate interests manifested in the way the city developed during the new century. Between 1890 and 1930, city leaders and residents, women as well as men, were mainly interested in building everything from libraries to schools and in developing a community culture that reflected both the rural and the urban, rodeos and opera houses. As shown in Chapter 1, Salinas City Council meetings and newspapers of the day reflected collective efforts on the part of city leaders to install electricity and gas power grids throughout the city, including Chinatown, and to build and pave streets and build sidewalks, to develop sewer lines, and to pass ordinances to provide clean water and protect public health. With support from the Women's Civic Club, the Women's Christian Temperance Union (WCTU), and various leaders from Asian communities, Salinas utilized Jesse Carr's donation of $5,000 (supplemented by a grant he solicited from the Carnegie Corporation) to create a public library that opened officially in 1909. The Salinas Rodeo was incorporated in 1913.

City leaders created a freeholder's charter in 1919 to fund needed city services and infrastructure, which relied on property taxes from the multiple new hotels and businesses in town more than from residents. The industrial garden idea did not work when industry was located outside of the city limits as evidenced by the Spreckels factory. Also in 1919, the city council decided that the mayor ought to be elected by city council members, who in turn were reduced from an eight-person to a five-person council and elected at large rather than from districts, something that would change only with the political challenges of the 1980s when demographic shifts forced the city to acknowledge a new Mexican American population who mainly lived in Alisal (annexed in 1963 after a decade of contentious battles). Leaders prioritized establishing schools, which were always integrated racially to include Asian children as photographs and school records showed. In one school photograph taken in 1923, there are eight Japanese American students pictured out of a class of twenty-three, a significant percentage of the class.[82]

Civic leaders used zoning ordinances to separate residential spaces from commercial and industrial ones, and segregated neighborhoods by race, as was the case throughout urban California—both in agricultural and non-agricultural regions. City-building meant cultural development too that signified an identity cemented in ranching and agriculture. It meant funding multiple newspapers and creating events and organizations supporting ranching and farming community culture for all the multiple groups that made up Salinas.

On the other hand, big agriculturalists like Claus Spreckels were not interested in any of this. He supported the establishment of public amenities in his own nearby company town, which was similar in its makeup to company towns established by Pullman and other industrialists in this period. Spreckels opposed immigration restrictions and especially anti-Chinese legislation at both the federal and state levels. He was not concerned about the racial or ethnic origins of his labor force any more than he was concerned about developing the city of Salinas, as long as he could rely on laborers to do the work he needed when he needed it at the lowest cost (and highest profit) to himself. That meant inviting a diverse population of laborers to the area, preferably divided by culture, race, religion, and language so as to make solidarity by class and organizing into unions as difficult as possible.[83] Many of these workers found living space either in housing provided by Spreckels or in nearby Alisal, where multiracial mixing led to interracial sex suggested by lurid newspaper accounts of the era, although interracial marriage was illegal in California until anti-miscegenation laws were overturned in *Perez v. Sharp* in 1948.

Spreckels was aided in his endeavor by international events. The 1898 Treaty of Paris, which ended the Spanish-American War, made the United States into an imperial power giving America hegemony over the Philippines, the Caribbean, and Hawaii, where laborers from all over Asia had been contracted to work on the rapidly expanding sugar plantations. In a strategy designed to control the massive labor force needed to produce the sugar, Hawaiian planters contracted laborers from a variety of places around the globe suffering widespread poverty such as China, Portugal, Puerto Rico, Korea, the Philippines, and, most importantly, Japan.

In the wake of the Treaty of Paris, these new U.S. territories generated a wave of immigration to the U.S. mainland, particularly to California, that would alter the demographics of the state dramatically and also challenge agriculture over wages and working conditions both in the field and in production sheds.[84] The aftermath of the war created a new stream of Filipino/a immigration to all parts of California now that the Philippines had become a U.S. possession, and Filipinos/as were "insular subjects" of the United States with free access to immigration in contrast to other excluded Asian groups.[85] These migrants included a new and more diverse contingent of workers, students, and elites who sought better economic conditions and education in America than they might have in their countries of origin. Filipinos/as who came to the Salinas Valley in the first years of the century formed a complex community made up of unskilled workers in the fields, but also an important contingent of labor contractors and educated professionals who made a strong, stable, middle-class presence in the city throughout the 1920s and after, as discussed in more detail in the following chapter.[86]

By 1914 there were over 75,000 migrant farm laborers in the state of California originating from twenty-six different countries of origin.[87] In Monterey County, this played out sometimes in dramatic fashion. In February 1904, "a disgruntled Italian" exploded a stick of dynamite under the house of Japanese immigrant workers who had been hired as replacements by the Southern Pacific Railroad, displacing the Italian immigrant workers from their jobs. The effort to "commit wholesale murder" against Japanese people was duly reported by the Salinas press in sympathy with the Japanese immigrants. The individual who was responsible, Pietro Farino, was prosecuted and jailed and described as "uncommunative [sic] and morose" as he awaited trial.[88] The local papers often sided with oppressed and exploited working classes, in contrast to the general population, which just as often disdained and abused them. It was evidence of the tension in these rural communities between needing and wanting more working classes to add to their labor pool (regardless of race) and resenting their presence.

JAPANESE SETTLEMENT

Japanese immigrants and Japanese Americans exemplified this tension. They were arguably one of the most important new populations from 1890 to 1920 in terms of the impact they had on California's politics, social dynamics, and economic life. As a result of their collective successes in agricultural production and marketing, Japanese immigrants and Japanese Americans were also deeply resented by Californians.[89]

A combination of high taxes and environmental catastrophes led to widespread poverty in Japan in the 1880s. According to an 1888 report in the *Japan Weekly Mail*, "the distress among the agricultural class has reached a point never attained."[90] This led to an out-migration of over 200,000 Japanese people (180,000 to Hawaii alone) between 1885 and 1924.[91] Between 1885 and 1910, over 30,000 Japanese workers (mostly men) came to California and in so doing replaced the Chinese workers as the main targets for anti-Asian backlash in the state.[92] An aggressive and newly empowered Japanese government protested fiercely against the mistreatment of Japanese immigrants in California, focusing specifically on the segregation of Japanese children in San Francisco schools, which led to an international incident that required the direct intervention of U.S. President Theodore Roosevelt and ended in the famous Gentleman's Agreement of 1907. The agreement negotiated by Roosevelt between the United States and Japan ended further immigration from Japan but allowed Japanese children into American public schools and prohibited racial segregation in other public settings. However, this agreement did not prevent the 1913 Alien Land Law in California that prohibited Japanese people and other Asians from owning land, a critical marker of belonging especially in agricultural environments such as the Salinas Valley.

Immigrant Japanese men who came to Salinas in this era were mostly teenagers and young adults who originated predominantly from the island of Kyushu in the southern part of Japan. They were also entrepreneurial capitalists just like their native-born American predecessors in Salinas. Like so many others, including Carr, they embarked on picaresque journeys before making their way to the Salinas Valley.[93] Unlike Carr, however, these young men would not benefit from friendships with American presidents to acquire wealth or social and political influence. After stretches in Mexico or Hawaii, they often arrived in San Francisco or Los Angeles, working their way through the Imperial Valley as migrant farm laborers; they sometimes traveled to Alaska, Seattle, and other parts of the Pacific Northwest and Northern California, performing any labor they could find in order to survive before finally landing in the Salinas Valley, which was one of the important destinations for them as a direct result of Spreckels and the growth of the sugar beet industry. According to activist historian and journalist Carey McWilliams, the Asian populations of California were both diverse and increasing dramatically throughout the early years of the twentieth century.[94]

McWilliams used the sugar beet (and cotton industries) to argue that agricultural production in California was modeled on the industrialized East, in which laborers were little more than cogs in the industrial machine. However, he overlooked distinctions between industrialists like Spreckels and, in places like Salinas, people like Carr (farmer, business entrepreneur, civic leader) and smaller farmers (including the Japanese immigrants and Japanese Americans) who produced beets for sugar, like their counterparts in fruits, nuts, grapes, and specialty produce and who were landowners themselves, using their American-born children to lay claim to property they were denied by law as unassimilable immigrants. Tenant farmers of all ethnicities did not necessarily perceive themselves to be part of a permanent, exploited working class. They may have worked temporarily as farm laborers and labor contractors, but these were families who shared a deep belief in landownership as a means to socioeconomic mobility and political acceptance—the same values and dreams as other Americans of their era. They were horticulturalists at heart, deeply connected to the land and their specific crops, and just as deeply bound to an ideal of civic life exemplified in the growth and development of Salinas. The permanent caste system that McWilliams (and John Steinbeck) worried about did not develop in agricultural California. White working classes usually found ways up the socioeconomic ladder when economies opened up. The availability of farmland and the support networks in Asian communities made it possible for enough members of excluded groups to move into property ownership (a definition of middle class in America) to make it appear that there was opportunity for all.[95]

As Japanese immigrant and Japanese American farmworkers established themselves economically in California, they often returned to Japan to marry women chosen for them by their families, or were sent picture brides, women also selected by families and sent to America on behalf of the young men. Thus, as in other parts of the state, the first Japanese immigrant laborers arrived in the Salinas Valley as early as 1898. Many of them were young men, whose presence led to the establishment of a boarding house in Salinas that year. They established the Japanese Mission Hall, which soon became the Japanese Presbyterian Church and a focal point for the growing Japanese immigrant and Japanese American community in the Salinas Valley.[96] The Asian population was clearly underreported by early census takers, but it showed an increase between 1890 and 1920, from 112 to

350. This included Chinese people as well as Japanese people (although it excluded Filipino/a immigrants and Filipino/a Americans who were given a separate category in the census as of both Asian and Hispanic origin). The numbers overlooked the increasingly large numbers of Japanese immigrants and Japanese American and other Asian American families who lived on farms and ranches just outside the city limits.

The Salinas Valley Japanese American Citizens League (JACL) published a chronicle of biographical sketches, *The Issei of Salinas Valley: Japanese Pioneer Families*, in 2010 that documented in vivid detail the migration experiences of Japanese Issei in Salinas by emphasizing the men as the founding members of families in Salinas. Like other immigrant community histories, this emphasis overlooked the critical role of women in the immigration process. Women may not have been the first family members of their families to migrate, but they were always important and even central to household strategies for economic mobility that often included out-migration.[97] The family stories in this chronicle illustrate both the complex nature of migration in California and how cities like Salinas became multicultural spaces for people whose identity was, first and foremost, agricultural. Here are a few examples.

Kichita Higashi, born in 1880, arrived in the United States via Mexico in 1913, where he worked in the silver mines, returning to Japan to marry Yaye Higashi, as arranged by his family and hers in 1919. He spent the 1920s in and around Hollister and Alisal, farming grapes, peas, and lettuce as a sharecropper before leasing land to grow lettuce on his own in north Salinas. He was the father of four children whose descendants remained in Salinas. Farming gave him both access to property and a gateway to a stable, upwardly mobile life in a small community of compatriots.

Heishiro Frank Hirozawa, born in 1877, apprenticed as a blacksmith in Japan but joined a circus troupe at age eighteen as a way of reaching Vancouver, British Columbia, and from there, America. He worked as a crewman for the railroad, which landed him in San Francisco. He sought aid from the Japanese Mission Hall, which connected him to the Spreckels family, who employed him first as a stable boy, then kitchen aide, then labor contractor in the Salinas Valley. He helped plant the rows of eucalyptus and walnut trees that still line Abbott Street linking the town of Spreckels to Salinas. His stepmother's niece, Yoshi Teraji, arrived from Japan to marry him in 1913 as arranged by their respective families. He and his young family embarked on a life of farming throughout the Salinas Valley, first as a sharecropper, then as a tenant farmer leasing his land to grow his own crop. An ambitious innovator, he was the first farmer in Salinas to grow celery. Heishiro and Yoshi had eight children, three of whom died in childhood. Again, we see opportunity, migration, and farming linked within the life of this family.

Heizuchi Yamamoto and Unosuke Shikuma, both born in Japan in the 1880s, became partners with two native-born Americans, Henry Hyde and Orrin Eaton. The Japanese immigrants needed American citizens as partners and official titleholders after the Alien Land Law of 1913 so that they could grow berries. Their enterprise, the Oak Grove Berry Farm, was subsequently deemed "the largest and most productive strawberry operation in the world" with, by 1919, approximately twenty families employed as sharecroppers to produce over 3 million baskets of strawberries per year. Moreover, they were responsible for a critical innovation in marketing and transporting their berry crop, inventing a pre-cooling van that allowed them to utilize ice "on the chassis of a Pierce Arrow truck to haul their berries to San José for shipment to the East Coast in refrigerated rail cars."[98] In this way, we see how a rural farming environment provided opportunity for innovation and property ownership in a world that was otherwise defined by racial exclusion in everything from citizenship to settlement.

The Hibino family also represented this model of complexity in migration with eventual settlement in Salinas. Frank Kosaku Hibino arrived in San Francisco sometime in the 1910s at the age of sixteen. His older brother and father had lived and worked in San Francisco and its outskirts for a decade prior to his arrival, but his father returned to Japan and passed away just as Kosaku arrived in America. Kosaku nonetheless remained in the United States attending San Francisco public schools, learning English and absorbing American customs and culture. Yet, San Francisco was a hostile environment for Japanese immigrants in the 1910s, and Kosaku soon left for the smaller (if not more inviting) community of Vacaville where he engaged in farm labor. In 1923, Kosaku returned to Japan, married Sen Kobayashi, the younger daughter of a large Japanese farming family, and subsequently moved with her to Vacaville to start a family. In Vacaville, Kosaku deviated from the pattern of farm labor that most Japanese immigrants followed and apprenticed himself to a shoe repairman. He moved to Salinas where he opened a small repair shop on West Alisal Street between Main and

Salinas Streets. His family lived above the store in downtown Salinas and raised three children—Chiyeko, Henry, and Mary—until the 1930s when the family moved onto a farm in nearby Soledad, having suffered losses due to the Great Depression. Henry Hibino would become Salinas's first Asian city councilmember and the first Japanese American mayor in 1973. The family is a powerful example of how an otherwise racially excluded group presented the appearance at least of inclusion in the rural setting of Salinas.[99]

The early Hibino family story also illustrated the ways Japanese immigrants in Salinas and in other towns in Northern California's agricultural regions experienced life differently than their cohorts in San Francisco (or Los Angeles).[100] Japanese people comprised only a tiny percentage of the population in smaller agriculturally based municipalities and were counted in the racial category "Asian" along with Chinese people, Sikhs, and Filipino/a immigrants and citizens. Although the Asian population in Salinas increased considerably from 1920 to 1930, it remained steady as 8.1 percent of the city population; the Asian groups generally lived in neighborhoods known for being multiracial. However, class mattered in this small agricultural town so that some integration by class superseded race in neighborhood settlement. On outlying farms and ranches, intimacy in living space was the norm, beyond racial boundaries. By contrast, in San Francisco and Los Angeles, Japanese migrants formed a significant enough minority that they were forced into separate and rigidly controlled sections of the city known in San Francisco as "Japantown" and in Los Angeles as "Little Tokyo."[101] The intimate living triggered fears of interracial relationships and marriage more so in places like Salinas, however, and Asian-origin residents recalled painful episodes of exclusion as teenagers and young adults when they became sexual threats to Anglo Americans.

Yet, Salinas's residents expressed fears mixed with admiration for Japanese immigrants' presence and their collective work ethic in the city and the surrounding agricultural areas. One Salinas educator admonished non-Japanese teenagers at a public forum in 1921 for being less willing to do manual labor than their Japanese American contemporaries, allowing "the Japanese to do the constructive work of this nature and then howl about more production when our own people will not produce to the limit. . . . [W]e shall need to look to our laurels or the Japanese will get ahead of us."[102] The "us" clearly meant Anglo American Salinas residents.

Japanese immigrant families were determined to acquire land and property, like other Americans, rather than remain as permanent members of the
non-landowning working class. They were able to accomplish their goals of
proprietorship before the 1913 Alien Land Law that disallowed landownership for aliens deemed unassimilable, which included all Asians. After that
legislation passed in California and in other states throughout the West
where Asians were immigrating in growing numbers, Japanese people felt
distinct hostility to their presence by native-born white Americans. There
is little evidence of overt anti-Japanese feeling in Salinas, however, at least
before Pearl Harbor, although like other rural communities in California,
Salinas's residents generally supported the 1920 initiative that strengthened
the Alien Land Law of 1913. When mentioned in the pages of Salinas's
daily newspapers, Japanese people were referred to with respect and even
deference. In July 1911, for example, the *Salinas Daily Index* reported as front-
page news the death of one Mrs. Sei Nishi, "wife of H. Nishi, a well to do
Japanese farmer" in the same way that the paper routinely reported deaths
of other prominent members of Salinas's white community.[103] As well, the
local newspapers printed regular updates on Japanese American residents
as part of their reports on social, economic, and political news of the day.
This included front-page announcements of visits by dignitaries from Japan
who came to Salinas.

Japanese immigrants and Japanese American residents of California
found ingenious ways to survive and even thrive in the oppressive environment of the 1910s and 1920s, such as leasing land or putting titles in the
names of their children who were U.S. citizens by virtue of being born in
America, according to the birthright citizenship clause under the Fourteenth
Amendment. They made strenuous efforts to show that they could fit into
American society by mastering English, adopting Christianity, dressing in
western attire, and enrolling their children in American schools. All these
strategies made for a successful immigration experience in the early years
of the century and were evident in the chronicle of the Issei produced by
the Salinas JACL, which showed photographs of families usually dressed
in western clothing, smiling, successful, with numerous children. Most
importantly, the Japanese families in the Salinas Valley did not necessarily
live in Salinas's Chinatown, but in north Salinas, or in Alisal, or on the
farms and ranches throughout the valley. They developed positive working
relationships with other Americans that remained so until the bombing of

Pearl Harbor and the subsequent incarceration of the entire population of Japanese Californians in 1941, which came as a brutal shock.

In the early decades of the twentieth century, Japanese residents of Salinas contributed to the transformation of agriculture in the Salinas Valley and occupied city space in neighborhoods in the north and east, which always remained multiracial and multicultural. They were business owners, farmworkers, labor contractors, supervisors, and keepers of boarding houses. They worked most often as tenant farmers to grow beets for processing in the Spreckels plant, or they grew lettuce, celery, and berries for markets nearby. More and more, Japanese managers supervised the increasingly multiracial workforce in the fields, and together with Filipinos/as became the middlemen in agriculture as labor contractors, an occupation that gave them the upward mobility to which they aspired.

The new demographic in Salinas (just as in other parts of California and the rest of urban America) coincided with the height of so-called scientific racism in American thought. The greatest intellectual and political leaders of the day espoused and championed it. This pseudo-science divided the human species into specific, measurable, and definable categories; northern Europeans occupied the highest rung of the human ladder with African Americans at the bottom but with multiple spaces in between for Asians, southern Europeans, and eastern Europeans. An individual's physical characteristics were used to determine everything from intelligence to character. Conclusions about groups of people based on head size and shape, skin color, facial features, even stature and size drove politics and policymaking on everything from zoning to immigration in the years from 1880 until the end of World War II, with consequences into the present day. This ideology was fundamental to what became known as the eugenics movement in American society and was integral to the Progressive movement that dominated American life and legislation in the 1890s through 1918. For many Progressives, citizenship status and opportunities for housing, employment, education, and any kind of upward mobility depended upon skin color and physicality rather than on character or intelligence.

In this, Salinas's residents were no different than anyone else in California or in America. However, and like other regional rural centers in California, its smaller size and the increasing multiplicity of groups that had room to spread out beyond the city center—in addition to its dependence on agriculture as its economic base—created a far more intimate environment than that of larger municipalities or smaller towns that had less diversity of population or less space to accommodate newcomers.[104] Intimacy did not lead to inclusivity, however. It was just harder to discriminate in a sweeping way when one had close working and living relationships with people of various backgrounds.

At the turn of the nineteenth century and throughout the early years of the twentieth, Salinas could be described as a California urban community aiming to create an industrial agricultural garden with itself as the center. It was a place clearly dependent on a farming economy and subscribing to an ideal of life that depended on a majority white, landowning population but also included people who hailed from all corners of the globe, including many parts of Asia. By the 1920s, Salinas's future as the model for a new version of rural America held both promise and challenges.

FIGURE 3.1   Lettuce fieldworkers in Salinas, 1936

SOURCE: LIBRARY OF CONGRESS, PRINTS & PHOTOGRAPHS DIVISION, FARM SECURITY
ADMINISTRATION/OFFICE OF WAR INFORMATION BLACK-AND-WHITE NEGATIVES.
HTTPS://WWW.LOC.GOV/ITEM/2017763125/

CHAPTER 3

A Lettuce Metropolis

SALINAS'S FOUNDERS AND RESIDENTS were a complex mixture of nationalities and racial and ethnic groups. The history of this and other towns and cities emerging in late nineteenth- and early twentieth-century California and the West challenges us to think beyond easy characterizations of the rural, agricultural landscape as white and homogeneous. Instead, we see emerging cities in a state of tension. We see the impact and influence of Chinese people who formed layered communities within Salinas and who contributed to city-building and identity formation. We see how Mexican Americans challenged white hegemony from earliest settlement, and the critical role Filipino/a immigrants and Japanese immigrants played as they created their own economic power structures and carved out communities within Salinas.

City life may have been based on a rocky kind of communalism, but it was also dependent on state and federal government from the nineteenth century onward—to support growth and infrastructure, access to national and international markets through increasingly sophisticated transportation systems, and a flexible and large labor force influenced by fluctuating immigration policies and international events. Salinas's city dwellers relied on the liminal space of north Salinas, Alisal, and the surrounding farms and ranches to smooth the way; these places offered a transitional landscape where new arrivals who labored in the factories, the packing sheds, and the fields found the social and economic opportunities that a multiracial city might afford them. They inhabited a world that was both identifiably rural and urban, multiracial, and dominated by a white power structure—all at once.

SMALL FARMS AND CITY-BUILDING

The new twentieth century marked a turning point in agricultural innovation and production that attracted "desirable horticulturalists" of European and Asian descent who were first and foremost also city-builders. The *Pacific Rural Press* encapsulated this moment of farming juxtaposed with town life: "One of the most important benefits which will accrue to the State [of California] is the growth of the towns . . . the cutting up and populating of vast tracts of land and the immigration of the practical farmer to California."[1] Importantly, the "desirable horticulturalists" and the "practical farmers" of California may not all have been white people, but many arrived as poor people. They created communities with complicated ethnic, social, and cultural spaces in which stability and comity prevailed. Salinas represented the poster child for just this pattern of city-building in California—based in equal measure on agriculture and a rough multiracial communalism, which that may have been based on white supremacy but left just enough room for people of various racial backgrounds to ascend the socioeconomic ladder, keeping the racial hierarchy intact.

Urban growth interwoven with agricultural development controverted the accepted narrative of industrialized corporate agriculture disconnected from community. The yearly summaries of farming for Monterey County showed that corporate agriculture happened *alongside* the development of small-scale farms and community building, not as a replacement for this pattern of rural-urban life.[2] The reports showed a long history of breaking apart massive properties formerly owned by large-scale landowners such as David Jacks, Claus Spreckels, the Espinosa family, and J. A. Trescony (all owned over 10,000 acres apiece).[3] Out of a total of 2,131,200 acres of land in Monterey County, 957,692 were designated for agricultural production in 1932 and divided into 1,891 farms.[4] By 1936 the number of small farms had actually increased to 2,100 and stayed consistent throughout the years of World War II because the production of lettuce and other crops such as carrots that could lead to good profits even when farmed on a small scale.[5]

Rather than just the consolidation of small farms into industrialized, corporate agriculture, we see a pattern of small farm persistence as influxes of migrants arrived in Salinas and the Salinas Valley from all over California; these migrants viewed farming (even tenant farming and field labor) as a way to enter the middle class. They found available land to buy at reasonable prices and produced crops for market that paid sufficiently in an era of improved technology and transportation, allowing access to markets thousands of miles away. Thus, the numbers of small farmers in Salinas and the Salinas Valley (who were of Mexican, Chinese, Japanese, Italian, Portuguese, and Danish descent, as well as Anglo Americans) remained fairly consistent throughout the 1930s, not all swallowed up by big corporate agriculture—at least in that era.[6] Most importantly we also see these farmers as civically engaged citizens whose sympathies alternated between alliances with large growers as members of the agricultural associations and with the farmworkers with whom they lived in close, even intimate proximity. As well, we see the growth of a new group of mostly minority contractors who formed a middle class within their respective ethnic communities and who tended to side with growers and shippers in ensuing labor disputes.

By the time of the Great Depression, all the defining aspects of Salinas town life that late nineteenth-century settler colonialists had dreamed about became reality. By the end of this decade, Salinas had become a town made up of people who identified with agriculture, whose shared belief in a vigorous, muscular capitalist economy based on values of landownership, thrift, hard work, and modest behavior drew them together into a communal pact that accepted to a great degree racial differences among themselves and rejected radical politics even as they supported a hierarchy with whites firmly at the top. Chinatown emerged as a relatively safe haven too for Chinese people escaping the hostility of Monterey and Pacific Grove. Linda Wong Gin recounted her parent's journey to Salinas in 1937: "They wanted to settle in Salinas because they knew there was a strong Chinese community here. Not like in Monterey. My mother had bad memories of the way she was treated in Monterey. But Salinas was more welcoming," she said, recalling a conversation she had with her mother about the family's history.[7]

Communalism and kinship tempered racism and class conflict as different groups participated in (and benefited from) the booming agricultural industry, most notably lettuce production. Cultural inclusion disguised a powerful and entrenched white supremacy and defined life in this small agricultural town shaping the growth of Salinas in the 1920s and 1930s.

LETTUCE

Between 1919 and 1940, Salinas's wealth more than doubled despite the ravages of the Great Depression on the American economy. The Grower-Shipper Association was organized when growers and shippers from all over the Salinas Valley came together on August 4, 1930 over dinner at the Santa Lucia Inn in Salinas and organized themselves into the Salinas-Watsonville Lettuce Men's Association (later changed to the Grower-Shipper Vegetable Association of Central California or GSVA; for simplicity, referred to here as GSA). The group elected a seven-person board of directors with H. L. Strobel serving as its first president. They focused much of their collective energy on wages. Wages were one of the only areas over which they believed they exercised control in a turbulent and uncertain context in which markets, transportation systems and even the weather determined profits or bankruptcy: "Shippers could exercise little control over price [of lettuce]. In the market . . . shippers were highly successful in putting down labor uprisings, which occurred rather frequently . . . field labor was the one factor market in which shippers were in virtual full control."[8] The GSA described their response to union activism as "putting down labor uprisings," which belied their insistence that they were negotiating with workers in good faith. In fact, individual growers responded harshly to anyone who threatened to organize: "Thomas Chung stated that 43 out of 96 [workers] had left and that he had kicked out all the trouble makers. . . . Mr. Harden reported every man had quit but all going back to work."[9]

The wealth that the GSA generated for Salinas meant that the city "again took the lead in building permits [for] the Pacific Coast," according to an analysis by W. W. Straus and company in 1929. In the month of December alone, Salinas "granted 33 building permits, the value of which was $89,215." In the entire year, 1929, Salinas authorities granted 606 building permits having a value of $1,380,679. This was at a time when nearby Monterey boasted the largest fishing industry in the nation valued at over $50 million, but that economy did not spur an equivalent development for the city, which granted only half as many building permits as Salinas in 1928 and 1929.[10] A series of Pacific Gas & Electric studies during the 1930s showed

Salinas leading the county in electricity and gas sold, which reinforced the perception of Salinas's economic prosperity and municipal growth in the first year of the Great Depression.[11] By 1935, Salinas celebrated "A record breaking 79 percent increase over last year for the period 1934–1935 by the City of Salinas in building construction."[12]

Although the Depression affected city life just as it did everywhere, Salinas was repeatedly described through the 1930s as "one of the chief prosperity 'white spots' of California during the depression era," in large part because the city benefited from the huge profits that came from lettuce production.[13] The income Salinas generated just from lettuce grew to $11 million in 1930 alone, up from its total earnings from agriculture of about $9.6 million in 1919.[14] One report noted

> At the height of the crop season $100,000 a day in cash comes into [Salinas]. Since the first of the year [1934] approximately $5,000,000 in good United States cash has been laid down on the barrel head in Salinas, Monterey County, population 12,000 for lettuce.[15]

A report in the *Washington Post* in 1934 applauded Salinas for its lettuce boom: "It doesn't seem possible, after hearing nothing but woe from the farm belt for 15 years, but there's an agricultural boom on here in the Salinas-Watsonville alley—a lettuce boom." The piece went on to liken lettuce production to the Wall Street of 1929 before the crash. The amazing thing to the reporter was that most of the success for Salinas farmers came without federal help:

> Here in the little Spanish-type California town they're getting rich out of lettuce—and without a penny's worth of help from AAA. They've done it themselves aided by market conditions, to which have been applied some Yankee horse sense.[16]

This comment belied the fact that Salinas Valley farmers and ranchers relied heavily on federally funded infrastructure to get their lettuce to markets in the East and that the most important lettuce producers were not "Yankees" but people of Asian descent, both immigrant and American citizens, along with Mexican Americans, who were responsible for the extraordinary growth and innovation of agricultural production beginning in the 1920s.[17]

Salinas and Watsonville farmers began experimenting with lettuce production in 1921. Although farmers often failed in growing, packing, and shipping this fragile crop at the outset, they overcame these challenges with both innovation and federally funded support for transportation systems that gave them access to midwestern and East Coast markets. The success of the lettuce industry created enormous prosperity for the city by the middle of the decade and mostly through the 1930s as well. According to E. L. Kaufman of the federal-state crop reporting service, lettuce was California's most important and most lucrative crop during the 1920s and 1930s, and Salinas was the epicenter of that growth.[18] Out of the total $80,499,000 crop return for California in 1929, for example, $23,000,000 came from lettuce with Salinas growing (and shipping) 65 percent of California's lettuce crop.[19] An editorial in the local newspaper enthused:

> While it might be a bit forward on our part to claim the majority of this crop, in view of the wide expanses of Imperial and Pajaro valleys planted thereto, it is NOT beside the question to opine that Salinas as the LARGEST single LETTUCE shipping center in the world and this same salad article being the biggest crop in California might indulge in a slight crow as to her "place in the sun" regarding vegetable crops. . . . Lettuce is king. Rah for King Lettuce! Rah for Salinas valley![20]

Lettuce (and all agricultural production) depended on new technology.[21] Claus Spreckels was no city-builder, but he had the means to develop the important new methods of irrigation that had been invented by Chinese immigrants and that effectively utilized canals and wastewater mixed with water from the Salinas River to irrigate 3,000 acres of beets for sugar production, and, at the same time, lettuce, cauliflower, strawberries, carrots, and other row crops.[22] By 1933, in the midst of the Great Depression, Ellis Spiegl, a Jewish American grower and entrepreneur, invested $25,000 in technology development. He revolutionized harvesting by developing machinery that

> conveyed . . . lettuce directly from the fields, where the cutters are at work, into large bins on truck trailers reducing labor costs by 75%. . . . In the packing sheds the lettuce is dumped from the bins onto conveyor belts and is conveyed to the trimmers and then the packers. The system

eliminates the previously used small field crates, in which the lettuce was often bruised from tight packing.[23]

Spiegl also invented "a new type of shipping crate lid which prevents lettuce bruising."[24] Technology led to prosperity, but prosperity was always mixed with uncertainty. Prices fluctuated, sometimes from minute to minute throughout the growing seasons of the 1920s, but particularly during the Depression years. Growers, packers, and especially shippers exercised little control over profits and found themselves at the mercy of unscrupulous buyers and wildly vacillating commodity markets.[25]

Farming was particularly difficult in 1932. Due to overproduction and dramatic price drops in that year, Bruce Church and Whitney Knowlton together with the smaller growers and shippers championed efforts to avoid the chaos of oversupply by creating a committee to "prorate" shipments. They faced strong opposition from their cohorts, F. J. McCann and Ellis Spiegl, two of the largest grower-shippers in the region who wanted free rein to ship as they wished.

A series of meetings proved contentious with members of the GSA grew frustrated with one another: "Mr. Storm said that he thought if the shippers could not get together now after all the work that had been done and after such a great majority were in favor of doing so, they were all a bunch of boobs and deserved whatever happened to them."[26] Members of the GSA spoke freely in their meetings, as comments such as these showed. They believed that the meetings were private affairs, at least until the 1937 La Follette congressional hearings shocked them into the realization that minutes of the meetings might be made public. After 1937, members either spoke more diplomatically or stopped recording the details of their disputes with one another with such a fine degree of accuracy.

Salinas's residents and businesspeople generally realized the economic danger of uncontrolled production and the benefits of strength in organization; they supported Church and McCann's efforts to organize growers and shippers to prorate their crops. In August 1932, the *Monterey County Post* warned that the county faced a possible loss of $9 million when "the bottom fell out [of the lettuce market] when shippers found few receivers willing to take lettuce even by simply guaranteeing their freight. The situation came as a shock. Good lettuce actually could not be given away, even where packing and crates were thrown in for good measure." [27] But Church's and

McCann's efforts to pass similar measures to prorate lettuce according to actual demand rather than speculation failed in 1932.

A year later, representatives from the Monterey County Farm Bureau and members from the Salinas Chamber of Commerce met to reconsider the issue through support for the Agricultural Prorate Bill under discussion in the state legislature. This proposal aimed to provide "compulsory control of produce whenever two-thirds of the producers of that commodity express the desire for that control." Imperial Valley grape growers initiated the measure, but according to this report, small farmers benefited most from controls over supply and demand. This initiative to bring the state in to help growers and shippers deal with unfair market conditions and unscrupulous buyers also failed, but it showed how eager growers were to use the power of the state and federal government to help them.

By June 1933, shippers led by Bruce Church reluctantly abided by a prorate agreement that suspended shipping until lettuce prices increased enough to make it worthwhile. Prices had dropped dramatically that year from one dollar ten cents per crate to a mere seventy-five cents. Church led a committee of eleven individuals from the Salinas community that would keep an eye on prices to decide if and when lettuce would be shipped. As the secretary of the GSA put it, this was a community endeavor rather than one that affected only growers or shippers: "All we desire is to get a ready sale of our crop at reasonable prices. We have planned this program for the benefit of the independent growers as well as ourselves and it is vitally important to everyone connected with, or dependent upon, the lettuce industry—including Salinas merchants and businessmen."[28] The prorate idea proved unsustainable, however, as not enough shippers signed on consistently to make it workable.

By 1934, lettuce production was back on the path of profitability due to the prescience of one Sam N. Beard, a producer broker who established the Growers Exchange. It was not an easy path forward. In 1933, Mr. Beard argued that shippers could not afford to "get panicky" just because buyers had become a little timid. Still he received little support as growers were always divided among themselves in the 1930s, rarely agreeing on a collective strategy.[29] "Mr. Beard stated that our weekly estimates would be discontinued as the shippers evidently did not know from one week to the next what they would get out . . . no action taken . . . Beard feared ruinous situation."[30] Growers and shippers were in almost constant conflict over even minor issues.

By the spring of 1934, the oversupply of lettuce "beat down the price and the Salinas shippers had to take what they could get,"[31] often fighting among themselves and undercutting one another in payments to workers in their efforts to find a path to profit.[32] The Association accepted Sam Beard's marketing agency, which prevented "Buyers at the other end [from] pil[ing] up shipments contingent on sale. . . . When Beard started operating . . . lettuce was bringing under $2 a crate. . . . Anything over $1.35 a crate is profit." One month later lettuce sold for $3.31. "Such prices were unheard of."[33] In this way, the boom and bust of lettuce became slightly more controlled by growers and shippers on the sending end, ensuring more stability for them and for the city of Salinas, which needed lettuce to be profitable to keep its tax base solid.

The Chicago-based Federal Market News-Service (FMNS), funded by the federal government, presented Salinas with another challenge in 1932 and 1933. The struggle over the FMNS not only showed how Salinas as a city depended on lettuce production but also how various groups in Salinas worked closely together to overcome hurdles toward the collective goal of prosperity based on agriculture, which all groups depended upon in one way or another.

The FMNS has been considered an integral part of the local lettuce industry for years. It was established only after a long hard fight against selfish interests controlled by big time gamblers on the Chicago Board of Trade and in other centers where speculation on crop futures is rife. . . . [I]t enables the farmer to know each day what the standard price should be for his product. Before installation of the Service speculators jockeyed the market at will. It is feared that there will be a return to this situation . . . virtually every product of the soil will be affected. . . . Salinas rallied in a desperate effort to protest against this loss.[34]

Clearly, Salinas's lettuce production story punctured the myth that rural California towns stood apart from the federal government. Instead, they depended on it.

The FMNS provided Salinas Valley growers and shippers with an essential tool in calculating prices that, in turn, might determine the quantity of lettuce worth growing. The threat of withdrawal of the Market News-Service inspired a delegation from Salinas to travel to Sacramento. That included Senator C. C. Baker and Fred McCarger: "McCarger stated appreciation of the lettuce industry as the principal business in the Valley and the desire of the Chamber of Commerce to help it and its operators in every way possible."[35]

Both growers and workers expressed fears that anything might derail a crop and send a farmer, packer, or shipper into bankruptcy, and consequently the contractors and workers too.[36] Growers conflated many issues in their discussions: gradations in wages for workers and tenant farmers, the influx of pests and diseases in crops to maintain land fertility, and how to control prices of the harvested vegetables and fruit.

Controlling labor costs became the one critically important variable that growers and shippers thought they could control, whether they were small farmers or large agriculturalists, but they hardly agreed on how to do this nor on a floor below which wages could not fall. Wages for workers might make the difference between success or failure, profit or loss, but those wages often meant survival or starvation for workers, especially for migrant labor in the 1930s. It was chaos in the context of plenty.

The lives of workers depended on the willingness of growers to include them in the assessments of profit and loss, which could be capricious. First and foremost, organizing into unions appeared to be one of the best ways to achieve a level of socioeconomic stability that allowed workers access into the world of agricultural entrepreneurship, as precarious as that was. Nonetheless, good wages meant finding the means to buy land, own a home, or create a business.

Yet, everyone involved in the GSA seized whatever advantage they had, and that meant keeping wages as low as possible and undercutting one another to do so. Still, most of the discussions at the meetings during the 1930s concerned how best to judge lettuce prices and control for volatility of markets and shipping rates.[37] Members of the GSA endlessly debated ways of cutting costs and maximizing profits in a chaotic environment where they believed that they had little control, and they were quite open about their feelings and fears. Every spring and summer throughout the 1930s, strikes threatened to derail the marketing of lettuce as workers used the urgency of the harvest to do what they could to gain an advantage—just as growers, packers, and shippers did. Both groups looked to the federal government for support.

GSA members worked together more readily to maintain standards.[38] The use of extreme terms like "disaster" and "catastrophe" showed how

dramatic and fraught some of these meetings became in the face of unpredictable markets and harvests, and they also illustrate how easy it was for
all sides to overreact to any labor dispute or new regulation. The growers,
shippers, packinghouses, ice-makers, and everyone connected to the production of lettuce hardly formed a homogeneous force; instead, they were often
at odds with one another in their effort to maintain power and control.

The growers and shippers kept a close watch on federal efforts to wrest
control over prices.

> This meeting was called to order to consider recommendations to make
> the Federal Government in line with its policy of Industrial reorganiza-
> tion . . . a meeting between Federal Secretary of Agriculture Wallace. . . .
> [I]t would be much better for our industry to make recommendations for
> putting its house in order than to sit by and allow the Federal Govern-
> ment to set up a dictatorship over it.[39]

The use of the term "dictatorship" and the endless debates about how to
utilize state and federal government denied the conflicts going on within the
GSA and its need for government action; they feared governmental interference and control, and they (mistakenly) believed in their own independence.
Local government, usually led by Dr. E. J. Leach, who served in various
capacities as mayor and city councilman in the 1930s, played an important
role as an acceptable government representative and intermediary, being
somewhat trusted by all sides.

By 1935, Salinas's residents congratulated themselves on overcoming the
volatility of the market: "The lettuce industry set a new record . . . after
prices climbed to a lofty peak . . . establishing the highest market quotation
in the past three years."[40] This prompted an editorial that also reported the
comments by former governor C. C. Young regarding Salinas's "enviable
position" as a "lettuce metropolis . . . in good financial condition."[41] Most
importantly, lettuce production generated growth in related industries in
Salinas that added to the city's taxable wealth.

> Endless ramifications of the lettuce industry are noted. There is the lively
> "shook" business—shook are the crates which are delivered knocked down.
> More ice is produced in the little city of Salinas—for packing lettuce—
> than in the large cities of San Francisco and Oakland combined.[42]

As a result of lettuce production—mostly by small-scale farmers from a variety of ethnic and racial groups in the city—Salinas exhibited consistent economic growth and stability in both the 1920s and the 1930s, despite the economic turmoil in the rest of the country.

THE PROSPERITY OF THE CITY

It was during the 1920s and 1930s that "the bustling city of Salinas" was known as the

> wealthiest community per capita in the United States, busy with indus-
> tries which are placing [Salinas] as one of the foremost of the progressive
> middle-sized cities in the world. [Salinas] high school is one of the finest in
> the country, costing a half million dollars to build. [Salinas's] two gram-
> mar schools were also built at enormous cost, and offer the growing boy
> and girl advantages that cannot be surpassed in any other community.[43]

Numerous newspaper articles reinforced this view of a prosperous city throughout the 1930s.[44] Banks in Salinas showed increases in revenue from $80 million in 1922 to $155 million by 1931.[45] In another piece demonstrating Salinas's general affluence, the writer reported that

> Salinas valley farmers bought $139,000 worth of automobiles in October
> 1929 alone. They have a new car for every 140 people . . . 46 percent bet-
> ter than the state average. Fourteen nationally known chain organizations
> have retailers in Salinas Valley. The per capita income for the year 1929
> was $831. The average income per farm is $9400 about 200 percent greater
> than the state average.[46]

Although these gushing reports indicated the persistence of a booster mentality reminiscent of late nineteenth-century efforts to increase both tourism and population, they nonetheless reflected the reality that niche agricultural production in the Salinas Valley generated enormous wealth in a short period of time. A good portion of the city's residents were able to weather some of the worst economic challenges of the 1930s, which left most of the rest of rural America destitute and desperate.

According to local analyses of agriculture in the Salinas Valley, Salinas had, in the decades of the 1920s and 1930s, the largest beet sugar factory in the world (capacity 5,000 tons daily), the largest strawberry farm in the world (124 acres) [that came about because of the effort, innovation and expertise of Chinese and Japanese farmers], the largest freesia bulb ranch in the world, which formed part of the important Japanese owned florist industry, and the only goat milk condensary in the world . . . a large cow milk condensary [dairy farming and ranching were largely Swiss Italian and Danish enterprises and] practically all the sweet pea seed that is imported to Europe. . . . [O]ther crops [grown successfully in the Salinas Valley] are: Lettuce, artichokes, cauliflower, tomatoes, celery, bulbs, apricots, pears, apples, berries, and the famous Salinas-Burbank potato.[47]

All of this agricultural production not only made an impressive list for the entire valley, but also served to enrich the city's coffers through taxes on businesses and industries tied to agriculture. Much of the new agricultural wealth came from innovative farmers who claimed a stake in the production of the land and who were mostly Asian American and newer European immigrants, who arrived in the Salinas Valley by way of other regions in California.[48] However, those who served in city government—from city staff to school board members to elected officials—were Anglo Americans. The new prosperity belonged to not only growers, labor contractors, packers, and shippers but also to townspeople who were engaged in medicine, law, and small retail businesses dependent upon and associated in various ways with agriculture.

Industrial and business development, as well as tourism associated with agriculture and with Salinas's prominence as the county seat, defined Salinas in the new century. The chamber of commerce routinely led the way, boasting the highest membership in its history for 1929 with 350 members; among other accomplishments for that year, it brought multiple conventions, meetings, and events to the city. The chamber created an advertising committee in 1926 that extended its reach to other California municipalities and drew attention to Salinas as a regional tourist and event center. Salinas's most important annual happening and identity marker was Big Week, or the Salinas Rodeo, which every July exemplified the strategies of the chamber of commerce.

At the invitation of Salinas Chamber of Commerce in 1929, over a hundred representatives arrived in Salinas "from all over the United States and Canada" to organize themselves into an umbrella group, the Rodeo Association of America, that would coordinate their respective rodeos so as not to conflict on the calendar. The president of the Salinas Chamber of Commerce pointed out, "We feel Salinas deserves a just amount of credit in Procuring this National convention and having our secretary, Mr. Fred McCargar (also publisher of the *Salinas Index-Journal*), elected to the office of its secretary."[49] In this way, Salinas's leaders through the chamber routinely patted themselves on the back for their work in ensuring that their city remained a focal point, not just in the region but also in the state. Dr. E. J. Leach (a local dentist), who was first elected to the city council in 1928 and then served as mayor for the next twelve years (with one interlude), led efforts to make the rodeo culturally inclusive and served stints as its president until 1956. Although his father had once advocated for strict tariff protections and restrictive immigration law aimed at excluding Chinese people, the son became a crucial mediator in most of the labor disputes of that decade.[50] His work for the Salinas Rodeo centered on bringing every entity of Salinas into the planning and coordination of Big Week, making it a central part of belonging in Salinas and ensuring that groups who were marginalized economically and politically felt that they were part of the community culturally.

The chamber worked hand in hand with the business community, regular citizens, ethnic organizations, the GSA, and the Central Labor Council (CLC, the organization for all unions in town), most of which were also chamber members to make the Salinas Rodeo the significant unifying event for the city, exemplified by their presence in the parade with sponsored floats.[51] Each year the GSA and the Central Labor Council sponsored prizes of several hundred dollars for rodeo championships.[52] The Salinas Chamber of Commerce made sure that floats showed the importance of lettuce to Salinas in the parade, "requesting . . . float[s] from the Lettuce Industry [to support various city-wide events]." The GSA and CLC made sure to maintain a presence at regional, local, and state fairs and combined forces to create a traveling lettuce exhibit: "Mr. McCargar suggested that the lettuce exhibit used at the State Fair at Sacramento be duplicated for the Monterey County Fair."[53] Russell Scott, president of the Salinas Chamber of Commerce in 1929, noted "During the year the Chamber of Commerce has had the occasion to work on several projects jointly with the Labor Council of Salinas and I compliment them for a very worthwhile effort in investigating and reporting the conditions of labor" in addition to "saving the merchants of Salinas several thousands of dollars";[54] he did not specify how workers saved merchants money.

Asian, Hispanic, and white small farmers and businesspeople identified as Progressive era women and men who envisioned a California (and an America) of homeowners, small towns and cities that shared attributes such as paved streets and sidewalks, churches, schools, and organizations dedicated to civic improvement and community uplift. These features of town life were built by middle classes, mostly women, but also by the multiple racial and ethnic groups integral to city-building although absent from local histories and city government, or sometimes included in Salinas's social life as equals with Anglo Americans.[55]

The year that the stock market crashed was a watershed for Salinas, but not in the same way as it was for the rest of the country. Instead of a downward turn in the economy as it was elsewhere, in Salinas the crash became a starting point for new growth and apparent prosperity. One front-page story a week earlier hardly anticipated the disaster to come, announcing the upcoming opening of a new bank and securing financing for a new airport "the [result of the] unbounded confidence of a group of agriculturalists and financiers of Salinas and Pajaro Valleys and of Monterey Peninsula."[56] Alongside this announcement, also on the front page, the paper prominently featured a photo of three new businessmen joining Salinas's thriving business community, while the editorial page announced the opening of a new J.C. Penney. In fact, every new business opening in Salinas made front-page news, usually attached to a large photograph of the businessowner.

Salinas's residents found businesses that relocated from rival Monterey particularly satisfying. For example, an article in the *Index-Journal* celebrated the following new business: "Taxable property in the value of several thousand dollars and a new business venture was added to the commercial life of Salinas when the Arcade Department store owned and operated by Mr. and Mrs. Dave Schwartz, late of Monterey, opened its doors in the Cominos building."[57] When interviewed, Dave Schwartz declared, "I've long had my eye on Salinas and Salinas valley as the 'coming' community in all of the coast valley region."[58] Like so many other retailers and entrepreneurs, Schwartz, who was Jewish, benefited from the wealth generated by agriculture that made Salinas a secure place to engage in business, but he also benefited from the community culture that welcomed diversity.

Women played central roles in reinforcing an image of Salinas as an affluent place based on community spirit.[59] Although every ethnic group in town had their own women's clubs, and all were acknowledged as important in Salinas, there was nonetheless a clearly understood distinction between white women's organizations as predominant and normative and other women's groups as marginalized.[60]

The social sections of contemporary newspapers in Salinas where women's activities took precedence reflected racial diversity if not inclusivity by the mid-1920s and throughout the 1930s. These sections did not focus exclusively on the doings of white elites as was typical of so many society pages, but also recounted news about the Filipina Women's Club, Danish and Italian social organizations, and Japanese and Chinese women's clubs and religious organizations—all of which directed efforts at organizing educational and social events. They held events that celebrated ethnic and cultural pride and hosted musicals, theater productions, and lectures by scholars from various colleges and universities around the state.[61] Salinas's newspapers also highlighted and promoted visits by Stanford faculty invited by various women's organizations and ethnic associations to enlighten community members about the history and culture of places all over the world, as well as give lectures on everything from agriculture to business to developments in public health and foreign affairs. Nonetheless, it was evident that the mostly white women's groups, such as the Business and Professional Women's Club, predominated in importance and prestige in Salinas and that the women's groups did not usually overlap in membership to include women of color.

Not only was every new business that opened front-page news, but it was used to demonstrate proof of full employment in the city and throughout the Salinas Valley, even as unemployment rates skyrocketed in the rest of the United States. One report in 1930 announced that a "New Grocery and Meat Store Opens . . . $10,750 week totals for building . . . five new structures were started this week. . . . Salinas canneries employ 700 people at one local spinach packing plant and put $210,212.18 into circulation."[62] On February 12, 1930, Salinas broke ground for a new six-story bank, the Salinas National Bank, which cost $260,000 to construct.[63] When Montgomery Ward bought the locally owned Farmers Mercantile Company in downtown Salinas, there was some sympathy for the family that was forced to sell to the big retailer, but it was tempered by enthusiasm for the new business enterprise and how that might add to an already strong local economy: "The transaction is looked upon as one of the most significant in the business history of Salinas. . . . [T]he new store will be much larger than the old one and will occupy . . . 22,000 square feet of floor space."[64] Many of these new retail establishments, particularly groceries, were owned and operated by Chinese Americans, Mexican Americans, Filipino/a Americans, and other minority groups who navigated racism to create a niche for themselves in the economy of the city.[65]

The H. P. Garin Company made Salinas its regional headquarters, moving operations from Gilroy to Greenfield in 1930, and it quickly became the subject for an enthusiastic editorial: "[Garin's company] has a payroll of $500,000. . . . Did you read Garin's statement of his unbounded faith in the future of this valley? Then you know how the biggest men in the produce game feel about it."[66]

Salinas seemed to withstand the worst effects of the Depression, thriving economically because of the power of agricultural production and specifically the success of the lettuce industry. "Two local banks, The Salinas National and the Monterey County Bank today announced they had declared dividends for their stockholders—the third Bank of America reported an increased volume of business."[67] Headlines such as the following filled the local press throughout the 1930s: "Local Banks Strong, Will Pay Profits: Financial Institutions End Successful Year After Holding Sturdy Position in Region" and "Integrity Held Certain Sign of Community's Strength to Withstand All Threats of Future."[68]

The newspaper accounts of prosperity may have been a bit over the top in their efforts both to reassure (and to rally) Salinas's residents. However, statistics about economic growth backed up their accounts and suggested some reasons why California generally (and Salinas in particular) became destination points for Americans trying to escape the worst effects of the terrible economic downturn. The population of Salinas proper increased from 4,308 in 1920 to 11,586 by 1940. Grammar school enrollment between 1923 and 1929 increased from 596 to 1,402, and dramatically so in the 1930–1940 decade, which also showed evidence of population expansion well beyond the city's original footprint.

Population growth stimulated new real estate developments, the building of new schools and golf courses, the construction of an airport, and multiple public parks and recreation centers, all of which were funded mainly (though not entirely) by newly prosperous horticulturalists invested in city-building rather than by the state. By 1935, according to the *Salinas Independent*, "All lines of businesses in Salinas flourished, business was good, new enterprises were established, farmers prospered, bank clearings increased, building increased and postal receipts increased, and there were no business failures."[69] The city raised $350,000 in bonds in the depth of the Depression to finance a new sewer system. A hard-fought battle to reorganize transportation led to the construction of an underpass in 1936 at a cost of $140,000 to the city but with subsidies from federal and state government that allowed better flows of traffic through Main Street, along with the construction of 33 miles of new street and the paving of 35 more. Salinas enlarged the city jail and created the new Parks and Recreation Commission in the 1930s, adding numerous parks and playgrounds to support the increasing population, many of whom had numerous, young children. The newly formed City Planning Commission instituted zoning ordinances that separated commercial and industrial areas from neighborhoods and preserved agricultural space, but also and ominously aimed to "protect both our fine residential and business districts against undesirable encroachment," a nod to the racially segregated neighborhoods that became normative in California and the nation in the 1930s. The report connected the prosperity of the lettuce industry to fortune for all, including the multiple racial groups who formed an important part of the business community, and the diverse workers, whose employment and wages from labor in the fields and packing sheds were used to support local businesses and also ensure upward mobility for themselves and their families.[70]

Referring to lettuce production as "green gold," Salinas's residents and civic leaders boasted that the prosperity they enjoyed came from their own efforts: "Sure it's a gamble . . . but we're winning and we're doing it ourselves without any help from Washington. . . . [Lettuce] means cash money here," a former inspector for the United States Department of Agriculture (and now lettuce farmer) Earl Wilson claimed in one report. "I got $175 an acre for 140 acres," he said. "When I think of those farmers in Iowa and Nebraska, I think we are all pretty lucky out here."[71] According to the *Washington Post*,

All of this money [from lettuce] has created boom time conditions here. Haircuts are 75 cents. The Cadillac dealer is doing the largest motor business in town. Del Monte, the famous resort less than 20 miles away, has

become the playground of Salinas, which was once its poor neighbor. . . .
One well known businessman here dropped $16,000 in a crap game the
other night.[72]

The wealth generated by lettuce production benefited growers, shippers,
packinghouses, and numerous other businesses and industries connected to
agriculture, but it did not extend equally to workers, especially those from
communities of color.

Salinas residents widely shared the sentiment that that they did not want
government intervention and support, even as the GSA became increasingly
dependent on government help in everything from regulation to transportation to labor. This noninterventionist view crossed ethnic and racial lines in
Salinas, but it ignored the real needs of workers for government help both
in ameliorating the harsh impact of the Depression and in protecting workers from exploitive practices in the fields and packinghouses. The workers
understood that they were at a disadvantage in negotiating with growers
and shippers. Therefore, underlying all the growth and prosperity was an
equally sustained push for unionization that was opposed by the GSA and
that would result in fierce labor battles in 1936.[73]

Despite wealth generated for growers, shippers, packers, and contractors,
their collective fortunes were still precarious, as they frequently admitted in
meetings and over association dinners. These meetings often became both
fraught and contentious, as we saw with the establishment of new marketing practices above. Lettuce production was always a gamble, dependent as
it was on weather and competition from growers in Arizona, Washington,
the Imperial Valley in Southern California, and even New York. "You've
got to remember," Earl Wilson acknowledged, "that about half the people
who go into lettuce go broke."[74] Costs such as crates for packing, waterproof
paper for packing, workers' wages, and icing to keep the lettuce fresh during shipping all had to be paid for and almost always in cash. Moreover,
controlling sales and distribution was a real headache and could (and did)
bankrupt any given grower in one season, especially the small farmers with
few resources to sustain them in lean years.

It was, after all, the Great Depression. In most American towns and
cities, people faced mass unemployment and widespread home and business foreclosures; many Americans lost all of their savings in short order.
Salinas's residents were not oblivious. The good economic news locally may

have played out on the front pages of the papers, but it was always alongside dire reports of turmoil, disastrous economic conditions, and the radical unionism that characterized the rest of California and the nation in the 1930s. Internationally, news accounts highlighted stories of the rise of fascist dictators and their aggressive behavior on the world stage.

Most importantly, migrants fleeing the Southwest made their collective presence known in Salinas. They flocked to work in the lettuce fields and packing sheds in determined efforts to restore their family economies in the face of the twin catastrophes of environmental disaster and economic collapse. They formed the bulwark of a new labor movement in the city that challenged narratives of prosperity.

PART II

Transitions

Conflicts and Opportunities, 1930–1965

FIGURE 4.1   Rodeo dance on Main Street, Salinas, 1940
COURTESY OF MONTEREY COUNTY HISTORICAL SOCIETY.

CHAPTER 4

The Ins and Outs
of Race Relations

BEGINNING IN THE 1920S, the entire city of Salinas shut down for several days the week before Christmas to honor Filipino war hero and martyr José Rizal. The local Filipina Women's Club organized the event in partnership with the Salinas Chamber of Commerce, the Business and Professional Women's Club, the Salinas Women's Civic Club, and a multitude of other mainstream local organizations. It felt like inclusion, but was it?

It was striking that this Filipino/a event was so clearly accepted as integral to Salinas's cultural and social calendar at a time in history when almost all that we know about Filipino/a American experience was that Filipino/a people were being targeted by mobs and as members of an oppressed agricultural workforce, vilified for their ferocious labor activism throughout California.[1] In Salinas and throughout Monterey County, Filipinos/as felt the sting of racism, as did other minority groups. Filipinos/as were beaten by gangs in Monterey and Watsonville and maligned in the press. Many single men labored in the fields without a chance for building families or for upward mobility. They lived mostly in neighborhoods in Salinas designated by ethnicity (and class), and they rarely held local political office or served on boards and commissions. Their organizations, particularly women's organizations, were defined by ethnicity and often separate from white groups, although the chamber of commerce and the Grower-Shipper Association had members who were not only Filipino/a but also Mexican American, Chinese American, and Japanese American.

Yet, what was happening in Salinas and other agriculturally defined California cities was that Filipinos/as (and other members of communities of color) believed that they were an important and valued part of the fabric of city life. According to one account by a Filipino American resident of Salinas, "Filipinos were highly regarded by the people of this community. Their credit was good everywhere because they paid their debts."[2] They were not all migrant fieldworkers nor were they all men; they were women and men who had put down roots as families and built communities complicated by class that intersected with one another and with whites. They became important stakeholders in Salinas and in other rural cities in California, just as did other Asian communities, Mexican Americans, and African Americans. They fundamentally changed the places that they chose to live. Race and race relations were not just about oppression or exclusion but complex mixtures of inclusiveness and marginalization in Salinas and elsewhere.

The celebration to honor Rizal exemplified the tension between cultural acceptance and marginalization. The event made front-page news in the local Salinas newspapers every year and generated a feeling of inclusion even as most Filipinos/as were excluded from the Anglo American social, economic, and political world in the city. Some may have established families and risen to the middle class mostly through their positions as contractor middlemen in agriculture, but they did not become growers, shippers, or owners of big packinghouses. Still, it is worth revisiting the celebration itself to appreciate just how prestigious and far-reaching it became in the years before World War II and how it exemplified the way cultural acceptance of racially excluded groups became a façade for actual inclusion, complicating our understanding of the experiences of communities of color. Salinas's apparent broad-mindedness in fact supported a system of white supremacy.

RIZAL DAY

The celebration began with a lecture series that was meant to educate the community about the importance of José Rizal. Selected orators chosen from among the best Filipino/a students from Salinas High School and Hartnell College enthusiastically depicted the life and heroism of Rizal in theater productions, musical performances, and oratorical displays. Numerous local and regional newspapers publicized all these events, which were well attended by thousands of residents from every part of the city and the state.[3] City leaders encouraged local merchants to "remove Christmas trees from the sidewalk curbs and supplant them with American flags" for the duration of the celebrations, which lasted several days. Prominent speakers and city officials lauded Rizal as "the greatest man of the Malay race."[4] The papers reported, "In addition to the large number of Filipino societies, with floats and marchers, a number of Salinas fraternal societies, will take part, as will also the Salinas fire department,"[5] which signified how the event blended definable Filipino/a culture and organizations with city entities such as the fire department float to show that the Rizal event was integral to Salinas's city culture.

The multiple stories over the course of several days described delegations of Filipino/a American groups arriving in Salinas from all parts of California—including Los Angeles, Stockton, Oakland, San Francisco, and Sonora—to celebrate Rizal Day with a "big parade" down Main Street, making this event significant at a state level. It was a dramatic parade, according to one observer:

> Each of the Filipino organizations carried flags and banners, and a large number of them escorted beautifully decorated and illuminated floats, depicting historical events, scenes in the islands, and expressing the hopes and aspirations of the Filipinos for ultimate independence under a just form of government such as that of the United States. There were in all fifteen such floats, several presided over by goddesses.[6]

The pageantry and drama, as well as the obvious praise for American democracy, all conveyed a sense of connectivity between Filipino/a, Filipino/a American, and American cultural and political ideals.

The event was hardly limited to the Filipino/a community, making this a collective enterprise by everyone in the city to show their sense of community and cultural solidarity with Filipinos/as and to demonstrate how integral the Filipino/a community had become to Salinas by the 1930s, despite the Filipino/a inspired labor actions that underlay agriculture between 1933 and 1936. Seventeen local organizations routinely participated in the parades with a grand marshal presiding, including the Elks Club, the Salinas Band, the American Legion, the Salinas Rotary, the Salinas Chamber of Commerce, the Exchange Club, the Fire and Police Departments, the Farmers Association, and many, many others from neighboring towns in the Salinas Valley. Notably, this collection of participants was expansive and included other ethnic organizations in the city as well as groups such as the Elks Club that were exclusively Anglo American in membership. As the event was always held in December and concerns over weather conditions limited choices for venues that could hold all the residents and visitors, the Salinas High School gymnasium was selected (over the outside rodeo grounds) to hold "indoor baseball and volleyball that were played by Filipino athletes [who had traveled from the Philippines expressly for this event]."[7]

The *Salinas Daily Index* reported the "Mayor of Salinas, Frank S. Clark, personally welcomed the delegations of Filipinos. . . . Dr. David Starr Jordan of Stanford University and Abdon Llorente, commercial attaché in San Francisco were among the prominent speakers at Salinas Union High School."[8] David Starr Jordan, a prominent intellectual leader in the eugenics movement (which was notable for its disdain for Filipino/a people as lower on the racial hierarchy than whites), made for a curious addition to the program. His presence nonetheless added importance to the event and luster to Salinas as the urban centerpiece in California's Central Coast region.

According to reports, the celebration of Rizal drew thousands of visitors to Salinas and involved multiple events, beyond the big parade down Main Street.

> The committee has completed a program for the entertainment of 2000 visitors. Athletes from the Philippines participated in competitions in baseball and volleyball. Events programmed include[d] a formal Ball in Foresters Hall in honor of the city's guests. . . . [T]he award of prizes will be made by Miss Milicia Villamor of Stockton who reign[ed] as queen during the celebration.[9]

The Salinas Filipino/a string orchestra entertained the crowds, and numerous individuals from Salinas's Filipino/a community gave speeches, including "Miss Eugenia S. Filomena [who] recited Dr. Rizal's [original] farewell address."[10] The tone and tenor of the celebration honoring Rizal, however, consistently was one of respect and appreciation for Filipino/a Americans. According to one report on the Rizal event,

> [T]he most inspiring program ever presented. . . . It was the 37th anniversary of the heroic death of Dr. José Rizal, beloved Filipino patriot. . . . The program was arranged by the Filipino Women's Club. Senator C.C.

Baker delivered the principle address a glowing tribute to the idolized Filipino martyr. . . . [T]here were many highly entertaining short talks as well as vocal and instrumental music.[11]

Performers, lecturers, and in keeping with tradition, the crowning of a queen for the event were described in press accounts in detail. The event ended as they all did with "the singing in chorus of the national anthems of the United States and the Philippines," indicating a shared sense of camaraderie and patriotic sentiment that brought both cultural traditions together.[12] Yet, Dawn Mabalon's depiction of Filipino/a life in the agricultural city of Stockton showed a very different experience, much less inclusive than in Salinas. Although the entire effect of the celebration of Rizal reflected inclusion, it disguised a deeper reality of exclusion in day-to-day life that mirrored Mabalon's depiction of Stockton's treatment of Filipino/a American residents.[13]

RACISM MODIFIED

Several accounts in the local press celebrated the patriotism of Asians and other people of color in the same way that Filipinos/as enjoyed. One editorial in the *Salinas Daily Index* compared ethnically different immigrants favorably with native-born Americans. Under the headline, "Citizenship Club of Japanese Parentage to Be Formed Here," the editor made the case that

[P]eople who come here from other lands . . . are more patriotic than our own nationals. . . . The flag means something to the woman or man who left another land where poverty and oppression was the rule. . . . In wartime they did not hang back but were the first to fight for the land of their adoption. . . . [M]ore to the point they register their names with the county clerk and vote in each and every election and that's a lot more than we can say for a great many people who were born right here in our own United States of America.[14]

Op-ed pieces such as this one reflected an ongoing tension over the very definition of American citizen in a period notable for a belief system that normalized Anglo Americans and assumed marginality for everyone else. At the same time, the combined pool of nonwhites had expanded rapidly in agriculturally based, smaller scale urban environments such as Salinas and defied easy categorization, especially when minorities expressed the same aspirations for home and business ownership, educational achievement, and patriotism that Anglo Americans did.[15] The struggle showed in the over-the-top editorials that attempted to demonstrate inclusion but not full equality. Groups might be tolerated or even celebrated culturally, but they still would not be considered as equals by Anglo Americans, who always held the reins of political, economic, and social power in Salinas, as they did elsewhere in California and the nation.

Individuals or groups who might be marginalized and segregated by race, ethnicity, gender, or class attended integrated public schools in Salinas, often lived in integrated neighborhoods, and even moved into business ownership and the professions as permanent and respected residents of the city.[16] Salinas's residents routinely applauded cultural diversity, but notably as part of an expression of American ideals. "Salinas citizenry is grounded in the best American soil . . . and that this blood, mixed with the sterling stream, which is fast making its appearance here, will serve to carry our city far on the path of progress."[17]

The evidence of acceptance and inclusion on the city's calendar of cultural events belied normalized racism in American life. An editorial in the *Salinas Index-Journal* summed up white America's point of view and linked race riots in Alabama to oppressions:

> A toll of nine dead in Alabama race riots. People in California cannot understand such things—cannot understand why whites should kill Blacks. But for that matter neither can the people of that region understand why it is that Californians object to the presence of Japanese, Chinese, Filipinos and other Orientals on the coast. And by the same token, neither the Californian nor the Alabaman can understand why the New Yorkers are worried over the problem of the ever-mounting tide of Italian and Russian Jewish immigration into that city. Nor for that matter can either of them understand how come the people of Minnesota and the Dakotas are upset about the presence of the Swede and the Norwegian in their midst.[18]

Thus the analysis suggested that oppression and even violence directed at any minority community forming a critical mass in a given American city was a normal and acceptable aspect of life in America and should not be judged harshly by outsiders.

Yet, in Salinas, this racist ideology was modified to create a situational reality in which "everyone had to get along with everyone"[19] to ensure the production and marketing of crops, which benefited the city in a holistic way. Therefore, besides the obvious racism in Salinas that came from shared beliefs in racial hierarchy with whites at the top, there was also evidence of active efforts toward communalism that enfolded all groups into Salinas's collective culture. Agriculturally based communities such as Salinas had to operate primarily as collectives—as communities of diversity in race, gender, and class—in order to sustain production of crops such as lettuce with a minimal amount of conflict over class and labor rights; this was needed to encourage the development of new crops and to foster creativity in new methods of growing, packing, and harvesting.

Numerous opinion pieces and letters to the newspapers reflected Salinas residents' complicated responses to new migrants of color, pulled into the region by the promise of work in agriculture. For example, when Judge D. W. Rohrbach argued for the removal of Filipinos/as from Monterey County in 1930, the editor of the conservative *Salinas Index-Journal* protested:

> In Salinas lettuce and other vegetables could not be grown without the labor of Filipinos. . . . This paper stands for white labor, when and where it can be had, but it has yet to be shown that white men will do the work in the lettuce fields which now is the lot of the Filipino. We are no great lover of ANY imported labor, particularly not the sort that will become our enemy in a military way . . . but we submit there are many angles in this case to be considered.[20]

Similar arguments were made in industrialized settings about biological determinism linked to specific work, but in agriculture this argument was given much greater weight and specificity; the belief endured through the twentieth century even after it was largely discredited in the manufacturing and industrial sectors.[21]

Labor was needed, and it did not matter if the laborers were people of color or immigrants who added diversity to the Salinas population. Workers of color who began as field laborers could make their way into the middle classes and join the collective culture of the city, while remaining a disdained population, whether they realized it or not, as was the case for the women members of the Filipina club who organized the Rizal celebration. Filipina women were respectable and made their case successfully to the Salinas City Council to celebrate their culture as a citywide event, but they were rarely invited to join the Anglo-dominated Business and Professional Women's Club in Salinas, the most prominent women's organization in town. Cultural acceptance and economic exigency in agriculture existed alongside prevailing views of race and racial hierarchy and anti-immigration feeling.

In the 1930s, the Salinas Chamber of Commerce attempted to strike a balance between the growing numbers of diverse groups in Salinas. Members decided purposefully to get along with one another:

> The matter of better service and friendly relations between the Filipino labor, Japanese labor and the American farmers was discussed and at the request of Mr. Alcantara and Mr. Agudo, Dr. Wiley Reeves moved that a committee of seven consisting of two Filipinos, two Japanese, two American farmers and one businessman be appointed as such a committee.[22]

The Salinas Chamber of Commerce was not made up of all white people and certainly not all elites. Throughout the 1920s and 1930s, the chamber included members of unions and minority groups that kept this important organization representative, even as it was weighed heavily in favor of growers and shippers in the labor disputes of the 1930s. The fact that the two Filipino/a Americans referred to in the above anecdote raised the issue of race relations in the first place suggested that the chamber might have provided something of a safe space for discussing race.

Salinas's residents viewed minorities as essential both to the local economy and to community life; they thought that if they only met congenially with one another all would be well. It was naïve but also revealing. Minority communities were not targeted by violence nor rendered invisible in Salinas. In agriculturally based communities, everyone worked and lived alongside people of different races, ethnicities, and social classes. Salinas's residents shared the racism of the rest of America, but they practiced a cultural inclusion that supported the façade of inclusion in all aspects of city life.

The chamber organized their multiracial committee on cooperation just two years after immigration restrictions—laid out in the infamous Immigration Act of 1924 (also known as the Johnson-Reed Act)—set extreme limits (or excluded altogether) immigration from entire regions: those whose populations were deemed racially undesirable and unassimilable, such as the entire continent of Asia; severe limits on all southern European and eastern European countries; Africa; and most of the Middle East. As an American possession, migrants from the Philippines were exempted from these restrictions, but they were reviled in most of California and the West. As one of the countries under the umbrella of the Monroe Doctrine and part of the western hemisphere, Mexico also was not affected by the restrictive legislation; Mexican immigrants continued to move in (and out) of California and the Southwest after 1924. However, whites treated Mexican immigrants no better than Filipinos/as in California and the West. Restrictive immigration based on national origin (race) clearly reflected Americans' widespread belief in eugenics, a movement based on pseudo-scientific racism in which whites were deemed closer to God than anyone else on the planet. Although they were allowed to enter the United States, Filipino/a and Mexican immigrants were treated as racially inferior, even as these workers filled increasingly pressing labor needs in industry and agriculture.[23]

The Filipino/a workers who came to California and to Salinas as "insular subjects" in the first years of the twentieth century did not enjoy the privilege of real citizenship that would have allowed them to send for wives and families as European-origin immigrants routinely did. As a result, on arrival at least, Filipino/a (and Mexican immigrant workers too) lived primarily in male-only, often rundown and unhealthy makeshift housing and labor camps, usually located outside of the city limits or in boarding houses and hotels in Chinatown during the lettuce harvests in spring and through the fall seasons.[24] Mexican workers came as part of a labor migration, but they were also fleeing the chaos and terror of the Mexican Revolution of the 1910s and its aftermath; and they lived in labor camps as well. Those camps were not only isolating: They were breeding grounds for everything from malaria to polio to typhoid and tuberculosis, all widely reported in the local press and the focus of public health initiatives by local women's organizations and city and county agencies. Numerous front-page reports documented public health efforts to contain and eradicate the various epidemics in labor camps, typically fusing the racial identity of workers with infectious disease.

On the one hand, we see a great deal of evidence of racism, openly expressed. On the other hand, and at the same time, there is an equal amount of evidence of genuine respect and acceptance for so-called nonwhite people from a variety of cultural traditions and ethnic groups. Filipino/a experiences in Salinas in the 1930s graphically showed how these apparent contradictions played out. Moreover, Salinas's example defied myths about the gendered nature of the Filipino/a communal presence. Men were more numerous, especially single men, but this was decidedly not an all-male community.

VIOLENCE AND CONDEMNATIONS OF VIOLENCE

Historians emphasize the frequency and violence of actions by whites (mostly men) directed at Filipinos/as in California in the 1930s. This was true. But what is often overlooked is the extent to which local communities denounced the violence. To fully understand and appreciate the experiences of Filipinos/as as well as those of other minority groups, we must look at the way local communities like Salinas both interpreted and acted in the wake of these violent actions.

Salinas's newspaper reports on violence against Filipinos/as showed apparent sympathy toward Filipinos/as and vilified the white perpetrators, perhaps just to give the impression that the community was more compassionate than it actually was. The *Salinas Index-Journal* reported "That race riot over at Watsonville last night. We have been informed that the bulk of those leading the attack were naught save pool hall habitués."[25] The paper emphasized whites as the aggressors and noted "armed bands of whites were shooting into Filipino houses," without mention that any arrests of whites were made. The paper announced the death of one of the victims, Fermin Tobera, twenty-two, on the front page in huge headlines that condemned the action as a "race riot." The piece noted further that officers under Chief of Police Robert Hastings "saved 30 Filipinos from being seriously beaten by the mob," which indicated that the Filipinos/as had some protection from authorities or that whites were being portrayed as saviors even though other whites clearly perpetrated the violence.[26] The report praised the police as rescuer heroes for standing up to racist whites at a time when police and sheriff's departments usually took the side of the white attackers rather than the Filipino/a victims, which again emphasized the positive side of white residents' behavior:

> About 8 o'clock a mob of about 500 whites took a Filipino community house on the San José Road by storm. Firing pistols and waving clubs the white men surged into the place. . . . Hurling rocks and firing revolvers they swarmed through the police and administered beatings to the Filipinos. . . . Just as they were preparing to set fire to the place Hastings and

his forces arrived. Backing up to the house they threatened to shoot the first man who made a move to destroy the property. . . . The mob melted away into the night muttering defiance only to turn up a short time later at [another] Filipino house on Van Ness Avenue. Here some of the islanders made a stand returning the fire of the whites with pistol and revolver shots. . . . Chief Hastings denied that the mob was made up of youths of high school and college age . . . "the situation is serious and will result in wholesale murders unless something is done about it immediately . . . all the Filipinos are in danger."[27]

It was notable that the report portrayed the Filipinos/as' collective efforts to defend themselves as an act of both necessity and heroism.

The American Legion was enlisted to patrol the streets of Pajaro and Watsonville to protect the Filipinos/as who lived there. The editorial the next day insisted "Salinas has kept aloof from the disgraceful mix-up at Watsonville, Pajaro and now in San José, in all of which places there have been inter-racial difficulties," suggesting that leaders in Salinas wanted to stay as much as possible on the good side of the Filipino/a community, on whom they depended for their agricultural work; and they wanted to make a distinction between Salinas and its neighboring municipalities, which were condemned for their open hostility to minorities.[28]

Although we are familiar with this particular incident of mob violence against Filipinos/as in Watsonville from numerous contemporary and historical accounts, it is less well known but equally significant that the Salinas community response was not only sympathetic to the Filipino/a victims but utilized law enforcement and stalwart community groups such as the American Legion to defend them, showing just how essential Filipino/a Americans were to Salinas's community life. Even more important, the report disparaged the white perpetrators as mobs and lowlifes—wild, uncivil, and not at all representative of Salinas's citizenry. Salinas residents wanted to be perceived within the region and the state as "liberal minded," whether they were or not, in no small part because their agriculturally based economy absolutely depended upon the Filipino/a American and other communities of color to support the production of crops for regional and national markets.

In another instance in 1935, the local newspapers reported that Fortunato B. Sampayan, who was described as a "Filipino ranch worker," was severely beaten by Billy Nissan and Kenneth Dutra, both white Salinas residents (but "youth," rather than respectable members of Salinas society, and likely Dust Bowlers) who hijacked Sampayan's car and commanded him to drive them to Los Angeles. When Sampayan refused their demand, they pulled him out of the car and beat and kicked him, injuring him so badly that he had to be hospitalized for several days. The paper showed obvious sympathy to Sampayan, detailed his version of the attack (omitted the two young men's side of the story), and emphasized that he was "a poor innocent victim." The paper reported that the two young men fled to San Luis Obispo after the assault (in Sampayan's car) but were apprehended and returned to Salinas a few days later to face charges: "[The two men were] brought before Justice Harry J. King . . . and arraigned. The court fixed bail at $500 each in default of which they were returned to jail. A date for their trial [was] to be fixed after Sampayan recover[ed] enough . . . to appear as a witness."[29] The newspaper supported the injured Filipino young man and described the white attackers described as "unruly youth" who deserved to be jailed for their crime against Sambayan. However, the sympathetic response to the young Filipino victim was not by chance, and once again the papers emphasized the difference between respectable Salinas citizens who would never behave in such an openly vicious, racist way and the young men who initiated this attack.

J. B. Sambayan, the injured man's brother, had filed the initial complaint against the two white men. A labor contractor in Salinas, J. B. had roots in the city (unlike migrant fieldworkers); typically a contractor had a family, with a wife who participated actively in cultural and social events. The wives of Filipino contractors became the backbone of middle-class Filipino/a cultural and social life in town, intersecting with other middle-class women's groups that were so essential to Salinas's social development.[30] Children of labor contractors attended public school along with their neighbors— Anglo Americans, Japanese Americans, Chinese Americans, and Mexican Americans—as enrollment lists made clear. Middle-class whites and members of Salinas's varied middle-class ethnic and racial groups respected the Filipino/a middle classes generally, even as they ignored or disdained migrant Filipino/a fieldworkers and treated them as degraded field labor.[31] Salinas residents understood that their entire economy depended on Filipino/a middle classes feeling included in the cultural and social fabric of the city, whether they were or not.

The fact that Fortunato Sambayan owned a car even though he lived in the labor camp his brother operated suggested a higher status than that of the two young white men who assaulted him, neither of whom were able to come up with the $500 to make bail. Unlike his assailants, Sambayan had roots in Salinas and shared middle-class status through his connection to his brother contractor. As such, his class trumped his racial identity when it came to meting out justice both in the court of law and in the court of public opinion.

A similar attitude of apparent acceptance was also extended to Mexican Americans expressed through editorials in the press that overlooked racist policies and practices in neighborhood settlement, law enforcement, education, and employment. In one piece, also in the *Salinas Index-Journal*, the editor attempted to diffuse stereotypes:

> Too often have Americans opinions . . . of the Mexican people have been solely based on their view of a group of railroad or ranch workers . . . too many of us go our way without stopping to think that there is charm, courtesy refinement, culture, music, art—all these things and many others among Mexican people, just the same as we have them. . . . [Moreover] the Mexican people are more given to sobriety than our own folks. . . . [W]e must not forget there were horse thieves and cutthroats on the northern side of the international boundary just as there were across the line.[32]

In this way, the editor reminded readers that it was wrong to attach stereotypes to an entire people, which was routinely done in this era. The editor's apparent challenge to racist thinking showed how living in an agricultural community made a difference in the way Salinas's residents treated racial difference. They were careful to maintain a semblance of inclusion to support an economy dependent on diverse populations.

Still, alongside these efforts to include, incorporate, and defend groups deemed racially inferior or suspect by whites, Filipino/a (and Mexican and other Asian) American residents often encountered open hostility from Salinas's white residents without the same sympathetic response generated by the attack on Sambayan or by the mob violence in Watsonville. Jimmy Ibarra who arrived in Salinas in 1928, recalled in an interview with a reporter from the *Salinas Californian* in 1974: "It was hard to be a Filipino back then. All Filipinos lived in labor camps and worked in the fields."[33] Although he was right that many Filipinos worked as stoop laborers and lived in single-sex labor camps, Filipino/a Americans also lived in the same kind of socio-economically complex community in Salinas as everyone else did.[34] Ibarra recalled that he worked ten hours a day for 25 cents. "There used to be lots of riots," Ibarra remembered. "Americans would burn down labor camps because Filipinos wanted higher wages. It was a big fight in Salinas in 1935."[35] This was true, but that fight became complicated when Filipino contractors sided with Anglo American growers against Filipino/a fieldworkers, as we will see in the next chapter.

Ibarra left the fields for a job working at a dry cleaning operation on Market Street in Salinas and remembered how marginalized he felt at that time. "If I would walk down Main Street, Americans would say 'Go home monkey, go back to your island. It was pretty rough. . . . At the Crystal Theater they didn't want us to sit with them. They made us sit on the sides or the balcony." That was hurtful indeed and clear evidence of the kind of racism defined as Jim Crow laws and practices that were commonplace all over the country at the time. He had difficulty finding housing. If the apartment owners were "American," they would not rent to him, he said.[36] His experiences and that of other Filipinos/as who lived in Salinas in the 1930s (but interviewed in the 1970s) might have also reflected the poverty they experienced in the marginalized and dilapidated neighborhood of Salinas's Chinatown circa 1970, which most certainly shaped their perspectives in the present as well as their memories of the past. Salinas could be both welcoming and respectful and rejecting and hostile—and could be those things simultaneously. Class mattered.

FILIPINO/A IMMIGRATION PATTERNS

Like Chinese immigrants, Japanese immigrants, and the nineteenth-century whites who arrived before them, Filipino/a immigrants generally came to Salinas by means of a circuitous route from their homeland, usually first by being recruited from the islands by Hawaiian plantation owners. Although Philippine schools taught English and American history and encouraged emigration, Filipinos/as were often disappointed at the treatment they received by white Americans. According to Gregorio Aquino, "When we were [in the United States] we found it was different than what they told us. We had to paddle our own canoe so to speak. We could not speak English very well. We did not know where to go."[37] Many people, racially marginalized or not, felt the same way in these years when urbanization and industrialization left hundreds of thousands of people, Americans and immigrants alike, adrift in a harsh environment without social safety nets.

Like so many of his compatriots in 1928, Philip Ben left the Philippines to work as a sugar technician in Hawaii. He wanted to attend San José State College, but the stock market crash ended his dream of upward mobility through educational attainment, and so he worked in the fields of Salinas instead and lived in a labor camp nearby. "I just came here to see what was going on," he remembered. Adelia Cacas arrived in Salinas also to attend school at what was then Salinas Junior College (now Hartnell Community College). She was ambitious: "I like to better myself. Usually when you were in the Philippines and you graduate from the U.S. you're somebody."[38] Filipino/a immigrants, both women and men, aimed for upward mobility, just like their counterparts among other immigrant groups. Young Filipino/a American women and men encountered an educational system in Salinas that welcomed them, even as they often felt disengaged from Salinas's society as young people, alone in the alien environment of America. Their individual and collective experiences depended on class, luck, education, and even on their individual maturity and marital situation. Racism always factored into their lives, but it was not the only thing they experienced, and it was not something everyone encountered in the same way.

Interracial dating and marriage were red lines in Salinas that prompted many acts of violence against Filipino American men in California and in the Salinas Valley. This situation, in turn, stimulated the revision of the multiple anti-miscegenation laws in California and throughout the West to include "Malays" as one of the groups expressly prohibited from intermarrying with whites.[39] However, interracial dating and marriage happened anyway, especially within the context of the multiracial subdivision of Alisal where Mexican, Asian, and Anglo Americans lived in close proximity.[40] Bill Ramsey described Alisal in the 1930s as a multiracial space with "a whole bunch of Chinese and Japanese. My sister's boyfriend was Mexican. There was a lot of dating," he recalled, referring to sexual relationships between young people from various racial groups.[41] The interracial relationships that Ramsey described were less common (perhaps even nonexistent) outside of multiracial spaces such as Alisal, especially in middle-class or elite areas of Salinas, which remained solidly white in population makeup.

Many Filipino/a immigrants and Filipino Americans strove to become labor contractors like their Japanese American contemporaries as a way to move up the socioeconomic ladder and out of fieldwork. However, relationships between contractors and the men they employed for fieldwork were complicated at best, and they reflected clear divisions by class within Filipino/a society.[42]

Pablo Abarquez had the means to travel to Stockton to collect workers and claim a place in Salinas's agricultural world that enabled him to escape fieldwork. His daughter, Estelle Ben, recounted her father's method of acquiring a labor force made up of his compatriots, "My father would go down Chinatown on Alvarado Street in Stockton and in an hour's time, sometimes less, he'd have that flatbed truck full with 20–25 men . . . a cot bed and a blanket their only possessions."[43]

Paul Olivete, who left Salinas in 1924 for Chicago, where he graduated from Blackstone School of Law, could find no opportunity to practice as a lawyer, and he returned to fieldwork in 1934. He nonetheless became a field supervisor for Bud Antle, one of the biggest agricultural growers in the Salinas Valley. "What is the use of bragging about your diploma if you do not practice it," Olivete reasoned. His educational level nonetheless gave him the chance to move out of the fields, but his race kept him from the higher level of employment that he earned and deserved.[44]

Felipe Sun arrived in San Francisco in the 1920s. He recalled how easy it was for Filipino American men to be recruited by unscrupulous labor contractors. He joined a group that worked in the fish canneries in Alaska before he found his way to Salinas to attend school and graduate from Salinas Junior College (Hartnell).[45] Ambitious Filipino/a Americans like Sun utilized educational opportunities to move out the fields to become part of Salinas's increasingly vibrant cultural and social community.[46]

Many Filipino/a immigrants were fluent in English (and usually Spanish too), but their strong accents made it difficult for American English speakers to understand them. More proficient English speakers were likelier to become labor contractors. Non-English speakers had to trust their more articulate counterparts, "some were honest, some not so," recalled Sun.[47] Moreover, they were often left vulnerable, without pay or the means to collect wages, as fieldworkers dependent on contractors, complicated by language difficulties, and without full citizenship status. Their helplessness increased when they worked for smaller farmers. "There were so many independent American farmers. . . . And so there were times the farmers would not pay us. . . . We could not insist, we could not sue them. We did not know how," recalled Aquino. Filipino/a immigrants and Filipino/a American workers blamed the Filipino labor contractors: "This may not sound good, but most of the contractors here were Filipinos vying for work. Some of them would cut the throats of each other by undercutting in wages. Then fights between one crew member and a Filipino would start. . . . That more or less divided workers here."[48]

In one particularly bitter dispute that ended with a lawsuit, the United States courts held labor contractors responsible for payment to workers, whether the growers paid the contractors or not, which was deeply unfair to the contractors. "Labor contractors who employ men to work in the lettuce fields are responsible for the payment of their wages, not the grower whose crops the contractor has agreed to plant, thin, cultivate or harvest," ruled Justice Harry J. King in the case of one Clementa Bautista. Bautista sued Leon de Asis, a Filipino labor contractor, after Asis failed to pay his wages. Apparently, this contractor hired Bautista to work for a vegetable farmer, but sometime late in the harvest the farmer went bankrupt (a common occurrence), and the contractor never received payment. So, in turn, Asis could not pay Bautista or the rest of the crew he had hired to complete the harvest. The contractor blamed the grower. However, the judge thought otherwise, and in doing so, he provided a window into the precarious place Filipino American contractors held in the city and the state in the 1930s. By making the contractor solely responsible for workers' wages, the court positioned Filipino/a Americans outside the realm of labor law, which gave workers power to sue in criminal court when employers did not pay wages due them. For fieldworkers, however, there was no direct link between themselves and the farmers who employed them, so the contractor (who depended on the farmer for workers' pay) was considered liable.

The interdependency highlighted the precarious nature of farming but also the racial disparity. Had the contractor shared the white racial identity of the grower, the result might have been different and perhaps in the contractor's favor. Contractors were seldom white, however. This was a niche occupation held primarily (if not totally) by aspiring Asian (Japanese, Filipino) or Mexican Americans. Fieldworkers counted on contractors, especially trusting those who shared their ethnic background, to pay them. Contractors depended on growers for remuneration. Growers, in turn, were often at the mercy of packers and shippers to buy their crops, and they, in turn, depended on always volatile commodities markets in Chicago and New York to make profit.

Power, profit, and privilege were not equally distributed as this incident made clear with the Filipino fieldworkers always left most vulnerable. Both race and class mattered, and the willingness of this Filipino American worker to bring his suit to court indicated that he believed that he held the same civil rights as anyone else, and the courts supported him. However, the fact that the contractor, who was also Filipino American, was penalized, rather than the grower, who was white and the source of the problem, suggested that racism tipped the scales.

Filipino American contractors used their English-speaking skills and permanent residency as a means for upward mobility, if not acceptance, in Salinas in the 1930s, just as Japanese American contractors did. But they may have failed to appreciate their fragile position as this case made clear. The court ruled that the contractor had to pay Bautista because Bautista actually worked for the contractor, not the farmer. The contractor had to wait for his own moneys due when the bankruptcy proceedings were settled. Although Filipino/a American workers lost wages amounting to thousands of dollars because contractors did not pay them, contractors lost too when farmers went bankrupt, and farmers lost when their crops failed to sell in the market. Nonetheless, it did not matter whether this was because of unscrupulous contractors or because growers defaulted contractors. The contractors "b[ore] the brunt of the losses."[49] The complexity of these relationships led to misunderstandings and perhaps obscured the extent to which race and racism affected outcomes, hurting minorities the most in any dispute.

Beyond Salinas's apparent cultural inclusion of Filipinos/as—exemplified by the celebration of Rizal and the uneven treatment of Filipino/a workers and contractors in Salinas's economic and social world—there was other evidence of Salinas's strenuous effort to show acceptance. The newspaper editorials led the way. When Filipino American Bernard L. Iazars died suddenly, his obituary emphasized his stature in Salinas as "businesslike, hard-headed, progressive, and enterprising,"[50] all characteristics valued highly by Salinas residents. Moreover, he played the important role of benefactor for the poor in Salinas, whether or not they were part of the Filipino/a community:

> Whenever he saw a case of distress his hand readily reached down into his pocket . . . to relieve it. This was for anybody and everybody whether Filipino or not. . . . [Iazars] gave liberally to Filipino charities. He encouraged Filipino dinner parties and sent [Filipino/a students] flowers when they graduated.[51]

Most importantly, Iazars demonstrated a keen business acumen: "He made money abundantly . . . as a leading Filipino pioneer and businessman [who] had arrived in Salinas [in 1916] owned a Filipino club on Market Street and managed the Manila Hotel on Main."[52] As someone who made money through business acumen, this put Iazars squarely within the circle of an approved and full member of the Salinas community, even though, as a Filipino American, he lived on the margins of respectable Salinas society.

SALINAS'S MULTIETHNIC INCLUSIVENESS?

Salinas's residents, politically conservative for the most part, applauded themselves for their embrace of diverse ethnic and racial immigrant groups. The conservative *Salinas Index-Journal* routinely described Filipino/a Americans as decent and honorable, with exaggerated praise:

> This is the story of an unnamed Filipino who is the kind of friend we all wished we had. . . . A Filipino named San Juan died of spinal meningitis, far from his native land and without any relatives to ease his last painful hours. All of his worldly possessions consisted of about $87 dollars in a local bank. This friend of San Juan's paid more than $250 out of his pocket for funeral expenses, and made every effort to clear up the dead man's business affairs. The normal person would have applied for the man's bank account as reimbursement for his expense and trouble, but not in this case. When the public administrator filed his petition for letters of administration of San Juan's estate, his surviving father and mother were named legatees. This friend, believing San Juan's family would need the money more than he, had willingly passed up any share he would have received out of kindliness for the bereaved parents. If this man was half as good a friend to San Juan's while that unfortunate was alive as he was when he died, then truly he had something which few of us can honestly claim.[53]

The piece did not challenge racial stereotypes so much as noted that people marked as racially inferior could be good, kind, and even morally superior to their white counterparts. Like the façade of cultural inclusion, Salinas's white citizens were keen to show their liberal attitudes within a strong belief in racial hierarchy and eugenics that justified severely discriminatory policies in both urban development (or lack of development), political representation, and educational and employment opportunities, which marginalized people of color.

Immigrants found mobility in retail business ownership and entrepreneurship in Salinas. When we look at the ethnic makeup of the business community, we see evidence that Salinas's entrepreneurs included Japanese Americans, Chinese Americans, Filipino/a Americans, and other members of ethnic groups ostracized in eastern cities, such as Jewish and Italian American merchants and professionals.[54] One analysis of Salinas's overall character as a community concluded that "Salinas is a hospitable city, where a certain freedom of action prevails. Its people are liberal-minded."[55] However, the apparent openness of the community came with a caveat:

> That does not mean, however, that it is not alive to the danger of obtaining a reputation of being a city where "everything goes." During this season of the year [the late summer and fall harvest season] our population is more mixed than during the winter, which is another reason for unusual care being exercised.[56]

Salinas was a diverse city with a fluid population. It was an urban space, but its multiracial population was all tied in one way or another to agricultural production and the rural. Salinas's white residents and business community were careful to strike a balance between apparent inclusion and distance from working-class people of color who might threaten the status quo.

Community events regularly featured speakers who encouraged "internationalism" and "courtesy to strangers" with ongoing plans for luncheons and dinners that were designed to highlight the benefits of ethnic diversity in the city.[57] There were well-advertised events and meetings celebrating every conceivable ethnic immigrant group in Salinas, such as the one honoring Greek independence (although the Greek population of Monterey County was negligible in the 1930s):

> Gathering here last Sunday . . . more than 300 Greeks from various parts of central coast section joined with Salinas Chapter of Old Order of Ahepa celebrating the 113th anniversary of the freeing of Greece from Turkish domination . . . [when] March 25, 1821 Greece threw off the shackles of the Ottoman Empire.[58]

It was easy enough to do this in order to present the city as one that welcomed diversity even as it also marginalized groups based on race.

Salinas became the center for Jewish life in the county as evidenced by the number of events, celebrations, and meeting notices that were featured prominently in the Salinas papers beginning in the late 1920s, particularly related to the local chapter of B'nai B'rith and Women's Fidelity Auxiliary (lodge number 1105).[59] David Schwartz, featured on the front page of the *Index-Journal* for opening a new department store in Salinas, shared his life story with the paper, which honored him as a man "whose career is the romance for which any American might be proud—a yarn which any American boy or girl might read with profit." Identified as a Romanian of Jewish ancestry, Schwartz "turned his eyes towards America" at age fifteen. He arrived in New York City around 1905 and studied both the English language and "Americanization." Like so many other immigrants to California at the turn of the last century, Schwartz meandered through Texas and the American South, working at odd jobs. He joined the U.S. Army around 1910 and spent time in the Philippines before he returned stateside to Monterey, where he met his wife and began his career as a retail businessman: "Today all his resources are centered in Salinas Valley—kingdom of 'green-gold'—which Dave asserts is the promised land of the future."[60] Again, as with other parts of California, Salinas residents welcomed Jewish, Italian, or other European-origin immigrants as whites, as opposed to marginalized communities of Asians and Mexican people.

Salinas's residents along with other Californians showed a clear admiration for European immigrant entrepreneurs in a decidedly anti-immigrant America of the 1920s and 1930s, but it was an environment that did not ostracize anyone who might be defined as white. When Victor Barlogio was elected mayor in 1933, the editorial board of the *Salinas Index-Journal* applauded the victory as evidence of Salinas's atmosphere of inclusion and merged this event (inappropriately) with the rise of Mussolini and the Italian fascists. An enthusiastic op-ed piece proclaimed "Salinas's New Mayor, Italy's Glory" and described the mayoral election as on the same scale as a boxing championship and Mussolini's accession to power:

> The *Index-Journal* joins with the rest of Salinas in extending congratulations . . . to Vic Barlogio. . . . [I]t is doubtful if there is anybody here who has a larger personal following . . . with Primo Arnera the new heavyweight

champion of the world and the next championship battle . . . to be held in the ancient Roman Coliseum, with Voliva predicting that Mussolini will be dictator of this country at the time when wheat sells for $48 a bushel, and with Vic Barlogio mayor of Salinas, anybody can see with half an eye that the former glory of Italy, when Rome was the capital of the world, has been most vividly renewed.[61]

Vic Barlogio started out as police commissioner, served out his term as mayor, then became Salinas's city manager and served on the city council throughout the 1930s. The Italian story in Salinas not only included the mayor, but also showed how integration into the city's social life was uneven for immigrant newcomers, with the outcomes uncertain. But for those European immigrants who might be defined as white, agriculture and its opportunities for economic entrepreneurship played a central role in making that social mobility and acceptance possible.

Salinas made room for Japanese immigrants and Japanese Americans in the 1930s in the same manner as it had for Filipino/a Americans, with an appearance of acceptance but a reality of marginalization. Japanese American cultural events were reported on frequently and positively in Salinas's newspapers.[62] When Japanese Americans wanted to build a new Presbyterian church, Salinas's non-Japanese residents rallied to support them:

> A financial campaign was opened this week by the Salinas Japanese Presbyterian church in an endeavor to raise $3000 from American friends and business houses of Salinas and the Salinas Valley which will be devoted to the construction of a new Sunday school building and gymnasium [for the purpose of improving] the physical, moral and spirited education of American born Japanese young people of Salinas Valley. . . . Although the Sunday school now has 100 pupils and eight teachers twice that number will be enrolled within a few years. . . . In closing their appeal the members said "We desire that the coming Japanese generation practice the teaching of Christ Jesus and so become good American citizens."[63]

The effort of Japanese American residents to blend into the American mainstream through religion and culture appeared to resonate with the wider Salinas community. But it stirred controversy if they dared to live in white neighborhoods or conflict with whites over labor issues.

The *Monterey County Post* referred to Usuke Uribe as a "prominent and highly respected resident of Salinas for 35 years," in a front-page article that announced his death in 1933. The report emphasized that his death was a loss for Salinas, not just for the Japanese American community.

> His death brought grief to his many friends of both races in this city . . .
> Throughout his residence in this city he was active among the people of
> his own race. . . . But Uribe's interests were not entirely devoted to the
> Japanese. He not only gained the respect of all his white friends for his
> outstanding integrity, but he was civic minded and he was always ready to
> help in any community project.[64]

In Salinas, this last ranked as the highest praise. It is notable that the paper referred to "both races" rather than admit that Salinas actually contained numerous other racial groups besides Japanese (and presumably) whites. As in the case of Salinas's Filipino/a American residents, we see evidence of both the city's racism, shared by Americans generally in the 1930s and also that it existed alongside a semblance of acceptance.

Like their counterparts in the Filipino/a American and other ethnically identified communities in Salinas, Japanese American–sponsored events routinely made front-page news in a positive way in the 1930s. For example, the *Salinas Index-Journal* heralded "The Japanese Association Maps Activity Program for the Year" and reported that "more than a hundred members" attended a meeting in downtown Salinas on Lake Street. First, a celebration of the origin of Japan in 2594 was planned . . . [and] a projected park for the Japanese section of the city [was also projected]."[65] This last revealed evidence of marginalization in a "Japanese section" of the city, demonstrating the common practice of neighborhood segregation by race.

Salinas's Japanese residents may have spent their entire lives in California, as did so many others who eventually settled in Salinas,[66] but they maintained strong cultural affiliations to Japan and demonstrated a consistent allegiance to their country of origin:

> Under the auspices of the Salinas Japanese Association the sons and
> daughters of Nippon in Salinas and vicinity held a celebration in the Lake
> Street Theater . . . to jointly celebrate the advent of the New Year and the

recent arrival of a crown prince in the royal palace of the Emperor and Empress of Japan.[67]

Although many of these events were listed in society pages, it is notable just how often they were deemed important enough to make front-page news; the newspapers reflected the care that city leaders took in treading carefully, understanding that they needed the goodwill of Japanese Americans to maintain their strong economy without the full inclusion enjoyed by white European immigrants. The fact that the city of Salinas warranted a visit from Japanese royalty was a testament to the size and significance of the Japanese American community in Salinas; conversely, the city was considered important enough to Japan that it became part of the tour of California for the monarchy.

Yet, just as with the Filipino/a American experience, Japanese Americans were subject to exclusions and mistreatment based on their race when they presented a challenge to white power and profit. H. K. "Harry" Sakata was a prominent lettuce grower, seed producer, and a full-fledged member of the GSA in Salinas in the 1930s. But in a GSA meeting in 1932, a discussion over tenancy targeted him and other Japanese farmers, in an attempt to keep them from competing with whites over lettuce by raising the specter of enforcing the Alien Land Law:

> Land rentals were discussed. . . . It was pointed out by Mr. Harden that some 6000 acres now in sugar beet . . . would be open to lettuce grow-ers. . . . Mr. Sears said it was most likely that the Japanese would take all such lands. . . . Mr. Harden suggested that a general investigation of the legality of Japanese leases might eliminate some of the competition. . . . A discussion of the advisability of trying to have the Alien Land law en-forced in this District, resulted in President Wing's agreement to consult the District Attorney in the matter and report his findings.[68]

This was an ominous sign of the racism not so far beneath the superficial inclusion. The minutes did not reveal a follow-up to that conversation, but even a consideration of enforcement of the Alien Land Law to preclude Japanese tenant farmers from competing with whites indicated the precarious nature of Japanese settlement in Salinas, a portent of what was to come a decade later. Like Filipino/a Americans, Japanese Americans faced both racial exclusions and apparent acceptance as they navigated space in Salinas's economic, political, and social order.

Salinas's residents nonetheless expressed their goal of assimilation mostly through public schools that were not explicitly segregated but reflected the racial segregation of neighborhood settlement. The local Salinas newspapers commonly ran stories about school improvements and enrollments, heralding how successful the diverse groups had become in showing their allegiance to America, their English proficiency, and the values associated with Anglo American ideals. For example, the *Salinas Daily Journal* reported that during a "A representative meeting of fathers deeply interested in the welfare of high school boys and girls," they were concerned about maintaining standards in skills and training for "all ages in the high school from thirteen to twenty-two." These fathers were worried about the "great difference here in the physical [and] intellectual range of students," who came to Salinas from all over California. "Out of the 309 students in school, 147 come from the city of Salinas and the rest from outside." The stated goal was to "mould them together and direct them under one system . . . aiming at the proper character training for the best citizenship," indicating that assimilation and incorporation were what Salinas residents, like the rest of California and the nation, sought to achieve, "regardless of origin of race or class."[69] One father advocated training "the foreign element in the community in citizenship, which means training the parents themselves. Train the children to love English if you want good citizens." He (identified as Mr. Burchell) urged that what was most needed was to create an "educated citizenship on the soil."[70] To this end, in 1930 Salinas created an Evening School, offering "Courses for the Foreign Born," with a curriculum that included levels of English language reading and writing and American history, American institutions, and a class on Americanization: "a course to give knowledge of standards, principles, and ideals of our government."[71]

By 1934, school enrollment at Salinas High School had expanded significantly, from about 300 to "739 with the freshman class leading as the largest, having 253 students," reflecting increased population in the city in the 1930s.[72] Salinas, like every other city in California and the nation, put great importance on education as an assimilation tool to create an Anglo American ideal, even as the city showcased its variety of ethnic culture in events, pageants, and parades.

Nonetheless, even with increased enrollments, the impact of the poor lettuce harvest in 1932 affected city funding for education, so that the booming lettuce economy that Salinas residents were so proud of belied an economic structure that changed from year to year with the markets and harvests. "School tax[es] were slashed . . . wage cuts for teachers and 'economies' [were implemented in schools]."[73] This policy was reversed two years later when teachers' wages were reinstated to their former levels as a result of greatly improved local economy that lettuce generated. "One third of the salary reductions given Salinas teachers was restored. . . . The board authorized the increase because of the rising living costs and because of the policy of the administration to increase buying power [in the context of the Great Depression]," announced the school board on May 11, 1934.[74] In the same meeting, the board decided

> not to employ any more married women teachers . . . [and] three teachers [presumably married women] now on a probationary basis would be released and no married women will be employed in the future as teachers, except those whose husbands are incapacitated from earning a living.[75]

Education may have been the primary means of assimilation of new populations and as such played a central role in the life of the city, but it was an area where budget cuts could be implemented quickly to offset economic exigencies during the precarious years of the Great Depression. Yet, even though teaching was one of the few professional occupations available to women—even women of color, at the time—it hardly offered them financial security regardless of their individual financial situations.

Taken altogether, race relations in Salinas depended on the need for diverse populations in agricultural communities to find ways to get along together and support one another in a climate that was defined by racism, statewide and nationally. Farming required interaction and interdependence that brought ethnically and racially different individuals, families, and communities into not just close working relationships, but also close living relationships. This may have led to cultural understandings and camaraderie that was generally missing in nonagricultural communities in America, but it did not mean that racism was challenged.[76]

Throughout the Salinas Valley as well as other rural parts of California, workers, tenant farmers, and owners lived and worked near one another regardless of race or ethnic background—adding to a familiarity and commonality associated with a city identity. In Salinas, race relations were anything but clear and simple; they were most often complicated by class division within and between groups. Neighborhoods roughly segregated by race, but not as rigidly as was the case emerging in so many other towns and cities in California in this period.[77] Communalism remained the ideal, if not the reality. Cultural inclusion papered over racism with its deep and damaging roots and effects.

Salinas's capacity to accommodate and absorb groups deemed racially and ethnically different was tenuous. However, it made for a relatively stable and peaceful city comprised of middle classes who demonstrated their belief that they were "liberal minded and fair" by including diversity in cultural celebrations and events on the city's calendar even as they maintained a clear racial hierarchy with whites at the top.[78] Filipino/a American, Japanese American, and Chinese American communities identified as part of the Salinas social mainstream. No one inside Salinas anticipated the events to come in the next decade that exiled the entire Japanese American population of the city and made them pariahs in a place they considered home. First, however, would come fierce labor battles that would tear at the fabric of the city.

FIGURE 5.1   Mary Martha Ramsey Day

COURTESY BILL RAMSEY.

CHAPTER 5

Labor Battles

IT WAS A FIGHT IN THE FIELDS that erupted in the streets of the city. This reality encapsulated the differences and similarities between the urban labor battles of the 1930s up and down the state of California (and the nation) and the labor battles in agriculture that led to the famous La Follette congressional hearings of 1937, which brought notoriety to Salinas and international fame to one of its sons, John Steinbeck. This reality also exemplified just how rural and urban blended in Salinas and in America itself.

What appeared to be a farming community in 1930 was also, and at the same time, an urban place, with cultural amenities such as an opera house, fancy hotels, and a wide variety of retail shops, professional businesses, and restaurants; and it was also beset by some of the same class and racial differences and conflicts that characterized city life. People who were residents of Salinas worked in some form or another in agriculture, but few of them were full-time farmers or ranchers. Many, like Bruce Church, who became one of the preeminent agriculturalists of his day, began adult life with a career in real estate, retail business, the professions, or in an occupation only tangentially connected to farming. "Everybody around here knows Bruce Church. He used to work in a real estate office for $100 a month. He decided to go into lettuce and found a partner with $4,000. [By 1934] Bruce Church cashed in lettuce heads to the value of $150,000," reported the *Washington Post* in 1934.[1] Many farmed or ranched as a hobby. Others used part-time work on nearby ranches and farms to supplement their incomes.

FIGURE 5.2   The Ramsey family in front of their home in Alisal, 1940
COURTESY BILL RAMSEY.

Yet, their identities as residents of Salinas depended equally on the city as a cornerstone for the Central Coast, its county seat, its urban center, and on the farms and ranches that encircled it. Salinas had no contiguous border with any other municipality: It was a city in the fields, and the people who lived there created a community that embraced both.

A NEW MIGRATION

Mary Martha Ramsey Day—a woman of resilience, fortitude, and remarkable good nature— embodied the migrant laborers who made up the crucial workforce in California agriculture in the 1930s and who became central to the history of the city of Salinas. Originating in the American Southwest, pushed out by the twin catastrophes of the Dust Bowl and the Great Depression, she and her people presented a clear challenge to the narrative of urban prosperity that defined Salinas in the 1920s and 1930s. She was also part of a wave of defiance, challenging the combined power of Salinas's growers, shippers, marketers, contractors, and local business leaders to provide equal pay to women workers in the packing sheds, livable wages, and better, more secure working conditions to all workers and their families.

Mary's family and others like hers also inspired John Steinbeck's graphic and compelling accounts of migrant farmworkers' desperate lives in newspaper stories (*Harvest Gypsies*) and novels (*The Grapes of Wrath*), which won him both the Pulitzer and Nobel Prizes and international recognition. He was deeply worried that California was creating a permanent underclass of agricultural industrialized labor. In his powerful collection of essays in *Harvest Gypsies* that would become the basis for *Grapes of Wrath*, Steinbeck interviewed a California agriculturalist who stated matter-of-factly that "The success of California agriculture requires that we create and maintain a peon class," which supported Steinbeck's worst fears.[2] This view of California's future as a state divided by class alarmed Carey McWilliams too. Journalist, activist, and union organizer, McWilliams's seminal book *Factories in the Field* was published just a few months after Steinbeck's *Grapes of Wrath* in 1939 and vehemently condemned corporate agriculture in California, which he likened to the worst of industrialism's exploitations of workers.

Steinbeck's and McWilliams's accounts and analyses, though accurate, told only part of the story of labor, class, and the southern migration to California, however. Migrants were not all white people as depicted by Steinbeck, nor did workers see themselves as part of a lasting caste system in California as McWilliams dreaded. As a result of what Salinas residents believed were lopsided narratives of labor relations, Steinbeck was despised by residents of all stripes in Salinas, and not just because he sided with workers or portrayed them as sufferers; Salinas residents believed he created a narrative of locals as greedy and cruel oppressors and workers as mindless victims. They thought that Steinbeck slandered his own people. Apparently, his books were burned on Main Street in the 1940s, according to numerous anecdotal accounts.[3]

The new migrants may have worked in the fields and packing sheds because they had no other options for employment, but they did not become sharecroppers or tenant farmers in Monterey County and were not part of a permanent working class. They were rural people who nonetheless continued to live as townspeople and to move up the socioeconomic ladder in short order by becoming small business owners and homeowners. They identified as both rural and urban. Salinas was an urban place beset with all the problems that the Great Depression wrought—homelessness and unemployment and the need to support those who suffered from the collapse of the national economy—but it was also the center of a vast (and lucrative) agricultural region that needed large numbers of seasonal workers to pick and pack and ship its produce for always fluctuating markets.

The very presence of the new migrant worker population doubled the size of the unincorporated subdivision of Alisal almost overnight and changed the complexion of the area from racially Asian, Mexican, and African American to predominantly white. The fact that the new migrants were Anglo American citizens (rather than noncitizen Asian immigrants) mattered enormously and propelled many of them, within the space of a generation, into the world of elite Salinas that excluded most people of color, who were lucky to make it into the middle class through small business entrepreneurship and home ownership.[4]

Both Steinbeck and McWilliams argued that only intervention and support at the federal level might thwart the development of a permanent caste system that threatened to destroy American middle-class life.[5] Steinbeck in particular made a sharp distinction in his descriptions of vastly different settings: makeshift migrant campsites where workers declined quickly into complete despair and destitution and more welcoming environments of federally funded labor camps where workers' families were met with communal support and camaraderie—keeping gardens and restoring their own sense of dignity and hope. According to Steinbeck, workers thrived with even a modicum of government intervention.[6]

Steinbeck's novels, particularly *The Grapes of Wrath* and *In Dubious Battle*, reinforced the importance of unions and organization as a necessary means to challenge the power of industrial agriculture aligned with government agencies that oppressed workers in the most absolute way. Yet, in both narratives, Steinbeck also exposed the corrupt machinations of union bosses and made a distinction between small farmers who often sympathized with migrant workers and large-scale agriculturists who certainly did not. Scholars of agriculture in the American West and in California increasingly argue for the complexity of both labor relations and race.[7]

For Mary Martha Ramsey Day, it all began in a small town in rural Texas. Mary recalled her childhood as one of hard work and privation, but also one of love and adventure. Her cheerful acceptance of the most difficult of circumstances likely came from her mother's example, a woman whom she described as "small" but resolute and fearless. Mary recollected, "I don't think [my mother] ever backed down from anyone or anything. . . . [She] wasn't afraid of anything except lightning [having been struck by lightning as a newlywed]."[8] Like so many other women who arrived in the Depression era, Mary's mother faced all the usual travails of motherhood in an era of economic uncertainty, multiple crises, and innumerable outbreaks of illness without access to medical care. On top of all that, she also contended with the challenges of travel with a baby, toddlers, and older children under extreme duress.

The family chose California as a destination because Mary's paternal grandparents had already relocated to Monterey in 1929, presumably to work in the burgeoning fish canneries but also for health reasons: "[The grandparents left Texas] because of Grandma Kate's health. She was an asthmatic." Mary vividly recalled the moment the family departed for California: "We had an auction sale on our farm and sold everything; household goods, farm equipment, and livestock." She described packing the bare necessities in "a Model B Ford," and together with her parents and nine siblings, which included a set of two-year-old twins and a six-month-old infant, "started for Salinas California."[9]

She described their harrowing journey west as a big adventure, which it may have seemed to her twelve-year-old self, but the trip must have pushed her mother and father to the brink of their ability to cope. They traveled in the middle of winter, but because "we were so tightly packed in the car the cold did not bother us." The family made it to Arizona in time for Christmas, which was spent picking cotton.

> [We] lived in a tent and we were within sight of the State Prison at Florence, Arizona. We did our cooking outside. . . . There was a prison break while we were there and the guards came by our place with the dogs and they told us that all women and children had to stay in the tent. I often wondered what protection we had in a tent.[10]

Mary described frequent automobile breakdowns and challenges:

> In the mountains in Arizona, all of us older children and my Father got out of the car and pushed because the car would not make it over the mountains. . . . Well, finally we got to San Luis Obispo. That car took a look at the mountain and wouldn't go anymore. Daddy called my Grandfather in Monterey and two of my uncles came to San Luis Obispo to get us . . . . [A]fter two months we arrived in Monterey.[11]

Bill Ramsey, Mary's little brother and the second to the last of the eleven Ramsey children, was born in Alisal in 1932 and would become one of the most prominent businessmen and civic leaders in Salinas. But he identified first as a poor Dust Bowl migrant.[12] Although the Ramsey family began life as small farmers in Texas, they did not aspire to a farming life in Salinas. Instead, they aimed to move up the socioeconomic ladder through work in processing and food production rather than actual farming.[13]

Entire families just like them lived in tents or built makeshift homes on the outskirts of Salinas in Alisal's Hebbron Heights, an area that also came to be known as Little Oklahoma, rather than the multiracial space that it was in these years and thereafter. Admitting that "poverty is not unheard of here" and that "poverty is always with us," an editorial blamed the migrant labor force: "The charities are having a heavy load thrust upon their shoulders because of migrants, and not because of established . . . residents," thus implying that such migrant laborers were unworthy of aid.[14] The problem of migrant farm labor in Salinas was a problem for the city. Migrant workers did not live on individual farmsteads or work as sharecroppers or tenants; instead, they lived in town and needed to be considered as a new resident population in Salinas, even as they worked in agriculture. It was a jarring disconnect for a city that prided itself on its wealth in Depression era America, as a "white spot" for its prosperity.

The Salvation Army stepped in to help "feeding and providing a night lodging for from 100 to 150 unemployed men who are daily passing through this city."[15] The newspaper report however warned Salinas's residents:

> If due to lack of funds, the Army should be forced to discontinue this work, the resulting conditions only become unthinkable. Can you imagine any worse condition than having these men turned on the streets of Salinas with no place to sleep and nothing to eat? Crime, panhandling and general begging would increase in such proportions that the actual security of our homes and property be in jeopardy.[16]

However, the piece included a call for citizens to help, as well as a plea for compassion and understanding:

> There is also the humanitarian . . . side of the situation. . . . [P]ersons compelled to ask for community aid . . . purely as a result of the depression . . . have always hitherto been self-supporting. They are normal and stable in their adjustment to society and as little social service problems as the victim of a shipwreck or earthquake.[17]

These were city issues, not problems that occurred in farm labor camps, suggesting that Salinas had more in common with Depression era Los Angeles or San Francisco or even San José than with unincorporated agricultural regions in California.

Although people of color often faced harsh judgment for being poor during the Depression, it was notable that Anglo American migrant laborers enjoyed a degree of respect despite their poverty. They were described as "hitherto . . . self-supporting" and as "normal and stable" people who just happened to be victims of bad luck and circumstances. The Salinas press applauded efforts by the Salvation Army to provide relief and called for donations to help the cause:

> Food clothing and shelter must be provided for them with as little offense to their dignity as possible. . . . During the past six months the Salvation

Army has given 19,025 meals, 10,391 nights' lodgings, 2,516 garments, 1,302 pairs of shoes and assisted 591 families (average four to a family). . . . The people of Salinas heartily and sincerely appreciate this splendid work.[18]

Still, messages were mixed at best. Californians generally despised refugees from the South during this era, famously posting sheriff's deputies to bar them from entering Los Angeles and other large municipalities. Reports in the Salinas newspapers echoed fears of other Californians about "indigents coming into this area," people who "drift." The poverty of Dust Bowlers bothered the citizens of Salinas less than their transiency. Although this city welcomed new populations of working people (especially if they were white), they deeply distrusted migrant fieldworkers. John Steinbeck recalled a conversation with a little boy in a migrant workers' camp: "When they need us they call us migrants, and when we picked their crop, we're bums and we got to get out."[19]

The areas outside of town included the kind of migrant labor camps that Steinbeck described so well in his novels and reports. According to County Welfare Director W. H. Leach (who popped up in Forrest Gump-like fashion in every area of political, economic, and social life in Salinas between the 1920s and the 1950s), there was real concern over the appalling conditions in the migrant camps located just beyond Salinas's borders. Leach described "alarming" living conditions with "More than 300 families are now camped in one spot alone along the river road south of Salinas while hundreds more are on private land."[20] He was less concerned about the welfare of these destitute families, however, than about the possibility that they might transmit disease to the larger population. "These families live in tents under conditions that are far from sanitary. . . . Children of these families attend schools in this county, exposing other children to whatever maladies they might acquire because of the unsanitary environment in which they live."[21] The board of supervisors held a special meeting to consider solutions to the "Migrant Problem," worried that "mass trouble is likely to occur if agitators go among indigents."[22] The concern linked the proximity of the camp to labor union organizing as well as public health, where neighborhoods and schools might be susceptible to infectious disease caused by the horrific living conditions of the camps.

What to do? One solution proposed by the board of supervisors and newspaper editorials was to force families to return whence they came, providing them gas to travel back. Although county officials sent fifty families back to their original homes, "daily there are more families arriving than leaving."[23] One editorial argued that government had a responsibility for these Americans: "While they are in the county they must be fed, and if they become ill, they must be treated. They are public charges from every angle and the taxpayers money must be used in keeping them alive."[24] But, they believed, the taxpayers of Oklahoma, not California, "should bear burden of supporting them," which blithely ignored the fact that the environmental and economic catastrophes made that prospect impossible. Moreover, it was an argument made in the context of widespread local prosperity, so this position felt doubly cruel: "This county is fortunate in having industries which employ practically all of the residents of the county, while other counties, states, and even sections of the country are burdened with caring for a larger percentage of their people."[25]

The county health and welfare officials discussed another proposal that would place migrant families in "concentration camps" that offered adequate housing, showers, food supplies, and medical care to meet basic needs along the lines currently carried out in San Luis Obispo.[26] Still, this plan meant marginalization rather than the integration of newcomers, which had been the common settlement pattern in Salinas since the 1850s and extended to newly arrived residents. The federally funded camps that Steinbeck described in *Harvest Gypsies* were certainly an improvement, however, and offered support for workers to regain self-confidence, self-respect, and a measure of economic stability, but it was not clear from the records here that the camps that Monterey County supervisors considered were funded by the federal or state government. They appeared to have been county efforts.

Diverse women's groups came together to provide emergency supplies of food, clothing, and even housing. Again, integration and incorporation of the poor all depended on perceptions by the larger community that the poverty and transiency were *temporary* conditions and that the newcomers shared community values. "Everybody became a good citizen," recalled one former Dust Bowler, "and we all grew up in a great community."[27] The emphasis on citizenship and community indicated that poverty alone did not disqualify individuals or families from Salinas's majority, but race may have. Salinas residents' perceptions of stability and commitment on the part of newcomers made the difference between persistent marginalization and eventual acceptance of someone into the fabric of city life—if, first and foremost, that person was perceived as white.[28]

DEVELOPMENT OF ALISAL

Almost all these new migrants settled—temporarily at first, and then permanently—in the unincorporated adjacent community of Alisal. Like the Ramsey family, they may have worked in agriculture, but they did not become farmers. Instead, they transformed the more affordable Alisal from a sparsely settled outskirts into a city space.

Although Alisal may have been thinly populated, people had been living there for centuries. In the early twentieth century, working-class families—Japanese, European-origin white, Chinese, Mexican, Filipino/a, and African American—intermingled in helter-skelter neighborhoods and on some scattered farms and ranches. Like Salinas itself, Alisal mixed rural life with the urban, creating community that blended both.

Alisal's residents worked through the board of supervisors to improve conditions, especially in constructing sewers and ensuring safe drinking water, but also installing sidewalks and paved streets as city dwellers. Elton Hebbron subdivided huge tracts of land for housing, and Robert W. Adcock bought land in Alisal in 1926—not to farm, but to found a water company and create a sewer system.[29] As the population of Alisal increased in 1934 and 1935, Adcock, along with "14 residents of the Alisal district . . . petitioned the Board of Supervisors to service an additional 90 homes and declared himself willing to pay one fourth the cost of connecting [them] while require[ing] the home owners to pay three-fourths of the cost of laying the mains."[30] Adcock also helped form the Alisal Chamber of Commerce with the aim of making a separate town. All of these were clearly attributes associated with a town identity. The migrant workers who came out of the Southwest did not intend to create farms. They put a great deal of energy into creating small businesses and organizing them into a viable community that eventually became part of Salinas proper.

Joanne Adcock Schmidt, born in 1930, remembered the vast, largely unpopulated landscape that mostly contained scattered farms and ranches but became transformed with the new, mostly white migration. In her words, "Dust Bowlers overran Alisal and that was the fault of the people who sent off all those [advertising] flyers."[31] A Mr. Jensen of Wells Fargo Bank, working in partnership with the GSA, advertised for 5,000 new workers in 1934, "setting forth the natural advantages of the country and the prosperity of its industries,"[32] which was viewed with horror by Salinas's Central Labor Council. It was the middle of the Great Depression, and union members in Salinas realized that the effort to bring in new workers was intended to depress wages.[33]

The Salinas Chamber of Commerce immediately "repudiated these ads and launched a counter campaign in support of the Central Labor Council . . . that there was no labor shortage in Central California . . . and that there were . . . between two and three [local] men for every job" ready and willing to work.[34] It was significant that the Salinas Chamber of Commerce, usually associated with business classes rather than workers, included a contingent of union people among its members and openly sided with them over the growers and shippers.

Adcock Schmidt noted that most Dust Bowlers who landed in Alisal (also called east Salinas) found "quick employment" opportunities: "When [Dust Bowlers] came over here they started working in the lettuce sheds and for Spreckels."[35] One report took issue with Steinbeck's portrayal of Dust Bowlers as itinerant laborers without the wherewithal to restore their family economies: "There's a book that burns East Salinas right up! The honest working people who own their homes and pay their bills get so mad they sputter" at their depiction by Steinbeck as destitute.[36] Their reality was more mundane: "If *Grapes of Wrath* had never been written, there would be no news in East Salinas whether it be called 'Little Oklahoma' or not. . . . [Rather it was] a typical California rural home settlement. . . . On gently rolling valley land between two ranges of mountains lies this loosely knit community of perhaps 5,000 to 8,000 people who came from everywhere," this observer argued.[37]

The article described the new residents of Alisal as "good lettuce workers," who

> found Hebbron Heights a good place to live. The acre tracts were . . . subdivided into lots about 50 by 120 feet, and they sold for $200 to $300. There were no costly building restrictions, the migrants were just getting a foothold and it was an ideal combination. They moved right in, buying lots and building houses and working for wages, and they had found what they came for.[38]

They built homes, not farms, nor did they intend to continue a life of farming, which had already proven far too risky to sustain families. They clearly aspired to become middle-class city people within the context of a rural, agricultural environment that offered them solid employment and upward mobility. The description of the area compared it to American urban life, with a dose of reality: "Hebbron Heights was no contribution to the City Beautiful idea, and its inhabitants ran into tough luck sometimes just as they do in Wall Street."[39]

For migrant workers to become full-fledged Salinas stakeholders, however, they needed enough money to contribute to the consumer culture that was as much a part of town life as agriculture. Besides improving their housing, "They are tearing down their tin can shacks and building neat houses as fast as they can afford to."[40] They had spending power too: "Salinas stores, which regarded [Alisal] as a joke are putting branches out here . . . so far as [the reporter] can see, [Alisal/Hebbron Heights] developed like any other subdivision that starts from scratch."[41] The fact that the reporter described Alisal and Hebbron Heights as a subdivision, albeit unincorporated, rather than as a place of farms and ranches indicated that residents perceived themselves as creating either a township on their own or becoming part of the city of Salinas. They were rural people, but they were also urbanites in the making.

Elton Hebbron noted that he had "gained a new faith in mankind" from his experience with Dust Bowlers:

> "I've never lost a cent on payments or had to foreclose on anybody. . . . The younger generation is practically all at work; some old folks are on relief but not many. The family feeling is strong, and the young people usually keep their old folks off the dole. . . . The working man and his family is the backbone of Salinas. They drive trucks or tractors, they work in the packing sheds . . . and in the fields. . . . Their wives work too and their sons and daughters, and they get ahead because they are determined to get ahead."[42]

The fact that these families moved to the Imperial Valley for a few months of work at the end of the harvest in Salinas Valley did not disqualify them from inclusion in Salinas life: "After April they'll be back in Salinas, working the 'long season' [the vegetable season lasted a full seven months] for the same boss and living at home, putting down more roots, paying taxes."[43] All of this depended on workers being paid high enough wages to allow them both stability and upward mobility.

Salinas's residents generally approved of those whose background marked them as not just as potential members of the middle class but also as permanent residents willing to put down roots. If they succeeded at showing stability, they were commonly welcomed. Class was usually seen as fluid. People who were poor or were defined as working class achieved middle and even elite status rather quickly (within their own lifetimes or at least by the second generation) by virtue of their racial identity as white people, but also because in an agricultural town like Salinas, a fluid economy and social system made for more elasticity and room to move upward socioeconomically. Their collective hard work and the wages that came from union membership also allowed workers opportunities to educate their children, acquire homes, and start businesses. First, they had to create and maintain a strong union.

LABOR STRIKES AND CONSUMER CULTURE

On May 9, 1934, the *Salinas Index-Journal* announced to its readers that a general strike called by the International Longshoreman's Association shut down ports from Seattle to San Pedro, the "gateways to the Orient," and brought almost all West Coast cities to a complete standstill. The paper reported that the unions were engaged in a "fight to the finish for more money and shorter working hours," which was an issue most Salinas residents supported in the interest of maintaining a consumer culture that required high wage levels and stability in the workforce, as shown by the article's placement on the front page. Alongside the report on the general strike, the paper announced "Salinas Sales Days," indicating an equivalency in importance but also the extent to which the city depended upon buyers, including from the working classes.[44] According to the article, Salinas Sales Days celebrated local retailers and encouraged residents to patronize local businesses in order to sustain them during the economic catastrophe of the Great Depression. The story predicted "merchandising history will be made in Salinas," exuding confidence (with many exclamation marks) that "thousands of visitors from all parts of the valley" would certainly arrive to shop and support the city's retailers (rather than traveling to shop in San Francisco or San José). "Gay flags and bunting, streamers and banners will be put up to transform Main Street into an inviting Wonderland of Merchandise!"[45]

They were not alone. The liberal local newspaper, the *Salinas Independent,* also urged communitywide participation in the shopping spree as an antidote to the Great Depression. One editor, Rolin G. Watkins, a tireless supporter of Salinas business and a booster for the city, wrote overblown editorials that urged residents to shop locally: "If we but center our interests upon Salinas [instead of shopping in San Francisco or San José] we are destined to become a great empire—small in acreage it is true but rich in monetary values."[46] He went on to make a case for Salinas as a place of producers: "It is not how much money you have as it is how much money you are producing. The worker bee ever commands more respect than the drone," merging consumer culture with labor force participation.[47]

What was striking about the juxtaposition of these two news stories was that 1934 was a boom year for lettuce production in the Salinas Valley and a moment of crisis when labor battles took center stage. The urban centers of San Francisco, Seattle, Portland, and Los Angeles were paralyzed by successful labor union activism that also divided their cities by race and class. Newspapers in those places reflected that reality even though the Salinas press did not. By 1934, cities like San Francisco and Seattle felt deeply the economic crisis of the Great Depression.

In Salinas an inspired new labor movement challenged the hegemony of the agricultural elite, although even union newspapers seemed terrified by the possibilities of chaos within this context of plenty. Lettuce production sustained the local economy despite the effects of the Great Depression and kept most (but hardly all) workers above the poverty line. In Salinas laboring people were much needed and appreciated for their part in growing, picking, and packing crops for market, but also for sustaining local businesses as consumers. For the latter they needed to earn high enough wages to allow them to purchase goods and services and move into middle-class life.

Union membership was normative and integrated into Salinas's community life, supported in public opinion pieces but also carefully disassociated from radical politics.[48] It was not only the conservative *Index-Journal* that advocated an energetic and activist capitalism, but the *Salinas Independent*, which defined itself as the "Official Organ of the Central Labor Union—AFL Affiliate." Through the *Independent*, union members expressed solidarity with merchants in town based on workers' power as consumers. They explicitly and frequently distanced themselves from radical politics and any hint of Communist affiliation even as they fought hard to achieve the measure of economic mobility so visible all around them among labor contractors, farmers, and businesspeople attached to the agricultural industry. To do that, they needed to maintain high wages and job security.

Salinas in the 1930s has been characterized by journalists and historians alike as a place in which white mobs attacked Filipino/a Americans for transgressing sexual boundaries, a city in which violent labor strikes happened regularly, and a region with a middle-class population that expressed collective disdain for the plight of the thousands of impoverished dust bowl refugees. However, this was a city that was also a multiracial mix of hopeful contenders to the middle class; it was a place where Japanese and Filipino/a American contractors joined forces with mostly white elite growers, shippers, and marketing people in opposing the labor activism of white women, and where packinghouse workers and working-class men—who were white, Filipino/a American, and Mexican American—did not see themselves as part of a permanent caste but as aspirants to middle-class lives of property ownership and status. After all, they observed socioeconomic upward mobility among their peers almost everywhere they looked.[49]

It all began with women just like Mary Martha Ramsey Day. The mostly white women lettuce trimmers, many of whom were new arrivals escaping the ravages of the Dust Bowl, went on strike in 1933, and in so doing became catalysts for both union organizing and the grower-shipper responses to it. The women packinghouse workers made up an important part of the approximately 3,000 members of the Fruit and Vegetable Workers Union of Salinas.[50] The women were upset about their earnings—5 cents less an hour than men who did the same job. Equal pay became a rallying cry for women during the numerous labor actions of the decade. According to minutes of the GSA, "The heart of the [1933] strike had been the demand for the same pay for women as for men in an organization in which the former constituted 70% of the membership."[51] Filipino/a American fieldworkers supported the women workers in the walkout in 1933 and in 1934, against the admonitions of their contractor-employers, thus threatening the lettuce crop and triggering growers' concern about the dependability of the labor force.[52]

The growers and shippers disdained the Filipino/a fieldworkers who supported the women packinghouse workers' demands for equal pay in the mid-1930s. They agreed to privilege white employment on racial grounds but also as punishment to Filipino/a supporters of women workers: "No Filipinos be employed on a job that can be efficiently done by white men," they agreed.[53] Although women sat at the bargaining table, their demand for equal pay was tossed aside over and over again both by the growers and shippers and their own union representatives who made agreements with the

GSA without advocating for women workers.[54] Women were also victims of blacklists. In the wake of the 1936 lettuce strike, "Mrs. Marvel Alberti . . . testified that she [and her children] had lived during the winter on a check of [only] $40 a month from SERA . . . and that when she applied for work she had been told that she had caused trouble during the strike and therefore was not to be employed."[55] Workers lived in constant anxiety throughout the 1930s as they attempted to challenge wage rates, and for women, pay equity.

NEGOTIATIONS AND STALEMATES

The GSA was formidable, but hardly an organized entity in the 1930s. Members met weekly at the downtown Jeffrey Hotel (by 1928 the tallest, most impressive building in Salinas) but rarely agreed on anything, heatedly debating everything from "shipping conditions . . . wage cuts . . . and [how to deal with] bad publicity." H. L. Strobel advocated that they "stand together in any of their problems and [in doing this] they would benefit greatly," but this rarely occurred. Still, with one exception, all the original twenty-two members agreed to pay $5 a month as "an admission fee" to move forward as an official association.[56]

Charles Moore was elected secretary, a position he held throughout the tumultuous 1930s. He took meticulous notes at every meeting and reported even minor comments and disputes. Moore reflected the concern by growers and shippers that any and all labor activism had to be suspect as inspired by anti-democratic, sinister forces "the third international and its effect on labor conditions," became a frequent topic for discussion. He expressed his sensitivity to newspaper accounts that reflected badly on growers who fought wage increases for migrant workers living in extreme poverty: "The question of the bad effect of wrong publicity was discussed."[57]

The decision in 1930s to cut wages because of intermittently lower demand for lettuce, considered a luxury food during the Great Depression, not only prompted vigorous debate but also how growers and shippers undercut one another when they agreed about a course of action in meetings but failed to carry them out in practice.

> It was reported that there were rumors that certain shippers had been paying 40 cents . . . some of them were [paying higher wages] through their foremen although the shipper did not know it. [Bruce] Church reported that McLaren changed his mind and will now pay 35 cents. . . . Mr. Spiegl

believes that no man is big enough to get along without the assistance of the others and the Association is too large to ignore the smallest shipper. Mr. Moore urged the members to cooperate because if they did not now the battle would start and there would be no reason that they would be forced to pay 50 or 60 cents an hour for field labor.[58]

A heated discussion ensued in which "various shippers accused others of paying 40 cents [rather than the agreed upon 35 cents] either directly or indirectly. . . . Mr. Church and Mr. Farley expressed grave doubts that a 35 cent wage could be maintained on account of the inability of the shippers to stitch an agreement among themselves."[59]

The tension in these discussions reflected the essential problem for the city. Growers, shippers, and marketing people in agriculture were also Salinas residents who needed working classes to function as consumers as much as laborers, either in the fields or packing sheds. They knew that in order to create a stable working class, wages had to remain relatively high and workers needed to feel valued, but in order to make profits for themselves, wages should be as low as possible, and in agriculture workers were not needed year round. It was a dilemma that erupted into violence by 1936.

The minutes from this September 23, 1930 meeting provided a window into how debates unfolded within the organization brought on both by competition among the members and by the lack of any kind of mechanism that might have been used to enforce policy once agreed upon, although there was seldom any agreement at all. Bruce Church played a crucial, but largely overlooked role in the 1930s; he sometimes singlehandedly worked to bring disparate groups of laborers, union representatives, contractors, and small and large growers and shippers together to negotiate over contentious issues regarding wages and working conditions, with the big picture in mind that Salinas needed workers who could also contribute to the city as consumers and full citizens.

The sheriff's department and city leaders were deeply involved in negotiations, as they were in all the other labor disputes of the decade, and they were clearly on the side of growers and shippers, not labor. The September 23 meeting included Police Commissioner Vic Barlogio and D. P. McKinnon: "Mr. D. P. McKinnon of the Sheriff's Office stated that the Filipinos recognized the fact that the Shippers would win their stand at a 35 cent wage . . . and that they considered that Valesques had skipped with their money and

left them in the lurch,"[60] which indicated growing mistrust among fieldworkers for both the contractors and the growers. As we saw in Chapter 4, the
contractors were directly responsible for paying the fieldworkers.

Despite their awareness that contractors were losing the trust of fieldworkers, the GSA members met with "Filipino labor contractors at . . . the
Chamber of Commerce . . . to discuss the situation with them. . . . It was
finally decided by all present that they would pay no more than 35 cents at
least until such time as they notified the secretary that they intended to pay
more."[61] The city of Salinas, the chamber of commerce, and growers and
shippers were clearly allies, something that was revealed repeatedly in the
investigations of Congressional Committees and journalists in the aftermath
of the 1936 strikes.[62]

Contractors and fieldworkers were also locked in conflict over wages and
working conditions that led to an impasse in the short-lived strike of 1934
and an indication that workers, just like their counterparts in the new GSA,
hardly made up a monolithic group. Contractors may have had working
agreements with individual growers and shippers, but they found themselves
at odds with the workers they were supposed to be representing and with
growers too when it came to enforcement. "Thos. Chung [a grower] spoke
of intimidation of his men by Filipinos in Salinas. . . . The contractors made
repeated [appeals] to humility and inferiority and said they were merely the
agents of the shippers and unable to influence the workers in their refusal
to accept 35 cents per hour."[63] Labor contractors exercised little power in
enforcing agreements over wages with growers and shippers. The contractors
made desperate efforts to maintain their position and power as go-betweens
in numerous meetings with the GSA director during the 1930s: "Mr. Canete
said that the Union had 1100 members and was formed by him so that the
Contractors would be able to keep in touch with the thoughts of laborers
and would be in a better position to control the labor in this district."[64]

Growers and shippers became frustrated over their inability to agree, and
on the contractors' inability to compel workers to follow through on wage
agreements. Workers were left out of consideration altogether: "The meeting was reconvened at the Jeffrey Hotel at 9:30 where discussion included
offers from F. J. McCann and H. L. Strobel to subscribe $5,000. And $500.
Respectively to a fund for the purpose of breaking the strike. Mr. McCann
also offered to hold out if Messers Harden and Storm would stand with
him."[65] The first strike action seemed to favor workers, nonetheless:

It was decided 18 to 7 to grant the strikers demand and pay 40 cents immediately. . . . Right after adjournment the shippers went back to the office of the Chamber of Commerce where President Strobel announced their decision to Filipinos, but with the explanation that 40 cents was granted for a limited time only and that it was not done through necessity but for the purpose of continuing the pleasant relations that have always existed between the Shippers and the laborers in the lettuce industry.[66]

This last comment was telling, indicating as it did that those who worked in agriculture in Salinas aimed for a relationship that was more cooperative than adversarial, and yet the agreement in favor of labor was explicitly a temporary one, portending further battles.

By 1932, it was clear that association members were reluctant to act as a body to enforce labor agreements. Individualists all, it was difficult if not impossible to prevent the numerous strikes that occurred almost every season—not just pitting shippers, packers, and growers against workers but against one another as well. Some believed in coordination and collective action and others wanted to go it alone, even as they identified loosely with one group or another. We see this lack of coordination played out in the failure of the 1930 strike as workers refused to conform to agreements contractors made and in the build-up to the 1933 and 1936 strikes as growers and shippers opted for a policy of independence from association agreement:

The request presented by Ray Sheeoe of some 25 Philipino labor contractors for consultation with this Association on the matter pertaining to field labor was denied on the grounds that this Association had last year refused to recognize an organization of the Packing house workers and that it is our policy to allow each shipper to work out his own labor arrangements independently of this Association.[67]

Letting each member of the association work out individual agreements with workers and contractors was the opposite of a unified organization.

GSA members advocated bringing in a new labor force from Mexico to compete with American workers and gain leverage over them, just when workers showed that they had the advantage in wage negotiations: "Mr. Moore suggested that it would be a good idea for our members to encourage Mexican labor to come to this section because of the growing restlessness of the Philipinos and their tendency toward organizing to dictate wages."[68] Some growers even attempted to bring in Chinese contract workers to replace the predominantly Filipino/a workforce: "Mr. Nutting reported that his experiment with Chinese labor was entirely unsatisfactory, that out of forty odd men he probably had ten or a dozen good hands . . . he said that the experiment probably cost him $500.00 and that he had abandoned it."[69] Growers actively sought to undercut labor organizing by Filipino/a workers, especially by replacing them with Mexican immigrant workers or anyone else who might be brought into the fields as competition. By 1935 construction of a labor camp for workers from Mexico was well underway.[70]

Because agricultural workers were excluded from the wage protections and organizing rights guaranteed by the National Labor Relations Act, support for Salinas fieldworkers had to be local. Thus, the GSA ignored Washington, DC's suggestion for wage "curtailments" and instead published support for "Mr. Spiegl's statement that he had raised the wages of all his employees 5 cents per hour . . . and the recent activity of both field and Packing house workers in organizing themselves."[71] These actions indicated a modicum of acceptance by the GSA that workers had the right to organize and form unions in agriculture despite their explicit exclusion from protections under the National Labor Relations Act.[72] However, the GSA had internal conflicts about wage rates and representation.

> The question of the recent demands by the Philipino Labor Council for an increase of from 20 cents to 30 cents per hour for field labor was discussed and . . . it was decided to appoint a committee to meet with the Philipinos. . . . [A]t the present time these people are divided as between their contractors and the individual laborer element. . . . [T]he Contractors are the conservative element and the others the radical group.[73]

The GSA continuously attempted to divide and conquer, making deals with co-ethnic contractors behind the backs of workers. Individual growers also obviously preferred to negotiate with contractors or even with laborers directly rather than deal with an organized and more powerful union, either in the fields or in the packing sheds.

An incident between the sheriff, district attorney, and labor organizers set the stage for new tensions in early 1933; the clash demonstrated how readily Salinas residents attributed union organizing to people outside of the

Salinas community rather than admit that Filipino/a (and all workers) had a solid claim to representation through unions, a right to livable wages, and to employment security and safe working conditions. In February, Sheriff Abbott had been called to investigate a stabbing at the Vierra Ranch labor camp. Abbott (who arrived with District Attorney Harry Noland) "overheard a white man [identified a Lawrence Newell] talking . . . in what they believed to be seditious talk."[74] The two men listened as Newell apparently "urged the Filipinos to refuse to work unless they were paid 40 cents an hour, urging them to oppose the capitalists."[75] Newell, and the two boys who accompanied him, "had been peddling papers carrying red propaganda. Both admitted they belonged to an organization which wished to prevent war and which feared the capitalists were planning a war."[76] Newell was quoted by Noland's stenographer, who was also present, as stating to the Filipino/a workers,

> We have spies in every branch of the United States. . . . [I]f there is no organization by April 1 [1933] we are going to have a revolution. We may have to take guns on our shoulders and fight for what rightfully belongs to us. Workers must organize to establish a system supporting the workers.[77]

Newell was duly arrested. Abbott and Noland likely invented Newell's pitch to the Filipino/a American workers (despite the presence of a stenographer).

City leaders confused labor organization with radical politics, which led them to fear, distrust, and overreact to labor actions throughout the 1930s. This, in turn, led to a pattern of cooperation among local law enforcement agencies that was justified by them as protection of American democracy and capitalism and was also normalized—long before the 1936 strike.

Lettuce prices declined in the 1932 season but rebounded in 1933. Nonetheless, markets remained precarious, and the Depression reduced consumer demand for this luxury produce. The GSA cut wages, which led to yet another round of protests and walkouts by workers who felt the effects of the economic crisis deeply. By October 10, 1933 a meeting of a few GSA directors (Church, Grainger, Harden, Nutting, Vertin, Eaton, Barkelew, Spiegl, Grande, Moody) considered a plan of action to deal with the predictable refusal of workers to accept wage cuts in the middle of the Depression.[78]

Growers tried to circumvent contractors by organizing "committees" of workers in their own packing sheds; they also eliminated union representatives, or as growers referred to them, "people who had no jobs."[79] The members of the GSA believed that in Salinas "conditions here were better than any other localities and that the wages we were paying would compare favorably with those paid anywhere else for comparable labor," but also that layoffs to maintain low wages "would cause little harm to growers or shippers"—indicating that growers and shippers were perfectly willing to sacrifice workers to depress wages.[80]

The workers fought back. "The strikers refused to allow the Shippers to meet with a committee composed of a representative worker from each of the sheds. . . . The condition that all shippers seemed to fear most was the closed shop ambition of the strikers."[81] Representatives from the National Labor Relations Board offered to become "involved and offered to negotiate but that time was necessary . . . and the public should not expect too much in the way of immediate efficiency."[82] The federal government simply had no power to enforce an agreement, and workers continued their 1933 strike to force grower-shippers to recognize a closed shop once and for all: "The strikers telephoned that they had turned down our arbitration proposal. . . . [T]hey felt that they could not be satisfied with anything less than what they were asking for."[83]

At this point, the GSA changed course and consolidated; instead of meeting strikers' desperate demand for a closed shop, they tried to disrupt the union altogether: "Mr. Jordan explained that his Company had never lost a strike and never would because they adhered to the principle that it was always necessary to start operations even in the sketchiest way,"[84] meaning the shippers decided to pool their products and resources as much as possible, splitting the costs and profits, just to get things going again.

Again the members of the GSA attempted to gain leverage over workers by bringing in immigrant laborers:

> Several suggestions were made as to what kind of labor to bring in and where to get it. Mr. Arena made tentative arrangements for upwards of 50 Mexicans from the San Joaquin Valley. Mr. Spiegl suggested bringing in a gang of professional strike breakers from San Francisco. . . . No action was taken.[85]

Three days later, George Creel, district manager of the National Recovery Administration, negotiated a settlement that did not include a closed shop.[86]

WORKERS' RIGHTS AND WOMEN WORKERS

Wages increased to 65 cents for packers and 40 cents for trimmers, but women still received less pay, which they contested to no avail. However, growers and shippers continued to disagree and even undermined one another: "Mr J.H. Grande [of Crown Packing] said that he would not be a sacrifice to the avarice of such shippers as Harden, Bruce Church, and Garin and served notice that he would repudiate his agreement to cooperate."[87] Workers also complained about lack of consistency by growers and shippers in satisfying the agreed-upon terms, especially when it came to rehiring striking workers. Workers identified GSA members (Gerrard, Sers, Sawdey & Hunt, Crown, McCann, and Ice Kist) as those that had not lived up to the agreement "that shippers had agreed to fire practically all workers in favor of strikers."[88]

By 1934, the GSA called a special meeting to find ways to employ locals in the lettuce fields and packing sheds. As usual, however, growers and shippers remained divided and suspicious of migrant workers. "It has been pointed out that the Shippers employing as much local help as possible reduc[ed] the strike likelihood, [and] the discouragement of migrants whose presence in the community is a potential social menace."[89] As a result, the labor force of the Salinas Valley slowly but surely was made up of members of the community and favored white, former Dust Bowl migrants who were quickly putting down roots in Salinas. Their work gave them the means to invest in homes and even some small businesses, leaving the fields and packing sheds altogether.

Still, Filipino/a labor remained central to the agricultural workforce in Salinas: "This Association was under obligation to the Filipino Labor Supply Association to negotiate with them . . . and that the Filipinos felt they should have an increase in wages due to the increased cost of food and clothing."[90] By the time of the August harvest season in 1934, shippers expressed trepidation over the organizing efforts of Filipino/a American workers in the Santa Maria Valley who demanded "35 cents an hour which was compromised at 30 cents."[91] A Mr. B. O'Brien of Santa Maria sent a warning letter to the GSA that Filipino/a organizers were on their way to Salinas:

[O'Brien gave] the 1934 License number . . . of two Communistic agitators as well as the names of Canete, Agudo and Mertulo who were also agitators in the trouble. . . . The Secretary [of Salinas Grower-Shipper Association] reported he advised the Sheriff and Highway Patrol of the names and number of their machine [and] the Communists involved, viz. Pedro Satuno and Amila Shanzek.[92]

Although there was no evidence of follow-up to this report, there was clear concern in Salinas over labor union activism from Filipino/a Americans; and there was always a willingness to attribute union organization to people outside of Salinas rather than admit that workers in Salinas had every reason to organize themselves.

The back-and-forth negotiations in 1934 included women workers at the bargaining table. "Miss A. Millan and Mrs. M. Durrart" joined their male counterparts to argue for "time and a half for holidays, sick leave pay during layoffs, hourly wages instead of piecework [and for employers] to furnish clocks in conspicuous places in packing houses," so that women could keep track of time at work on their own.[93] The shippers did not agree to any of these demands "except that instead of time and a half for Sundays and Holidays . . . any employee [could] decide for himself whether he would work on those days without prejudice to his future employment."[94]

The GSA created an "arbitration board" as another means to settle disputes and circumvent union organizing. Some shippers voted to increase wages by 5 cents because "it was understood that shipper W. B. Grainger had already increased wages," and also that a small increase in wages might reduce the power of unions because "it would convince workers that the shippers would, of their own initiation, do the right thing."[95]

Salinas's residents accepted labor unions as another interest group in support of capitalism, but many (though not all) panicked when labor appeared to be under the umbrella of the larger political movements of the 1930s. Both the Monterey Board of Supervisors and the City of Salinas passed anti-picketing legislation in 1934 and again in 1936 in reaction to what they perceived as radical labor activism. The Fruit and Vegetable Workers Union (FVWU)—with the support of the Central Labor Council, the Salinas Chamber of Commerce, and the *Salinas Independent*—vehemently opposed those ordinances and tried to soothe overly reactive voices that American labor was first and foremost devoted to democratic ideals, which included a capitalist economy. Under this combined pressure, both the Salinas City Council and the Board of Supervisors rescinded the measures within days. However, these ordinances demonstrated the extent to which labor issues intersected with local governments in the 1930s and the suspicion labor organizing provoked when it was perceived to be linked to larger political movements in California in the 1930s.

City government and agriculture intersected in Salinas. There was little distinction between what was going on in the fields and packing sheds and what was happening in urban life. Salinas fundamentally depended on agriculture to fund its city services and support local business, and its citizens worked in every facet of agriculture or engaged in businesses supporting it, as evidenced by the involvement of city leaders in every aspect of agriculture: Salinas Mayor Leach also served as an arbitrator on the Monterey Industrial Relations Board: "We should confer with Dr. E. J. Leach . . . as he had been appointed the seventh disinterested board member and chairman of the ILRB."[96] He was hardly a disinterested party, however, linked as he was with growers, shippers, and businesspeople tied to agriculture.

> It was again explained [to the Filipino Labor Union and Vegetable Pack-ers Association] that the shippers would not delegate their authority to leave a decision to a committee or anyone else. . . . After lengthy discussion . . . Chairman Leach said that [labor] demands could not be met. . . . Sheriff Abbott called and stated that he would lend every assistance possible to preserve peace and protect those who desired to proceed about their business in an orderly manner.[97]

City government leaders and the sheriff's department had a vested interest in agricultural disputes and were almost always on the side of the growers and shippers.

Abbott deputized citizens and brought in "sixty additional officers [from] the California Highway patrol."[98] As tempers flared and negotiations came to a standstill, Bruce Church once again stepped up to urged cooperation: "[Church] spoke in favor of mediation . . . he had prepared an agreement whereby both unions [Filipino and VPA] would return to work . . . and points under discussion [including setting up a grievance committee] would be submitted to the Monterey County Arbitration Board."[99] Church and attorney Joe Bardin tried to make a compelling argument for both sides to agree to support arbitration over conflict: "A prolonged period of indecision would fill the community with Communists at a time when there is danger and definite trend toward radicalism as evidenced by the large vote for Upton Sinclair in the recent primary."[100]

In the wake of the general strikes in 1934 up and down the coast of Washington, Oregon, and California, Salinas's residents (including workers) recoiled in horror from the threats of communism, authoritarianism, and fascism that some labor organizers from outside the area personified to them. The representatives from the Congress of Industrial Organizations (CIO) prompted harsh retaliation just by their presence in the community. One opinion piece in the union newspaper, the *Salinas Independent*, expressed the fear from working people that any link to communism would undercut their demand for higher wages and equitable treatment:

> To those ignorant of the matter let it be said now that some of the public . . . refers indiscriminately to members of organized labor as Reds. Nothing could be further from the truth. . . . [T]here is a direct effort, especially among the Fruit and Vegetable Workers . . . to weed out the Communists and would-be agitators.[101]

By 1935, prices stabilized. The *Salinas Independent* marked 1935 as "the greatest lettuce year [that] poured into the channel of trade of the district $50,000 weekly" and emphasized that everyone benefited from the good lettuce economy, not just growers and shippers: "Everyone profited in some degree from the small boy in Chinatown who carried a shoe shining kit to the big merchant on the main thoroughfare."[102] The difference between volatile markets in 1933–1934 and the widespread prosperity of 1935 was notable both for the full employment and full union membership: The FVWU boasted "several 100 per cent sheds" by June 1935.[103]

STRIKE OF 1936

The 1936 strike happened in this particular and complicated context. Salinas's residents were enjoying unprecedented good fortune due to the success of the lettuce industry during the Great Depression, yet each year was unpredictable and depended on uncertain markets. City leaders were focused on developing transportation systems, adding new housing, and building important infrastructure, notably a new sewer system. They expanded communal activities around the central event of the year, Big Week

or the Salinas Rodeo, that gave residents a strong sense of identity as farming and ranching folk within an urban environment. The schools absorbed
multiple native-born and immigrant populations into a communal identity as a successful agricultural town. They became a union town too.

As with all the other strikes in this decade, deeply divided interest
groups drove debates on all sides. The 1936 deadlock began as the Filipino
Labor Supply Association contractors—J. B. Sampayan, Pablo Tangonan,
Angel Malendres, and John Cacas—negotiated wage rates for Filipino/a
workers apart from the Fruit and Vegetable Workers Union.[104]The
Filipino/a American contractors responded that negotiations with contractors representing Filipinos/as should be kept separate: "Mr. Sampayan
said that a wage increase now was needed in order to bring the best grade
of Filipino labor into the valley to replace the inefficient work now done,
particularly by Mexicans and white people."[105] Filipino/a American contractors were willing to undercut packing shed workers, Mexican workers, and Dust Bowlers in an effort to claim predominance for Filipino/a
Americans, who were in the process of forming an important community
within Salinas, indicating that workers were split by race and ethnic identity as well as by class.

Besides controversy over a closed shop or "preferential hiring" supported by packinghouse workers but opposed by growers and shippers,
equal pay for women trimmers in the packing shed remained one of the
main issues of debate in the fall of 1936. In early August the GSA decided
to "leave the question of equal pay for men and women trimmers to the
union."[106] By the beginning of September, the GSA decided to support
equal pay, but with a peculiar rationale: "After full discussion of the union's
proposal to pay men and women trimmers the same rate, in which it was
brought out that this might work a hardship on the women, it was decided unanimously . . . that this request be granted as long as the women
seemed to want it."[107] Women workers clearly did not consider equal pay a
"hardship" since they had been demanding such a measure for the past six
years. GSA also agreed to "allow overtime at time and one-third after 8:00
P.M. if a shipper was not delayed by rain or frost in which case overtime
should start at 10:00 P.M."[108] Bruce Church suggested that wages ought to
be raised even higher, to 65 cents, "and thus nullify to some extent at least,
the main argument of the union in soliciting members."[109]Again, this was

a clear effort on the part of the GSA to do anything possible to undercut union organizing.

Within a few days, September 4, 1936, it had become clear that resolution was impossible, and workers would strike: "President Sbrana stated briefly the present situation being a strike condition" and advocated that shippers break the union by "dry pack[ing] the lettuce to [its] destination or to some other point in California to be packed with ice."[110] Some GSA members supported letting the strike play out, perhaps hoping that workers would exhaust themselves in the effort, and growers might again reassert authority over unions. "[Church said] it is wrong to risk bloodshed with the resultant loss of public opinion; that he feels the best course is to take no action whatever, letting the sheds remain closed until the workers get ready to come back under a reasonable contract . . . [Grainger, of W.B. Grainger Packing Company, agreed with Church:] It is just as brave to sit tight as to fight."[111]

However, the discussions among association members indicated that growers and shippers should regard any union activism as anti-American and act aggressively to crush them: "American [sic] was never developed by lying down," argued F. V. Birbeck. Walter Farley agreed that the GSA "should not lie down before Revolutionaries . . . the issue is Communism." E. E. Harden claimed, "This situation is part of a statewide plan to make Salinas a closed shop,"[112] also revealing a tendency to view union activism as a sinister New Deal government conspiracy. The Central Labor Council tried to intervene and find a way out of an increasingly polarized situation. The council had credibility with the GSA: "It was established that the Central Labor Council does in fact represent all of the labor unions in Salinas and particularly the more conservative craft unions [associated with the A F of L]."[113] It was to no avail: 3,200 members of the Fruit and Vegetable Workers Union went on strike on September 4, 1936.

A week later, the editor of the *Salinas Independent* admonished growers, shippers, packers, fieldworkers, and packing shed laborers to submit to arbitration to resolve their disputes, as they had done in previous years, or risk economic disaster for everyone in town:

> There is not one man woman or child in this entire area who is not affected directly or indirectly by the closedown of the huge lettuce

industry. Soon this cessation of business will hurt; sweep cupboards bare; cause forfeit on payments of homes; lose thousands of dollars in a rising market; dig into small businesses that can ill afford such prolonged losses.[114]

Citing a "definite and American precedent" in 1934, in which a board of arbitration made up of "the two disputing groups and their complement of neutrals" settled the conflict without resorting to lengthy cessations of work, the editor advocated

> the machinery for arbitration be set up and put in motion swiftly; that an understanding be reached promptly which would permit immediate resumption of operations . . . and that without further procrastination [the strike] be settled along true American principles in the unemotional atmosphere of the council chamber.[115]

In this way, the *Independent*'s editor brought almost all of the ingredients together in the vegetable stew of city, labor, and lettuce in September 1936—omitting, however, women's rights. He made clear that agricultural production, particularly lettuce, involved everyone in town and that all would be adversely affected by the strike. Therefore, it behooved all sides to end the dispute quickly, which, he argued, was all due to a mere misunderstanding anyway. It was not to be.

Just five days after the editorial in the *Independent* called for an end to the "misunderstanding," the streets of Salinas erupted in violence. Crates of lettuce that shippers attempted to send to market fell off a truck and were then destroyed by striking members of the Fruit and Vegetable Workers Union. The following day strikers were met with "grenades and projectiles [that] spurted gas onto the grounds of the Central Labor Council temple as strikers gathered to partake of their evening meal in the soup kitchen . . . The gas barrage of hungry strikers climaxed a day of deputizing scores of citizens and arming them with pick handles, gas bombs and other weapons."[116] An apparently intoxicated "special deputy" shot two male strikers in the legs. Another striker, Rose Lloyd, suffered a lacerated knee and required hospitalization. In response, strikers attacked Henry Strobel, president of the Farmers Association, and the two deputies who tried to defend him. All were hospitalized with serious injuries, and nine other strikers were arrested. The violence got the attention of Secretary of Labor Frances Perkins, who sent an emissary, Walter G. Mathewson, to attempt to resolve the dispute. Mathewson finally left Salinas over a month later without an agreement. It also prompted outrage statewide among union members and organizers who advocated a general strike for all of Salinas.[117]

All this happened in the middle of the city and involved everyone who lived there. Moreover, race and class complicated the battle lines. Japanese American farmers and packers not only supported the GSA during the strike, but also used their packing sheds for Filipino/a American strikebreakers to trim the lettuce, which inspired the wave of violence.[118] Filipino/a American contractors (Sampayan, Tangonan, Malendres, and Cacas) had agreed secretly to a wage increase with the GSA on September 9 (behind the backs of the FVWU), which undercut their own workers.[119]

After planning was underway for Filipino/a American strikebreakers to work in the sheds, Walter Farley complimented H. K. Sakata in a directors meeting for a "splendid job" in supporting fencing off packing sheds to safeguard the strikebreakers:

> During this period a fence was constructed in Watsonville around the J.G. Marinovich and Travers and Sakata sheds. This fence . . . was of double construction, the outside of the fence being barbed wire and the inside of the fence of solid wooden construction ten feet high. Delivery of dry pack lettuce put up in the fields [and] shipments have gone forward.[120]

A week later, the GSA reported that "On the morning of [September] 29th a concerted attempt was made to drive the Filipinos from the fields by intimidation on the part of striking shed workers," indicating further that Filipinos/as were involved on both sides of the issue—as strikers and activists but also as strikebreakers aligned with the GSA.[121] Both Japanese packing firms—Sakata Farms (Travers & Sakata) and Matsura & Marui—remained active members of the GSA throughout the 1930s, fully supporting efforts to control workers and wages; similarly allied was the Chinese-owned firm Sing Wo Kee & Co, represented by Joe Gok.[122] Furthermore, during the September 13 GSA meeting, Art Sbrana "reported the cooperation of the Japanese Association" as a community in supporting growers and shippers.[123]

Although the contemporary reports of riots were disputed by local news organizations, they tore up Salinas and divided its people. The *Independent* deplored what it believed was the sloppy reporting from San Francisco that oversimplified and exaggerated events in Salinas: "The fight seems to have developed into a dispute between the metropolitan newspapers of San Francisco . . . and the Salinas people, including the strikers, the shippers and the community at large who have been the sufferers."[124]

Many of Salinas's citizens joined forces with the sheriff's department to act as special deputies and violently attacked their fellow citizens who were striking workers. However, hundreds of other Salinas residents held a mass meeting at Salinas High School condemning the violence and supporting the right to unionize and to strike: "An impromptu mass meeting of [800] citizens," calling themselves the Citizens Welfare League and led by George Pollock, argued "they were not connected with the lettuce industry" (meaning that they were neither grower-shippers nor workers on strike) and "launched vigorous protests against officers and special deputies,"[125] thus showing their collective disdain for the actions of those who bullied striking workers. The Citizens Welfare League brought City Manager Vic Barlogio into discussions with both sides to avoid a repeat of what was beginning to be termed "bloody Wednesday."[126] They met repeatedly during the entire strike advocating "equal protection for everyone instead of a few" and launched their own investigation looking into use of excess force against strikers by the sheriff's department and its recently deputized citizens.

As the strike deepened in early October 1936, both the Monterey County Board of Supervisors and the Salinas City Council passed anti-picketing ordinances "with penalties for 6 months in jail or $500 fine or both" that the Central Labor Council and the *Salinas Independent* strenuously contested.[127] Notably, the GSA objected just as strenuously to the anti-picketing ordinance as "contrary in plan to the American traditions [and] so extreme as to curtail, if not deny the right of free speech and the right of assemblage,"[128] which was a surprising contrast to the more commonly expressed anti-picketing views of the GSA.

By October 23 with no settlement in sight, The FVWU narrowly defeated one final offer proposed by the GSA, much to the chagrin of many members who had become weary of the strike and were depleted financially. According to the *Independent*,

The action came as a decided blow to a number of F & VWU members, who though staunch supporters of organized labor, feel that the
strike . . . was theoretically lost, and feel that men with homes to maintain and families to support should be allowed to return to their jobs
without the stigma of "rat" being applied to them.[129]

Although the strike accomplished little for workers, the National Labor
Relations Board held hearings on April 12, 1937. The hearings accused the
GSA, Associated Farmers of Monterey County, Salinas Valley Citizens
Association, Western Growers Protective Association, and law enforcement
officers from the cities of Salinas, Monterey, Watsonville, and the state of
California of twenty-nine charges of "anti-labor practices." These included

Unlawful searches and seizures, use of secret headquarters from which a
reign of terror was directed, unnecessary use of tear gas and nauseating
gas, tear gas bombing of the Labor Temple, use of deputized vigilantes . . . restraint of trade, and extensive blacklisting after the strike.[130]

These were harsh words and strong accusations indeed and succeeded in
putting the GSA on notice that the federal government had a vested interest
in the well-being of workers in agriculture.

The strike occurred after decades of effort on the part of all of Salinas's residents to build a city central to the regional political economy—
and one with a common purpose: to create and maintain community
at all costs. This communal effort was carried on from all sides and
included virtually everyone in town. The city aimed to bring together
workers from every ethnic group and at every skill level, in kinship with
merchants, city leaders, growers, packinghouse owners and workers, ice
producers, and other tangential businesses related to agriculture and
shippers throughout the 1930s.

Acting collectively, they sought to create a viable and important city and
community, to make agriculture work to benefit Salinas's citizenry—all of
them. It came as a surprise, however, that the *Salinas Independent* seemingly
brushed off the 1936 strike as a minor irritant instead of a game changer in
industrial relations: "The Fruit and Vegetable Workers Union has had its
trials, suffering two strikes of short duration,"[131] read an editorial in 1937

(just a few months after the violence in the streets). Instead, the editorial focused on the investment in the city by union workers and their value to the community, even breaking down their financial contribution to the local economy:

> More than two and a quarter million dollars are spent in the Salinas district every year by the fruit and vegetable workers connected with the lettuce industry alone. . . . In a general division among 500 business houses . . . a conservative estimate this immense payroll put into circulation $4,493 to each merchant [in Salinas] during the season.[132]

Russell Scott, president of the Salinas Chamber of Commerce, noted that "For every man doing labor in Salinas there is employment created thereby for five others,"[133] presumably in terms of supporting the laborers' housing and living needs. Salinas was a place that prided itself on respect for workers as integral to a thriving agricultural community if the workers in question were residents-in-the-making, not migrant laborers, and it was better if they were white. As permanent residents and tax-paying citizens, union members' wages contributed mightily to the local economy as the *Independent* underscored under the headline "Vegetable Folk Pour $2,246,400 into City Yearly."[134]

Most telling, all the workers—Japanese American, Mexican American, Filipino/a American, Chinese American, and Anglo American—identified themselves as integral members of Salinas's community as stakeholders who claimed inclusion, and, if white, they had a good chance of achieving it. They expressed their feelings as community members, explicitly stated in a special edition of the *Independent* in 1935, which reported that labor union organization was directly linked to "industrial peace" and that Salinas workers themselves were integral to the economic well-being of their community: "Union workers are, VOTERS and TAXPAYERS here, [and] are rearing families in our community educating their children in our schools and . . . form a part of our solid citizenry."[135] The report in the *Independent* emphasized just how widespread and important union membership in Salinas had become, naming numerous trade unions and concluding with a ringing endorsement of the Fruit and Vegetables Workers Union that represented packinghouse workers:

We have seen the development of the Butchers Union, the Barbers Union . . . all of the A.F. of L. Unions with almost 100 per cent organizations. The Building Trades too have shown an unprecedented organization and development. The Retail Clerks, Bartenders, Musicians, and several others have become strong factors in the economic development of this district. Likewise, the Fruit and Vegetable Workers Union has developed from an organization of lettuce packers into an Industrial Union with a strength almost unequaled in any open shop industry.[136]

Despite the strong support for labor and union membership, and the city's desire to unite for a common purpose, the ethnic and racial lines remained fuzzy during and after the 1936 strike: Not all Filipino/a American workers supported the strike; most strikers were white and from the Dust Bowl; and Japanese American residents overwhelmingly supported and were members of the GSA.

By 1937 (and throughout the contentious La Follette civil liberties committee hearings), Salinas's residents, embarrassed and shocked by the harsh national spotlight, wanted to move on from the strike story. The local news focused on development, namely the construction of an underpass that facilitated access to Salinas for visitors and locals alike. The increasing population of Alisal also generated attention, as city leaders hoped to encourage annexation through improved housing and newly created infrastructure.

The labor conflicts quickly receded into the background of Salinas's community life. Regardless of racial or ethnic identity, almost all Salinas residents believed that they had a shot at middle-class life. Individuals and families from all groups focused their energies on educating their children, acquiring land, buying homes, and creating businesses. Most Salinas residents supported unions and appreciated union membership as a means to achieve the American Dream, even as they feared and disdained the more radical activism of the era. On May 9, 1940, the *East Salinas Pioneer* reported that Salinas Mayor Dr. Ed Leach had proclaimed "Union Label Week: "Insomuch as the union label is the best consumers assurance that the article so marked is made in America under fair working conditions by adult workers receiving American standard of wages."[137]

This was a city deliberately imagined as an agricultural urban center for the Central Coast region that included a diverse and multiracial population who managed to live together in a rough sort of comity despite their obvious socioeconomic differences, the crises of labor and the Great Depression, and the racism that was the hallmark of American life in the twentieth century. The end of the 1930s appeared to signal a new era of inclusion. But race relations in Salinas were complex, and World War II upended the social order of the city.

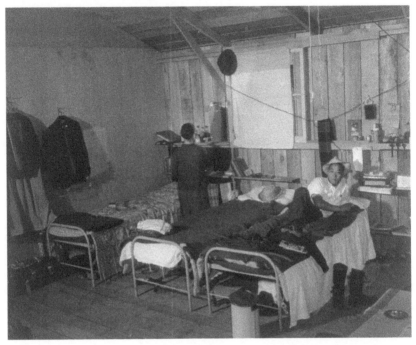

FIGURE 6.1   Evacuees of Japanese descent at the Salinas Assembly Center; they would be transferred to a War Relocation Authority center for the duration of the war.

CHAPTER 6

War and Its Aftermath

PEARL HARBOR PAPERED OVER DIFFERENCES of class and race in Salinas—unless one happened to be of Japanese descent. The *Salinas Californian* enthusiastically reported on the diverse citizenry now enlisted in every branch of the armed forces, tracked their whereabouts, and printed excerpts from letters home, often on the front pages. World War II allowed Salinas's residents to shift their collective focus away from labor conflicts and put their energies behind the war effort. International politics and the progress of the war replaced labor issues in the local press. The main local newspaper, the *Index-Journal*, which acquired the *Monterey County Post* and was renamed the *Salinas Californian* during the 1940s, devoted its front pages to coverage of the war. The liberal union paper, the *Salinas Independent*, ceased publication at the outset of World War II because its editor and publisher were drafted into the military.

The city expanded its boundaries and its population during the war years, and even more thereafter. "Since 1933 the city has been annexing outlying areas like mad and it's been difficult to keep up with the changes in the city limits."[1] Russell Scott, Salinas city attorney who presided over the annexations through the 1940s, oversaw as many as thirty-nine separate annexations that increased the city's footprint from only about 0.005 square miles in 1874 to 0.08 square miles by 1933 when the city added 51,935 acres of Romie Lane Territory. By 1940, the city was 3.2 square miles. Its assessed valuation in 1940 was $12,606,203.[2] "The growth of Salinas has indeed been phenomenal," one assessment concluded in 1940.[3]

All this expansion and attention to the war effort affected life in the city. Family stories reflected its impact. The Gattis family had arrived as part of the Dust Bowl migration and settled in Alisal when it was a sparsely populated, rough subdivision with little in the way of infrastructure or development. As a young boy, Jim Gattis remembered his wide-eyed impression of the transformation of Alisal into a military training ground: "We lived at one point on Natividad Road. It was out behind the Rodeo grounds. They were training medics out in the field. It was fascinating as a kid to see the military operating."[4] Jim's fascination with the military stayed with him. He went on to become one of the founding members of the annual California International Airshow, Salinas, which celebrated military prowess through demonstrations with groups such as the Blue Angels and the U.S. Air Force Thunderbirds, and in the very same place in Alisal that he recalled as a child.

Albert Fong, born and raised in Salinas but too young to remember the war, nonetheless emphasized the extent that Chinese Americans in Salinas came together as a community to support the war effort. They agonized over the invasion of China by Japan and responded by joining the U.S. military: "The fathers, uncles, brothers [of most] Chinese families in Salinas served in the military. There were the Chin brothers, the Chos, the Tyes, the Lees, and many, many others," Albert Fong stated, naming families who traced their roots in Salinas to the late nineteenth century.[5] Albert, a leader in Salinas's Chinese American community, serving as president of the Chinese Association of Salinas, was also a leader in the city itself, including serving on Salinas's Library and Community Services Commission. He noted that the U.S. policy relaxing restrictions on Chinese immigration during and especially in the postwar period made a difference, too—if not in numbers of new immigrants, then in a collective feeling among Chinese Americans that they now really belonged to the community as Americans.

Inclusions, however, always came with a caveat. Chinese Americans, as other Asians, still experienced marginalization in Salinas's economic, political, and social life and tended to live in segregated neighborhoods through the 1960s. Newspapers in Salinas nonetheless prominently featured photos of young men of Filipino, Chinese, Italian, Jewish, and Mexican descent as American soldiers engaged in combat in the Pacific and in Europe. Just like the rest of America, Salinas's residents felt fully integrated into the mainstream because of their collective identity as Americans (without hy-phenation) with the advent of war.[6]

INCARCERATION AND ANTI-JAPANESE SENTIMENT

That nationalist embrace included unreservedly surrendering their Japanese American friends and neighbors to the federal government's (clearly uncon-stitutional) program of internment, which people of Japanese descent prefer to call "incarceration," a more accurate descriptor for what happened to them. Although editorials in the local press had opposed the mistreatment of Filipino/a Americans a decade earlier, the silence was deafening when thousands of Salinas residents of Japanese descent, citizens and noncitizens alike, were rounded up, registered at the Armory (also called the Assembly Center, located in the middle of town), and sent to the rodeo grounds, then forcibly incarcerated outside the state for an indefinite period.

Non-Japanese residents of Salinas remembered the pivotal event of arrest and incarceration not as something traumatic for the community but as a natural consequence of the bombing of Pearl Harbor and the subsequent U.S. declaration of war against Japan. Many residents recalled the moment matter-of-factly. According to one resident, who was a child at the time, "We had gone to church. After church my cousins and I were sent up to a little candy store and we heard the Japs had bombed Pearl Harbor. Obviously they were the enemies."[7] It was "obvious" to all that the "they" included Japanese nationals living in Salinas, who had nothing to do with Pearl Harbor, as well as Japanese American citizens—men, women, children, young and old people—who had lived and worked in the community as friends, neighbors, and fellow compatriots since the 1890s.

It was as though the Japanese people in Salinas evaporated in plain sight. As shown in earlier chapters, people of Japanese descent had integrated themselves into every aspect of community life by 1940. But it was always tenuous. They were resented as much as admired for their collective work ethic, which made them innovative and successful agriculturalists (despite restrictive legislation), and for their outstanding achievements as scholars and athletes in the local schools. Japanese American cultural celebrations and events were featured on the front pages and society pages of the news-papers, just as were the events for every other ethnic group. Not only that, but the newspapers regularly printed positive stories about visits from Japa-nese dignitaries who sought to calm fears about Japanese aggression in the

Asia-Pacific region, which Salinas residents appeared to accept at face value, even when Japan invaded Manchuria in 1931 and in the aftermath of the infamous Rape of Nanking in July 1937. "We always got along fairly well with our fellow townsfolk," recalled James Abe, a former lettuce grower and long-standing Salinas resident.[8]

However, aggressive actions by the Japanese military in China and in the Pacific islands were well publicized and influenced Americans' perceptions of Japan as a belligerent nation-state long before Pearl Harbor, including in the minds of many Issei.[9] When former picture bride Nami Hashimoto returned to Japan with her husband's ashes in 1940, she refused to register her two youngest sons with the Japanese government, citing the Rape of Nanking to explain her reluctance—even though her two eldest sons were already living in Japan, registered as Japanese citizens, and enlisted in the Japanese military. One of her younger sons returned with her, and the other was killed in action fighting for Japan during the war.[10]

In Salinas, many people of Japanese descent dismissed or overlooked evidence of racism directed against them and usually sided with growers and shippers (mostly whites) in labor disputes, even those who were tenant farmers and laborers. As shown earlier, although people of Japanese descent maintained membership in the GSA, white members raised the specter of enforcing the Alien Land Law behind their backs as a means of preventing Japanese and Japanese American farmers from claiming newly available farmland (even as tenants) for lucrative lettuce production.

One rare instance of pushback came about when the local newspaper acknowledged the incarceration. The paper described the effort of Gertrude Waterman, dean of girls at Salinas High School, to ensure her Japanese American students received their high school diplomas. According to the *Salinas Californian*, which reported on the graduation ceremony for the high school on June 5, 1942,

> More than 250 Salinas high school seniors [out of a class of 322] received diplomas in impressive patriotic exercises. . . . Because of war conditions however, not all members of the class could be present. . . . Some 46 Japanese seniors were unable to attend and will receive their diplomas, yearbooks and special awards at the Rodeo grounds assembly center. Others already at work on defense jobs or moved to other sections of the country were likewise unable to be present.[11]

The piece suggested an odd equivalency between students who were absent because they chose to work in the defense industry (or move elsewhere) and the Japanese American students forcibly incarcerated at the Assembly Center at the rodeo grounds (as shown in the photo at the beginning of the chapter). Still, Waterman made sure the incarcerated students received diplomas, according to her friend and contemporary Ruth Andresen:

> She was very determined that the Japanese children graduated in 1942. They were all out at the Rodeo grounds so she got all the caps and gowns and diplomas and handed them out. It was very important. . . . You don't often use the term "noble" with respect to a woman but I thought Gertrude Waterman was noble.[12]

The fact that such a simple, righteous gesture of support for students penalized solely on the basis of race was considered an outstanding act spoke to the extreme racism of the times directed against everyone of Japanese descent, from babies to elders, and whether or not they were American citizens.

Although it might be tempting to see a linear path of racial hatred and exclusion based on the brutal incarceration of the war years, the historical relationship between Salinas's Japanese American and non-Japanese Salinas residents was a complicated mixture of acceptance, admiration, resentment, and apathy. Just like relationships among everyone else in Salinas, the experiences and relationships between Japanese and Japanese American residents and others depended on gender, class, occupation, and places of residence, but generally people of Japanese descent participated fully in the Salinas communal enterprise whatever their citizenship status. Japanese American families interacted intimately with Anglo, Filipino/a, Chinese, and Mexican Americans especially when they lived in the unincorporated subdivision of Alisal. The over 400 families of Japanese descent living in Salinas in 1940 lived in both "the Japanese section" of town located to the north and east of the city, but also in multiracial neighborhoods. Ten families were listed as property owners.[13]

Yet, despite superficial levels of comity and acceptance, Asian groups created a separate sphere in Salinas. Chinese, Japanese, and Filipino/a Americans but also some Sikh and Korean Americans shared boundaries in neighborhoods and patronized one another's stores and professional services. Doctors, dentists, accountants, and attorneys of Chinese or Filipino/a descent, for example, depended on residents of Japanese descent to support their respective professional practices, and in turn, Japanese American shopkeepers and professionals counted on a clientele from the larger community of Asians more than from whites or other ethnic groups to sustain their businesses and professions.[14]

On the other hand, many residents of Japanese descent remembered antipathy between Asian groups that was not always visible to outsiders. Kay (Endo) Masatani's "parents did not allow her to associate with the Chinese," reported her friend Larry Hirahara. He commented that Chinese families also did not encourage their children to associate with the Japanese. "[Masatani] had a Chinese childhood friend, Helen Lee. After they left Chinatown, on the way to Lincoln School they would walk together and be friends at school. Until they returned to Chinatown when they no longer spoke to each other." Parents also made sure their children knew their own cultural traditions, including language school. "[Masatani] went to Japanese School at the Buddhist Temple after school Monday, Wednesday, and Friday. Along the way to school she stopped at Aki Toya Store . . . to buy senbei (Japanese rice cracker treats)." However, extracurricular activities included typical American activities such as music and dance too. "Since her family had businesses, she was able to take lessons in tap dance and piano," which included students of other ethnic groups and placed her in the ranks of the middle class.[15] It is doubtful, however, that white Salinas schoolchildren took classes in Japanese or Chinese language or culture. Cultural learning was not reciprocal. Anglo Americans assumed primacy, and also assumed that their culture was the normative one.

After Pearl Harbor—and regardless of class, gender, or citizenship status—all people of Japanese descent appeared to non-Japanese Salinas residents (including other Asian groups), just as they did to Americans generally, as imminent dangers to the security of the nation. In the wake of the attack by Japanese fighters in Hawaii and the hysteria that followed, Asian American, Mexican American, and Anglo American Salinas residents no longer hid their resentment and fear of Japanese Americans; they overwhelmingly supported Franklin Delano Roosevelt's Executive Order 9066, issued on February 19, 1942, which called for the compulsory incarceration of all people of Japanese descent, citizens or not. Within two months of that order, over 120,000 people of Japanese descent were forced out of their homes and businesses up and down the West Coast, even though over 70 percent of them were American citizens. They had less than a week to dispose of all their property.

One survivor of the incarceration commented on the sense of extreme isolation Japanese people felt at that moment: "The only national group that supported us were the American Friends, the Quakers, not even the ACLU (American Civil Liberties Union)."[16] Most narrators who remembered that time recalled feelings of shock, disappointment, confusion, and isolation at the treatment they received by the American government and Americans generally. The careful cultivation of even superficial acceptance in Salinas disappeared, replaced by disdain and indifference to the plight of hundreds of Japanese resident families who were forced to leave homes, property, and lives behind for the unknown, all in a matter of a few days.

In rare instances non-Japanese Americans took responsibility for safeguarding property belonging to Japanese Americans. The Hashimoto family had the good fortune to retain their family property with help from a local attorney: "We boarded up our house and put our car on blocks and stored it in the garage with our appliances. We had a refrigerator and other appliances. We owned our house. We didn't sell it. We gave the keys to a trusted friend, Stacy Irwin."[17] Irwin paid the property taxes on the home, but not with her own money. She received the funds from the Hashimoto family, who sent it to her out of the paltry salary they earned working in the camps, thus saving their home and property from seizure by the federal government for nonpayment of taxes, as so many other Japanese Americans experienced. She also took care of young Mas Hashimoto's dog, which she sent to the Poston Camp in Arizona with help from Greyhound bus drivers, a circumstance Hashimoto recalled with gratitude decades later. It meant a lot to an imprisoned child to have the comfort of his pet, but it was notable that a small act of kindness in the context of enormous unfairness and cruelty was given exaggerated importance and treated with excessive gratitude.[18]

It was more common for families to lose everything, however, even after their neighbors promised to safeguard their possessions. According to Marcia Hashimoto, whose family lived in Woodland, California, when Pearl Harbor occurred, "The Woodland, California sheriff told my parents to store everything in a warehouse and he would guard it. But then he died of a heart attack. When my family returned from Amache Camp [in Colorado], everything was gone. We had nothing left."[19] Hers was the more typical experience of Japanese families whose neighbors took advantage of their sudden leaving to appropriate homes and possessions without consequence.

Salinas residents turned on their Japanese neighbors in part as a response to the news of the capture of 108 Salinas members of Company C, 194th Tank Battalion, stationed in Manila, who were then forced to join the infamous Bataan Death March (only 47 of the Salinas guardsmen survived).[20] Although most Salinas residents understood that the battalion was stationed in Manila, news about the death march did not leak into the press (and public knowledge) until after the end of the war, so hostility against people of Japanese descent cannot be attributed to that event alone.[21] Once the news of the Bataan Death March came out, however, it only intensified Salinas residents' collective scorn for all people of Japanese descent and opposition to their return to the Salinas community after the war.[22]

The Pearl Harbor attack had the opposite impact on Filipino/a Americans. When the Japanese attacked Manila on the same day as Pearl Harbor, any doubts about Filipinos/as being loyal Americans disappeared. Filipino/a Americans were welcomed (even celebrated) on the Monterey Peninsula. Special training grounds were built for the Philippine Scouts at nearby Fort Ord, which joined their American counterparts in training there. The Philippine Naturalization Act passed Congress in May 1942, allowing Filipino/a immigrants to become U.S. citizens, which they did en masse. The Fort Ord military newspaper, *The Panorama*, included a special section known as "FILIPINOTES" that highlighted Filipino exploits as brave fighters in the common cause of defeating Japan, and also informed Americans about Filipino/a culture and community life in positive terms.[23] Although some Filipinos/as befriended Japanese neighbors and friends before incarceration and after the war, most did not; they remained solidly identified with the American community united against all people of Japanese descent.[24]

The experience of incarceration disrupted life in the most profound ways for Japanese residents of Salinas. There is no evidence of organized resistance to the executive order on the part of Salinas's Japanese American community, who, with notable exceptions, appeared to have complied with sadness. Those who objected were referred to as "No-No's," "Resisters," and "Pro-Japan" within the confines of the camps.[25] Interned Japanese and Japanese Americans who wished to show solidarity as loyal Americans saw the objectors as a problem. When the War Relocation Authority separated the objectors from the rest of the prisoners and sent them off to a separate camp at Tule Lake, one survivor recalled, "We were happy when the pro-Japan group was sent to Tule Lake so we loyal Americans could get on with the war effort, [which included] selling war bonds."[26] Comments such as these are painful reminders of the patriotism of people who were so cruelly assumed to be dangerous traitors or potential traitors. Clearly, many held fast to their sense of belonging as Americans, even in the face of brutal mistreatment by the U.S. government.[27]

The vast majority of local Japanese Americans remained loyal to the United States despite banishment and ostracism. Marcia Hashimoto recalled that her parent's adamant loyalty included a clear understanding that the treatment of people of Japanese descent was morally wrong, unconstitutional, and a lesson to their children to remain vigilant as citizens of the United States: "My mother wanted us to remember this incarceration and understand that we are American citizens and have the right of protection under the Constitution. We should not let this happen to anyone else."[28]

The Armory was a registration center for incarcerated Japanese people from all over California. Located in downtown Salinas, the nearby rodeo grounds was one of the most significant detention centers and departure points for Japanese Californians sent to incarceration camps. Yet, this huge undertaking, right in the middle of the city, was largely ignored in the local press. Although an announcement on June 22, 1943 indicated that a Dr. Lechner would "speak at the Salinas High School at 8:15 on the Japanese situation," there was no content given nor was Dr. Lechner identified as representing a particular organization or agency.[29] Bill Ramsey recalled the matter-of-fact acceptance of incarceration among Salinas's residents and its small blip on the radar of the community: "They were our neighbors before the war. Then the war happened. Then they were our neighbors after the war."[30] Nine years old at the time, Bill could not have fully appreciated the tremendous suffering, tension, and continued animosity directed at his former neighbors and friends, especially when some returned to Salinas in the postwar years.

Mas Hashimoto, on the other hand, understood all of it. Like Bill Ramsey, he was a child at the time of Pearl Harbor, and he remembered in painful detail his older brother's death at the Salinas Assembly Center, which he referred to as "our first prison."[31] Hardly a neutral way station, it was a terrifying place for the people who had absolutely no idea why they (as American citizens) were being targeted by the U.S. government, nor what would happen to them, nor how long they would be away from their homes and businesses. Mas Hashimoto's mother had recently been widowed. She was forced to manage on her own as a single parent with three underage sons, a situation that was emotionally agonizing for her. One of her sons, Noriyuki, aged thirteen, suffered a severe head injury while playing baseball at the Salinas detention center, but "didn't want to worry [my] mother so he went under the barracks and quietly died. . . . [W]e left his ashes in the mortuary in Salinas. The first thing we did when we returned was [to] pick up his ashes for burial."[32] Noriyuki was obviously aware of his mother's lonely anguish and was willing to "quietly die" rather than add to her troubles by complaining about his injury. This tragedy, ignored in the local press, symbolized how Salinas's larger community rendered Japanese lives invisible and inconsequential after Pearl Harbor.

Even in his eighties, Mas recalled (in detail) life in Poston, Arizona, where he spent the next three years and three months of his childhood.

> We lost our privacy along with our civil rights. Our family of six lived in a room that was 20 x 25 feet. We ate dust. We lived with dust. Privacy was nonexistent. We did have flush toilets though. [By contrast, the Salinas Assembly Center had outhouses, which women and men were forced to share.] After we were there for a year, they [military authorities] must have thought "Well we should have education for the children."

Mas described how the War Relocation Authority hired local teachers to instruct the incarcerated children: "The [teachers'] pay was better [in the camps] than in the local area [so] white teachers came to teach us. . . . Most of them were kind and considerate." He emphasized the creativity of imprisoned Japanese people in making the best of a terrible situation. Inmates found building materials in the "wood piles [leftover from building barracks] and made furniture," he recalled. Marcia Hashimoto kept a woodcarving made from scrap wood, a gift to her parents from a friend who was also confined in the Amache Camp in Colorado. In several camps, women made brooches from seashells they collected and presented them as gifts of appreciation to family members, friends, and the medical staff at the camps.[33]

The Japanese people installed irrigation systems in the camps to grow vegetables to supplement their meager government rations. They taught irrigation techniques to Indigenous People living on a nearby reservation.

Indigenous People expressed sympathy for the Japanese prisoners and seemed to view their plight as similar to their own forced removals into designated reservations a century earlier. Indigenous People formed close bonds with the incarcerated Japanese Americans, Mas Hashimoto claimed. "They saw what happened to us as the same thing that happened to them."[34]

The war's end meant that Japanese Americans could return to Salinas and begin to recover from the trauma of incarceration. Yet, Japanese American families clearly felt the hostility that remained in Salinas in the war's aftermath, and many were reluctant to resettle in a place that made no pretense of wanting them back. Only 25 of the over 300 original Salinas Japanese American families returned after incarceration when it officially ended in May 1945.[35] The Salinas Chamber of Commerce conducted a poll of local residents to ascertain whether Japanese American survivors ought to return to Salinas; 769 residents responded in opposition to the prospect of the Japanese people returning and sometimes expressed great anger and bitterness against their former neighbors and friends, disregarding all evidence of Japanese American patriotism as well as the fact that most people of Japanese descent were American citizens. Only one person, attorney George Pollock, voiced approval for Japanese residents to return. Many respondents made additional comments on their surveys, including Louis R. Jenkins, secretary of the local plumbers and steamfitters union: "I was looking at the High School graduation class pictures in a studio window the other evening, and it certainly was a pleasure to see no Japanese faces amongst our children, and in years to come I sincerely hope that Japanese faces will never appear again."[36] Numerous others echoed Jenkins's anti-Japanese sentiment. "We hope that we never see another live Jap on the Pacific Coast," wrote William Casey. "We don't want any of them back at all," agreed farmer Tony Garcia and his wife. "There are no loyal Japanese," asserted banker Oliver Bardin, while hotel owner W. L. Young proclaimed, "the only loyal Jap perhaps is a dead one." The chamber questionnaire was widely publicized, creating the (deserved) impression of general hostility for Japanese Americans in Salinas.[37]

However, a petition published by the *Monterey Peninsula Herald* and signed by 440 Monterey County residents (including John Steinbeck and his close friend, the marine biologist Ed Ricketts) advocated for the return of Japanese Americans to the Monterey Peninsula in the name of "democratic values."[38] It called into question both the morality and constitutionality of the removal and incarceration of Japanese Americans in the first place. Noting that the War Department "has authorized all persons of Japanese ancestry whose loyalty has been investigated and attested by the Army or Navy Intelligence or the F.B.I. to return to their homes," the petition argued forcefully that among the returnees "will be veterans of this war and relatives of Americans, who are now fighting for democracy on all our war fronts." The petitioners asserted that the Japanese Americans "had made their homes [on the Monterey Peninsula] for many years and had been part of the life of this community. Their sons are making the same sacrifices as our own boys." Finally, and in upper case for emphasis, the petitioners affirmed that those Japanese Americans who had enlisted in the armed services had shown unquestionable bravery and loyalty to the United States and that the U.S. government had established beyond all doubt that their families showed loyalty to America as well: "We the undersigned then believe that it is the privilege and responsibility of this community to cooperate with the national government by insuring [sic] THE DEMOCRATIC WAY OF LIFE TO ALL MEMBERS OF THE COMMUNITY."

Those few Japanese Americans who returned to Salinas initially found some refuge in a hostel located at the Salinas Japanese Presbyterian Church located on Lincoln Avenue, which James Abe, a Buddhist leader, and Reverend Thomas Woodbury Grubbs, a Presbyterian minister, co-directed an effort to reintegrate survivors back into the community. "We heard rumors that an attempt would be made to keep us from opening," Abe remembered. "A city health department officer came and told us we couldn't have people living at the church as toilet and bathing facilities would be inadequate. He told us he would be forced to order the hostel closed if we violated the city health laws." Public health officers were not alone in their opposition to the hostel. "Several others who said they were city officers also inspected the place and told us not to open," Abe explained. However, both Reverend Grubbs and Abe stood firm in supporting Salinas's Japanese American returnees by offering transitional housing: "[Reverend Grubbs] said he wasn't convinced that officials would move in to block what was clearly an emergency situation, but if they did, he was perfectly willing to go to jail."[39]

Three men, who had been prisoners of war in Bataan and high school friends of James Abe, approached him about the community's resistance to the hostel and defended the rights of the Japanese American people to return to the city. "They said 'Jim, if anyone comes around and lifts a hand to bother you, you just call us up and let us know. We'll take care of them,'" which was a rare show of support on the part of Salinas's non-Japanese residents.[40] But these few positive examples of welcome hardly dispelled the overwhelming hostility to the Japanese Americans who returned to Salinas after the war. Many who had been incarcerated found some refuge in San José.[41] Many others originally from Monterey and Salinas regrouped and established a new community in nearby Seaside.[42] They formed small businesses, usually in landscaping or gardening, choosing to avoid both farming and, for the Monterey families, fishing, which had been their primary means of livelihood before the incarceration.[43]

Seaside, adjacent to Fort Ord, more easily incorporated Japanese Americans and other minorities (especially those in multiracial families) in the immediate postwar years. Fort Ord was designated as a "compassionate duty" military base to signify that it was a more welcoming destination for minority and interracial military families than other bases in the United States at mid-century. Thus, mostly African American but also other minority and multiracial military families were deliberately stationed there, creating a far more diverse town in Seaside, with integrated neighborhoods well in advance of other towns or cities in the nation as a whole, but in many ways similar to the more mixed-race and integrated populations of military towns elsewhere in the country and abroad.[44] The postwar Japanese American community in Seaside included interracial couples and families, particularly Japanese women married to American military personnel (often minorities themselves) who had been stationed in Japan.[45]

Those Japanese American families who returned to Salinas focused on rebuilding their lives and supporting their elderly Issei family members. They resumed educations and found employment where they could. One teenager, alone in Salinas, recollected her feelings of isolation and marginalization in an interview with Salinas resident and Japanese American community leader Larry Hirahara in 2019:

> She had no place to stay. She became a House Girl. Like a nanny, she cooked, cleaned, and took care of a [white] family's children. She was also attending Salinas High at the time. She felt discrimination [at school]. Only . . . 6–7 Asian girls . . . would associate with her. But she graduated and later completed business school. The family of the house she stayed

at had family friends that would often visit. Those friends were a family that was affected by the Bataan Death March. When this family visited, she was told to hide in the back room and not come out.[46]

Her experience showed how the bitterness and pain of the war years extended well into the postwar.

Nonetheless, by the 1960s Japanese Americans had recovered somewhat from the trauma of incarceration and even repeated their prewar settlement patterns of living in Salinas proper, in integrated neighborhoods if they could afford to. One Mexican American Salinas resident explained, "Most of [the Japanese] lived [within] Salinas [city limits] when the families came back," alluding to the continued pattern of racial segregation by neighborhood, which put most Mexican Americans in Alisal rather than in Salinas.[47]

USO AND ALISAL

During wartime, non-Japanese Salinas residents focused their attention and energy on building the first United Service Organizations (USO) in the United States.[48] The establishment of the USO drew soldiers and residents of the larger Monterey Peninsula to Salinas, not just for entertainment but for shopping and business too. Located in the heart of city center on Lincoln Avenue, Mayor Edmund Leach declared a city holiday to celebrate the dedication on December 9, 1941, which happened just two days after Pearl Harbor.[49] "Because of our proximity to Fort Ord it was quite a feather in the cap of Salinas. We were just a small agricultural town, so having the first USO became an important indicator that we were on the map," recalled one longtime Salinas resident.[50] The USO quickly became the social focal point for Salinas's residents:

> Young ladies were invited to attend the dances and they were encouraged by church groups and school groups to do so. They were carefully chaperoned. Women in the various church organizations would accompany them and while they danced with soldiers stationed at Fort Ord, the older women served refreshments. Everything was kept very proper.[51]

Multiple announcements of wedding engagements between soldiers stationed at Fort Ord and residents appeared regularly in the *Salinas Californian*, proof indeed that the USO had a welcome impact Salinas's social life.

More concerning to Salinas residents was the area around Lake Street on the outskirts of town, which proliferated with houses of prostitution, gambling parlors, bars, and liquor stores. The high rates of sexually transmitted diseases regularly announced by the Monterey County Department of Public Health showed that Fort Ord impacted every city in the county—in adverse ways too. One report issued in July 1944 noted a measles epidemic with twenty-two cases reported that month, but syphilis came in second with fifteen new cases and gonorrhea third with eleven new cases, far surpassing any other communicable disease in Monterey County, even when a serious typhoid epidemic broke out in the labor camps located nearby.

Equally concerning, local police departments struggled with the issue of "victory girls." In a meeting in Salinas celebrating the fourth year of the presence of the USO, Judge C. Lloyd Colby informed the group of the work of Traveler's Aid in assisting young women drawn to the Salinas USO. He reported that he saw

> 8–10 . . . cases per week . . . girls from 18 to 27 years of age [in his court-room], who follow soldiers from their hometowns are without funds and often have to be taken into police custody for their own protection. . . . Whenever possible Travelers Aid takes responsibility in sending the girls to their homes or takes a hand in rehabilitation of those who wish to go to work and become useful citizens.[52]

The problem of young women who attached themselves to Fort Ord and the USO became even more worrisome in the postwar period, contributing to the perception of the base as a mixed blessing for the entire area. It brought increased attention and federal funding but also the same problems of gambling, prostitution, and prevalence of bars and high crime that every other military installation brought to bear on surrounding communities.[53]

Economically, the entire county benefited from federal attention and largesse during and following World War II, and Salinas's leaders took advantage of it as a way of enriching the city's coffers and expanding the city's footprint. Jim Gattis vividly remembered the new economic opportunities available during the 1940s, particularly for anyone willing to work in agriculture because of a dire need for labor during the war. He recalled, "A lot of people weren't finishing school [because] you could go drive a lettuce truck and make a hundred dollars a week. That was a lot of money. I was working in the packing sheds before that so we could make money during high school."[54] Bill Ramsey echoed Jim's experience, remembering how his family first lived in a tent in the Lunsford Labor Camp and were grateful for the bags of groceries that the Salvation Army left for them when they returned from church on Sundays, contrasting that reality with his family's economic stability in the war years: "People were making money. It was a small world and the common denominator was lettuce." Bill remembered his father and uncles traveling to the Imperial Valley to follow the harvest, but they always returned to Salinas. By 1940, "My Dad bought a home on Midway Avenue [in] Alisal . . . a step up for us [from life in the labor camp]," he remembered.[55]

Everett Alvarez Jr. also described family migration patterns that ended with settlement in Salinas, and like other former residents, emphasized the opportunity in agriculture during the war years. He traced his family roots to Mexico and the Southwest, linking his personal history to such events as the Mexican Revolution and the Great Depression.

> My grandparents came from Mexico around the turn of the century. On my father's side, around the time of the Mexican Revolution. Somewhere between 1900 and 1910. . . . My father was born in Arizona. His father worked in the mines. . . . The Sanchez family [his mother's family] lived in Castroville when Mom and Dad met. My grandmother had been awarded some money. She was in a car accident. So she bought land in Alisal . . . around 1937, around the time my parents were married.[56]

That chance collision with a milk truck (sometime in the late 1930s) led to a fortuitous break for the Alvarez family. They had migrated from Arizona and Southern California to take advantage of available work in agriculture in Watsonville and Salinas Valley in the 1920s but struggled to gain a foothold in the area. However, fate intervened. The milk company settled with Simona Sanchez (Everett's grandmother) for enough money to allow her to purchase land in Alisal. They built a home for themselves and units that they rented to the new Dust Bowlers flooding into the area. Simona's daughter, Soledad, lived in one of those units with her husband, Everett Alvarez. In 1937, just a year after the contentious lettuce strike in Salinas, Soledad and Everett welcomed Everett Alvarez Jr. into their large extended family that included a network of aunts, uncles, and cousins throughout the area. "My grandmother owned property maybe half an acre at the most with three cabins. We lived in one of them." The Alvarez family became landlords to the mostly white refugees from the Southwest who lived among a diverse population on the outer edges of Salinas.

With the outbreak of World War II, the Alvarezes followed opportunities for employment in the lucrative defense industries springing up in larger municipalities such as San Francisco, Oakland, and Los Angeles. The entire Sanchez and Alvarez clan moved to San Francisco's Mission District to take advantage of good jobs in defense.

> When the war broke out my father and all his cousins packed the families up to move to the Bay Area to get jobs. . . . My father worked at Bethlehem Pipe and Steel in their shipyard. One or two families got jobs later across the bay at Kaiser shipyards. They all went to work as welders. . . . We moved to the Mission District, . . . [but the family soon returned to Alisal, and Everett] grew up with the Grapes of Wrath kids.[57]

In the spring of 1940, a new community newspaper, the *East Salinas Pioneer*, announced its inauguration with the motto: "By the People, for the People, and with the People of East Salinas," indicating that Alisal had become a genuine community of Dust Bowl migrants, Asian groups, and Mexican Americans all its own. In one typical announcement for a bridal shower given in honor of "Miss Lois Wilkerson of Juanita Boulevard," the guest list included women whose surnames (Espinola, Miguel, Izora) suggested either Filipino/a or Mexican descent along with guests with Anglo American surnames, supporting numerous anecdotal accounts of life in Alisal as a multiracial social space. Everett Alvarez observed that Alisal circa 1940s was a place of real racial mixture: "Growing up was pretty neat in Alisal. It was inclusive. It was a heterogeneous mix. Okies, Arkies, Filipinos, Chinese. There were a couple of Chinese girls in my class." However, in Everett's recollection, ethnicity and class intersected, with most Chinese people solidly in the middle class by 1940. "The Chinese families were the merchants," he recalled. "The Filipinos and Japanese worked the land."[58]

The Alvarez family's story emphasized the easy way Alisal was settled by families who arrived in Salinas between 1929 and the 1940s, including some migrant workers and mostly members of an aspiring working class who found space, place, and an opportunity to become stakeholders in this agricultural urban center, especially during the lucrative World War II years. According to Everett, "The homes [in Alisal] were basically put up by migrants who came and worked there [in the 1930s]. Some of them had corrugated tin roofs. These were families who came out in the Dust Bowl phase, who moved from Camp McCallum into permanent residency in east Salinas."[59]

Residents of Alisal may have been poor on arrival but quickly settled in, building homes and businesses in short order as they became permanent residents in Salinas, where land was cheap and abundant, and economic opportunities beyond fieldwork and constant migration beckoned. Jim Gattis's story provided a perfect example of this common family trajectory:

> I just have memories of numerous places we lived. Each season we moved to a different place. Then we would go back to Arkansas. We lived in a rental house roughly 600 sq. feet with a couple of bedrooms. Nobody had a room to themselves much less a bed to themselves. . . . There were 34 of us, 1935 to 1941.

Most importantly for the Gattis family, Salinas offered a chance to end the pattern of migratory life and settle down—not least because of the thriving agricultural economy during World War II. In this, Jim did not feel unique in Alisal: "Everyone lived pretty much the same. It was rough in those days [the 1940s] in Hebbron Heights and Alisal."[60]

Alisal became an attractive potential asset to Salinas, which coveted the area to its east, now almost equivalent to Salinas in both population and business development by 1940. However, also in 1940, Carey McWilliams, who was chief of California Housing and Immigration, issued warnings that Alisal's rapid population growth and lack of zoning or regulation endangered its residents and all of Salinas. Alisal, according to McWilliams, was "without a public sewer system . . . with the corresponding danger to adjacent water wells and to the water wells serving the Salinas public." McWilliams went on to report that many of the houses were still merely "shacks and lean-tos unfit for human habitation."[61]

That dismal view of Alisal was vehemently disputed. Enthusiastic reports in the local press described:

> A community of neat, freshly painted homes . . . fronted by well-tended lawns . . . [and] distinctly an asset to the county. . . . Today more than 3500

of the 300,000 depression and Dust Bowl refugees in California live in that community and their record is most reassuring. There is scarcely a case where a migrant . . . and his family . . . has not been able to make the grade. It is a matter of record that migrants into Salinas since 1933 have re-invested more than $100,000 of their earnings in permanent improvements.[62]

All of it was based on the availability of employment in agriculture—not just fieldwork but a variety of occupations in packinghouses, shipping facilities, ice plants, and the myriad small business enterprises tied to farming that ratcheted up during World War II and the postwar.

THE BRACERO PROGRAM

Throughout the war years, the GSA became formidable and strategic, just like its counterparts throughout California and the Southwest, and even referred to itself as a "union" rather than an association.[63] The membership of GSA declined during the 1930s, but membership "more than doubled [between] 1941 and 1946 [from] 23 members to 52."[64]

Growers, shippers, and packers paid attention to their image. They set up a formal public relations program to counter the fallout from the 1936 lettuce strike and the findings of the La Follette congressional committee in 1938.[65] They contributed to the expansion and development of Salinas with philanthropic works supporting schools, libraries, and, most importantly, marshaling forces and raising substantial funds to construct Salinas Valley Memorial Hospital. They also reached out to nearby universities such as the University of California, Davis, to improve growing and harvesting produce, introducing the latest technology into their methods of production and harvesting. They organized a research committee to create partnership projects with "various scientists from the University of California" who established sites in Salinas to experiment with new, more efficient ways of growing and harvesting produce that might increase production, expanding markets nationally and internationally but also reducing costs, especially for labor.[66]

The GSA also connected to power centers in Washington, DC, as well throughout California in Sacramento, Los Angeles, and San Francisco.[67] GSA representatives often and regularly visited these centers of government and worked with important agencies such as the Office of Price Administration to influence policy concerning price setting and rations during the

World War II years, and with the Immigration and Naturalization Service concerning labor negotiations with Mexico throughout the decades of the 1940s through the 1960s.[68] In one meeting held shortly after the end of World War II, GSA Secretary Jack E. Bias reported "There were over 500 bills effecting [sic] agriculture in the legislative field this past year,"[69] which reflected the GSA's awareness of what government agencies were doing in relation to agriculture and their efforts to sway policymakers in their favor.

Although the GSA operated haphazardly throughout the 1930s, everything changed with the war. Almost every meeting involved reports on how to deal collectively with a host of new state and federal regulations and agencies and the challenges of agricultural production in wartime—from prices for crops, to wage rates and labor, to production, transportation, and marketing of agricultural products. Most of all, they focused on labor, determined to exercise complete control over recruiting and wages. That came to mean lobbying the federal government to create and sustain the Mexican National Program, commonly known as the Bracero program.[70]

Although GSA members concluded that it was in their best interest to work with (rather than against) state and federal government agencies and legislators in creating regulations that impacted them, they nonetheless remained deeply suspicious of government control, especially with regard to labor: "C.B. Moore talked [to the GSA] on Mexican labor and the chances of securing such labor for another season. . . . [H]e felt agriculture was going to have to fight control as . . . Washington wanted to control agriculture so long as the war lasted and even after the war was over if possible."[71] This became a recurring theme throughout the 1940s as tensions over federal and state involvement in labor issues increased. Again and again, the group regarded any federal or state regulation over labor, production costs, or transportation as "really a regulation of profits," and because of that perception of government as a sinister force determined to control them, the group believed that they needed to remain vigilant.[72] More concerning, the Salinas GSA routinely sent one of its members to Mexico City to negotiate directly with "officials in Mexico City in regard to Mexican nationals,"[73] an action that appeared to go behind the back of the federal government and was quite possibly illegal.

The crisis of World War II was also a labor crisis in Salinas as growers and shippers turned to migrant laborers from outside of the United States. During the war years, growers grew so desperate for labor that they created a special committee headed by predominant shipper J. T. Merrill to take charge of field labor. Merrill engaged in negotiations with both the Mexican government concerning the importation of Mexican workers and with the military concerning the use of as many as 10,000 German POWs in the field, some put to work growing guayule, discovered in South America, and considered for a time as a potentially profitable way to grow rubber to support the military.[74] The GSA was also considering importing Puerto Rican workers.[75]

By 1945, John Jacobs, representing the Western Growers Association in Phoenix, reported to the Salinas GSA that "everyone in Washington looked favorably upon the importation of Filipinos from the Philippine Islands but stated that now it was necessary to secure the approval of General MacArthur."[76] Apparently this plan did not pan out because by August of that year, the GSA minutes highlighted that field labor was an ongoing problem: "The foreign labor problem is an important one. All foreign labor must be out of the country by January 1 and if Congress does not pass additional appropriation there will not be any recruitment of Mexican labor and at the moment there seems no other source to obtain field labor."[77]

The tone of the conversations among members of the GSA indicated an almost complete lack of compassion or sensibility that they were discussing fellow human beings who happened to be in a different position within the interconnected world of agriculture. The respect that American packinghouse workers, contractors, and drivers demanded and received as they negotiated wages, hours, and working conditions was painfully absent when workers were Mexican nationals. In the conversations over "labor," workers were reduced to a commodity along the lines of farm equipment as they became bargaining chips in U.S.-Mexico relations. Again and again, the solution to labor shortages came in the form of the Bracero program, described by sociologist Christopher Henke as "too good to be true" for growers, allowing them to effectively sustain, consolidate, and even increase growers' control over farm labor.[78] The GSA admitted as much: "The Shippers of the Salinas Valley have been most fortunate in obtaining a sufficient number of Mexican Nationals to care for their crops and harvest them this year. . . . There has been less difficulty with labor . . . than for the past several years."[79]

The Bracero program, started in 1942, brought a new population of workers into Salinas, but unlike their Filipino/a American, Mexican

American, and Dust Bowl predecessors, they were left out of the life of the city in every way. Mexican nationals who became part of the Bracero program worked in the fields on a temporary basis to get the crops in but had to return to Mexico after the harvest ended. They did not have standing as immigrants to become American citizens or even permanent residents. Controversial from its inception until the program ended in 1964, the Bracero program brought noncitizen workers into agriculture, not just to fill a necessary gap in the labor market due to the loss of workers to military service during wartime, but in the eyes of labor, to undercut wages, reduce the negotiating power of unions, and guarantee a labor force without making a commitment to workers' inclusion in the larger American community. Workers were issued temporary "passports" that allowed them access to work but also required that they leave the country when the crop was finished. Braceros were never on a path to citizenship like other international immigrant workers who had been arriving on American shores since the 1600s. That did not mean that some former Braceros did not stay. They did. Others returned to the United States after an interlude in their home states in Mexico.[80]

GSA members feared labor shortages, but they also worried about excess labor "brought in too early," which would create "an abundance of labor" that, in turn, would leave growers in the position of supporting workers: "There was some danger that the border [with Mexico] might be closed leaving workers stranded on the American side."[81] The presence of migrant Mexican fieldworkers—men isolated from the cultural constraints of family or community—also alarmed Salinas citizens in general.[82]

Supposedly, Mexico guaranteed the men sent over to participate in this program that they would not be subjected to discrimination of any sort, including racial segregation in housing, and they were to be paid the prevailing wage.[83] However, growers who employed Braceros determined their wages, not American labor unions. Braceros were routinely housed apart from the community in racially segregated and often squalid labor camps that had been abandoned by Dust Bowl migrants. The 1949 Agricultural Act codified the program, and the 1951 Migrant Labor Agreement (Public Law 78) further strengthened and legitimized it. The GSA in Salinas supported both pieces of legislation that guaranteed 200,000 Mexican national workers every year. Between 1942 and 1964, some 4.6 million Braceros entered the United States to work in agriculture throughout California and the Southwest.[84]

Family stories showed that although Braceros were forced to return to Mexico when their work in the fields ended with the harvest, many nonetheless came back to Salinas, started families, and became important community members. Diana Lizbeth Soria recalled her grandfather's journey from El Moral, Zacatecas, at age twenty. Margarito Soria was married and had one child at the time. He described his home in Mexico "as not even considered a pueblo, because it was so small, but it was still a beautiful place to live. You would feel the fresh early morning breeze to the sound of crickets at night"; there were only about twenty-five other families living there, and it was accessible only by horse. He expressed trepidation about becoming a Bracero. His granddaughter Diana explained that it was "a difficult transition for him not knowing what life was going to be like on the other side." After a stint picking cotton in El Centro, California, Soria came to Salinas to work in lettuce, broccoli, and cauliflower. Diana marveled at the harsh conditions and low pay: "It's hard to believe how much hard work they would do and how low the pay wage was for it. . . . The farm work was only 30 cents an hour." Soria lived in a labor camp with about 200 other men, divided into four groups, each group working for different growers. The men traveled to and from work by bus. Soria considered himself lucky to work for a "*patron* . . . [who] made sure the Braceros were in good working conditions under his supervision," but he felt alone:

> Their camps were isolated, which meant that my grandfather did not really go out and get to know the town of Salinas. . . . Most Braceros did not associate with Mexican Americans. Mexican Americans who worked in agriculture saw Braceros as a threat and refused to communicate with them in Spanish. This made most of the Braceros feel discriminated towards their own people.[85]

Despite his memory of discrimination, Diana's grandfather returned to settle permanently in Salinas in the 1950s. His family and extended family eventually became established members of the community.

Diego Ruiz's paternal grandparents experienced extreme hardship as Braceros, but like Diana Soria's family, returned to Salinas, raised their families, and integrated into the Mexican American community after their terms as temporary workers ended. According to Diego, "Herminia Alvarez Ruiz, wife of former Bracero Raymundo Ruiz, remembered the arrival of her husband as he returned from completing his contract in the U.S. 'I did not recognize him, he was very skinny, darker than usual, and was exhausted. I had to ask if it was really him.'"[86] The Ruiz family blamed the Mexican government for the plight of the Braceros as much as they blamed American growers and the American government:

> The Mexican government was to blame. According to the agreement of the program, the government of Mexico withheld 10 percent of earned income from each Bracero in a special bank account that was never released. The reason for this deduction was to deter possible permanent settlement in the U.S. However, Braceros were never made aware of this "bank account" and thus, the money mysteriously disappeared for them. In order to catch a ride back to his hometown of Santiguillo in the state of Guanajuato, Reymundo told his wife Herminia that he had to sneak into a train headed for Mexico. Upon his return home, he had only $15 and a sewing kit for his wife to knit a dress.[87]

Diego's maternal grandfather, Eugenio Martinez, who completed consecutive contracts in the United States, was paid $24 twice a month. Diego reported, "My grandfather's biweekly check should have been in the range of $50–55. . . . [When asked about her husband's pay,] Hermina Ruiz recalls never receiving any money . . . She wondered what her husband was doing on the other side of the border."[88]

As these family stories illustrated, Braceros did not benefit much, at least in the short term, from their employment in the United States. They lived in the shadows in Salinas, isolated in labor camps well outside the city limits. Then, on June 17, 1958, tragedy struck and brought Braceros into the collective conscience of Salinas's community. A group of fifty Braceros transported in an illegally converted truck suffered severe injuries and death when someone lit a cigarette, which ignited two gas cans nearby. The truck blew up. Fourteen workers were killed, and seventeen others were severely injured. It was the worst non-collision traffic accident in the nation's history according to the National Safety Council. Historian Lori Flores described the accident as generating widespread indignation among Mexican Americans in Salinas as it showed how callously these men had been treated. Yet, GSA members felt little responsibility (or remorse) for the tragedy: "The Executive Vice President commented briefly on the recent bus accident in Soledad. . . . It was pointed out that the bus involved was a new one and had nothing wrong with it."[89] No one spoke to the loss of life or expressed compassion for the men involved or for their families left behind.

A few years later, on September 17, 1963, a Southern Pacific train traveling north collided with an unregistered truck transporting fifty-eight Braceros at the intersection of Thomas Ranch Road and Highway 101. This time, thirty-two Braceros were killed and twenty-four others seriously injured. Again, the tragedy garnered national attention and condemnation that these workers were being treated more as commodities than human beings, but there was little other evidence in the local press or among their GSA employers to indicate any sympathy or attention to Braceros' living and working conditions that put them in such danger.[90]

Unions objected strenuously to the Bracero program, which they correctly perceived was designed to undercut organizing and wages. The National Farm Labor Union (NFLU) led by Ernesto Galarza challenged the Bracero program directly and became a target of the GSA for doing so.

> Let me sound a note of warning. . . . The vegetable workers union is frantically and persistently writing and wiring the Secretary of Labor Tobin, as well as the President, demanding that no more Mexican nationals be imported into Salinas Valley. Why? Because the shed workers feel that [packing lettuce in cartons in fields rather than in packing sheds results in] a great deal of work . . . taken away from them and given to Mexican Nationals in the field.[91]

The GSA did not take concerns from union members seriously, passing them off as "just another effort on the part of [a Mr. Galarza] and the discredited National Farm Labor Union to cause trouble. . . . [W]e sincerely hope that the Labor Department will find no fault [with GSA] but no one knows, with the present labor-loving administration in Washington, what might happen."[92] The federal government could hardly be described as "labor loving." In fact, as historians Deborah Cohen and James D. Cockcroft argued, postwar immigration policies in the form of the McCarran-Walter Act and the 1940 Alien Registration Act, along with the Taft-Hartley Act, served agriculturalists' interests in suppressing labor activism.[93]

As was the case in the 1930s, union organizing was dismissed as antidemocratic and anti-American, and it was blamed on outsiders rather than understood to be a logical response to balancing the power of the GSA with the power of labor unions. GSA spokesmen urged growers "to instruct their foremen or camp managers to expel any outside agitators who might come into their camps and to instruct their foremen to keep [the GSA] posted on any activities of the National Farm Labor Union."[94] The NFLU continued its activism, despite the efforts of the GSA to thwart it, which distressed GSA members: "The National Farm Labor Union was still active in the district and . . . they had sent a contracted Mexican national to the Labor department in Washington with unfounded complaints against growers of bad food, pay, and working conditions."[95] The GSA specifically identified Ernesto Galarza, leader of the NFLU, as culpable in influencing policy at the national level, which they believed (correctly) challenged and put in jeopardy the entire contract labor system, something the GSA depended on by the 1950s.

They were right to fear Galarza. A strong and powerful activist and visionary, he was born in 1905 in Mexico. Galarza and his family became part of the stream of migrants in the early twentieth century who fled the Mexican Revolution but also worked as farm laborers and became the backbone of agriculture in the Southwest and California. However, unlike most young men of his generation, Galarza not only graduated from college but also earned a Ph.D. He dedicated his life both to a passionate activism and to scholarly production that linked labor rights, not just in Salinas and the Salinas Valley but also throughout California, to a bigger, broader effort for Mexican American civil rights. As a resident and activist in nearby San José, Galarza attacked segregation that kept Mexican people confined to deplorable conditions in San José's barrios. He traveled up and down the state challenging the power of growers, utilizing his union to overturn the harsh and exploitive conditions in the agricultural fields and packinghouses, where most Mexican immigrants and Mexican American people were employed. He objected strenuously to the importation of labor from Mexico (or anywhere else) that served growers' purpose of maintaining low wages and brutal working conditions. Yet, he was not a Salinas resident and had no particular affiliation with the city or its residents. By contrast, the Community Service Organization (CSO) in Salinas was comprised of insiders, important members of the Mexican American community of long-standing in the city.

The CSO had roots in Chicago and Los Angeles. In 1940 labor organizer and activist Saul Alinsky founded the Industrial Areas Foundation to advocate for workers' rights in Chicago. He hired Fred Ross to organize workers in Los Angeles area and in the Imperial Valley of the California Southwest. In turn, Ross, together with Antonio Rios and Edward Roybal, created the Community Service Organization in 1947, which not only focused on the plight of workers but specifically Mexican American workers, and dealt with the larger problem of Mexican American civil rights. Beyond the workplace, the CSO addressed inequality in immigration policy, slumlike living conditions in barrios, lack of representation in politics, and mistreatment of Mexican Americans in the courts and in the media. The CSO became an important advocacy group and garnered attention throughout California, including César Chávez and Dolores Huerta among its members. In Salinas, families of long-standing—such as the Casarez, Chavez, Gutierrez, Zermeno, and Sanchez families—joined the CSO and spearheaded efforts to support Mexican Americans in their collective fight for equal rights, engaging with growers and shippers over wages and working conditions.[96] They linked with other CSOs in California to confront inequality in the justice system, the media, and, most importantly, in the fields and packinghouses.[97]

This group of self-defined "rabble rousers," including the Sanchezes and Alvarezes, supported workers' rights, including the rights of migrant laborers and Braceros, and challenged discriminatory practices in Salinas's neighborhoods, employment, the justice system, and schools, especially over the issue of bilingual education. They focused as well on eliminating segregation in housing and expanding public health to poorer sections of the community. As middle-class residents of the city, they engaged in building a community based on equity and civil rights, which would be a hallmark of the 1960s and 1970s through the United Farm Workers movement led by César Chávez.[98]

In response to efforts by the CSOs and Galarza's NFLU to put an end the Bracero program, GSA members toyed with the idea of importing Filipino/a contract workers from the Hawaiian Islands: "The Secretary announced 4,000 or 5,000 alien Filipino laborers available in the Hawaiian Islands for contracting. . . . [T]he bond for these men would be about $75.00 per head."[99] This compared with the much less costly "$10.00 per head for transportation" of Mexicans workers who were part of the Mexican National Program.[100] Growers hoped Hawaiian Filipino/a workers would give them a competitive edge over union workers and Braceros: "This competition with Mexican Nationals might result in an agreement with Mexico which would give growers a few advantages."[101] However, after a trip by GSA member S. V. Christierson to Hawaii, it became clear that it would be "a waste of time [and] practically useless to try to recruit these workers, because wages in Hawaii had gone up after the war and unemployment decreased significantly, making it impossible for growers in Salinas to compete." Christierson concluded, "To me, our only hope is federal legislation permitting contract workers from the Philippines, Korea, and Japan to come in under bond for a period of 2–3 years."[102] Despite protests over the power of the federal government in labor relations, the GSA sought federal support in obtaining a workforce they could control.

Growers also hired Mexican undocumented workers, referred to in deeply disparaging terms as "wetbacks" or "wets," to supplement what they feared was an ongoing labor shortage in the postwar years. It was another example of the tendency to regard workers as mere commodities, rather than human beings who deserved respect for the critically important work they did that supported the entire industry. However, visits to the fields by representatives from U.S. Government Employment Services, checking "the extent to which wetbacks are employed with the Mexican Nationals," alarmed members of the GSA because under the provisions of new legislation, "the Ellender and Poage Bills [made] it a felony to employ wets." Instead of ending the practice of employing noncitizen workers, "a group of grower representatives [lobbied] to have the felony provision amended to make it a misdemeanor rather than a felony."[103] Their effort simply to reduce penalties rather than stop the practice of importing labor spoke to their self-awareness that they were wrongly undermining American workers.

The GSA justified their actions by making the argument that American citizen workers who lived in Salinas "do not wish to drive thirty miles to be in the field at 5:00 or 5:30 in the morning and [do] . . . a tremendous amount of stoop labor . . . working for only three hours then lay off the rest of the day."[104] Furthermore, the hiring of American packinghouse workers to do fieldwork would constitute "an absolutely prohibitive cost." Mexican nationals spent much of their workdays in "weeding, thinning, [and] tying carrots," tasks for which citizen packing shed workers would have to be paid union wages and would require growers to accede to decent working conditions, including offering healthcare and childcare. Again, we see a growing tendency among the GSA to treat fieldworkers as less than the human beings that they were, more akin to farm equipment or livestock. It was a far cry from the pride that union members in packing sheds expressed and the respect they demanded and received in the 1930s.

The Central Labor Council of Salinas joined the National Farm Labor Union in their objection to the presence of Braceros in Salinas, but they framed their argument as a public health problem and a threat to democracy, language that they no doubt hoped would resonate with the GSA and the public rather than challenge Bracero labor more directly as a threat to their own wages and job security. At one board of supervisors meeting over the issue of housing for Braceros, the Central Labor Council hired attorney J. A. Bardin to argue against building labor camps because this would "invite excessive and cheap labor into this area, where ample labor already exists."[105] Furthermore, "labor men pointed out that a camp would be an easy target for agitators." Labor Council President A. S. Doss ratcheted up the argument against the board proceeding with the building of another labor camp for migrant fieldworkers, threatening that it would "be the focal point of disease, of strikes . . . its dynamite!"[106] They might have thought that this language would resonate with both GSA members and with Salinas residents generally.

The GSA should have understood from the conflicts of the 1930s how important it was to integrate workers into agriculture as stakeholders in the city, both to protect their own interests and to support their view that Salinas welcomed working classes. They did some of that, at least to demonstrate a show of respect for workers. The GSA created a committee to support fundraising for cultural celebrations in Salinas and invested in a wide array of social welfare enterprises, including increased housing construction, infrastructure, and roads to benefit their workers and the community as a whole.[107] In 1952, growers donated funds to "be used for the erection of a building suitable for a Child Welfare Center" in nearby Watsonville.[108] The workers in question, mostly working mothers, labored in packing sheds but lived primarily in the unincorporated Alisal and needed childcare nearby when they were on the job.[109] The GSA treated the mostly white union packing shed workers with far more respect than noncitizen Braceros or any migrant field laborer who lived in male-only camps with the barest minimum of food, clothing, or healthcare.

At about the same time that labor issues became central in Salinas, revisions to the McCarran-Walter Act of 1952 led to the passage of the important Immigration Act of 1965. This new and sweeping legislation opened the door to formerly excluded nation-states (including the entire continent of Asia) and contained the important restrictive provision that for the first-time limited immigration in the western hemisphere.[110]

Still, a caveat in immigration law allowed for some workers known casually as "commuters," who lived both in Mexico and the United States, to move back and forth across borders with special "green cards" that allowed them free access to temporary employment in both countries. Workers from Canadian and Mexican borderland communities took advantage of the commuter status that the green cards allowed, but it was only controversial on the U.S.- Mexican border because living costs were so much lower in Mexico (in Canada they were equivalent to the United States). Mexican laborers worked for far less than their U.S.-born counterparts, infuriating union members on the U.S. side. Unions (including both Teamsters and the UFW) repeatedly and strenuously challenged these loopholes in the immigration system throughout the 1950s and 1960s, but their efforts failed on the grounds that "[as] plaintiffs [they] lacked legal standing to sue" so the merits of the law were left unresolved after the passage of the 1965 legislation.

Yet, after 1965, Mexican workers who sought employment in the United States (even temporarily) often arrived without status, as undocumented, an illegal presence rather than an accepted part of the workforce as they traditionally had been. This led to another kind of crisis because their act of border crossing was now considered illegal, a felony in the United States.[111] In 1969, Senator Ted Kennedy introduced legislation that seemed to offer a compromise solution and would require periodic labor certifications. This compromise was favored by labor unions but opposed by the agricultural community as being "extremely detrimental to agricultural workers in view of its provision to restrict the return of Mexican Aliens . . . to their former jobs in the United States."[112] The result was a flurry of raids on people suspected of living and working in the country without legal standing.[113] Many labor contractors left the contracting business entirely rather than house undocumented workers and risk committing a felony offense.[114]

The wrangling over migrant labor came about in the context of a dramatic sea change in population movement in America—from the rural South to northern and western cities. It began during the Great Depression, extended through World War II, and picked up speed in the postwar and through the 1970s. New federal immigration policies added a level of international immigration to a surging population in California. Salinas felt its effects too.

REPLENISHED POPULATIONS AND
NEW IMMIGRATION POLICY

Population changes in California were first brought on during the Great Depression and in the build-up to World War II. Millions of individuals left rural America (particularly the South) to work in the burgeoning new manufacturing plants and shipbuilding industries associated with the military in the urban North and West. As a result, California towns and cities exploded with new population between 1940 and 1970, especially in cities that became sites for shipbuilding and war industry production such as Oakland, Richmond, San Francisco, Los Angeles, and San Diego.[115]

The newcomers did not resemble their prewar counterparts ethnically or racially. Instead of mostly European-origin people and some Asian immigrants, most of the new arrivals were of African American and Mexican descent. They tended to be native born rather than foreign born because restrictive legislation of 1924 reduced international immigration to a trickle. In Salinas, this meant far fewer Chinese, Japanese, and Filipino/a immigrants but more and more Mexican American families who came mostly from Southern California, Texas, and other parts of the Southwest, first as migrant farmworkers, then as permanent residents. These women and men, born in the United States and having lived there for generations, also had children who were American citizens. They were family people, determined to become stakeholders in the city, just as their Anglo American, Asian American, and Mexican American counterparts had over the previous hundred years of settlement. Like the others before them, they mostly settled initially in the east Salinas area, still the most affordable part of Salinas.[116]

With the end of World War II, the McCarran-Walter Act opened the doors to a new population of Filipino/a, Chinese, and Japanese immigrants. The 1965 Immigration Act (known as the Hart-Celler Act) that followed over a decade later allowed for family unification and the end of the quota system, which led to a surge of new international immigration that transformed California. In 1960, California's population included a mere 1.3 million foreign-born residents who made up 9 percent of the population. After the legislation of the 1960s and the new immigration policies, that figure had risen to 6.5 million, or 22 percent of the population by 1990, including approximately 3 million people who were undocumented, mostly from

Mexico, because of the new limits on western hemisphere migration. In Salinas, the Chinese, Japanese, and Filipino/a American communities were replenished and reinvigorated by the new arrivals, but they were challenged too, as these newcomers did not share the deep roots or understandings of their co-ethnic counterparts.

Salinas became a destination for both new populations of diverse Asian groups and Mexican and Mexican American population in the postwar years. From a tiny population of 13,917 in 1950, Salinas's population increased to 28,957 by 1960. By 1968 the population of Salinas had reached 57,000, making it the most populous city in the California coastal region between San José and Santa Barbara. It reached 58,896 by 1970 and 76,402 by 1978. By 1980, Salinas grew to well over 80,000, and by the end of that decade, the city's population had passed the 100,000 mark. The increase was not due to immigration alone, but also to the annexation of Alisal in 1963, which increased the population from 31,200 to 50,000, and Santa Rita in 1975, which boosted population from 69,500 to 71,630.[117]

Salinas grew both in geographic size and in population. Most significantly, its ethno-racial makeup changed from a population that was 90 percent white in 1960 with smaller but significant minority populations of Asian Americans and a small percentage of Latino/as, to a minority-majority city that was 38.8 percent Latino/a by 1980 and 60 percent Latino/a by 1990. Most of the new arrivals were ethnically Mexican, predominantly native born and citizens of the United States, although there were a fair number of undocumented newcomers too.

But, in contrast to the other groups who had arrived in the first hundred years of Salinas's history, inclusion would not be as seamless for the new population of Latino/a people streaming into the city beginning in the 1970s. As Charlotte Brooks claimed in her analysis of San Francisco, "some people deserved inclusion in the suburban lifestyle that symbolized American freedom, and some did not. In California the deserving increasingly included Asian Americans, while the undeserving were, more often than not, African Americans and Mexican Americans."[118] A breakdown of Salinas's multiple Asian communities supported Brooks's assertion. In Salinas, a new and fuller integration of Asian groups into the mainstream of Salinas's political, economic, social, and cultural life happened after World War II as a result of new immigration policies that welcomed them.

Japanese American Postwar Experience

The Japanese American community of Salinas expanded and integrated during this period. Japanese American residents originally immigrated to the Salinas area in the late nineteenth century and had lived in and around the city working mostly as farm laborers in the production of lettuce and berries. But many became tenant farmers and labor contractors in the early years of the twentieth century—that is, before they were all forcibly removed during the incarcerations of World War II. However, at war's end, there was a dramatic shift in U.S. foreign policy initiatives toward Japan, and Japanese Americans, through the Japanese American Citizens League (JACL), vigorously worked to ensure basic civil rights and citizenship privileges for Issei (Japanese Americans born in Japan).[119]

Among the JACL's successful efforts were overturning the Alien Land Law and the part of the 1924 Immigration Act that excluded anyone from any part of the Asian continent; ensuring Japanese American expatriates living in China, Taiwan, and Manchuria inclusion in the 1953 Refugee Relief Act, which allowed over 200,000 war-displaced people entry to the United States;[120] and adding a quota for Japanese immigrants to the 1952 McCarran-Walter Act. By the time the Hart-Celler Immigration Act passed in 1965, Japanese Americans were poised to reestablish their presence in California and in the Salinas Valley.

By 1974, almost 60,000 Japanese Americans lived in the Central Coast region. They were businesspeople and professionals, but they also maintained a significant presence in agriculture, particularly in the flower industry. They usually arrived in Salinas by way of the East Bay and San Mateo County, having served internships with more established flower growers there and utilizing networks among themselves to secure loans to buy land and start businesses. By 1974, Japanese Americans owned almost all of Monterey County's twenty-five nurseries and owned fifty separate but related companies, many of them in and around Salinas.

Most importantly, they reinvigorated the Salinas Japanese American community with their numbers and powerful presence.[121] Although Salinas's Japanese Americans participated fully in the economic and cultural life of the city, they maintained their cultural integrity through the Buddhist Temple on Soledad Street and the Lincoln Presbyterian Church. Their cultural events such as the annual Obon festival drew the whole Salinas community.

These culturally specific celebrations continued to serve as a relatively easy way for Salinas residents to reflect inclusiveness without having to address inequality in political representation or exclusion in social life.

One of the strongest indications of changing times for Japanese Americans can be seen in Henry Hibino, a descendant of nineteenth-century Japanese settlers who survived the incarceration camps in the 1940s. The Hibino family had originally arrived in Salinas by way of Vacaville in 1904, first as shoe repairmen, then as farmers. Henry Hibino's son Kent still cultivates the land north of town that the family first acquired in 1937 as tenants but now owns. Henry Hibino recalled his return to Salinas after the incarceration during World War II as a less than welcoming time. "They didn't like Japanese people here," he said in something of an understatement. However, that all changed over the course of the 1960s, as Salinas's Japanese American residents enjoyed a new level of acceptance in the postwar years, as evidenced by such apparent inclusions as an invitation to join the Elks Club: "I played the game. I thought sure I'd like to join the Elks Lodge," Henry mused, speculating that "maybe 'Papa' Nunes" had sponsored his membership.[122] The Elks Club had an official policy of excluding Asian Americans from membership. His awareness that he was "playing a game" showed that he understood all too well that his invitation to join the club belied the racism underlying its exclusionary policy.

Henry Hibino was first elected to the city council in June 1971, recruited by a group of local businesspeople (Bob Ames, Joe Stave, Bill Bryan—all local attorneys, and Syd Gadsby who owned the only music store in town). According to Henry, this group "scouted people" who might want to participate in local government. Henry "felt that everyone should do charity work and public service" and so was amenable in 1970 when asked to run for office by this cohort of local businessmen. He was elected easily and served from 1971 through 1979, which included a term as mayor. According to news reports of the time, Henry Hibino was heralded as "the city's first non-Caucasian councilman. . . . The Japanese American farmer came in first with 4,633 votes in a community which had once led a statewide crusade in the 1940s to block return of Japanese-Americans to California."[123] Decades later, he mused that "I must have been out of my mind" for accepting the mayor appointment during the tumultuous years of the 1970s. Nonetheless, the active recruitment of Henry Hibino was an indication that city officials, all of whom were white and male, understood that they needed to showcase inclusion even when it was more apparent than real.

It might have made more sense to recruit someone from the growing Latino/a population of Salinas, but recruiting someone from the Japanese American community, now reestablished after the cruel expulsion during the war years, seemed a safer choice. Hibino recognized this for what it was. He joined forces with white businessmen, eyes wide open, having experienced firsthand the dark side of American politics in his experience with World War II and the incarceration; now he was willing to be part of the political establishment as a way of showing solidarity with his fellow Salinas residents, who were trying to make amends by including him as a Japanese American representative—not just in politics, but in the elite social world that the Elks Club represented. In fact, as mayor, he would be the city's titular head. Henry Hibino became mayor of the city in 1974, just as Salinas prepared to celebrate its centennial anniversary of incorporation as an American city and during the contentious farmworker strikes. The Bank of Tokyo opened a branch on Main Street that year too, also evidence of a new era of acceptance for Japanese Americans and other Asian groups.[124]

Unlike the Hibinos, Andy Matsui and his family did not have deep roots in the community; they came to Salinas as part of the new postwar migration. Born into a farming family in Nara prefecture outside of Kyoto 1935, Andy left his family's farm in 1961 to apprentice with Japanese American flower farmers in Redwood City. Innovative and ambitious, he focused on growing chrysanthemums the American way, out of pots rather than in the fields as the Japanese farmers did. After several years of apprenticeship and with a loan from the Bank of Tokyo, he purchased 50 acres of land in Salinas in 1969. Together with his wife Mary and their four children, the Matsui family farmed both chrysanthemums and roses successfully through the 1970s and 80s, blending into Salinas's Japanese American community and the agricultural elite, at least in terms of economic class. The family maintained an important presence in the city through support for the local community college and numerous nonprofits.

When the cut flower industry experienced a downturn due to competition from Latin American flower growers due to NAFTA in the 1990s, Andy Matsui invented a new industry in floral agriculture—potted orchids. In doing so, he attained the kind of prominence that only the biggest international agricultural giants held. Andy, like so many other wealthier Salinas residents, left the city for residence elsewhere in Monterey County by the 1980s. This move followed a pattern motivated by fears over the changes wrought by Salinas's new predominantly Latino/a demographic, its economic challenges and political controversies, and the pull of elite and attractive neighborhoods elsewhere on the peninsula, which now welcomed Asian Americans (but not African Americans) where they had once been excluded.[125]

The Matsui family's story, unlike the Hibino story, was new and a direct result of the more liberal American attitudes toward Japanese Americans and the consequent immigration policies implemented after 1965. By 1980, 750 Japanese Americans resided in Salinas, 13.4 percent of its Asian American population, making it the largest Japanese American community in Monterey County.[126]

By looking at Japanese American experiences through the lenses of both family histories, we see examples of how a revived Japanese American community played out in Salinas. Japanese Americans sustained their cultural integrity, while enjoying the positive effects of postwar American views of Asian groups and benefited from the policy work of the JACL that allowed for a resurgence of immigration from Japan. By 1970, newer Japanese American immigrants had replenished the community, sharing mainstream American values of individual enterprise and political involvement. These more recent Salinas residents did not have to combat the overt racism and discrimination in employment, education, and neighborhood settlement that earlier generations faced (and remembered).

Chinese American Postwar Experience

Like Salinas's Japanese Americans, the city's Chinese American residents had expressed their own sense of belonging to the political and social community by 1970, but they remained apolitical. "We stayed out of politics because of the Exclusion Act," explained Linda Wong Gin, a Salinas native whose father Herbert K. Y. Wong and partner George Lee established the American Meat Market on the corner of Pajaro and Market Street in the 1930s. After her father passed away in 1963, Linda's mother became the co-owner of the enterprise.

Although the Chinese Exclusion Acts were nineteenth-century measures long since overturned, it is telling that the older community of Chinese Americans retained an unusually strong institutional memory, indicating their awareness that policy and public feeling might, at any moment, revert to the bad old days of Chinese persecution in California and the West, which it did very recently.[127]

The 1970s marked a more welcoming climate in terms of immigration policy for Chinese Americans in Salinas and throughout California, just as it had for Japanese Americans. It was a time when then-President Richard Nixon, with his Secretary of State Henry Kissinger, were opening diplomatic doors to China in significant and dramatic ways.[128] Every overture by Nixon and the State Department was noted in Salinas and applauded in both editorials and on the front page of the *Salinas Californian*. The Chinese American population of Salinas reached 675 by 1980, 12 percent of Salinas's Asian population, and, like their Japanese American counterparts, they made up the largest concentration of Chinese Americans in Monterey County.

Although Chinese American residents did not run for political office, they were among the first minorities in Salinas to be included on city boards and commissions and in staff positions in city government. Beginning in July 1971, the city made explicit a new policy "to ensure broad community representation." Soon after that announcement, York Gin and Frank Chin, community leaders and entrepreneurs, were appointed to the Recreation-Parks Commission and to the Health and Safety Board, respectively.[129] Like the recruitment of Henry Hibino, welcoming York Gin, Frank Chin, and other Chinese businessmen into the circle of governance in Salinas allowed white city leaders to show that they embraced minority representation without giving up the levers of power or including anyone from the growing Latino/a community.

Chinese Americans in Salinas approached controversial issues such as Chinese language education with an eye to accommodation rather than conflict. In the 1970s, San Francisco's Chinese American activists waged a fierce political battle with whites and African American activists who wanted to integrate San Francisco's public schools by busing mostly African American children into white neighborhood schools (rather than the other way around). For Chinese Americans, busing thwarted their efforts to sustain bilingual education in public schools by spreading Chinese American children out among multiple school systems, making the hiring of Chinese language teachers fiscally unsupportable.

However, bilingual education was a nonissue for Chinese Americans in Salinas.[130] Even though Linda Wong Gin and other narrators emphasized the importance Salinas's Chinese American parents placed on their children's education in Chinese language and culture, they would not openly demand bilingual education in public schools. Instead, they created their own language school. Recalled Linda:

> It was very important to the parents that the children learn Chinese. . . . Cantonese was taught only in Chinese School and no tuition was charged in the early years. Mandarin was only taught after I became Principal in 2015. Children were required to attend [Chinese School] daily after regular public school.[131]

Chinese Americans in Salinas maintained their own language schools outside of the usual public school system rather than demand that the public schools incorporate a bilingual education program, which they feared might have triggered a backlash against them.

By contrast, according to Bill Meléndez, Salinas public school teacher and president of the League of United Latin American Citizens (LULAC) at the time, "I saw teachers relegating Spanish speaking students to a lesser education and I reached out [to organize]." His efforts eventually led to a successful lawsuit requiring bilingual education in public schools in Monterey County, something Salinas's Chinese Americans even refrained from supporting.[132] To be fair, the Chinese American population of Salinas was only a small fraction either of the San Francisco Chinese American population or of the growing Latino/a population in Salinas, and more recent immigrants mostly spoke fluent English, thus having less reason to demand bilingual language teachers. Still, it was significant that Salinas's Chinese Americans declined even to join their counterparts in San Francisco who aligned with LULAC and other Spanish-language advocates in demanding bilingual language teachers in public schools. They stood apart as well from the growing Chinese-speaking immigrant population from Southeast Asia that settled in nearby Seaside and Marina, who advocated for bilingual education in public schools in Monterey County alongside LULAC.[133]

Unlike the Japanese Americans whose occupations tended to remain mostly in agriculture, Chinese Americans in Salinas generally directed their economic energies into small business enterprises, particularly restaurants and grocery stores. They became dominant grocery purveyors and still carry on the small, established markets that have mostly withstood the invasion of the giants such as Nob Hill and Safeway into the area. Their success in the retail trades ensured Chinese American families entry into middle-class life throughout the postwar years. Just as the Japanese Americans experienced an increasing sense of inclusion based on race and class, Salinas's Chinese Americans created a "flourishing really close-knit" community now infused by new immigrants.[134]

Linda Wong Gin recounted her parent's journey to Salinas in 1937: "They wanted to settle in Salinas because they knew there was a strong Chinese community here. Not like in Monterey. My mother had bad memories of the way she was treated in Monterey. But Salinas was more welcoming," Linda said, recalling a conversation she had with her mother about the family's history.[135] The family avoided settling in Chinatown, however:

> My mother did not want us kids or my Dad to be a part of Chinatown because the tongs really ran it. She thought they were really bad people . . . gambling, prostitution, that sort of thing, although the [tongs] did positive things too. They founded the Chinese American Citizens Alliance (CACA) to help immigrants with legal issues . . . but my mother didn't even like the idea of donating cash to keep the association alive [because of their unsavory business activities].

Nevertheless, Linda's father, Herbert K. Y. Wong, was a founding member of the CACA chapter in Salinas, and he remained an active member of CACA throughout his life. Members of CACA frequently met in the rooms above the family grocery store.

Linda described the Chinese business community in the 1950s and 1960s as one dependent on agriculture, mostly without actively engaging in farming, particularly during the years of the Bracero program, 1940s through the 1960s: "My family owned a grocery store on the corner of Market and Pajaro, the American Meat Market. All along that strip there were [Asian] businesses. There was a Japanese clothing store next to us. There were a lot of Chinese restaurants," she recalled. "We supplied food and meat to many of the labor contractors. I remember working at the store as a young girl and serving the Braceros when they came to town [to shower, sleep, and recreate]. They were all really nice people. They were family men. They really looked out for us," she said.

Like Blanche Chin Ah Tye's merchant family (discussed in Chapter 2), the Wongs (through CACA) participated in Salinas cultural events, such as the rodeo. CACA raised money to build the Grand Sweepstakes trophies for the rodeo, which lined the walls of the Chinese Community Center in Salinas. Yet, the family also experienced the painful impact of racist restrictions on housing. Linda's parents originally bought a home in the multiethnic neighborhood of Capitol Street, which is located near the center of town and across the street from Roosevelt Elementary School: "There was a Spanish family, the Perezes, who also lived there. Mrs. Burgess, around the corner—her husband was Italian. Everybody was open and friendly. I don't remember any Japanese families or Filipinos." She described a neighborhood made up of mainly "Caucasian, Spanish, and us and the Lees [who were also Chinese]. We always felt safe and comfortable in Salinas. We felt part of the community," she claimed, even as her family was excluded from living in many neighborhoods.[136]

That feeling of belonging to the Salinas community was more illusory than real. Linda recalled:

> Neighborhoods were restricted in the 1950s. I know it because my mother mentioned that. Our house was only a two-bedroom house. She told me "I wish your Dad would purchase a home on the other side of Main Street" but [we] couldn't. They weren't selling to Chinese in those days. . . . So they just stayed where they were. When my brothers came along, they converted the dining room into a bedroom. . . . I know we could've afforded to live somewhere else, but we stayed there.[137]

Neighborhood settlement exposed racism that cultural exclusions papered over.[138]

Linda's family may have been excluded from living in the Maple Park neighborhood because of their race, but their retail grocery business allowed them to claim middle-class status:

> I do remember we had a housekeeper. A person came when I was about 9, 10 years old. She did all the washing, cleaning. I think she was Hispanic or white. After her came another older lady. This lady was Caucasian, and we really liked her . . . because she would read to us. We were the first Chinese family who could afford a T.V. so we had a lot of visitors.

Besides home and business ownership, these were all indications of a degree of economic stability and upward mobility associated with being a member of the middle class, and class mattered a great deal in Salinas. Other Chinese American families lived in the wealthier white areas of the city by the 1960s.

The newer population of Chinese immigrants were well educated, often graduates of California colleges and universities, and part of a class of professionals in Salinas. Unlike the Wongs, Dr. Harry Chong and Dr. Emma Dong lived in the prestigious Maple Park subdivision and socialized among the cohort of mostly white doctors who also lived there. Their son, Dr. Byron Chong, also a physician and current resident of Salinas, recalled the neighborhood as an integrated racial space:

> We bought a house from Ellis Spiegl [who was Jewish and also one of the most prominent members of Salinas's Grower-Shipper Association] in 1952 in Maple Park. We were pretty much upper middle-class people. . . . There were other Chinese families [in Maple Park], but not so much Filipinos or Mexicans. They lived a little east of that.[139]

Still, Byron claimed that Maple Park was slowly integrating in the 1960s based on class: "One of my best friends in Maple Park was a Filipino guy. I knew he wasn't white. There were Jewish kids there too," he explained.[140]

Linda Wong Gin had no personal memory of racism directed at herself in Salinas, beyond her mother's recollection of their being excluded from buying a home in the elite neighborhood of Maple Park. By contrast, Byron Chong—whose family enjoyed a level of acceptance and inclusion in Maple Park based on their status as part of the medical community—recalled painful microaggressions as a teenager:

> When we were kids, we had birthday parties and invited the whole class. But when I got into junior high school I stopped getting invited to these parties, and I thought they worried about Chinese kids getting too close to the girls. I started figuring out they didn't want the kids around the white girls.[141]

Byron remembered conflict with Mexican American kids too: "In junior high school there was a larger influx of Hispanics . . . that would have been around 1955. I just remember kids saying, 'Ching Chong Chinaman' and they would say things in Spanish about us." His upper-class status might have contributed to tensions within the Chinese community as well.

He remembered routinely being called "banana" by his peers in the 1960s, signifying that he was Asian on the outside but white on the inside. It was clearly meant as an insult.

Yet, the appearance of acceptance and inclusion showed in the way Salinas celebrated Chinese culture. When the Chinese Community Center officially opened on April 17, 1961, "Local residents thronged the block long area [to watch] the spectacular Lion Dance," according to the *Salinas Californian*.[142] Serving as master of ceremonies, H. W. Wong (no relation to Linda Wong Gin) welcomed dignitaries from all over the United States. Senator Fred Farr called the new building a "great landmark in the growth of our country," praising Chinese contributions to American economic, social, and cultural life and demonstrating their acceptance and respect in Salinas. Then-Mayor Art Atteridge, District Attorney Bert Young, and Judges Anthony Brazil and Elmer Machado joined City Manager Thomas Dunne and Chief of Police Ray McIntyre in attending the opening of the center. Skits by Chinese actors and various banquets lasted over the course of two days.[143]

The city could point to these celebrations as evidence of inclusion, even if they marked the Chinese community as a separate sphere. They are also evidence of the ways in which Salinas residents created an impression of unity, cohesion, communalism, and common purpose. Byron vividly remembered the annual celebrations as affirmations of Chinese American life in Salinas: "The Chinese Association Building or Chinese Community Center on One California Street was our center. We were all Chinese together. We celebrated Chinese New Year. We usually celebrated Chinese New Year as a 2-day event . . . they would have all the Chinese food, movies."[144]

The 1970s initiated a new political era for Salinas's Chinese American community. As residents celebrated Chinese New Year on January 12 of that year, with York Gin "passing the gavel" as president of the Chinese Benevolent Association to Tommy F. C. Li, the group collectively vowed "improvement within the Chinese community relationship continuing to build a better image in the bigger community."[145] It was a signal of the Chinese American community's willingness to actively engage politically and economically with non-Chinese communities in the city—not merely for cultural events. And despite increasing integration of neighborhoods, social life in the city remained strictly segregated along racial lines.

The experiences of the Chongs and the Dongs, compared to the Wongs and the Gins, exemplify the changes in treatment in Salinas for Chinese

Americans. New migrations of Chinese families had no memory of mistreatment of Asian Americans in California. Like the subtle but clear distinctions in perceptions and experiences between the Matsuis and the Hibinos, these newer Chinese American families infused the community with perspectives that often conflicted with the older Salinas residents. Byron Chong came from a well-educated professional family who lived in an elite neighborhood and expected to be treated the same way as whites of his class. His family did not come from poverty or fieldwork, nor were they subjected to any obvious, collective discrimination. Byron was perhaps far more sensitized to any form of racism directed at himself than someone who might have a shared memory of this as a commonplace occurrence. Linda Wong Gin's parents had roots in the working-class Chinese American communities of Monterey and had connections to San Francisco's Chinese American community. She had deep family memories of racial discrimination that her parents shared with her and even expected that it might resurface (she was right); but she was not as acutely attuned to microaggressions as Byron, whose family had no experience with California's anti-Chinese policies and its impact on individuals and families. Together, these Chinese American families recreated a community like that of the Japanese Americans—divided both by class, experience, and stage of migration—which determined how they were treated by others in Salinas and how they perceived themselves in the community and the city.

Filipino/a American Postwar Experience

A similar pattern of inclusion and replenishment happened for Filipino/a Americans in Salinas. Governor Ronald Reagan met with leaders of Filipino/a American communities throughout California in March 1970, which led to the creation of the California Filipino-American Coordinating Conference (described in the local press as a "Filipino Power Group"). They met in Salinas "in order to hear the needs and-or complaints of Filipinos in Monterey County."[146] First on the list of "asks" that Filipino/a Americans made was "Appointment of capable Americans of Philippine descent to policy-making positions in government." Scholarships for Filipino/a American community college and college students, housing for the poor and aged in the community, "decent housing for farmworkers," and "inclusion in the War on Poverty Programs" also made the list of urgent needs for Filipino/a Americans in Monterey County.

By 1970, Filipino/a Americans made up the largest community of Asian Americans in Salinas with a population of 3,514 that was twice the size of the next largest Filipino/a American community in Monterey County, Seaside, which had a population of 1,666 Filipino/a Americans, largely made up of military people connected to Fort Ord.[147] Just like the populations of Japanese Americans and Chinese Americans in Salinas in the 1970s, Filipino/a Americans enjoyed a level of acceptance that contrasted with their (at best) conflicted status in the decades before the war years. Before the war, as we have seen in earlier chapters, middle-class Filipino/a Americans enjoyed some privilege based on their socioeconomic standing, especially for the prominent Filipina Women's Club, but their working-class cohorts were routinely discriminated against in both employment and housing and marginalized in local politics. By the 1970s, however, immigration reforms led to increased immigration and a new, replenished community in Salinas. Many Filipinos arrived as professionals and middle classes in the 1970s with very different perspectives from those who came from the ranks of labor contractors or fieldworkers.

The Salinas Filipino/a American community was intensely hierarchical, with professionals and those who made up the successful class of contractors at the top of a socioeconomic pyramid.[148] Filipino/a Americans were concentrated in some neighborhoods, but also spread out through Salinas based on class. Religion and ethnic organizations bound them all together: "The two most important Filipino church associations in Salinas remain the Filipino-American Catholic Association and the United Filipino Presbyterians," both of which served as institutional connections within the community and as evidence of racism. White-dominated Catholic and Protestant churches excluded Filipinos/as from membership or forced them to sit in back pews.[149]

Sociologist Edwin B. Almirol studied the experience of Salinas's Filipino/a community. He divided its members between "the old timers," who arrived as uneducated, unskilled laborers, and the "post-war immigrants," who were "highly trained professionals."[150] The "old timers" were "reconciled . . . to working in hotels, restaurants, canneries, and farms [where they experienced] intense racial discrimination." These immigrants still felt deeply connected to the Philippines politically and culturally. The "post-war immigrants" had a different perception of life in Salinas. They "believed that the social climate was . . . tolerant of minorities. To the American born [children of these newer immigrant families] America is . . . home."[151] Almirol argued that although class was an important dividing line in the Filipino/a American community, region of origin in the Philippines was at least as important:

> The Tagalogs regard themselves superior to all the different Filipino ethnic groups . . . and look down on the Ilocanos as *barrio rubes* . . . and the Cebuanos as . . . lazy. . . . [T]he Cebuanos and Ilocanos consider the Tagalogs *mayabang* (proud show-offs).[152]

Filipino/a American narrators agreed with Almirol's assessment.

Ron Cacas, whose father John was a labor contractor from the 1930s through the 1960s, explained the significance of region:

> Inherent in our culture regionalism was very strong. Most men came from northern region, Ilocano. My father was from the northern part. The invasion [from Japan during World War II] was in the Visala [region], the southern part, where my mother originated, so it was like a mixed marriage. They didn't even speak the same language. We considered them from two different cultures.[153]

This was a distinction completely lost on Salinas's non-Filipino/a population, which saw the Filipino/a American community as a homogeneous whole.

Many Filipino/a Americans who arrived as workers found a path to middle-class life through the niche occupational ladder of labor contracting. Their story mirrored that of other Asian American minority groups who immigrated in the early years of the century, began lives as fieldworkers, but used the unique opportunities agriculture afforded them to join a middle- class mainstream in Salinas through landownership— all the while holding onto a cultural integrity that formed the basis of their social lives and cushioned the racism that kept them marginalized.

Like other Filipino/a Americans in Salinas, Ron Cacas marked World War II as the critical turning point in American views of his community:

> I think World War II was a major factor in changing the attitude towards Filipinos in Salinas. Our brothers were fighting on Bataan, everywhere, right alongside the Americans, on the side of America. They were heroes. I

remember going to the movies and seeing John Wayne and Filipino fighters with him. I felt really proud about that. I felt American.[154]

Ron lived in a multiracial neighborhood in Salinas in the 1950s, which he defined as middle class:

I grew up on Romie Lane. The neighborhood hasn't really changed. It was always middle class. We owned our home. There were the Riddles next door. They were Caucasian. The Barnards lived there too. The father was a supervisor at PetMart and the son, Pete, and I became so close that he came to Arizona and stayed with us.[155]

By 1947, the family had profited enough from their position as labor contractors that they were able to buy a ranch in Arizona, which Ron compared unfavorably to life in Salinas because he missed Salinas's urban character and its strong Filipino/a community: "My Dad expanded his business to Arizona, so he bought a farm ranch there. . . . We thought Salinas was cooler because it was a city. . . . [W]e were the ONLY Filipinos in grammar school and high school in Arizona. Here in Salinas there was a real Filipino community."[156]

Ron described a vibrant Filipino/a cultural life that included excursions to the beach and parties. "We were part of the Filipino marching band on Independence Day—all that stuff—dances on Saturday. And when I say picnics it was a big event and sponsored by the whole Filipino community, which was very well established." Often, the events centered on fundraising to support celebrations that were central to Filipino/a identity: "It was fundraising that would go on all weekend. They had dancing, blackjack tables (they waved the rules on gambling because it was a fundraiser). We roasted a pig." Within the community, fraternal organizations connected Salinas Filipino/a residents to others throughout the state and the nation: "The name was Caballeros de Masalon. That was the biggest Filipino fraternal organization in the United States," which Ron described as "one of the largest, most affluent, most progressive . . . [linking] Filipinos who were extremely active in Salinas community activities. This was in the 1950s and 1960s."[157]

His perception of a vibrant and complex Filipino/a American community life in Salinas was replicated in other agricultural towns in California with large and long-standing Filipino/a populations such as in Stockton. According to historian Dawn Bohulano Mabalon, Filipinos/as in Stockton also "created distinctively Filipino/a American traditions . . . [with] dances, plays, sports tournaments, parades" that were organized to celebrate both Filipino/a and American holidays and "sustained Filipinos" especially "in times of hardship and sacrifice." Mabalon cited one Filipina resident of Stockton who described these celebrations as "'the happiness of our people.'"[158]

Susan Aremas, born in Salinas in 1948, recalled a solid, prosperous Filipino/a community with roots stretching back to the 1920s, which grew from mostly working class to middle class by 1970 and had become an integral part of Salinas's economic, social, and political life. Like Ron Cacas's father John, Susan's father had little education when he left the U.S. military after the end of World War II. But instead of labor contracting and a smooth path into the middle class, Susan's father worked in the fields. Her mother, like Ron's mother Adelia, had some college education; also like Adelia, Susan's mother was a long-standing member of the Filipina Women's Club, an organization that played a central role in Filipino/a American community life.

Susan's parents benefited from the availability and affordability of housing in Alisal during the 1950s and bought a home there, but unlike the Cacas family, the Aremas family experienced racial discrimination. She recalled the painful experience her family endured when they tried to purchase a home in Alisal: "In 1948 my Dad saved money to buy a home. . . . We applied for it, but we found that there were petitions being sent around to bar us from living there. The people who objected [to the family buying into the area] were mostly [whites] from Oklahoma," she recalled.[159] Susan remembered her parents fighting back: "My parents said 'We also deserve this.' They told our friends come on over and we'll try to break through." However, financing was also a problem: "In those days there were no loans for Filipinos," she indicated in a reference to federal, state, and local policies that discriminated against most minority groups. The policy denied minorities mortgage-backed home loans and effectively prevented them from building wealth through home ownership, something that became commonplace among whites in the postwar era.[160]

Eventually the family succeeded, along with other Filipino/a American homeowners:

About 6 [Filipino] families [lived] just on East Alisal street alone. . . . There were sections on East Alisal and Williams that was open housing, [but Filipinos/as] couldn't even touch South Salinas [in those years].

Still her parents persevered. "They bought their house in 1953 [when] I was four years old. We lived in that same house for twenty-seven years." She described the neighborhood that she grew up in as mostly undeveloped and poor even today:

> Look at the area. There were no expensive houses. There were even Quonset huts then. In front of El Sausal Jr High it was all Quonset huts. Across the street were mostly fields.[161]

Susan admired her parents' perseverance and the closeness of the community, which was both empowering and supportive for all of them: "They worked hard at saving. Our house is still there. We were very close families. Our parents were godparents to all of the children. The Villegas, the Anchetas, we were very close families."[162]

In contrast to Ron Cacas, Susan Aremas was acutely aware of race: "I know I'm American," she said, "but I don't look American and my parents aren't American, so it was a struggle." She noticed that Filipino/a immigrants who arrived during that period in the 1970s did not share her self-consciousness as being part of a marginalized racialized minority group:

> They just wanted to assimilate and fulfill that American dream. What were their struggles? No question was made [about their acceptance] in the 1970s and 1980s [Salinas]. There was hardly any struggle for them. They had houses, cars, [access to good] schools.[163]

Susan related her family history as a long, ongoing effort to overcome obstacles of both class and race: "My dad was just a teenager with no education. My mother was a little more fortunate she went to a little bit of college, but she came from a very, very poor family and was the only one that made it here. They worked hard at saving." After she graduated from college and returned to Salinas to work, she still identified mostly with the people she grew up with:

> I wanted to come back to the community because I related more to the families. I didn't think I would fit in with an upper class. South Salinas was known for all the doctors and professionals. I didn't grow up with that, and I liked being with a working-class community.[164]

Susan described her early years as a young student in Alisal as being first and foremost multicultural, but she was also uniquely privileged in large part because of the efforts of Virginia Rocca Barton who became a champion of education in that community and a strong advocate for Alisal generally: "It was very mixed when I was growing up. I went to Barton school when Virginia Rocca Barton was superintendent. There were Chinese, Japanese, whites from Oklahoma, and a few Mexicans. The 1950s were a surge of Filipinos." Susan described a warm, supportive school environment in which students of all ethnicities thrived—so much so that she was determined to become a schoolteacher herself: "Alisal School District was in the forefront of education in those days." She described Virginia Rocca Barton as a powerful figure who drove policies that supported the multiracial community:

[She] invited all the diversity. She had ethnic nights and people would bring potlucks. There was a precursor of gifted program. . . . It gave us the confidence that we were not only special but had the potential. There was a piano in every room. We had music teachers, art teachers. Our teacher taught us Spanish. I went on to major in Spanish with her influence. They were the ones who steered me in that direction. I became a teacher too.[165]

As a student at Salinas High School, Susan recalled a multiracial mix: "I had friendships from a mixed grouping. Our class was really big, about 560. There was a little bit of separation by class, but all the guys were into sports. Some of the girls too. It was a good time. I socialized with the Louises, the Wongs, the Gins," she said naming Chinese American students.[166] During the 1950s and until the mid-1960s, all of Salinas's students of high school age attended Salinas High, which functioned much as it always had in bringing Salinas's diverse communities together, just as Bill Ramsey, Jim Gattis, Everett Alvarez, and other narrators remembered about high school life from the 1940s. "High school was pivotal," remembered Susan Aremas, using language similar to the Dust Bowl kids of the 1930s and 1940s. "It was an exciting time. People ran for class offices. Our group was pretty involved and active . . . in campus organizations, football games, all the activities." After college and teacher training at San José State, Susan returned to her community:

I wanted to teach at Bardin [her alma mater], but they didn't have any positions . . . but Mrs. Barton called and found a position for me at Fremont [also in the Alisal School District] and that's how I got my job. I taught twenty-seven years at Fremont and six years at Creekside [which was in a more middle-class area of Salinas outside of Alisal].[167]

Susan Aremas's account thus emphasized that in her view the Filipino/a American community of Salinas had expanded and solidified its presence in the postwar years. Salinas remained a place defined by diversity of population, notably by Asian American communities that had become replenished and reinvigorated, but it was also more complicated by new migrations in the postwar era.

Still, the biggest changes in life for Salinas residents came about with the annexations of land, especially of Alisal in 1963, and with the civil rights and environmental rights movements of the 1970s. Both led to huge dislocations in city life, serious intercity conflicts that had lasting effects, and a new political order in Salinas that threatened the racial status quo that had existed since the 1870s.

PART III

Accommodations

Power and Pragmatism, 1965 to the Present

FIGURE 7.1   César Chávez at a UFW rally in the Salinas Valley, circa 1970

CHAPTER 7

Expansion, Activism, and Civil Rights

THE COMITY THAT SALINAS RESIDENTS had carefully constructed in the first hundred years of incorporation broke apart in the 1960s and 1970s as battles over expansion, environment, and labor exposed fissures in both intergroup and intragroup relations. Although residents claimed that all were welcome as members of the community, the proposed annexations of the 1960s showed the disdain Salinas residents had for residents of Alisal. Environmental activists from the Anglo American community clashed with business owners (sometimes within the same family), over clean air, clean water, and industrialization. The Chicano/a civil rights movement, centered as it was on farmworker issues, pitted growers, shippers, and Salinas residents of all racial groups against fieldworkers and activists, who also represented all racial and ethnic communities in town.

ANNEXATION OF ALISAL

"It was after the war that people started discovering Salinas. That was when Valley Center was developed. And then second was Sherwood Gardens," recalled Ruth Andresen, a Stanford-educated geologist who arrived in Salinas in 1952 as the wife of a prominent obstetrician. Born in 1920, she marked the establishment of both shopping centers as a turning point for the city's growth in the 1950s, but in her view the real "benchmark" for Salinas was the construction of the Salinas Valley Memorial Hospital, "the best hospital for the whole county [and] the most modern one between San Francisco and Santa Barbara. It was state of the art."[1]

The new library in the heart of downtown by "world renowned architect" Welton Becket also symbolized Salinas's postwar transformation into a modern municipality. It was a collective effort "sponsored by the Salinas Women's Club . . . [and] public support. Everybody was right behind that new library, the best, the first and the only," in Monterey County and the region.[2] The architect explained in remarks celebrating the library's official opening that "the design of the building was to conform with the shape of the valley: flat and wide at the front and tapering at the back," signifying a sensitivity to Salinas as strongly identified with landscape and place in the region.[3]

The economic indices validated Ruth Andresen's perception that the postwar was transformational, marking a significant turning point in Salinas's identity and growth. By the end of January 1947, the city had annexed both the Rodeo Tract (182.40 acres) and the Monterey Park Tract (80 acres), which included both residential and business areas with plans to subdivide the sections for housing and business development.[4] A few years later, Salinas Mayor E. J. Raffeto made a strong argument for annexation and consolidation of other unincorporated areas surrounding the city, increasingly centers of population growth: "The advantages of a strong community, tied together for maximum effectiveness, far outweigh the small costs resulting to taxpayers for annexation. If this area is to grow industrially, we must present a united front to those businesses we are asking to locate here."[5] Raffeto was referring to the annexation of Alisal, which had become an important subdivision of the county. By the end of the 1940s, the tax benefits of annexing areas around the city appeared to far outweigh the costs of building infrastructure that supported populations of working classes who lived there.

The goal for city planners, government officials, and residents alike remained consistent: ensure that Salinas was the urban center of the entire Central Coast region. "[Salinas] became the trading and merchandising center for an area that extended beyond the artificial county boundaries . . . [and assumed] a hub position," according to an economic analysis of the city.[6] Although economic analyses credited agriculture for Salinas's wealth and status, studies also emphasized that agricultural production alone could not support a strong economy year-round. The annexation of agricultural lands for industrial development and housing proved problematic, however:

Since the Second World War, Salinas's growth has spread rapidly into the surrounding green fields. The encroachment of subdivisions upon rich agricultural soils is a cause of concern to the produce industry, which depends on the products of those soils. The produce industry is the industrial backbone of Salinas, and any substantial weakening of it will have serious consequences.[7]

The issue became increasingly contentious as downtown merchants joined farmers and ranchers who clashed with city officials over land use. Under the auspices of the "Greater Salinas Committee," an election was held November 1947 to annex the area south of Main Street, which became Valley Center, which Ruth Andresen mentioned. The mayor and city council wanted to annex this area because it was increasingly being developed anyway, but without annexation the city lost tax revenue when new residential, commercial, and business development used city services but did not pay city taxes.[8] In a veiled reference both to growers, who opposed annexation of even marginal agricultural land, and to the vocal merchants along Main Street, who feared that new shopping developments like Valley Center would siphon business from them, the proponents of annexation argued, "We must not let less than 2% of property owners stop the growth of Salinas." With slogans such as "Zoning Is Not a Tool to Be Employed in Economic Conflict!" the group convinced Salinas voters that annexation and subsequent development would reduce taxes for everyone, increase property values, and add to Salinas's prestige. "New, fine, highly restricted, and beautifully developed" housing was also planned on newly acquired land. The measure passed.

The use of the term "highly restricted" was meant to convey that neighborhoods would continue to be racially segregated.[9] J. Morgan Kousser examined real estate advertisements in Monterey County, from the 1940s through the 1970s, to investigate the extent to which cities in the county restricted housing by race.[10] He found evidence of systemic, purposeful racial restrictions that led to the creation of politically, socially, and economically unequal spaces. According to Kousser, Anglo Americans settled primarily in Monterey, Carmel, Pacific Grove, and Pebble Beach and enjoyed a high degree of socioeconomic mobility and political power. Nearby Marina and Seaside struggled at the lower end of the political and economic spectrum as primarily places where African Americans, Asian Americans, and some Mexican Americans lived. Isolated from these other peninsula communities geographically, although still the county seat and urban center of the region, Salinas presented a more complicated, even haphazard settlement pattern. In Salinas, Kousser found evidence of multiracial tracts and neighborhoods, as well as racially restricted subdivisions, even in Alisal. He also found plenty of neighborhoods and subdivisions, even in wealthier parts of Salinas, that were unrestricted by race and that increasingly made room for people of Asian and Mexican descent if they could afford to live there.[11] There was only a tiny population of African Americans in Salinas, confined as they mostly were to Seaside and Marina in the postwar era.[12]

In Kousser's study of Salinas, homes were advertised as "beautiful" or "attractive" and "modern" when they were in a "restricted subdivision" or a "restricted district or tract." One Salinas realtor asked *Californian* readers, "Would you like a really nice five bedroom modern home, located on a corner lot in a *restricted* district in Alisal surrounded by other nice homes?" (emphasis added). Over and over again in Kousser's study, realtors emphasized the attractiveness of homes located in all-white neighborhoods, tracts, and subdivisions, including in the so-called multiracial space of Alisal.[13]

By contrast, places that were not racially restricted were advertised in less glowing terms as "a good buy" or that could "be sold to any nationality." One realtor offered a "4 room furnished house" for sale in the Boronda district of Salinas for a "small down payment." She was specific that "Mexicans and Filipinos can buy," implying that Mexican and Filipino/a people could not buy homes elsewhere. Another realtor advertising "lots in Alisal that might be subdivided [without] restrictions to Filipinos, Chinese or Mexicans." But in an ad for a new subdivision in the "beautiful Mission Park" subdivision of Salinas, the promotional literature promised, "The same restrictions will prevail here as in any other high class subdivision in the city [Salinas], racial restrictions, etc."[14]

By the 1950s, Salinas's Anglo American population made room in neighborhoods for some Chinese and Japanese families, even as they continued restrictions against Mexican Americans, African Americans, and Filipino/a Americans. For example, Dr. Harry Chong and Dr. Emma Dong lived in the prestigious Maple Park subdivision of Salinas, as discussed in Chapter 6, based on their status as members of the elite community of physicians, but other people of Chinese descent who were retail business owners were excluded from Maple Park.[15] Despite the prevailing racial restrictions of neighborhoods, Salinas residents saw themselves as progressive regarding race relations. The Interracial Council of Monterey County included Salinas residents who were "concerned with the problem of housing racial minorities." They organized a meeting, which included the showing of a 1945 Frank Sinatra film *The House I Live In*, that was notable for being one of the few Hollywood films to challenge racism. Local realtors were invited as part of the consciousness-raising campaign against racism in Salinas.[16]

Racial restrictions did not apply so much to business development, although Chinatown was an acknowledged Asian retail and professional center. Nonetheless, as Salinas expanded its retail footprint, race was far less a consideration in office and retail space than it was in housing. The area south of Main Street became part of the city in 1947 and inaugurated a new era of breathtaking expansion and development. In August 1947, developer R. T. Tustin Jr. broke ground for Valley Center, which included a Sears, J.C. Penney's, Lucky grocery store, and Thrifty drug store. According to the press, "The development [projected for completion by 1949] will have five acres of buildings, 15 acres of parking lots, and 55 acres of residences. . . . Novel features of the center when completed will be the day center and medical building . . . patterned in a small way after the Mayo and Scripps clinics."[17] Yet, those new shopping centers and industrial plants paled in significance to the annexation of Alisal.

As the city bolstered its self-image as the urban hub for the Central Coast, it needed to show population figures that might generate federal (and state) investment. That is why annexing Alisal assumed such strategic importance in the postwar era, and why it had been attempted (and failed) in 1949, 1950, and 1955 before finally succeeding with a 72 percent voter turnout in 1963.[18] Loss of the Wrigley chewing gum plant to Santa Cruz in 1950 was blamed on the failure to annex Alisal. In an editorial that referred to annexation as the unification of the communities of Salinas and Alisal, overlooking that these were unequal spaces, the *Salinas Californian* opinion page editor lamented that it was "Too bad . . . Salinas was not a united city [because] Wrigley may have come here instead of Santa Cruz, which IS united. . . . [T]hey sensed that Salinas was a split community not pulling together."[19] Touting the benefits of the company, the piece described Wrigley as "a beautiful concern—one that will employ 300 white clad, cosmetic free women. . . . It is the sort of good, clean factory we need and a payroll of $1,500,000," which insinuated that the "white clad" employees would also be white people of a respectable middle class ("cosmetic free"), rather than people of color or anyone who came from the gaudier-clad working classes that overused makeup.

The editor expressed hope that with the December 19, 1950 vote for annexation of Alisal, "We believe Salinas will be a big united city at the annexation election. . . . It must consolidate if we are to make progress. . . . Our 35,000 population in case the Alisal population is annexed would look mighty good in the record as new district offices, terminals, and warehousing for the west coast."[20] Population growth generally was considered an unqualified asset in the 1950s and 1960s that might draw lucrative businesses and industries to a given city and enhance its standing. These promotional pieces showed the way Salinas's residents aspired to be the central, major city in the Central Coast region.

Thus, by 1950 Salinas had drastically changed its attitude about Alisal. Once disdained for its chaotic settlement of "shacks" and marginal groups of mixed-race migrant laborers, the local and national press now enthusiastically described Alisal as "a community of neat, freshly painted homes . . . fronted by well-tended lawns . . . [and] distinctly an asset to the county."[21] Observers touted both evidence of upward mobility of former Dust Bowl refugees and also the sheer numbers: "Today more than 3500 of the 300,000 Depression and Dust Bowl refugees in California live in that community and their record is most reassuring. There is scarcely a case where a migrant . . . and his family . . . has not been able to make the grade," implying a middle- class, white population that would fit right into to the rest of the city socially. Analysts noted that the upward mobility of the migrants enriched the city too: "It is a matter of record that migrants into Salinas since 1933 have re-invested more than $100,000 of their earnings in permanent improvements."[22] A clearly defined community, Alisal boasted its own newspaper, the *East Salinas Pioneer,* and earned its own special section in the main Salinas newspaper, the *Salinas Index-Journal.* Alisal residents came together to organize the Alisal Civic Improvement Association, which added sidewalks, other infrastructure such as stop signs and street lighting, and established both a sanitary district and fire district. The Civic Improvement Association also purchased school buses and established a childcare center.

By 1946 the population of Alisal had increased to over 14,000 and the area included a theater, bank, and post office. Alisal residents also formed their own chamber of commerce in 1946.[23] Alisal's business and residential developments grew almost exponentially. The community thrived culturally and socially too. The Alisal school district hired teachers and administrators at a brisk pace and appropriated almost any available structure as classroom space. Alisal had become an attractive potential asset to Salinas, now almost equivalent to Salinas in both in population and business development. Joining the two communities through annexation drove political discussions throughout the 1950s. Although most Salinas residents favored annexation, most Alisal residents opposed it.

The top concern for Alisal residents debating annexation was how to effectively improve infrastructure, namely the sewer system, which was originally meant to serve a population of only a few thousand but had grown to 16,000 by 1950. The population needs for efficient waste disposal and clean water outstripped the capacity of the sewer system, but residents debated which entity (county, local residents, Salinas) might be the best choice in addressing the problem.

The independence of Alisal schools came in second out of a long list of concerns over annexation with Salinas. Alisal teachers feared that their tenure might be at risk if they were swallowed up by Salinas, and they also worried about equitable representation on the school board. In response, the state attorney general got involved in the tenure issue promising teachers that their tenure status was protected. "Tenure of teachers in the Alisal school district . . . was assured by the state attorney general and District Att[orne]y Burr Scott, legal advisor to all schools in Monterey County."[24] In the same article in the *Californian,* Alisal residents were guaranteed that their voices would be heard on the school board: "The Salinas city council will propose a charter amendment following annexation to increase the city school board from three to five members in order to assure representation of Alisal taxpayers and parents." The council made clear that elections would be held so that Alisal residents could vote on the amendment and run for election to the school board.[25]

The triumph of Alisal's school district in remaining independent of Salinas's jurisdiction came about because of the partnership between York Gin, a prominent member of Salinas's Chinese American community, and Virginia Rocca Barton, Alisal's preeminent educator and champion for Alisal students. Determined to protect Alisal students from being relegated to second-class status, Barton believed that Alisal's schools needed to remain self-governing. She was right to be worried. Alisal's forward-thinking bilingual education program, for example, was not going to be replicated in the Salinas schools, which privileged whites (especially those from elite agricultural families) and native English speakers.[26] Salinas schools showed both class- and race-based bias in teaching and in assessment of students.[27] Barton had the full backing and support of York Gin, whose Chinese American family roots in the area stretched back to the late nineteenth century and who had risen to prominence both within the Salinas Chinese American community and as president of Alisal's chamber of commerce and the school board. Gin recognized Barton's leadership capacity, plucking her out of the classroom first to appoint her as principal and then as superintendent of schools.

Barton arrived in Alisal as a newly minted teacher in 1940 where she taught fifth grade and inspired students and families with a combination of toughness and loving support for those at the margins of society. She embraced Dust Bowl students: "I was up and down the aisle letting them know how good they were. . . . [M]y number one goal was to make students feel important and worthwhile," she recalled, bristling at the term "dumb Okies," which is how Alisal kids were often referred to.[28] She could be a strong disciplinarian too. After one locally famous schoolyard fight among eighth grade boys, Barton called a meeting of all eighth graders and with her hands on her hips dared anyone who continued to engage in fist fighting to "fight with me." The students responded to the diminutive twenty-four-year-old's challenge with horror. "We wouldn't fight with you. We love you," one of the students replied. Her angry confrontation did not end the schoolyard skirmishes, but it did show how valued she was within the community.[29]

Barton showed an equal empathy for Latino/a students. In 1950, she set up a school for the 150 Latino/a children who lived in nearby McCallum Labor Camp. This included instituting a bilingual education program for students and teachers, which was one of the only initiatives of its kind in California.[30] At an Alisal school board meeting in 1953, someone asked, "Is it possible to teach a foreign language in the elementary school?" To which superintendent Virginia Rocca Barton replied, "Of course." Thus, in the Alisal school district, Spanish-language bilingual education became the norm, twenty years before activists or educators demanded it at the state level.[31] One teacher, Mildred Ramos, who helped to implement the new policy, recalled that the concept of teaching in Spanish came about purposefully, thoughtfully, and with a clear action plan. The 1953 initiative put "great stress . . . on acquiring a speaking vocabulary, on developing the correct pronunciation, intonation and inflection and all the other skills pertaining to oral communication." Ramos recalled how unpopular such a program was at the time, and how difficult it was to implement: "It wasn't easy," she remembered, "but then pioneering seldom is."[32] Ramos noted further that only five years after starting the program,

> It is not at all unusual to walk into a fifth-grade room at Alisal school in Salinas and find the children at the chalk-board doing simple arithmetical skills in Spanish. Likewise, the sixth grade teacher may be giving class room procedure in Spanish and the children responding to her instruction with admirable facility.[33]

Ramos published her assessment in an article in the November 1958 issue of the *California Teachers Association Journal*. In glowing terms, Ramos evaluated bilingual education as a success, carried out within a very short time frame— its benefits to students, teachers, and the community beyond dispute. She described happy classrooms and "astonishing results" that resulted almost immediately.[34]

By contrast, the principal of Salinas's Lincoln Elementary School, Josephine DiCarli, was described by former pupils as a "politically astute" administrator who "seeded most of . . . the towns' growers, doctors, lawyers, and Main Street businessmen . . . onto the academic track because of who our parents were." That meant that the children from working-class and non-English–speaking families were designated in "B" and "C" classes, rather than the "A" group, and they were given to understand that they were never going to achieve the professional and business success or high social status of their "A" group peers.[35] The Salinas public school system thus sustained an inequality that thousands of working-class and minority children contended with for the rest of their lives. Decades later, according to attorneys who challenged the tracking of minority students into second- and third-tier classes, Salinas and Salinas Valley's entire public school system policy were "tantamount to a life sentence of illiteracy and public dependency and a permanent stigma of inferiority."[36] Everett Alvarez Jr. did not feel particularly targeted by racism but acknowledged it nonetheless: "I didn't know any better. I never noticed anything. That was our world."[37]

Jim Gattis remembered being acutely aware of the class divides reflected in his life in Alisal and his view of Salinas as a boy: "[Alisal] was literally the other side of the tracks. . . . When I went to a friend's house [in Salinas] I was really impressed. I had never been in a house like that before." Everett supported Jim's perception of a great divide between Salinas and Alisal in which class and race intersected to create distinctive and unequal communities. Everett described Salinas as a "different world" that he experienced as a middle schooler venturing the "two to three miles from Pearl Street to downtown. Walking on Alisal Road, I crossed a slough and passed a flat lettuce field. Once you got past the railroad tracks there were sidewalks and gutters. Salinas was upper scale." He defined class in terms of the clothing he and his fellow students from Alisal wore: "We had one set of Levis and you'd wear them all year," in contrast to the "kids from Salinas [who] had nice cashmere sweaters and Dockers."[38]

Albert Fong, president of the Chinese Association of Salinas and vice president of the Chinese American Citizens Alliance, Salinas Chapter, whose family dated their settlement in Salinas to the late nineteenth century, noted that although Salinas and particularly Alisal were multiracial, racism was evident: "My family and friends were this group that had to get along with the whites and the Mexicans. . . . Yes, there was discrimination but you do what you can do to survive." His family were property owners and landlords: "We [bought] properties in Alisal and the older parts of Salinas."[39]

Everett Alvarez believed that sports served as a great equalizer for youth in Salinas: "We were athletic. I became part of the guys that played football and ran track. We were pretty much integrated. We all played sports, basketball, clubs, I hung out with the kids who played sports. We are friends to this day." He acknowledged, however, that "There were some parents who didn't let somebody date somebody." On the other hand, Everett offered the example of his friend Jerry Sun as evidence of a more open and inclusive racial environment in Alisal than in Salinas in the 1950s: "Jerry was part Filipino. He was athletic [and] the student body president. Mr. Popularity. I never thought twice about it. Married a white girl from Alisal."[40]

Everett made a clear distinction between the settled families who populated Alisal and the migrant farmworkers who lived in the labor camps:

If you continued going out East on Alisal Road it went out to a camp that had been built as a camp for Japanese families [who had been incarcerated there during the war]. After they had moved Japanese families [to Poston, Arizona] they converted the camp to housing for farmworkers. It

was different from the kids at camp McCallum. The kids from camp Mc-
Callum may have been discriminated against but we were not.

This was not true, as was evident in the Salinas school system and in the
housing restrictions, but Everett was correct that class and race intersected
so that discrimination was worse (and in his telling, more obvious) if one
came from a migrant family than if one came from the middle class like he
did. He recalled teenage girls from migrant families placed in elementary
school for the short period of time they lived in Salinas, working in the fields
with their families and marrying young with little or no education. Many
other Salinas residents with roots in Alisal echoed Everett's account of the
place as a multicultural and multiracial space with important divisions along
class lines both between Alisal and Salinas and within the city of Salinas.

Although residents of Salinas perceived the annexation of Alisal as a good
outcome for everyone, and were generally oblivious to their own classist and
racist bias, Alisal residents had good reasons to be skeptical of the alliance
as fundamentally unequal. The Salinas City Council needed to sweeten the
deal to "join communities," as proponents often called annexation, if they
wanted the residents of Alisal to vote in their favor. They offered up a wide
range of city services that Alisal residents might benefit from if they voted
to become part of Salinas rather than incorporate as a city unto themselves
or remain under county control as an unincorporated space. The language
of "joining communities" signified an effort to showcase a changed attitude
on the part of Salinas's residents and leadership—an acknowledgement of
equality despite decades of scorn that Salinas residents had inflicted on
residents of Alisal based on race and class.

It was good economics for Salinas to expand the city's boundaries. By
1950, according to reports in the *Salinas Californian*, Salinas would receive
almost $100,000 (equivalent to $1 million in today's dollars) in state grants
and subventions "if the two communities joined forces." In addition, based
on a population increase of approximately 17,000, "the state would grant an
additional $50,000 from the motor vehicle in lieu tax and $46,000 from the
gas tax fund."[41] The annexation of Alisal finally happened on June 11, 1963,
with a vote of 1,748 to 648. It marked the moment that Salinas defined itself
as a metropolitan center too. "We couldn't remain so close to Salinas and
not be part of an incorporated city," argued Sally Gutierrez, one proponent
of incorporation and organizer of the "Right Way, Alisal" campaign.[42]

In 1963, when the initiative to annex Alisal finally passed, the City of Salinas added 1,119 acres of land to its footprint (it would now be 7,067 acres) and $13 million in assessed valuation (making its new assessed worth $84 million). Its population added 16,500 new residents, totaling 47,700 and nearly doubling the population.[43] The investment promise Salinas city leaders made to Alisal in the 1960s included expensive infrastructure projects such as new sewer systems, improved streets and safety initiatives, more libraries and public schools, to name only a few—all of which needed to be maintained over time. These initiatives were widely advertised in the years leading up to annexation and contributed greatly to Alisal residents' vote to join Salinas rather than remain an unincorporated part of Monterey County or incorporating as a city themselves.

Immediately following the vote to "join communities," Salinas's council members and staff felt intense pressure to follow through on their promises, routinely proposing various new tax measures at meetings, such as the 5 percent tax on utilities in June 1969 (opposed by local industry and the Grower-Shipper Association).[44] Almost every city council meeting after 1963 included discussion and support for infrastructure and development in Alisal and on the east side of town, although little of it actually happened due to competition for resources from other areas of Salinas and the fiscal restrictions of the shrinking economy of the 1970s.

INDUSTRIAL EXPANSION AND ENVIRONMENTALIST RESPONSE

By the end of the 1960s and with the annexation of Alisal completed, Salinas was promoted as the Central Coast's urban hub. The city officials not only expanded its footprint but began aggressively marketing its geographic location. Built on a vast wide and flat plain with plenty of water, and without contiguous borders with any other municipality (still unique in the nation for a city of its size), Salinas appeared to be the perfect spot for industrial development. Under the auspices of the Monterey County Industrial Development (MCID) Committee, Salinas's business community enticed industry into the newly annexed outskirts of town.

Most importantly, annexations and increased population made a compelling case for federal and state investment in highways and infrastructure in Salinas and Monterey County.[45] The nonagricultural industries that located within city limits not only added to Salinas's tax base but also offered employment opportunities and encouraged new, middle-class settlement in the city for middle-level managers. These new residents would become the clientele for professionals in Salinas, including Ruth Andresen's obstetrician husband. All this growth happened at a remarkable pace between 1950 and 1970.[46]

At first, the new investment, development, and people appeared only as an asset. Numerous articles in the local press breathlessly announced every new industrial and manufacturing plant that located in the vicinity of the city, claiming to invigorate city coffers with new tax revenue. For example, when Pacific Lincoln Laboratories chose to make Salinas its West Coast headquarters, its representative listed five reasons for doing so: "Transportation services . . . climate . . . central location of Salinas in relation to major markets . . . reception by the members of the [Salinas] Chamber of Commerce industrial committee [Monterey County Industrial Development] . . . proximity to the Monterey Peninsula."[47] Indeed it appeared that Salinas would take advantage of every aspect of its location, including the vast, still vacant surrounding landscape that allowed huge industrial plants the room to build and expand.[48]

The working-class population that increasingly defined the city needed employment throughout the year and, most importantly, needed an avenue into the middle-class world of home and business ownership that Salinas offered. Olga Reyna Garcia explained how important those new employment and housing opportunities were to families who had labored for years as migrant workers and how promising Salinas appeared to them:

> My parents, Ismael Reyna and Juanita Serbantez, decided to come to Salinas because . . . they wanted us to stop traveling. . . . There was plenty of work, we didn't have to move around. My elder sisters worked at nurseries. Dad got a job at Firestone. The possibilities were plenty. The valley was beautiful and we liked it here.[49]

The chance for migrant workers to move out of the agricultural fields and into year-round, stable employment enticed Olga's family as much as it did the middle-level managers who were also moving into Salinas.

There was a dark side to the industrial expansion, however, that met unexpected resistance from mostly white, middle-class women in Salinas whose husbands brought the industries to the city in the first place. Industry came with a cost to the environment, which sparked environmental activism at the local level. In Salinas, this activism was led by Ruth Andresen. She recalled that the support for unbridled growth and industrial development ended in the early 1960s in the context of a nationwide awareness of the severe consequences of pollution, brought about by such publications as Rachel Carson's *Silent Spring* (1962).

Ruth described the air in Salinas with acerbic wit and irony: "When you get up in the morning, you had the most delightful chocolate wind [emanating from the Nestlé and Peter Paul plants]." Although Salinas boasted good regulatory control, according to Ruth, "The air pollution people [tried] to get industry to clean up, but it costs money to put [in] filters and scrubbers." Industrial leaders understood the need for a clean environment, but it would adversely affect profits, which discouraged compliance. As Ruth explained, "to get excess money out of the budget when it wasn't absolutely required . . . well that's a business decision so you don't do it if you are going to keep your profit margin." As long as compliance with regulation remained voluntary, it did not happen. She recalled, "These agencies were all doing a good job but they didn't have any enforcement arm."[50]

The air pollution was bad enough, but the threat of an oil refinery coming to Monterey Bay generated a wave of controversy in Salinas and the entire Monterey Peninsula in 1965. This news led to a full-scale uprising in support of the environmental movement led by Ruth Andresen and a significant cohort of mostly Anglo American, middle-class Salinas women, as was the case in the rest of the nation where fights for clean water generated new waves of activism. On the Monterey Peninsula, oceans and polluting fisheries had been a point of contention for decades.[51]

According to Ruth, when the Humble Oil Company decided to build the refinery near Moss Landing, Salinas residents feared the worst—not just the threat of oil spills but also deteriorating air quality, which was already severely and negatively impacted by the industries in operation. As a geologist, Ruth was well prepared to explain such complex processes as wind and ocean currents and how an accidental oil spill at sea might damage community life all over Monterey County. She began giving community lectures on wind and ocean currents throughout Salinas and the county to generate support for environmental activism that would be needed to counter the power of business and industry:

It was an educational process. . . . People did not relate that the smoke coming out of Firestone had anything to do with dirty curtains. Then there was always this idea that if you wanted to get rid of something you dumped it in the ocean. The fact that these currents sometimes just turn around and bring everything back on shore came as a big shock.[52]

Ruth's work inspired groups of women to organize and resist, and they focused on the oil refinery.

Businessmen might have been concerned about the environment too, but they remembered the Great Depression and were determined to ensure full employment through industrial development come what may. They prioritized anything that might avoid another economic catastrophe "They went from war and distress to [employment] and all of a sudden their first home," Ruth explained, by way of rationalizing the work of the Monterey County Industrial Development Committee in attracting any and all industry to Salinas, including the refinery. Still, their wives, who came from polluted eastern cities, were willing to challenge their husbands so as not to repeat those mistakes in their adopted homes in California. Ruth recalled:

It was homemakers that didn't want to live in a soiled environment. So many of these people had come from eastern cities where they had coal and they had refineries and they remembered in their childhood what the condition of those cities was like. I remember sulfur dioxide and the smell of rotten eggs from Tulsa. The ones from Pennsylvania and those urban areas just were beside themselves with the threat of refineries coming right here.[53]

The proposed Humble Oil Company refinery would produce 50,000 barrels of oil a day. The danger was that the oil had to be transported by means of a "heated pipe to the refinery on the shore. Now can you imagine how many oil spill potentials there were?" Ruth posited. Moreover, the refinery would exacerbate poor air quality, already damaged by industry: "In the Salinas Valley the wind blows down the valley during the day and at night when the ground cools the wind blows up the valley and out to the ocean. With that unfiltered smoke coming out of the refinery the Salinas Valley would never have had a clean breath of air."[54] Ruth's vivid clarification of how the refinery was a disaster in the making created a movement in Salinas.

The battle lines were sharply drawn between MCID and the women activists with the Salinas Women's Club, the American Association of University Women (AAUW), the Medical Auxiliary for the Monterey County Medical Society, the Salinas Civic Women's Club, and the Salinas Business and Professional Women's Club—a who's who of middle-class, mostly white women's organizations that formed the backbone of Salinas's civic culture. They were joined by book clubs, craft clubs, and ethnic women's organizations in town.

The refinery needed the approval of the Monterey County Board of Supervisors, which led to an angry exchange at the meeting on September 3, 1965. Ruth Andresen described the process:

> We had a terrible fight to deny the refinery . . . [At first,] the Planning Commission turned down the application to develop [a refinery] and then it went to the Board of Supervisors and that's when we got all the people out to testify. . . . The hearing went on for thirteen hours and it didn't break until 3 o'clock in the morning. They put loudspeakers around the whole courthouse so everybody could listen. You couldn't get into the Chambers it was so mobbed. Nonetheless, the Board of Supervisors approved [the refinery] 3 to 2.[55]

The women did not give up, however, and began to collect signatures to appeal the decision. When that failed, the women resorted to economic pressure. "We had everybody cut up their credit cards for the gas company and send them to Standard Oil," Ruth recalled. The women's goal was to become enough of a nuisance that the company would give up. Their strategy worked. "The refinery ended up at Benicia where they have had continual trouble ever since. We won. We were such a deterrent that when the EPA started enforcing the smoke scrubbers to be put on P. G. & E., they [PG & E] did it because they knew they would get protests if they didn't."[56] Ruth's environmental activism defined what environmentalism looked like in the 1960s and 1970s. It was white; middle class; led and powered by women in cities and suburbs across the United States; laser focused on clean air, clean water, and clean energy.[57]

Environmental activism in Salinas occurred in a much larger context of vigorous activism in general across the nation. It was an era of national rights movements, mainly African American civil rights but also anti-war protests, feminist rights, and gay rights, all of which had a tremendous impact on life in California, whose citizens often led and defined those rights movements. Furthermore, in California, civil rights activism was not limited to the struggle of African Americans but also, and importantly, included activism of multiple Asian groups and Mexican Americans.[58] Mexican American civil rights activists predominated in agricultural communities such as Salinas. Their battles made purposeful connections between labor rights and racial justice. According to the *Salinas Californian* in its end-of-year assessment of the most newsworthy events in the city, "The 1970 news year in the Salinas Valley was dominated by a complex, emotionally-charged farm labor unionization struggle [that] kept the Salad Bowl of the Nation on the front pages. And it's not over yet."[59] The newspaper was referring to the efforts of the United Farmworkers Organizing Committee (UFOC, later changed to UFW) led by César Chávez and Dolores Huerta, both of whom had family roots as fieldworkers and in civil rights before coming to Salinas. Their activism has been explored and analyzed by a range of scholars who are in dispute about the successes and failures of Chávez and Huerta but are unanimous that their work had a truly historic and significant impact on the collective consciousness of Americans.[60] The UFW was bigger than Salinas. As numerous scholars observed, it became international in its scope.

CIVIL RIGHTS AND LABOR RIGHTS

On July 24, 1970, César Chávez demanded that growers recognize his union (UFW) as the sole representative for all fieldworkers in the Salinas Valley. However, three days later Chávez learned that most growers had already signed contracts with the Western Conference of Teamsters. Olga Reyna Garcia described the pressure workers felt to join the International Brotherhood of Teamsters Union, which she characterized as a company union: "The company asked us to sign up to work under the Teamsters or not come back the next day. Most of the workers were living in company housing so they had to do what the company said," she recalled. One member of the Grower-Shipper Association who participated in the collective bargaining with César Chávez explained, "We were trying to negotiate a labor contract, but every time we came to an agreement, they [ratcheted] things up. They didn't want a business deal, they wanted social revolution."[61] He was correct. The UFW was not merely trying to raise wages and improve working conditions; they were also trying to energize Mexican Americans and to lift people up from what they perceived as their place at the bottom of the social order—not just in the city of Salinas but also in California and the nation too.[62]

At first, many Salinas residents were perplexed that civil rights for Mexican Americans became defined by the labor battles of farmworkers. Most Salinas residents were connected to agriculture in some form or another and perceived labor rights as a business issue separate from civil rights and anti-racism. They felt unfairly targeted by the UFW. "Fieldworkers were such a small part of the agricultural system in Salinas and the Salinas Valley," argued Ruth Andresen, who now found herself on the establishment side of the activist struggle. "Chávez was a thorn in the side of multiple businesses," she claimed. "All of them were interdependent. The strikes and boycotts affected all of them and everyone lost. The UFW strikes had a domino effect on this city. . . . It wasn't just the man with the hoe."[63] It was arguable whether everyone lost. Most Mexican American residents of Salinas felt empowered by the UFW. The civil rights battles of the 1970s brought a new set of political actors into leadership positions in Salinas and gave Mexican American residents a general sense of pride and purpose.

Olga Reyna Garcia was still a teenager when the UFW came to Salinas under the direction of Dolores Huerta and César Chávez. Like so many other Latino/as in the city, this civil rights movement deeply impacted her and affected her choices and outlook for the rest of her life. Olga had recently graduated from high school in 1970, but like so many of her cohort, instead of college, "we continued to work in the fields with no other thoughts of leaving."[64] It was difficult, mind-numbing labor. Olga described her work for a cauliflower company and in the strawberry fields:

> [W]e didn't pick much. Salaries were low conditions were hard. Companies didn't have restrooms, everyone drank from the same cup (a cut up metal can with a wire handle). No breaks. Lunch was taken in the field among the rows of cauliflower. . . . [But the UFW offered hope.] We started hearing announcements about our right to have a union and a better lifestyle with clean working conditions and many other changes. They would always finish by saying "Sí Se Puede, Viva César Chávez!"[65]

Olga noted that the UFW events were festive affairs with music, dancing, and speeches, and she reported that Chávez treated workers as equals: "He

[Chávez] would always call us compañeros, he would include himself as a campesino and people were attentive." She was particularly impressed that a woman, Dolores Huerta, took a leadership position in the movement. "Dolores Huerta . . . spoke to the crowds in the same spirit as César Chávez . . . [she] could negotiate a contract herself. She has won the respect of many. She was the backbone of the movement! Viva Dolores Huerta!"[66]

After efforts at compromise failed, Chávez declared war on both the Teamsters and the growers: "The [Salinas] Valley's roads blossomed with the red and black strike banners of thousands of UFOW pickets."[67] Olga joined the fight. "The Salinas Valley strike was on," she remembered with a feeling of having made the right decision. "The time was right. Those were times we just knew we were doing the right thing." She considered César Chávez "a great leader" because of his advocacy of nonviolence. The strikers were frequently attacked by both Teamsters and Salinas residents who were angry about the unrest, but they were instructed to refrain from fighting back. "When we were attacked, we could not fight back, violence would beget violence."[68]

Lucy Pizarro glowed when remembering César Chávez: "He made us feel proud. A lot of people came here because they knew he made things better for workers. We had benefits and higher wages because of him,"[69] she said. Phyllis Meurer, an Anglo American who later served on the Salinas City Council, recalled being "awed" by the "vast sea of red and black flags people waved" that symbolized the UFW at an outdoor gathering in August 1970 at Hartnell College that drew a crowd of more than 3,000. She felt inspired by the changes in the works that the new and newly energized arrivals to Salinas seemed to promise.[70]

Others in Salinas remembered the times differently, however, and vividly recalled being attacked and chased out of the fields by striking workers. The *Salinas Californian* described the situation in the fields as akin to "combat conditions." Jack Armstrong, born and raised in Salinas and a descendant of several of Salinas's founding families, noted with consternation how César Chávez and the farmworker movement not only upended the city's identity in the most profound and public way but also appeared to come out of nowhere. In a reference to Larry Itiliong and the strikes in Delano in Kern County, led by Filipino/a Americans between 1965 and 1970, he recollected how surprised everyone was when the UFW arrived in Salinas: "We were blindsided by Chávez. Delano seemed so far away."[71] For most white Salinas residents like Jack Armstrong, but also for the multiple Asian American communities in Salinas, César Chávez hit the city like a sledgehammer in 1970. "He started with the grape harvest you know. . . . It felt like civil war. It was bad. It was very bad," Ruth Andresen remembered.[72]

Ruth recalled a cruise she took to Alaska during the tumultuous period of the 1970s. She was enjoying the spectacular scenery with a group of fellow travelers when she made what she considered to be an innocent conversation starter. "This salad reminds me of home," she told the group she was lunching with. When asked where home was, she replied, "The Salinas Valley, 'salad bowl for the world!'" To her horror she was met with a verbal assault on Salinas generally and herself personally as "despicable" for the mistreatment of farmworkers. Ironically, her fellow tablemates came from Chicago, where civil rights activists, including Dr. Martin Luther King Jr., had recently been stoned as they marched peacefully through the city to protest racial injustice.

Ruth was too shocked to reply to these Chicagoans, although she remembered that the "abuse continued after I left the table." She avoided them for the rest of the trip, but the incident stayed with her, filling her with indignation that Salinas and its people had been so badly misrepresented. To Ruth (and to many other non-Latino/a residents of Salinas), it felt like a drumbeat of unfair and negative media accounts had painted the whole city in the worst possible light as a consequence of labor issues, perhaps even permanently damaging its reputation as an attractive destination for families and businesses.[73] She and other narrators blamed Chávez for showcasing racism, invisible to most whites. Many Salinas residents believed that civil rights and labor rights were being wrongly conflated in the UFW movement:

> Except for that Chávez there were no racial problems. We really disliked Chávez for what he was doing [and for being] disruptive. . . . He hit right at the peak of the harvest. Anyone who has put seeds in the ground had all their income taken from them by this rabble-rouser. They lost revenue. He hit when we were the most vulnerable.[74]

Yet, Chávez and other civil rights activists intended to disrupt a racial order that privileged whites at the expense of everyone else. That was the whole point of the movements of the 1970s.

On September 17, 1970, Chávez raised the stakes and called for a boycott of "all lettuce grown by Salinas based produce firms." On October 8, Superior Court Judge Gordon Campbell demanded that Chávez call off the boycott of Bud Antle farms or face jail time. Chávez refused to comply with the judge's ruling and was subsequently jailed. He became "the most celebrated prisoner in Monterey County history," according to the *Salinas Californian*. His arrest drew the attention and backing of civil rights advocates such as Coretta Scott King and Ethel Kennedy who endorsed Chávez and the UFW on national television and through widely disseminated interviews. Salinas Latino/a residents were proud to have such validation and support: "Incarcerating César, brought publicity and support. Ethel Kennedy was here in Salinas to speak with him personally. Those are memories that can't be forgotten," recalled Olga Reyna Garcia.[75] She remembered Chávez's dramatic arrest but also the embrace he received from the community: "Every night there would be candlelight vigils. An altar was set up, and there were people there with César Chávez. Teatro Campesino would perform skits and speakers always kept our spirits up."[76]

However, other Salinas residents remembered the moment less positively: "When Ethel Kennedy came to town, she brought the Catholic bishops with her and they stood on the back of the trucks at City Hall. There were some good Catholics in town that dropped their contributions then and there. It was a business issue. They felt it was mixing business and religion and it was blackmail. It wasn't a good scene," according to Ruth Andresen.[77] Ruth was referring to the involvement of the United States Bishops Committee on Farm Labor, whose chair, Bishop Joseph Donnelly, routinely sat in on negotiations between the UFW and growers.[78] She also captured the confusion of non-Latino/as who did not understand (much less share) the view that the UFW and Chávez were leading a necessary civil rights movement. This was most often expressed as a comparison with the Teamsters: "The Teamsters are a trade union. Chávez's group is a civil rights movement,"[79] said one unnamed representative of the GSA, stating the obvious. Numerous interviews with members of the GSA who had participated in the negotiations reinforced their collective condemnation of the UFW as fomenting a (repugnant) social revolution rather than negotiating a good faith labor contract.[80] Ruth Andresen noted that the aim of the GSA was to maintain control: "They [GSA] would meet with workers but not the UFW. They wanted to control their workers is what the truth of it was, rather than have an intermediary like Chávez."[81]

Chávez's choice of Salinas was fortuitous for the union, at least in the short term, as Lori Flores made clear in her analysis of the Mexican immigrant and Mexican American experience in the Salinas Valley. By the time Chávez arrived, according to Flores, Mexican American activists were already successfully challenging inequality, largely through the organizing efforts of the women and men of the Salinas chapter of the Community Service Organization (CSO): "The 1970 strike was not an outburst of political consciousness and activity led by Chávez. Rather it was the outcome of years of work by men and women who believed they had grounds for dreaming."[82]

However, until the farmworker movement attracted a whole new population of Mexican American workers and activists to Salinas, the members of the CSO simply did not have the numbers to mount an effective political challenge to the entrenched majority in Salinas. Membership in the UFW reached its peak in 1975 with almost 70,000 members statewide but then declined precipitously, so that its membership was only 20,000 by 1990, only to recover and increase again to over 50,000 by early 2000.[83] Matthew Garcia and other scholars credited the UFW and Chávez for important victories in Salinas, even as they failed to achieve the same gains elsewhere and eventually imploded as an effective labor union, due in large part to conflicts over strategy and Chávez's personality.[84]

For its part, the Grower-Shipper Association was organized, protective of its interests, and actively engaged in shaping legislation in its favor, but it was hardly a homogeneous entity. In fact, serious infighting during the labor crisis of 1970 led to defections and ostracism in the group, particularly with Bud Antle and the Antle corporation over his choice to sign with the Teamsters unbeknownst to the rest of the membership.[85] Increasingly, growers and shippers consolidated into mega-corporations rather than operate independently as they had done in the past.[86] Nunes Brothers Farms, for example, became part of the corporate giant Interharvest, which undercut Tom and Robert Nunes by signing a contract with the UFW behind their backs. It prompted both men to resign. According to Robert Nunes:

> We'd been running Interharvest for two years when United ordered the company to sign a contract with the United Farm Workers union. . . . [T]he company feared a boycott on its lucrative banana business. Tom and I disagreed. . . . We were told to either "go along or step aside." . . . We chose to step aside. I left my office in the morning.[87]

The brothers went on to found another agricultural firm, the Nunes Company, but their story showed that the growers and shippers in Salinas were beset by infighting as much as the UFW was. Neither group comprised a completely united front.[88]

As the produce industry developed throughout the 1970s, it became much more sophisticated and technologically oriented in crop production, but much less diverse in its workforce.[89] Whereas in the 1940s through the early 1960s mostly white Dust Bowl migrants, multiple groups of Asians (Chinese, Japanese, Filipino/a, and South Asian Americans), African Americans, and Mexican immigrants and Mexican Americans made up the workforce, by 1970, Mexican immigrants and Mexican Americans predominated in both the fields and in the packinghouses.[90] Much of the labor force was made up of undocumented workers from Mexico in the 1960s through the 1980s; this was the case despite obvious concern about legal status, because growers' feared labor shortages. Ben Lopez, employed by the GSA to serve as a liaison between workers and growers, routinely gave updates on labor issues and needs: "Ben Lopez reported there was a considerable shortage of labor about three weeks ago. . . . At the time of the shortage, from 450–500 people were available for day haul and last week there were 980. He expected another shortage to occur in September after the youngsters return to school."[91] The growers relied most heavily on Mexican immigrants, undocumented workers, and students on summer break to supply their labor force during the strikes.[92] Several GSA members introduced resolutions throughout the 1970s "evidencing our members' dislike of using any but U.S. citizens or Legal aliens for farm labor work."[93]

The GSA worked hard to get ahead of any state legislation that might curtail its power to control the labor force: "[The GSA] was of the opinion that the timing was right to prepare a bill that agriculture can live with rather than have organized labor submit a collective bargaining bill that agriculture cannot live with."[94] By the end of the 1960s, growers, shippers, and other members of the GSA in Salinas tried to circumvent direct confrontations with workers that might lead to a breakdown and to a strike by advocating a series of initiatives meant to address the most pressing needs of labor, such as the need for housing and unemployment insurance.

Growers understood the need for some supports, such as farmworker housing, but struggled with the details and often denied culpability when confronted with the horrific living conditions for workers and their families.[95]

Their response to a request for temporary housing showed their effort to collaborate with city, state, and federal governments to respond to the pressing need for worker housing:

> The Monterey County Housing Authority . . . secure[d] approval for 100 units with heaters to be built in King City next year. Such units are available for six-month periods to farm workers with the opportunity of being extended 2 or 3 weeks . . . it might be better to build one-fourth the number of houses and have them solidly built for year-round use. In view of the fact that the project is in motion, the Board [considered] it advisable to support it in principle with the addition that we recommend more permanent housing . . . we support housing.[96]

However, nonprofits rather than the GSA or government agencies stepped into the void in Salinas to solve the housing issue. The persistent efforts by farmworkers and their families to obtain land and settle permanently in Salinas showed that their struggle went well beyond labor organizing. Like every other group that came before them, Latino/a families meant to claim space in Salinas in the 1970s and become integral members of the community.[97] They focused on settlement and created the Community Housing Improvement Systems and Planning Association (CHISPA), which made housing availability and affordability their priority. CHISPA was originally composed of thirty-two families, led by Sixto Torres, which had spent the better part of the 1960s traveling to pick crops from Texas to the Pacific Northwest. This group was joined in the housing effort by other activists, such as Edward Moncrief—a former priest who had previously marched with Chávez but become disenchanted with the UFW's direction. California Rural Legal Assistance (CRLA) and the Central Coast Counties Community Development Corporation (CCCDC) provided both legal and technical assistance in transforming former labor camps into communal housing settlements and farms on the outskirts of the city. San Jerardo was the most famous of these enterprises that gave farmworker families housing and taught farming techniques. Through sheer force of will and persistence, these activists obtained a $1.8 million loan from the Farmers Home Administration (FmHA) in 1974 to rehabilitate former labor camps on the outskirts of town, where Dust Bowl families and Braceros once resided, and turn them into permanent housing; the families moved into their new homes in 1978.

San Jerardo happened over the objections of agriculturalists, however, who wanted to use the labor camps as farmland, but the fieldworkers succeeded in claiming space and securing permanent homes and landownership, both of which defined what it meant to belong in Salinas.

CHISPA gave farmworkers access to housing, and with that, a permanent stake in Salinas as community members. The association built and renovated 2,268 single-family homes and apartments in Salinas and surrounding areas and has become one of the largest private, nonprofit housing developers in the region. According to Torres, "It's real. . . . If you can put a family into a decent home, you've changed their lives forever. The parents are proud. The children grow up in a stable environment. What's the alternative . . . people doubling up in garages, ten individuals on a crowded floor?"[98]

Besides housing, farmworkers needed job security. The GSA also tried to answer those demands with a proposal for unemployment insurance. On March 3, 1969, the Salinas GSA voted unanimously to "endorse in principle the theory of extending Unemployment Insurance to [all] agricultural workers as expressed in the proposed bill by Alan Patee."[99] This was an initiative meant to counter the lawsuit by California Rural Legal Assistance (CLRA) filed against Harden Farms by employees Antonio Dorado and Ramon Romero to force Harden Farms to pay unemployment insurance. Again, small initiatives such as these did not so much solve the bigger problem but paper over it.

On the other hand, safety issues did not extend to concerns over the impact of pesticides on the health of fieldworkers, at least not in the 1970s. The GSA fought against the imposition of any legislative restrictions on pesticide use. In the 1970s this meant DDT, which was then considered essential in crop production: "On June 19th [1969] John Marcroff of D'Arrigo Bros. Co. of California and Joe Jensen of Merrill Farms went to Sacramento [on behalf of GSA] to present testimony to the Senate Agricultural Committee Hearing in opposition to three DDT Bills."[100] However, former fieldworkers remembered harsh working conditions that included contact with pesticides. "We would receive the effects of the planes spraying the fields with pesticides," Olga Reyna Garcia related in something of an understatement. It became a matter of record that new housing developments and elementary schools in minority neighborhoods in Salinas, as well as the vegetable fields where fieldworkers labored, were routinely exposed to dangerous levels of pesticides. However, this issue did not stimulate the same vigorous resistance from Salinas's environmentalists that industrial pollution or the threat of the oil refinery had previously; this was because the pesticide issue had become too heavily identified with the Chicana/o civil rights movement, which many environmentalists opposed.[101] For their part, the UFW continued their efforts to improve the lives of fieldworkers, including establishing the Clinica de Salud del Valle de Salinas, which provided primary care and dental services to farmworkers.[102]

Alongside these efforts to ameliorate conditions for farmworkers, members of the GSA were focused on eliminating their dependence on large numbers of workers by developing cutting-edge scientific and technological advances into the growing and marketing of agricultural products through partnerships with universities in California.[103] Almost every meeting in the 1970s included discussion of collaboration with the University of California, Davis, as part of a strategy to remain technologically forward-looking in planting, harvesting, shipping, and marketing as well as choosing crops that needed less labor. On July 14, 1970 the GSA unanimously approved an investment of $100,000 for research (the equivalent of over $700,000 today).[104]

Innovation in technology on the part of growers and shippers effectively undercut the UFW. One attorney and negotiator for the GSA, Terrence O'Connor, explained that although the UFW and other unions succeeded in forcing wage increases for farmworkers, the higher production costs for growers inspired them to make important technological advances limiting the need for human labor in favor of machines and robotics, although many forms of agricultural production would always require a human touch such as the picking of strawberries and the harvesting of tomatoes, both delicate crops.[105] According to O'Connor, unionized workers lost jobs, and growers and shippers fundamentally reorganized in the wake of the pressure brought on by the UFW and the advanced new technology that followed. The UFW responded to innovations in production by forcing an agreement that "no seniority workers will be displaced or lose work as a result of mechanization."[106] Yet, job losses due to technological advances were difficult for the UFW to fight against as they did not violate contract or subcontracting agreements, so could not be challenged on those grounds. Although the UFW had been able to successfully negotiate better contract deals for workers than the Teamsters had, the workers were not able to enjoy those gains because many agricultural jobs relating both to fieldwork and processing had been downsized and even eliminated.

The UFW was a civil rights organization more than a labor union, but that did not mean that other minorities in town supported its goals or strategies, however committed they were to civil rights. Asian American groups generally recoiled at the bluntness of UFW activists' demands for socioeconomic and political power, antithetical as this was to everything Salinas represented, which was a carefully constructed appearance of acceptance by the dominant Anglo American population based on an embrace of cultural diversity instead of political or economic power sharing or social inclusion. Salinas may have been a majority Anglo American city in terms of population makeup, but communities of Asian Americans (Chinese, Japanese, and Filipino/a Americans) as well as a small community of African Americans lived there too. Each community had its own agenda, its own complicated history, and its own trajectory by 1970—and these identities were at the same time tied into a larger identity with the town as a whole, as an agriculturally based urban center.[107]

Although many Salinas residents admired Chávez and the new movement on an individual basis, community leaders from the city's various ethno-racial groups pointedly did not weigh in publicly on either side, often denying even the existence of any structural racism in their city. Salinas's Filipino/a American residents divided over the UFW, and like their counterparts in the Japanese and Chinese American communities, either supported or disapproved of Chávez and the farmworkers as individuals but did not take a public stand either way as a community. Much of what Chávez advocated did not resonate for Filipino/a Americans in (or out) of agriculture by 1970. The foremen and contractors, who functioned as "field representatives" for growers and shippers, tended to join the Teamsters Agricultural Workers Organizing Committee (TAWOC) rather than the UFW, in part because of pressure from growers to do so, but also because the Teamster policies seemed more in line with foremen and contractors' interests. For example, the UFW wanted control over the hiring and firing of workers, but Filipino American foremen and contractors fought to maintain their authority over hiring practices as a critical tool in sustaining their own positions as the powerful intermediaries between workers and growers, which the Teamsters supported.[108]

In another example, the UFW fought fiercely to eliminate use of the *el cortito*, or the short-handled hoe, as a "back-breaker for farmworkers and not essential to effective hoeing and thinning of crops."[109] Filipino American foremen and contractors, however, considered the use of the hoe unimportant "and [did] not feel that the short-handled hoe has any relevance to them." In fact, contractors and foreman believed "the longer hoe will be less effective." Furthermore, Filipino/a American foremen and contractors felt that the whole issue of the short-handled hoe did not even concern them: "[The short-handled hoe] was for the Mexicans to worry about." They separated themselves from the UFW by claiming a higher status in the agricultural workforce that aligned more with growers than with fieldworkers and revealed their sense of superiority over Mexican American workers in their work ethic: "We are foreman now and we are out of it . . . the reason the Mexicans refuse to use it [the short-handled hoe] is because they are not really hard workers."[110]

As a result of the obvious disdain that Filipino American foremen and contractors expressed for Mexican fieldworkers and union organizers, the UFW accused Filipino foremen and contractors of engaging in "sweetheart contracts" that favored growers and "declared that [foreman and] labor contractors [were] inimical to the interests of laborers," a damning assessment that made clear that Salinas's middle-class Filipino/a American community would stand apart, at least as a group, from the battles of the UFW in spite of their proximity in organizing experience and shared history of oppression with Mexican American fieldworkers throughout California.[111]

As a student at San José State in the late 1960s, Susan Aremas, a Filipina American, became involved in the Filipino/a civil rights struggle and took issue with the prominence given to Chávez, Huerta, and other leaders of the farmworker movement who eclipsed those in the Filipino/a American community: "It wasn't César Chávez at the helm," Susan contended. "It was the Filipinos [under the leadership of Larry Itiliong]. Without the Filipinos César wouldn't have gotten very far."[112] Nonetheless, Filipino/a American college students joined with Mexican American, Anglo American, and multiple other Asian American groups of their generation in the civil rights protests of that era: "The college groups were together. We were protesting with the grape strike" but became disillusioned by Chávez. "The Filipinos were left hanging because César wanted to go in a different direction," Susan contended.[113]

Yet, according to Aremas, the UFW had little appeal even for working-class Filipino/a Americans in Salinas. "The Filipinos had moved on up" by the 1970s, "so, we didn't see UFW as a big moment. We wanted to be part of South Salinas," which was the wealthier and whiter part of town.

She linked socioeconomic mobility with anti-labor, at least for Filipino/a Americans: "The ones who bought houses in Alisal went over to bigger more expensive homes. They wanted to get out [of fieldwork]. . . . By the time [of the farmworker movement] most of the Filipino men who had worked in the fields had transitioned to the military and to other occupations," Susan claimed, by way of explaining why few Filipino/a Americans in Salinas supported the UFW.[114]

The irony in the battle over labor and race in Salinas was that many of those who opposed the UFW came from the ranks of former strikers from the 1930s. As an example, a Mr. & Mrs. A. C. Cole wrote a letter to the GSA dated February 1979 when negotiations again broke down and led to violence on both sides of the labor issue. The Coles lived in a modest home at 140 Central Avenue in Salinas. It was a multiethnic working-class neighborhood located two blocks from Market Street. This self-identified "Okie" couple had taken a small step upward socioeconomically by living in this part of the city rather than on the east side.

> We wonder, what happen to the grower-Shipper.??? We remember when Okies were trying to get a living wage. The grower-shipper brought in goon squads from L.A. Shot tear gas and mustard gas down Main St. Where no strikers were. But you yellow bellies must be afraid of Communistic "Chavez" All the red flags fly up and down streets by ways and hi ways. Where is your guts.
>
> We guess you will work to put Commie Jerry back in office or make him president: We lived through the 1936 strike, have from day to day record. So why don't you guys get on the ball. Stop Chavez. The ex-service men are getting fed up with the red flags flying. Why not picket Chavez.[115]

The Coles at first appeared to identify with the UFW strikers, even citing mistreatment by the GSA, accusing the organization of bringing in "goon squads" to harass and terrorize them in 1936, using tear gas and mustard gas to inflict pain and suffering on innocent people who happened to be present on Salinas's Main Street—a place where "no strikers were" marching. However, the writers quickly took the opposite standpoint, siding with growers and angrily denouncing Chávez and the UFW, not acknowledging race (strikers in the 1930s were mostly white but also included Filipinos/as) but political ideology, which may have felt safer to them: "But you yellow bellies must be afraid of Communistic 'Chavez' All the red flags fly up and down streets by ways and hi ways. Where is your guts." Ironically, the Coles also faced the threat of being labeled communists in 1936 because the California Highway Patrol had inadvertently placed red flags along the roads to Salinas, which looked to local residents like a signal for a Marxist takeover, causing panic and overreaction.

Nonetheless, the Coles, and so many other non-Latino/a Salinas residents, hurled the worst insult they had against the UFW—that it was a communist organization—because of the symbolic red flags the strikers planted everywhere and routinely waved in the marches that dominated newspaper headlines in the city. The Coles and those opposed to the UFW also viewed then-Governor Jerry Brown as a UFW sympathizer, although he explicitly and publicly remained neutral. Further, they accused the conservative, largely Republican membership of the GSA of having unlimited power and conspiring to support Brown—not just as California's governor but also to "make him president" of the United States. They ended their letter with the demand that the GSA "get on the ball," "Stop Chavez," even "picket Chavez" and the UFW.[116] The Coles, as well as many others who were not associated with the GSA and who had no real idea about the makeup or goals of the association, clearly believed that only the GSA was powerful and trustworthy enough to save them from the so-called communist threat that Chávez, the UFW, and Democratic Governor Jerry Brown represented. They sent their letter to the GSA rather than to the Salinas City Council or to another government agency.

Despite the commonly held assumption (voiced by the Coles) that government was allied with labor organizers, particularly with the UFW, farmworkers had experienced a long history of hostility by government agencies and legislators. Farmworkers were not covered by the 1935 National Labor Relations Act, in part to appease southern senators who wanted to prevent African American agricultural and domestic workers from union organization. And there were measures enacted in the 1950s and 1960s that also weakened labor's the position, particularly in terms of Mexican American civil rights.[117]

Yet, the Coles were correct that government shifted in favor of civil rights activists (including labor rights) in the 1960s and 1970s. A California Superior Court injunction against the United Farm Workers that had made UFW strikes an illegal offense was successfully challenged when the

California Supreme Court overturned the ruling in 1972 in *Englund v. Chávez*. Here judges sided with the UFW and declared that an "employer's recognition of a minority union as the exclusive bargaining agent of his employees constituted an improper 'interference with' a labor organization proscribed by federal law."[118]

Public support for minority rights gained momentum in the 1970s even as it was challenged by new initiatives from a growing conservative movement in California.[119] When growers along with other conservative groups in California attempted to pass Proposition 22 in 1972 challenging consumer boycotts, a strategy that the UFW had utilized successfully throughout the 1970s, the measure also failed.[120] The Chicana/o civil rights movement that the UFW embodied culminated in the passage of the California Agricultural Labor Relations Act (ALRA) of 1975.

The UFW did not always fulfill the high expectations that some workers hoped for. Maria Belen Loredo recalled that "nothing really changed in the fields or work camps where [she and her family] lived. Things mostly stayed the same until the 1980s when [they] got restrooms."[121] Similarly, Lomeli Delgadillo concluded that the farmworkers "weren't really affected by the UFW or the ALRA in the long run."[122] Although anecdotal and controversial (many farmworkers expressed opposite opinions), recent scholarship on the history of labor and agriculture conceded that "most union organizing, and bargaining efforts proved to be short-lived."[123] This was reflected in membership rolls, which plummeted at least until the early 2000s when many workers transitioned out of the fields altogether and did not feel the need to belong to the UFW.

On the other hand, as the 1970s came to a close, a new generation of Mexican American activist politicians rose to prominence in Salinas and changed the dynamics of the city in fundamental ways. The open wounds of the 1970s healed and led to a reconfiguration of social and political power as Salinas became a global agricultural powerhouse and a majority Latino/a city.

AGRICULTURE IN THE 1980S AND 1990S—THE DISRUPTORS

The agricultural industry rebounded from the challenges brought on by successful consumer boycotts during the Chávez era that damaged their reputation as well as their bottom line. They made changes in every area, including increasing wages and adding benefits, at least for packinghouse workers.

Fieldworkers faced a tighter labor market as technological advances in harvesting lessened demand for their labor. Marketing strategies that targeted specific regions of the country meant efficiency and higher profits too.[124] Agriculture also transformed sales by cutting out the produce brokers, the one-time critical link between growers and consumers: "The produce brokerage industry was a mighty industry. They bought most of the produce. In the 1990s they were under huge attack because they were middlemen. The market wanted to squeeze out the middleman and work directly with grower shippers and cut out the brokers. This was no longer the buying hub of the produce industry."[125]

The way produce was sold in stores shifted from bulk to packaging, which created an entirely new labor force. "We used to ship over 400 truckloads a day of iceberg out of Salinas Valley. That got eroded to 250. . . . [T]he processor started processing chopped convenient bags. Some of those people were growers. Dole. Fresh Express. Church. Earthbound Farms created the Spring Mix."[126]Some workers found higher-paying jobs and stable, year-round employment in these new processing plants. "The reason this was able to take place was that labor was quiet," Tom Nunes explained as he described the surges of immigration in the 1980s, when Central Americans, displaced by war and environmental catastrophe, swept across the U.S. southern border. These desperate migrants usually faced a harsh reception on the American side, and most were turned away. They felt forced to cross illegally, creating the general perception that the borders were porous. As a result, growers in the Salinas Valley had leverage and less incentive to negotiate with the UFW or any other union. "We had an abundance of labor," Tom recalled, "Chávez was gone. Unions were quiet. We had plenty of labor. We had the right climate. Economically the country was doing okay."[127] He described the era as one without control or regulations over hiring practices or labor rights and one in which "the environment was right." Growers became confident and powerful by the 1990s. "We had the Amnesty [under the 1986 Immigration Reform and Control Act]," he said, as a way of explaining their access to labor and their collective ability to control the labor force.[128]

Robert and Tom Nunes had grown up in Chualar, California, a farming town a little over 10 miles southeast of Salinas.[129] Like so many other ethnic Portuguese families who settled in Monterey County, the Nunes brothers descended from immigrants from the Azores and spent their childhood and adolescence "being close to the dirt," working for their parents on the family produce farm that was established by their father in 1930. As young children, they made deep and lasting friendships with other farmers' sons and daughters: "Old alliances are an important part of our business . . . one breaks or betrays them at great risk." This defined the culture of agriculture in the Salinas Valley from its earliest incarnation to the present day.[130]

Quiet and soft-spoken, and immensely proud of his family and company, Tom Nunes explained that to be a farmer in the post-UFW era meant so much more than paying attention to labor issues. It also meant being flexible, creative, and connected to every single element of farm production and being well informed about marketing, sales, consumer demand, and price. He described the preoccupations and hazards of agricultural life: "Every grower is concerned every hour of his waking life with the weather and the prices paid for his product . . . potential demand, price movement, and where it all might be as his crops came in."[131] Tom Nunes added that branding became a central feature of the transition from commodity production to identity marketing, so that instead of just growing and selling generic heads of lettuce, growers and shippers created salads and vegetables with labels such as Foxy Lettuce, Fresh Express salads and spinach, Earthbound Farms Organic salads and vegetables.[132]

Large firms—such as Bruce Church Company and Taylor Farms through Fresh Express, the Nunes Brothers through Foxy Brand, the D'Arrigo Brothers, and the Ramseys at Mann Packing—made quick assessments of consumer needs and switched to prepackaged salads and vegetables over the course of the 1990s.[133] The most dramatic outcome for agriculture was "the emergence of the processing plants," according to Tom. In a few short years, growers stopped selling produce in the way that they always had and instead began selling "value added chopped lettuces in the bag," which altered every aspect of agriculture in spectacular fashion by 1990. This new method of packaging utilized a "keep-crisp" salad bag that maintained oxygen levels and expelled carbon dioxide so that salad and other produce might retain its color and freshness without the use of preservatives.[134] These prepackaged salads became hugely successful as busy consumers could buy salads already put together, prewashed and cut, or spinach and other produce or pre-peeled carrots, making food preparation that much easier, convenient, and efficient for middle-class consumers. It was also healthier and safer, given that it was locally grown and organic, without harmful preservatives or pesticides.

Although the per capita consumption of iceberg lettuce dropped from 26 pounds in 1990 to 12 pounds in 2018, packaged salads and vegetables, now with a 14-day shelf life rather than the day or two that head lettuce had previously had, made up for it.[135]

Widespread use of new technology initiated a renaissance in agriculture in Salinas by the 1990s, at least for some of the most successful growers and shippers. "Follow the money," suggested James Lugg, a scientist working in conjunction with the Salinas agricultural community and the University of California, Davis, by way of explaining how Salinas's agricultural community fared during this era.[136] By the 2000s, lettuce and other produce were grown and packaged more efficiently, requiring far less field labor, and were sold at three-year, fixed-priced contracts, which eliminated both price variability and anxiety over profits for growers and shippers. This "created great wealth for a very few" of the larger firms.[137] Although there was an abundance of small growers, specialized growers, and cooperatives in the 1970s and 1980s, by the 1990s and 2000s they had been were swallowed up by larger firms, and the traditional cooperatives had all but disappeared.[138] Larger grower-shipper firms such as Taylor Farms dominated, and many smaller enterprises such as the Nunes Brothers and Mann Packing were acquired by corporate agricultural giants such as Dole and Del Monte, respectively, although some of them regrouped in new forms and established their own brands.[139]

The 1994 North American Free Trade Agreement (NAFTA) also shook up agricultural production in important ways. Markets opened along the NAFTA highway that stretched from South America through Canada, but there was increased competition for agriculture at all levels in the United States. For example, NAFTA played an important role in the freezer industry, which moved to Mexico, and in the floral industry, which moved to South America. Multiple agriculture-related businesses in Salinas were negatively impacted by the agreement. "Growers don't move. The crop moves in the free market system of produce. If they [growers in South America] produce something for a dollar and it costs us 3 dollars who can last longer in the market? We couldn't compete in frozen or canned food. They could hold their markets down."[140]

Growers lost the competitive edge in products such as asparagus and green onions that could be grown far more cheaply in Mexico and easily traded and transported north because, as Tom Nunes explained, "labor was so much cheaper" in countries south of the U.S. border, particularly in Mexico. Nonetheless, he claimed that growers in Salinas and the Salinas Valley "had other things emerging."[141] According to Tom, "We had replacement crops that took their [asparagus, green onions] place—wine grapes in the foothills, strawberries grown in local Blanco area, iceberg lettuce, cauliflower. Strawberries started to emerge. Another item that emerged was romaine. Iceberg was king in the 1970s and 80s but we developed romaine hearts by the 1990s," by way of explaining that even large agricultural firms in Salinas were impressive for their capacity to quickly accommodate to changes in markets and readily adapt.[142]

The conglomerates were not as nimble, however. Although many local growers and shippers profited, they also attracted the attention of international corporations such as Del Monte and Dole. Although those takeovers increased the wealth for some local family-owned firms, the conglomerates did not invest in the city either financially or in terms of philanthropic initiatives as the Salinas-based companies had always done. For example, when the Nestlé Company abandoned its factory in 1994, it was taken over by a local shipper, Bruce Church, who spent over $12 million renovating the plant. Although his company maintained offices, farms, and plants nationwide, Salinas remained the headquarters and home to its executives. The Church family stayed deeply connected to the city, as did the Taylors.[143] This was a common practice for most Salinas agricultural families; they supported local philanthropy, community culture and events, and hundreds of nonprofits in the city.

Agribusiness had become increasingly global by the 1990s, but—at least in Salinas—it was also intimately connected to the community. Still, for all their collective philanthropy, the large Salinas agricultural families, like those in other urban centers in agricultural California, generally and fiercely supported the most conservative political candidates: those who distrusted government at any level. This created a deep divide in city and regional politics. The most far-reaching outcome for the UFW and Chicano/a civil rights movement in Salinas was in politics, not in the fields.

FIGURE 8.1   Swearing-in ceremony at the Salinas Police Department, 2017

CHAPTER 8

Politics and Empowerment in a New Era

THE IMPACT OF THE CHICANO/A CIVIL RIGHTS and environmental rights movements, together with the urban expansion of the 1960s and 1970s, had long-term (and unexpected) implications for Salinas. The rights movements brought about real and positive political change and empowerment that should not be overlooked or minimized. The ideals expressed in civil rights led to changes in political representation, economic equity, and even in the way law enforcement was imagined. Furthermore, the annexations of marginalized spaces like Alisal led to an overall sense of responsibility for development and an inclusiveness that did not exist previously. None of the highest aspirations of those years was completely fulfilled, but the effort was evident and paved the way for major positive changes in the context of a new political climate beginning in the mid-2000s.

Jack Armstrong recalled Salinas's downtown culture when he was growing up in the 1940s: "Everything was centered on the 300 block of Main Street," he recalled.

> Doctors, bankers, CPAs, all the professionals and businesspeople had their offices in the center of town. They all knew one another and would go to the Elks Club around the corner for lunch every day. They played cards, joked around; then it was back to work. It was a tight group. Very congenial.[1]

After Jack returned to Salinas in 1952, newly married and newly employed by the Bruce Church company in sales and marketing, he could already see the changes that were coming to the city's functioning and to its downtown.

Throughout the 1970s and 80s, many white professionals and business-people abandoned their downtown offices. The Elks Club moved out of the center of town, and the grand downtown hotels closed their doors, no longer functioning as the primary gathering places for professionals, Ag folks, and businesspeople. Instead, professional offices and banks spread out over the south and west sides of the city, and the new Corral De Tierra Country Club, originally built in 1959 and located well outside the city limits, became the social gathering spot for local elites.

Jack Armstrong was surprised by the proliferation of shopping centers throughout the decades of the 1960s and 1970s, which became a hot button political issue as they drew residents and visitors away from Main Street. Although these malls breathed new economic life into Salinas, the developments—such as Valley Center located south of Main Street, the expanded shopping area even further south of town, and the Northridge Mall in 1974 on the north end along Highway 101—were controversial because they all bypassed downtown Salinas and left consumers bereft of the Main Street culture that Jack remembered so fondly. No longer did everyone shop together and interact intimately across class and ethnic lines, giving the appearance of communalism.

CHANGING POPULATION

By the 1970s the demography of the city had shifted enough to make Jack Armstrong and other middle- and upper-middle-class Salinas residents of Anglo, Asian, and Mexican American descent feel more than a little uncomfortable, which they demonstrated by moving their families out of Salinas's central neighborhoods. The new housing developments such as Creekbridge to the north of town and Toro Park and Corral di Tierra (among others to the south and west) complicated the city's carefully constructed neighborhood identities.

Neighborhoods were no longer within easy reach of one another, making communalism that much harder to achieve. "Salinas was a city of neighborhoods,"[2] recalled Ruth Andresen, describing the city prior to the 1990s. Neighborhoods had been traditionally defined both by race and class, with elites living in Maple Park, around Salinas Valley Memorial Hospital, and on the south side of town. Chinese American families tended to avoid living in Chinatown if they could but formed the bulwark (along with Filipino/a, Japanese, southern and eastern European, and Mexican American families) of the multiracial, working- and middle-class neighborhoods on the north and west sides of town. Alisal remained the destination for poor and working-class families of any ethnicity but increasingly became known as a center for Latino/a family life by the 1970s. Neighborhood and settlement mostly reflected the mixture of ethnicities that characterized Salinas. Ethnically focused organizations and religious centers, the Buddhist Temple, various Catholic and Protestant churches (defined by the ethnic makeup of their respective parishioners), and the Jewish synagogue in town reflected the cultural diversity of Salinas within the context of a predominantly white social, political, and economic order.

The changes Jack Armstrong and so many others felt in Salinas began in California generally with the population increases first brought on in the build-up to World War II. Salinas mirrored other California cities in population change and also in how long-standing residents of all ethnicities responded to this new browner and blacker population: with a wave of suburban growth based in large part on racially restrictive settlement patterns that led to the establishment of newly developed all-white subdivisions and suburbs.[3] Lucy Pizarro was one of those new arrivals, but she recalled Salinas in that era as a mostly positive and inclusive environment in which to live and raise a family. Born in 1944 in Durango, Mexico, she was only twelve years old when her father died suddenly, leaving her mother to care for seven children. As the eldest, Lucy felt a responsibility to support her mother and siblings. When a cousin living in Canoga Park, California, sponsored her immigration to America in 1966, she jumped at the opportunity to earn far more money than she could possibly earn in Mexico at that time. She mostly babysat and sent almost all her earnings home to her mother.

By the time she was twenty-one, Lucy had fallen in love with Domingo Pizarro, who happened to be visiting from the Salinas Valley where he was employed as a packer in the Spreckels Sugar factory. Lucy moved to Salinas and began raising a family of three children. It was hard at first. "I was totally alone," she recalled of those early years in Salinas. The growing family lived in Alisal on Dennis Avenue in a multiethnic neighborhood that included a "nice old couple from Iowa." She recalled Alisal in the late 1960s and through the 1970s as a "beautiful, clean, peaceful" environment where she was made to feel welcome and at home. "There were a lot of families with kids [who] played freely in the streets. There were a lot of Mexicans, Filipinos, and whites there and we all shared food." The Spreckels factory gave Domingo Pizarro steady employment and good wages so that the Pizarro family could buy their first home by 1972. By 1973, Lucy was able to sponsor her siblings and mother, and the family was reunited in Salinas.[4]

In 1980, the Pizarro family's collective place in the city was cemented when Lucy established what was to become one of the most important gathering places for politicians in Salinas: Chapala Restaurant: "I was a cook, dishwasher, everything. My kids would help after school. They would do their homework, eat and clean tables, do whatever was necessary." But this arrangement was unsustainable, and after a few years she hired nine paid staff. After the 1989 Loma Prieta earthquake destroyed the first restaurant, Lucy rebuilt and flourished. Nicknamed "Little City Hall," Chapala was used for fundraisers, meetings, and events of all sorts by city councilmembers, county officials, even then-Congressman Leon Panetta—anyone who wanted a connection to the Salinas Latino/a community knew to schedule an event there. It was a symbol of a new ethnic identity for Salinas as it was transforming demographically into a majority Latino/a city.

Simón Salinas's family arrived at about the same time that Lucy's family did, but his experience in Salinas was a little less welcoming. He and his family had arrived in Salinas by way of Watsonville as part of a larger out-migration from Texas in the 1950s:

> My brothers came to the area in the 1950s to work in the fields. The rest of the family stayed in Texas. But then in 1963–64 the cotton harvester was invented so there was no need for so much labor [in southern states] and we fanned out . . . hundreds of thousands of families, not Mexicans but American citizens. We were all born in the U.S.[5]

In contrast to Texas's labor surplus in the mid-1960s, Salinas was experiencing a labor shortage at the end of Bracero program. Despite technological innovations that were supposed to decrease the need for a large labor force, its delicate crops of lettuce, carrots, tomatoes, onions, and other vegetables still needed prodigious numbers of field laborers, especially during the harvest seasons.[6] The Salinas family settled in Watsonville, where Simón exceled in school. He remembered his school years in Watsonville as positive but also recalled dividing lines between the Mexican American students who came from Texas and were both poor and migrant laborers and those who were native Californians who were working class and traced their family roots back for decades. "We were made to feel like intruders to the extent that even the cafeteria workers disdained us if we were eligible for free lunches."[7]

With support from his high school counselor Michael Sullivan, Simón won a scholarship to Claremont College in Los Angeles. Sullivan proactively recruited migrant farmworker children for acceptance into many of California's small private liberal arts colleges, which were predominantly white in the 1970s. While at Claremont, Simón became president the Movimiento Estudiantil Chicano de Aztlán (MEChA), at one point joining his peers in taking over the financial aid office when the school threatened to eliminate Chicano/a, African American, and Asian American study centers. The centers provided essential support for minority students, particularly those who came from families that had little experience in higher education, and most importantly trained them in activism that they utilized after graduation. Simón later became chair of La Raza Law Students Association at Santa Clara University, earned a law degree in 1984, acquired a teaching credential at San José State, then quickly became immersed in Salinas politics. "I was teaching elementary school and we [Mexican American community activists] felt like we wanted to participate, and we got involved with the local politics here."

By the late 1970s, Californians showed their fear of and resentment toward the newer Brown and black populations (who were also poorer than more established residents) through a series of propositions meant to exclude them from housing, restrict employment opportunities, curb immigrants' civil rights, and require English language as a standard in the state.[8] They also left the state. Between 1991 and 1992, fully 41,000 native Californians moved out of state. The decades of the 1970s were also marked by an unwillingness of majority white Californians to support public schools outside of their own neighborhoods, or to subsidize the new minority-majority cities and suburbs. Whites showed this by means of a series of tax revolts, which culminated in the passage of Proposition 13 in 1978.

Proposition 13 froze property taxes at their 1976 valuation (as long as the property was not sold) and barred city governments from allocating funds from property taxes to meet their own needs, granting that power to the state. Moreover, local government needed a two-thirds approval from voters if they raised even sales taxes, thereby stripping California city governments of the power to add critically needed revenue—even for basic city services and development projects. This happened just when the cities were trying to serve a new and growing population that was also poorer and in need of education, housing, and medical care. Proposition 13 proved catastrophic to cities like Salinas, which had just added Alisal, one of the poorest subdivisions, to its city boundaries.[9] To make matters worse, federal and state development and infrastructure funding dried up in the recessions and economic downturns of the 1970s.

At the local level, in Salinas the numerous industrial and manufacturing plants that offered year-long employment to thousands of Salinas's residents started to leave the city in favor of sites abroad with larger workforces, less environmental regulation, and lower taxes, putting a further dent in the city revenue. Like so many other municipalities across the country in the 1970s and 80s, Salinas suffered the twin impacts of lack of federal and state government funding and the loss of a substantial commercial and industrial tax revenue. Nonetheless, in contrast to other parts of the country suffering from recession, Salinas enjoyed a stable economy based on an expanding and profitable agricultural sector that remained its economic bedrock, allowing for business growth and expansion of professional services outside of the limited space of downtown.[10]According to Vern Horton, a Salinas native who was also an integral member of the banking and business community,

> It was economically pretty good. We didn't see foreclosures [during the era of strikes and boycotts of the 1970s]. The Ag industry was the major sustaining catalyst, but small businesses drove everything. We didn't see any major defaults on any loans. Housing development was strong. Salinas was an outlier [during the national recession of 1973 and through the 1970s].[11]

Most of the newcomers to Salinas, like the Pizarros, settled in east Salinas, which remained the most affordable part of the city and Monterey County. Part of the grand bargain Salinas promised with the annexation of Alisal involved Salinas's commitment to invest in this subdivision and in the settlements and neighborhoods along the east and north side of town. The expensive infrastructure projects were also promises made to a predominantly white southern population of former Dust Bowlers, rather than to the newer, growing Latino/a population that was rapidly displacing them and, at the same time, creating an entirely new identity for the city.

Alisal became predominantly Latino/a in its population makeup; it also remained working class and underdeveloped compared to the rest of Salinas through the 1970s and beyond, despite efforts by the city to make improvements and invest in the community. We cannot know the extent to which the complexion of the population might have affected moneys spent there, but we do know that Alisal was not ignored by the city council or by numerous county agencies. Many initiatives were proposed and adopted. Funds were built into city budgets regularly to develop the area and improve daily life for its residents.

The Hebbron Heights neighborhood, which consisted of about 60 acres of land—roughly bounded by East Market, Terrace, Madeira, and Division Streets—received particular attention. City Manager Thomas Dunne (vilified by many for his support for development projects that decimated Main Street businesses) consistently advocated a public-private partnership in developing the area. He sought federal and state funding to improve the neighborhood's infrastructure, add elementary schools and parks, and build multiple-use housing.[12] Dunne argued that development in Hebbron Heights should be prioritized and responded favorably to grassroots activism: "in view of the interest expressed in property reuse by the Filipino community (a housing project and cultural center)."[13]

However, he did not tie development in Alisal to general development, so the community remained marginalized and separate from the rest of the city as "the other side of the tracks." As an example, in July 1971, the city council voted to rezone "a parcel of land located at 645 Williams road for multi-family housing," in their continued effort to support the growing population of east Salinas by providing more housing, but multi-family units as opposed to single-family developments.[14] Two weeks later, the city decided that working-class families needed rental apartments rather than single-family homes, without seeking their input on the matter. Had the city investigated, they might have learned that working-class Salinas families wanted single-family homes with gardens and yards for their children to play in, just like middle- class and elite families did. Nonetheless, the council approved the rezoning of the entire area on Mae Avenue between Del Monte Avenue and Sherwood Lane and all along Del Monte Avenue to be rezoned from "single family residential" to "multiple residential" and "duplex residential," so long as everything remained single-story.[15]

In 1975, the city council approved funding for a park in Hebbron Heights, a "$100,000 city playground. And Salinas went a step further by declaring Hebbron Heights the priority target for federal community development funds."[16] By 1977 "federal job funds [provided] the extra boost that permitted . . . a $650,000 East Salinas Branch Library [and] a $141,268 street improvement project in Hebbron Heights."[17] But there was no vision for how these improvements might serve to integrate Hebbron Heights (or Alisal) into Salinas proper. There was little effort by Salinas's residents from southern and western neighborhoods to visit libraries or parks in Hebbron Heights, and residents of Alisal did not feel particularly welcome in the recreation centers or libraries located outside of their neighborhood.

Many grassroots nonprofits sprang up to render support to the eastside community. For example, the Salinas Valley Anti-Poverty Council (SVAC), a service center directed by Guillermo (Bill) Villasana and founded in 1967, offered residents mostly from Alisal support in finding employment, filing tax returns, and dealing with various state and federal social welfare agencies. In an effort to require Anglo American conformity, SVAC offered classes in "Americanization, English as a second language, health, tutoring, homework study groups and homemaking," but no classes in Spanish language or Mexican culture that might have encouraged non-Latino/a groups to learn about and appreciate the new majority community in their midst. The center "was also active in the effort to find a solution to the youth gangs in the East Salinas area," an issue that would gain attention in the ensuing years and eventually lead to an unsavory depiction of the city as generally crime-ridden and unsafe.[18]

City leaders supported grassroots programs designed to bring Latino/a young people into the circle of Salinas city life, but their plans were not based on reciprocity. No one made the effort that Virginia Rocca Barton once did to bring Anglo American or Asian American youth into a wider circle that might have given all young people more of an appreciation of cultural differences and the sense that it was worthwhile to learn about every culture. Assimilation in Salinas, as it was throughout America, was a one-way path to a white cultural norm.

Still, it was noteworthy that city government at least funded minority organizations. One group, called the Salinas Warlords, successfully demanded financial support from the city to "address problems in Alisal faced by Mexican American youth."[19] The Warlords were also funded through Lyndon Johnson's War on Poverty program. Ray Banuelos, the Warlords' leader, was frequently mentioned as a spokesperson for the group in discussion at council meetings.[20] The Warlords advocated for the empowerment of young people who felt disengaged from community life based on their socioeconomic circumstances and ethnic identity as Latino/a people. The original program director, John Day (who was replaced two years later in 1970 by Francisco Garcia), defined the Salinas Warlords' goals as "rehabilitation and crime prevention," rather than using a less negative term such as "cultural empowerment," signifying that identity as a young Latino male was inextricably linked to criminal behavior. The group addressed problems such as "school dropout, youth relationships with police, [and] the whole spectrum of community and home problems of young people and particularly of minority youth"—all negative descriptors rather than more positive associations connected to the Chicano/a civil rights movement, such as educational attainment or voter registration or affiliation with organizations such as MEChA, which had inspired and empowered emerging Chicano/a activists such as Simón Salinas.

Instead, the Warlords focused on race relations connected to crime. According to Day, "it could in the future find itself concerned with such problems as housing, prejudice, and 'the lack of sensitivity on the part of the community to the human needs of so many of our youth.'" This last at least implied that there was so much more to address than criminal activity for young Latino/as in Salinas. Although the Salinas City Council members listened and answered with financial support, their response (like the response of the federal government to many of the programs of those years) called attention to the problems of communities of color, rather than to their positive contributions. This only increased a sense of marginalization and inequality among the very people who might have benefited from a truly inclusive approach that celebrated diversity and considered a Latino/a majority to be a positive development for the city.[21]

The Warlords received funding from the Salinas City Council to pay the annual rent of $4,800 toward a Warlords youth center at 242 Williams Road in exchange for physical labor, among other conditions. It felt patronizing to the young people. The city council reconsidered its rental agreement with the Warlords following reported incidents of disruption and littering at a Warlords-sponsored Halloween dance at El Sausal Junior High, but the proposal to cancel funding was struck from the agenda after two dozen youth spoke about the continuing need for city support. The young people had to fight continuously for funding.

Months later, the Salinas Planning Commission sponsored a second youth center for the Warlords at 536 E. Market Street through the Monterey County Antipoverty Coordinating Council; this center provided "a variety of activities to keep youth off the streets such as dances, table tennis and boxing . . . group discussions and drug abuse counseling." Again, the language clearly suggested that the youth were a problem population, rather than a great addition to the city, further marginalizing them.

The organization finally fell apart completely after it declined an offer of $74,000 in federal funding. The Warlords argued that they might be compromised if they were tied financially to federal aid, indicating the group's sensitivity to being treated as mere recipients of funding. Their decision not to accept federal funding appeared to be arrogant and shortsighted to other residents and led the Salinas Union High School Trustees to withdraw their consideration of a $43,944 grant of "in-kind services to the East Salinas delinquency prevention program." This moment is a good example of the effort both at the grassroots and government (city, state, and federal) levels to respond to issues relating to inequality in the city; but like so many other government-sponsored programs in the 1970s, their heavy-handedness and negative outlook doomed them from the start. Community members were not allowed to define their own problems or to work in equal partnership with city leaders. Without a more positive and inclusive vision that might include an appreciation of the new demographic as a positive for Salinas, these piecemeal efforts were fated to fail.

An example of that happened at Salinas High School in October 1971 when a group of white youth (who were not students themselves) taunted a small group of Latino students gathered outside of class. A melee resulted with multiple students injured. Principal Jack Carolan accepted full blame for the incident, which he suggested was due to Latino/a students being marginalized on campus, making them targets of white youth. He agreed to institute more bilingual programs and add staff to serve as better communicators. Yet, violence between groups of whites and Latino/as increased over the next two decades, in large part because Latino/a ascendancy in numbers was resented by whites rather than embraced. White youth were not taught to see and value the Latino/a students as equals and as assets to city culture from whom they could learn.[22]

Housing remained the most pressing problem for Salinas in these tumultuous years. It became increasingly clear that the city urgently needed new and better housing for the north and east sides of town, housing that allowed for apartments, duplexes, and developments that might accommodate a surging population. In October 1969 the Salinas City Council considered bids to build new housing subdivisions "intended to be a compact homes development for lower incomes, price ranges expected to be from $15,000 to $17,000. City Manager [Thomas] Dunne said this is the first compact housing development brought before the Council and felt there is a real need for it."[23] The proposal for the subdivision, named Las Casitas, passed.

City council meeting minutes throughout the 1970s showed the council voting consistently to rezone both agricultural and industrial land for both commercial and residential purposes, often for low-income housing and apartment development, but there was also a real push to create more shopping nearby so that residents did not need to drive long distances for basic needs. Those development plans conflicted with the belief by others who thought that affordable housing would lower property values and that shopping outside of Main Street, defined as "leapfrog development," would decimate downtown culture. Those opposed to the development were ultimately unable to stop such projects because of the dire need for housing and infrastructure and the inability to raise revenue from any other source. Shopping malls outside of downtown became the only hope for city government trying to navigate an impossible situation. Citizens were also deeply worried about the appropriation of some of the richest agricultural land in the state for development of any sort. A burgeoning resistance movement at the grassroots level that included environmentalists and some of the more established agricultural landowners mobilized in these years to challenge housing projects and shopping centers alike, often running directly against the needs of the new and newly dominant Latino/a community. In 1974, over 4,000 Salinas residents attempted to stop leapfrog development with a demand for a referendum to put the measure to a vote but were unsuccessful in their subsequent court challenge.[24]

The conflicts over development strained relations in the community to the breaking point, but it might have been prevented. Had city government, led by City Manager Dunne, made efforts to include all groups in the development decision-making process, they might have been able (in partnership with the city council) to create a holistic vision of the city, taking each groups' concerns and needs into account and thereby leading to better planning and fewer conflicts. To be fair, top-down planning in most cities in California in the 1970s and 80s led to similar bitter conflicts within communities all over the state.[25] Organizations such as CHISPA, an outgrowth of the Chicano/a civil rights struggle, might have been useful partners in helping local government solve the conundrum of a need for housing, shopping, and development, along with the need to preserve agricultural land and a city culture based around Main Street. In Salinas, including residents from Alisal on city staff might have led to better engagement with the community and better planning outcomes.

New highways and shopping centers did not destroy Salinas (or many other municipalities in California), but they did deprive them of a tax base and drove many municipalities to the brink of bankruptcy. They also decimated the community culture that places like Salinas had so painstakingly built up for almost a century.[26] The high-handed decisions of federal, state, and local governments and planning departments to focus money, attention, and political energy into developing transportation systems and shopping centers—which bypassed Main Streets—left many places in California, Salinas among them, out of the most lucrative new developments. Most importantly, these piecemeal policies needlessly divided cities along class and racial lines leading to decades of discord.

Northridge Mall became the very definition of leapfrog development and a firestorm for Salinas. In July 1968 the Salinas City Council voted 4 to 1 to approve the annexation of 232 acres of land north of the city to create a new shopping mall anchored by the Emporium department store. It promised to solve the revenue problem by bringing in badly needed property taxes to the city coffers but was strenuously opposed by Main Street business owners Raymond Little, Robert Firth, and Herman Rothstein, who were supported by City Councilman Richard Wallace.[27] Northridge Mall opened in 1974, and with that development, Main Street lost its place as a lively social and business center; by 1980, the downtown area had become a site for the homeless and criminal activity. The revival of Main Street would not happen until the early 2000s when city leaders and policymakers, having learned from previous mistakes, included the community in every step of the development decision-making process.[28]

The new development projects of the 1980s, on the other hand, were meant to counteract the limits in state funding first and foremost, not bring the community into the planning process. In February 1968, Governor Ronald Reagan had unveiled a new budget that promised to "hold the line" on property taxes even as it increased spending on education, welfare, and medical aid for a state population expected to "cross the 20 million mark by July 1, a growth of 477,000 in a single year."[29] At the same time, the city council considered whether to rescind its traditional exemption from licensing taxes for "growers and manufacturers," but ended up voting unanimously to continue the practice as a perk for establishing industry in the city that paid significant property taxes to support a growing population and infrastructure. Thus, both state and city governments appeared to be on a collision course between meeting the needs of citizens and hamstringing themselves from raising revenue.

There just wasn't enough government money or local taxable revenue to come close to fulfilling the obligations of city government to its people in the 1970s. The farmworker movement, as it played out in Salinas for more than a decade, came about during serious economic downturns in America beginning in 1969, including a stock market crash in 1973, which led to a deep recession that lasted throughout the decade. Combined with high inflation rates and high unemployment, the 1970s through the 1990s marked a time when Salinas, along with most other California municipalities, scrambled to add revenue just to maintain basic services and infrastructure, as minutes of the council meetings graphically showed.

This confluence of new demographic and economic pressures and policies caused a crisis in Salinas. Almost every single council meeting from 1963 forward advocated an improvement project for Alisal that depended on a combination of local, state, and federal funding, but no one thought of including the community in the discussions of how to meet these new challenges that the loss of federal and state funding created. The city had to get creative, which mostly entailed fashioning new public-private partnerships with developers and with the agricultural and business community who were in the strongest economic position to provide support, but not imagining a more comprehensive vision of the city that would bring everyone, including the poorest residents, into the decision-making and planning process.

One example of how this played out came with a report from the Neighborhood Betterment Committee. Its chairman, Wayne Pierce, argued for the necessity of public housing: "[T]he committee is thinking in terms of 150 units on three or four sites in different school districts and that such units should be in the form of townhouse apartment complexes with recreational facilities with units of from two to six bedrooms."[30] The city planned to build that much-needed housing in Alisal with help from the federal government. The city also wanted to limit occupation to these new Salinas residents, rather than opening it up to anyone in Monterey County. John Jones, representing the Monterey County Housing Authority, "pointed out that [all] public housing must operate within guidelines set forth by the Federal government," which would not allow limitations as to who resided there. Thus, Salinas could not operate as an independent entity because it relied on federal (and state) funding, even to build a rather modest housing development promised to Alisal. So, time and time again, city councils, planning departments, and city officials turned to the wealthiest members of the community for help (primarily agriculturalists in the form of growers and shippers) and to outside developers (primarily those interested in building shopping centers) rather than seek funding from the usual state and federal government agencies, who were unable or unwilling to provide it or to bring in diverse members of the community to plan. This set in motion a trend toward a skewed public-private partnership that would grow in the coming decades and cause controversy, when the city partnered with elites from business and agriculture (but excluded everyone else) to sustain and create infrastructure, housing, and shopping centers as a way of maintaining its tax base, which was sinking due to the lack of government support.[31]

Despite efforts on the part of city government to address the housing shortage and need for development in Salinas in the 1970s, the areas where Latino/as resided remained underdeveloped compared to other parts of town. Worse, Latino/as on the east side were completely excluded from all planning and decision making. Planning decisions were also made, as we have seen, area by area, rather than to benefit the city as a whole. Salinas lacked an overarching sense of what it would look like as a newly expanded entity, both in land area and as a Latino/a majority population.

SOLEDAD PRISON

In 1970, just as César Chávez announced plans for a grape and lettuce boycott in Salinas, nearby Soledad Prison erupted in racial violence. Salinas's intimate connection to Chicano/a civil rights and, at the same time, to the prison system encapsulated what was happening in the rest of the country. The emergence of a carceral state focused on the mass incarceration of minorities who were actively engaged in vigorous civil rights activism, namely Latino/as and African Americans.[32]

Soledad Prison was conceptualized as a model for reform and rehabilitation when it was first established in 1946. At that time, the California state legislature approved the purchase of a 936-acre site near the town of Soledad (approximately 22 miles south of Salinas). Formerly used for growing guayule (rubber), the area was intended to be a state prison for "older, more stable offenders" who might live and farm there while the prison buildings were under construction.[33] At a cost of $10 million, it was part of a $43 million statewide initiative, a "penology program" to house 1,800 inmates "incorporating all the new techniques" that the California state legislature developed to prevent recidivism. Soledad Prison was described in the local media as "virtually a little town within itself" that included chapel, hospital, library, and facilities meant for rehabilitation. It also contained a dairy farm, piggery, chicken farm, and truck garden that included grain production, all of which meant self-sufficiency rather than reliance solely on taxpayers for financial support. Inmates were given access to educational opportunities and vocational training, including music, orchestra, and Spanish-language learning. Two hundred inmates were allowed outside prison grounds daily for on-the-job training.[34] Newspaper reports applauded the new facility in glowing language: "Gone are the days, when a convict was regarded as an animal to be caged, then beaten into line. Gone are the rockpile and torture chambers."[35]

Inmates were tasked with everything from fighting fires to reconditioning used toys to be distributed to disadvantaged kids at Christmas. The local baseball team, the Salinas Buffets, played against the Soledad Prison team in 1950 and continued to do so throughout the 1960s, making inmates feel part of the community.[36] In October 1950, "eager" inmates set a new record for donations to the local blood bank and were rewarded with a relaxed schedule and a "holiday feeding system."[37]Construction work on the prison provided jobs for Salinas residents, increasing employment in the city 33 percent from what it had been in 1949.[38] The want ad sections of the papers for the 1950s and 60s were full of openings for roofers, plumbers, and construction workers of all sorts to help build and operate the facility, boosting the economy of the entire region as city leaders intended.

However, less positive stories about the prison appeared in media accounts beginning in the early 1960s too. Although articles praised exhibits of crafts and art made by inmates, reports of stabbings and eruptions of violence (often blamed on San Quentin culture to the north) became more common in reports about Soledad. By 1965, violence at the prison often made front-page news in Salinas, replacing the positive spin of the earlier years that had played up the rehabilitation of inmates through education and work and contributions by inmates to the well-being and economy of the city.

African American inmates were blamed for the violence in unmistakably racist language. In February 1965, "Negro gangs" were accused of "attacking two white men" with homemade knives, killing one of them: nineteen-year-old Paul Drummonds, who was in jail for burglary. The district attorney's office blamed the incident on "racial tensions" within the prison, without assigning any blame to the white instigator or referring to him as anything more sinister than a "white man," while the Black inmates were automatically assumed to be "gang members." According to an assessment of the incident, "The Negroes were reacting from the death of Malcolm X," who had been assassinated at a rally in New York the day before, but that was mere speculation and also evidence of media disparagement of African Americans generally as reactive and violent.[39] All of a sudden, it did not seem like such an asset to the city and surrounding area to have located a prison facility in their midst, notwithstanding the employment opportunities it provided for the multiple communities of the Salinas Valley and Salinas itself.

By 1965 reports of violence on the part of prison guards replaced the congenial relationships touted in the 1950s and early 60s. Guards attacked inmates with tear gas, abused them in "strip cells" or solitary confinement, and engaged in routine beatings and cruelty that were reported regularly in the local papers. Yet, these clear violations of inmates' civil rights and humanity did not inspire any reaction whatsoever from the Salinas community, which, just a few years earlier, had welcomed the inmates in sports contests. Rather, letters to the editor identified with brutal guards and prison personnel in racist language most often directed against African Americans incarcerated at Soledad. In August 1966, five inmates from the prison sued Soledad for civil rights violations and described their treatment at the hands of guards as akin to "medieval conditions" where they were kept in "filthy, smelly, unsanitary [spaces] to a pronounced degree."[40] Again, Salinas residents remained silent.

In 1970, the violence escalated, garnering national and international attention. On January 13 of that year, a prison guard killed three inmates during a so-called brawl that erupted in the recreation yard. In retaliation three days later, a guard was beaten to death and "hurled off the upper tier of the Central Facility wing." Another guard was stabbed to death in July 1970 and three more inmates were killed (apparently by fellow inmates) in the "racially tense prison." Racial tension, rather than the brutality of guards, was named as the cause of the violence.[41] A few months later, in January 1970, three African American inmates—George Jackson, Fleeta Drumgo, and John Clutchette—were accused of murdering a white prison guard. They were responding to the shooting of three other African American inmates by a prison guard a few days earlier, but the killing of three Black prisoners did not garner the attention or sympathy that the killing of one white prison guard did. At Soledad Prison, as elsewhere throughout the country, African American lives mattered much less than white ones.

By 1970, Soledad was no longer a place for rehabilitation but teemed with racism that was complicated by the growing presence of Latino inmates, who tended to join forces with white inmates against African American prisoners. One African American inmate accused prison officials of using white and Latino inmates to serve "poisoned" cafeteria food to Black inmates: "food with feces, spit, urine, crushed glass, and cleanser powder."[42] Guards clearly favored whites and Latino prisoners over Black inmates, who were at the bottom of the hierarchy within the prison system.

As the 1970s came to a close, the conflicts revolved less around African Americans and focused almost exclusively on two groups of Latino gangs: the Norteños and the Mexican Mafia. The Norteños, or the Nuestra Familia gang, was formed to protect the rural California northerners who were becoming increasingly ostracized by the main Latino/a prison gang, the Mexican Mafia, a gang that was originally formed ostensibly as a counter to African American gangs.[43] Norteños relied on family networks outside of the prison to maintain power and engage in gang activity. The families apparently settled in various neighborhoods in East Salinas and fought with one another to move up the chain of command or murder suspected "snitches." The Norteños also identified with the UFW and used the black Aztec eagle as a symbol of membership, although the UFW did not have any connection to gang members and disavowed gang activity.

Still, the presence of gang activity both at Soledad Prison and on the streets of Salinas became conflated with both the labor movement and with the new majority Latino/a population in the minds of many Salinas residents. It also drove many families out of Alisal, such as the Pizarros. Lucy Pizarro described East Salinas in the late 1970s as "stressful" because of the news media reports on crime. "The problems started around 1978. I wanted my kids to go to private school [to escape the violence], so I moved to south Salinas. We were the second Mexican family to live there," a signal that racially restrictive housing kept Mexican American families out of south Salinas until well into the 1970s.[44] Lucy Pizarro's story is an example of how a new population associated with gangs and Soledad Prison complicated life for Salinas's residents in the 1970s, especially for Latino/a families.

POLITICS AND POWER

Salinas faced a real challenge as the 1980s approached. Concerns over race and racial tensions became tied up in debates over equitable development and representation in the city council where decisions over spending took place. It became increasingly clear that the white, male business elite living lived on the south and west sides of town did not represent most of the population, which was Latino/a and working class and lived primarily in the city's east and north sides. The election of 1987 changed that dynamic and marked a decisive turning point, permanently altering the political climate of city. One observer likened Salinas politics in 1987 as an unstoppable force toward equality, "a train that is moving and it will keep moving. It's a freedom train. Or a change train. Or maybe an empowerment train," he said.[45]

A young lawyer, Anna Caballero, arrived in Salinas 1979 as part of an energetic cohort of attorneys working for California Rural Legal Assistance (CRLA) to support farmworkers and their families in battles ranging from voting rights and representation to bilingual education. Anna recalled the political climate of Salinas in those first years of the 1980s: "When I got to Salinas it was very polarized. If you were Latino/a you were for farmworkers and if you were Anglo you weren't, and there were very bad feelings about the union and its organizing activities."[46] She was correct in her assessment of the two communities generally (Anglo American and Latino/a), although neither was as homogeneous as they appeared, but she overlooked the significant role multiple Asian groups played in Salinas's political, social, and economic life and how these groups added a complicating factor to power and politics in these years. After all, Henry Hibino, a Japanese American Salinas resident, served on the Salinas City Council between 1971 and 1979, with one term as mayor, which belied the depiction of Salinas's government as dominated only by Anglo Americans. As well, Chinese businessmen Frank Chin and York Gin, among others, had been appointed to commissions in city government such as Parks and Recreation and Health and Safety. Salinas was always multiethnic and multicultural, even though inclusion might have been more façade than real. There were multiple racial dividing lines, with class and gender adding complexity to the divides.

Anna Caballero faced a deeply misogynistic culture both in Salinas and within the Latino/a community, as was the case throughout 1980s America. She was the only female attorney at CRLA when she arrived. "The only Latinas in the office were secretaries, and they were very opinionated about what I should do and what I shouldn't do, which meant I shouldn't go out and have a beer with the guys and I should go home and make dinner." She came from the Los Angeles area and was unprepared for a "really weird attitude about the difference between men and women and the difference between what was appropriate for Latino/as and non-Latino/as [in Salinas in the early 1980s]."[47] Even in Los Angeles, however, the political (and socio-economic) gains from the feminist movement had only just begun to take root and inspire change by the 1980s.

Anna balked at having to trade in her pantsuits, which she preferred, for skirts and dresses. She attributed that imperative to life in an agricultural town, which was a far cry from the more sophisticated, urban environment of Los Angeles where she attended law school or even the San Fernando Valley where she grew up—both places more liberal minded in terms of women's roles and attire: "I realized I had to go out and buy suits that had skirts," she recalled. She also remembered having constantly to remind her peers that she was their equal:

> When I walked into court I was routinely asked if I was the court inter-
> preter or the court reporter as opposed to being an attorney and so I had
> to fit into a system that was hostile to attorneys, that didn't really appreci-
> ate women attorneys, [and that was] hostile to farmworkers.[48]

It was a heavy burden to carry. She believed that she could be accepted by colleagues and judges, if only she assumed some of the cultural habits of her white, male peers. Like most professional women of her time and place, her belief that her behavior or dress could overcome deeply ingrained, structural sexist and racist attitudes was perhaps naïve. Nonetheless, she took up golf and studied football as a way of finding common ground with male judges and attorneys:

> I needed something to talk to the judges about. . . . And if you're going back into chambers and they're having a conversation about the football games over the weekend and you don't know what their teams are and what schools they graduated from, you're just sitting there listening to conversation instead of being a part of it. . . . [I]t was a really big transition to come to a place like Salinas where things were very polarized along race and along gender as well.[49]

Nevertheless, she persevered. Anna became well enough respected by 1982 to be appointed to the Planning Commission where she dedicated herself to learning about land use and development. She was poised to make a difference in Salinas politics five years later when a pivotal political event took place in the city—the transition to district elections—that would finally give Salinas's Latino/a community its place in city government.

In the 1987 election, the conservative candidate Russell J. Jeffries who favored "slow growth" won the mayor's race by a wide margin, beating Alan Styles, who closely aligned with developers' interests. Styles came from the east side and traced his roots in Salinas to the Dust Bowl migration. His support for development came about because his part of town desperately needed housing and infrastructure, which required partnerships between local government and private developers, something the city had committed to with the annexation of the area in 1963. Thus, through Styles the east side did have a voice on the city council. However, it was not a Latino/a voice. Even though he lost his run for mayor, Styles kept his city council seat by narrowly beating Hal V. Thompson (by a 42-vote margin).

Planning Commissioner Caballero had supported the politically conservative Jeffries, even though most of the rest of Alisal residents supported Styles. When Jeffries became mayor, he wanted to fill his vacancy on the city council by appointing Caballero. It would have been a politically expedient move. With this appointment, the new Latino/a majority population in Salinas might have at least one minority representative on the city council, something they had long demanded. As well, by elevating a woman to the city council, the council could be seen as progressive by the entire community.

It was not to be. Phyllis Meurer and Alan Styles both declined to support Caballero's appointment, joining the rest of the council in allocating the vacant seat to Thompson instead. This was partially an acknowledgement that Thompson had lost his council seat only by the tiniest of margins, and Caballero had not even run for office, although she was well known in Salinas and enjoyed a solid reputation as hardworking, fair, and a strong leader during her five- year tenure on the Planning Commission. Both Jeffrie's failed attempt to include a minority representative on the council in that moment, and Meurer's reluctance to support his effort, proved prescient.

The appointment of Anna Caballero might also have undercut a surging movement to challenge minority exclusion in city government through the courts. Although William Meléndez, president of LULAC (League of United Latin American Citizens), and activists in the Latino/a community claimed to have "no hard feelings" about the decision to replace Jeffries with yet another white male councilmember, it became clear to the community that the old adage "no one gives up power without a fight" held true, and they fought back. Led by attorney activist Joaquin Avila, who had just won a similar case in nearby Watsonville, the effort to use the courts to force inclusion through redistricting gained momentum throughout California during this time. Monterey County attracted Avila's attention because it had been intensely scrutinized by the federal government ever since the 1968 presidential election, which revealed gross under-participation by minorities in voting throughout the county and almost no representation in local government at either the city or county levels. With a majority Latino/a population and no representation in city government whatsoever, even after a series of failed efforts, Salinas made a good case for Avila. Even though the east side's economic interests were represented in the city council through councilmember Styles, the issue became entirely about race and racism.

By August 1987 Simón Salinas, Fernando Armenta, and Marta Granados initiated a lawsuit, with Avila's backing, to force the city to institute district elections that might open the door to representation for the Latino/a majority. Anna Caballero, however, did not join the lawsuit, much to the chagrin of activists such as Philip Tabera and Jesse Sanchez. She might have believed that her years of work with Salinas's white establishment politicians and business community as a member of the Planning Commission gave her needed credibility and a better chance of electability to the city council under an at-large system than confrontation with city elites and siding with Latino/a activists in a lawsuit forcing district elections.

Simón Salinas's disagreed. He attributed his and others' activism to the farmworker movement, which gave him a sense of pride and empowerment: "We were products of the farmworker movement, the 1960s Chicano/a movement in L.A. and throughout the Southwest. There was real organization," Simón explained. "Now we had a group of middle-class professional Chicano/as come back [to Salinas]. We had attorneys and teachers—folks that were now going to start organizing and mobilizing."[50]

Simón was careful not to present himself (or his community) as too disruptive in the late 1980s, although he certainly shared the ideology of Chicano/a civil rights activists who would be confrontational if it was needed: "We wanted to get people to embrace change so that we don't have the fires and the rioting. We didn't want to tear it all down. [We asked ourselves,] How do we open it up so that everyone can get to the table?"[51] He feared that the city might erupt in violence and worked to convince other activists that they could change the power structure in Salinas from the inside:

> The system is malleable. . . . We can get in there and we can start bringing in our input. That is why district elections [were so important]. This gives us an opportunity to elect someone from the neighborhood who understands the potholes, understands where kids need to congregate and the need for recreational centers. . . . We had to deal with this change [in population from white to Latino/a]. It's coming. Whether you like it or not. It's coming.[52]

Simón explained that his moderate, professional cohort "the intelligentsia of the Mexican American community," believed in the same kind of visionary pragmatism that defined everyone else in the city going back to the late nineteenth century. Overlooking structural racism, these activists truly believed in the ameliorative power of a democratic government and, just as importantly, that there was room for them within political power structures. However, when Simón proposed district elections to Mayor Russell Jeffries, the mayor responded (rather dramatically) that district elections "would only happen over his [the mayor's] dead body."

It was at this point that Simón Salinas joined with Fernando Armenta and Marta Granados in the Avila-backed lawsuit, which was enough to force the city council to hold a public meeting on the subject. The meeting convinced the council to put the matter to a vote and hold a special election to let voters decide whether to elect the council by district or at large. After that meeting, Simón recalled, "They did give us something that gave us hope. [They were willing to] put it to the vote of the people. We were willing. What did we have to lose? If it fails, we can always go to the Supreme Court. Watsonville had that precedent."[53] Salinas, Armenta, and Granados dropped the lawsuit in response to the city's willingness to institute a special election on the issue.

The vote for district elections passed with a 100-vote margin in December 1988. Simón recalled, "We won by 106 votes. And where did the votes come from? The Alisal."[54] The elections that followed in 1989 made Simón Salinas the first Mexican American city councilmember in the city's history.[55] District elections did indeed empower the Latino/a community politically by producing city councils in the ensuing years that were made up predominantly of Latino/as, not only from the east and north sides of town, but also from the south and west, which became increasingly ethnically and racially integrated in the 1980s and 1990s. Given the predominance of the Latino/a population (by 2010, Latino/as made up fully 80 percent of the population of the city), at-large elections may have produced the same result. It was not at all clear that district elections alone led to a fairer outcome or to democracy with a small "d," but there were significant, immediate consequences for the city.

In 1988, Simón Salinas defeated his opponents in District 2, Juan Uranga and Deloris Scaife-Higgins, in a hard-fought race. Uranga, like his spouse, Anna Caballero, may have lost votes in District 2 in part because he failed to support the Avila lawsuit, which was widely popular there. Simón reflected on the outcome of that critically important election. It marked a shift in political representation in Salinas, but it was not the radical turn of events that white, conservative city councilmembers had feared. Simón recalled that even conservatives in Salinas city government came to appreciate the value of district elections that gave representation to east Salinas's by now mostly Latino/a community. In a prescient analysis, Simón explained to his colleagues on the council, all of them (except for Phyllis Meurer) white men from the south and west sides of town: "I told the more conservative member of the council, attorney Bob Taylor, that this was good for you, for the Anglo community because you are becoming the minority now. You are going to want to have a place at the table when you are the minority."[56]

Simón indicated that the fear on the part of Anglo American councilmembers was that "We would become like the ward system in Chicago. But we didn't."[57] His vision of his city showed an optimistic worldview that minimized evidence of racism in favor of the power of pragmatism to make real change.

In conversation with Simón, Phyllis Meurer agreed. "That was one thing I was happy to see. We had a much better picture of communitywide needs [because of representation by district on the council]. We really listened to each other."[58] Simón emphasized that the city council, now expanded from five to seven members due to the new election results, worked well together because they understood that "we all represent the city, not just our own district," but that was an overly optimistic view that depended on the composition of the council. When there was less comity, as happened in the mid-2000s, there was also more self-interest. He described a positive, cooperative political environment:

> Phyllis was there to listen to our concerns. I [explained] we have a lot of needs in east Salinas. I need signal lights right now. People are dying. We need to understand we are councilmembers for the whole city. We have to prioritize east Salinas to the extent that I got four or five intersection signal stations where the rest of the city got one or two. And, in turn, eventually I am going to support north Salinas south Salinas if that becomes a priority. We all understand that. I think everybody made it clear that we represent the city of Salinas. I don't just represent District Two. Now I am a councilmember so I would go to south Salinas to talk to kids, schools.[59]

Phyllis Meurer explained that in the context of the late 1980s, it was still a relatively small community in which people freely accessed all parts of the city for work, school, and recreational activities and as a result felt ownership for the entirety of Salinas. "Those of us who had kids would go to recreational programs in another part of town," she said by way of explaining that intersections, stoplights, and transportation systems throughout the city mattered to everyone. "What was good for the district was good for the whole community," she argued. Phyllis attributed much of the good feeling on the city council in the immediate aftermath of electing its first Latino member to Simón's personality as a calming member, rather than the "radical UFW revolutionaries" white members worried about:

> We had a pretty good consensus on that among the councilmembers when Simón was first elected. . . . Simón doesn't talk as if it's my way or the highway, but it's "let me share with you the perspective of my community . . . and we'll make better decisions overall." None of the five city [councilmembers] got removed [as a result of district voting]. We went from five to seven so we added two seats instead [of councilmembers fighting over five seats]. The mayor was still elected every two years and the transition, I think, was smooth.[60]

Thus, a semblance of compromise and camaraderie prevailed in the aftermath of this hugely transitional election, creating a city council based on district representation in Salinas. However, racism was still a problem in Salinas, just as it was elsewhere. Simón recalled confronting the absurd and hurtful bigotry by city staff:

> Having been the first Mexican American city council member I could sense some of the hesitation some of the perception that some of the department heads said. I would hear sometimes "He's going to make us pledge allegiance to the Mexican flag." For crying out loud, I was born in Texas. The panhandle! I think they thought here comes a different face, a different color.[61]

Nonetheless, Simón largely ignored the microaggressions at city hall and spent his energy on rectifying the fiscal inequity that kept his part of town marginalized. One of his first efforts was to create parks in east Salinas, and to do so by bringing the entire city together on the project:

> One of my first projects after Prop 13 was a little tot lot on the César Chávez library [grounds] right there on Bardin and William. The city didn't have a lot of money [because of Prop 13] and so they said here is a hundred thousand. You figure out how to raise the next hundred thousand.

Simón brought in groups such as the Salinas Jaycees and the "low rider car clubs" partnered with parent designers to create a tot lot for children in

Alisal.[62] It was a small endeavor, but successful, and showcased a community-minded spirit that he had hoped for with the representation of Latino/as such as himself on the city council.

However, things were less congenial within the growing Latino/a community, at least politically. In the aftermath of the 1989 election, divisions within the Latino/a community became public and antagonistic, particularly between Anna Caballero and her spouse Juan Uranga on the one side, and Jesse Sanchez, a self-proclaimed leader in Alisal, on the other. After losing to Simón Salinas, Uranga withdrew from actively pursuing a political career in deference to his spouse's political ambitions.

Besides her advocacy work at CRLA and activism with the Alisal Betterment Committee, Anna Caballero had been a member of the Salinas Planning Commission since 1985 and was already well regarded within the Salinas business community and at city hall; she also remained a powerful figure in east Salinas's political life. When the couple, along with their three children, moved out of the east side and into a new housing development to the north, Creekside (District 6), Caballero ran for a city council seat in 1991. Jesse Sanchez accused her of having "a carpetbagger image. . . . When Uranga loses, a couple of months later, they move to District 6 and she decides to run."[63] Caballero's response was to accuse Sanchez of holding a grudge against her husband and wanting to exercise complete control over east Salinas politics: "This harks back to the days Juan was running. Jesse wants to be kingmaker. He doesn't want anyone else participating if they're Hispanic unless he chooses them."[64] Sanchez, born and raised in Salinas, distinguished himself from residents like Caballero who had arrived as part of the Chicano/a civil rights movement. As a result of the bad feelings between them, Sanchez supported Caballero's opponent from District 6, Lily Cervantes, who subsequently dropped out of the race to study for the bar exam. Notwithstanding Sanchez's refusal to support her, Caballero won her city council seat unopposed.

As a first order of business in June 1991, the new Salinas City Council (now comprised of Steve Ish, Jim Collins, Mayor Alan Styles, Phyllis Meurer, Simón Salinas, Anna Caballero, and Fernando Armenta) authorized spending $10,000 to conduct a demographic analysis of the city to ensure a fair redrawing of voting districts now that district elections had become Salinas's new reality. According to local population counts used by the Salinas City Council (but that differ slightly from official census data), between 1980 and 1990 the population of Salinas grew from about 80,000 to over 114,000, with significant increases in the Latino/a population. In 1980, the racial breakdown in Salinas included 52 percent white and 38 percent Hispanic/Latino/a. By 1990, that was reversed: 38 percent white and 50.6 percent Hispanic/Latino/a.[65] By 2000, the shift was even more dramatic. The population exploded to well over 150,000, with a Hispanic/Latino/a majority of 63.8 percent and a white population of 24.6 percent. Asian people made up 5.9 percent of the population in 2000 and African Americans 2.9 percent.[66]

The results of the 1990 citywide census showed that districts needed to be redrawn in Salinas to conform to federal statutes. According to federal law, redistricting was required when a population was not correspondingly represented in government according to its numbers. Thus, in Salinas, Latinos/as "who constitute 51 percent [in 1990] must form the majority in three of six districts."[67] Salinas not only needed to be divided by districts, but its districts needed to be redrawn to truly represent its population that was now majority Latino/a. Representation could no longer be left to chance.

After a committee presented several options involving the creation of a new Latino/a- majority district that might eliminate either the district represented by downtown businessman Steven Ish or the one represented by Phyllis Meurer, the matter came to a vote. Although Fernando Armenta and Simón Salinas voted to support Meurer in retaining her district, preferring her on the council to Ish, the other councilmembers prevailed, with Caballero, Styles, and Collins choosing Ish. Both Salinas and Armenta were taken by surprise at Caballero and Styles's decision to support Ish over Meurer. Salinas and Armenta had a strong, well-established working relationship with Meurer and wanted to see the city council less business oriented. Caballero, Styles, and Collins preferred the old model and may have hoped a business-oriented city council might help the city thwart the financial pressures brought on by Proposition 13 and fiscally conservative federal and state governments.

Meurer's supporters presented three separate ballot measures in the November 1992 election that challenged the decision, but all failed. After contesting its legality, Meurer gave up. She resigned from the city council in February 1992. African American businesswoman and political activist Deloris Scaife-Higgins was appointed in her place. Gloria De La Rosa replaced Scaife-Higgins on the council in the next election and began her nearly thirty-year career as a councilmember. Phyllis Meurer retreated from politics and became the executive director of the John Steinbeck Foundation.

Thus, the election of 1987 had consequences for the 1992 outcome on the city council and thereafter. Meurer's unwillingness to vote in favor of Caballero's appointment in 1987 might have had an impact on Caballero's decision to join Ish and the other councilmembers in 1991, which left Meurer without a seat on the council and eliminated her from contention as a potential political rival for Caballero. After all, Meurer, the first woman to hold a council seat since Ruth Wing in 1947–1951, had the same progressive views and shared the same constituency as Caballero, so might have posed a political challenge going forward.

The council's decision not to appoint Anna Caballero, or anyone else from the Latino/a majority community in east Salinas, to a vacancy on the city council in 1987 strengthened the lawsuit filed against the city two months later that claimed racial discrimination in representation. The publicity surrounding that lawsuit elevated the political profiles of both Simón Salinas and Fernando Armenta (perhaps at the expense of other activists in the community who were not given such prominence or publicity), which not only led to their subsequent elections on the Salinas City Council, but also to their respective elections to the Monterey County Board of Supervisors a few years later, and then to statewide offices and thirty-plus years of careers in public service.

That election also provided Caballero a springboard for her long political career, spanning over thirty years; it included eight years as mayor beginning in 1998, two terms in the state assembly beginning in 2006, and an appointment by Governor Jerry Brown to secretary of the Business, Consumer Services and Housing Agency in 2011. However, in the political climate of Salinas in the 1990s, Caballero's unwillingness to join or even support the lawsuit by Salinas, Armenta, and Granados added to the political divides already apparent within the Latino/a community (particularly with Jesse Sanchez) that festered throughout that decade. Anna Caballero felt (correctly) that the men on the council begrudged her for her place and power instead of offering support: "The interesting thing is that the people who have been the most resistant [to her politically] have been Latinos/as. . . . They can't get over a woman being in a leadership position. Their resistance is there. . . . Even on the council," she recalled.[68]

Finally, the election of 1987 appeared to mark a turning point in race relations, as Simón Salinas had hoped. The Salinas City Council would never again be the exclusive bastion of white men from the south and west sides of town.

Local businesspeople and elites from the agricultural community had little to fear from the new council in 1991 and thereafter, and although they stayed on the sidelines, they made their interests known in financial support for candidates who shared a conservative, anti-government worldview.[69] Simón Salinas and Anna Caballero were civil rights activists, but they were also moderates, pragmatists, and optimists who had a stake in the system as it was. They did not aim to overturn or disrupt. Caballero described herself as a "logical, practical thinker," rather than an ideologue, whose five years of work on the Salinas Planning Commission "gave people an opportunity to see how I think and that I could make rational and logical choices and that a lot of the things I was looking for were what is in the best interest of the future of Salinas."[70]

Both Anna Caballero and Simón Salinas's styles of political engagement were cooperative rather than confrontational, soothing the fears of the white businessmen who dominated Salinas politics and social and economic life at that time. Anna and Simón both believed in compromise and negotiations over the increasingly loud and demanding voices emanating from the progressive left in the Latino/a community. They also faced off against the increasingly strenuous objections of environmentalists (and some smaller agriculturalists) wishing to preserve farmland at all costs as they focused on the urgent need for housing and development throughout east Salinas.

CITY GOVERNMENT IN THE 1990S

Salinas city government and the new city councils of the 1990s and 2000s encountered both crisis and budget shortfalls, brought on by both natural and human disasters, including the Loma Prieta earthquake and the widely publicized gang violence that marginalized Salinas and discouraged tourists from venturing there. Like its neighboring city of Seaside, also a minority-majority community, Salinas bore the harsh economic and social consequences of long-standing structural racism that was ingrained in American society, although it was usually denied even by those most impacted by it.[71] This was the American story—commonplace inequality felt severely in most minority-majority communities in California and the nation.

In Salinas, the economic problems began just as political transformations on the city council were underway when a budget shortfall of $1 million was discovered in 1987, and the city had to institute a hiring freeze in response, angering staff and residents alike. Almost every department lost its leadership to retirement, in part due to the fiscal turmoil. Roy Herte, who assumed the role of city manager between 1988 and 1990, faced a barrage of criticism for the fiscal shortfall, as well as for the resignations, high crime rates, and low morale at city hall, especially from the police department.

Dave Mora stepped into the city manager's role in 1990, just when the city council had transformed from majority white and male to majority Latino/a and female. It was also just a year after the devastating Loma Prieta earthquake almost destroyed Main Street. Mora explained,

> I was attracted to Salinas because it was a demographically diverse city. It was majority Latino. . . . It was very apparent walking in that the Latino population was attempting to have more political influence. And that is my background. . . . It was the first time Salinas had a city manager who identified as nonwhite, much less Latino.[72]

It would not be the last. Ray Corpuz, who was Filipino American, would take the helm as city manager in 2014, with the similar purpose of reinvigorating city space and making sure city government represented minority residents and women.

It was important to Mora that city government, like the newly elected city council, reflected the population of Salinas. He focused on hiring a racially and ethnically diverse staff especially at the highest levels:

> City staff [unlike the city council] was not representative of the community, at least at the senior level [in 1990]. One of the advantages that I had [was to fill] six key vacancies within the [first] 6 to 9 months [of my tenure]. My instructions to the recruiters were "I want a diverse applicant pool." I would describe my career as implementing social equity and social justice as much as possible.[73]

He did. By January 1991, Jorge Rifa assumed the position of assistant city manager. Rifa, Mexican American like Mora, came to Salinas by way of Compton in Los Angeles and Soledad in south Monterey County—both places, like Salinas, with majority Latino/a populations. Mora hired African American Dan Nelson, formerly of Richmond and East Palo Alto, to serve as Salinas's police chief, overseeing a department of 135 officers. After Nelson retired in July 1999, Mora replaced him with Daniel Ortega, a thirty-year veteran of law enforcement and another minority member. Julia Orozco, also of Mexican American descent, became the new library director. After she retired, Mora replaced her with another Latina, Elizabeth Martinez, in 2007, who remained in that position until she resigned in 2014.[74] Neither John Fair, the new director of Public Works, nor Richard McCarthy, the new director of Parks and Recreation, were members of minority groups, but both had lived and worked in majority Latino/a cities (Sacramento and El Paso, respectively), like Salinas, at the heart of rural, agricultural regions.

Mora stayed out of the political fighting that ensued almost as soon as he began work but emphasized that despite disputes in city government the 1990s, "I was lucky enough to have city councils that worked well with one another in spite of their differences. Everyone got along and were careful and discreet about revealing city politics and policy to the general public."[75]

The biggest challenge for any city manager in the era was to balance need with vastly shrinking budgets. In his 1993–1994 state budget, California Governor Pete Wilson proposed "shifting $2.8 billion in property taxes from counties, cities, special districts and redevelopment agencies to school districts . . . [forcing] local governments to either dramatically cut programs and services or seek local tax hikes to make up the difference."[76] The end result was a loss to local municipalities of nearly $4 billion. Not all municipalities experienced that loss of revenue equally. Those that had transformed into minority-majority cities such as Oakland and Compton felt the effects of the budget cuts most severely because of decades of racist policies and practices that effectively excluded them from the wealth that white-majority communities enjoyed as beneficiaries of federal and state largesse.

Wilson's initiative came on the heels of a ballot measure, Proposition 218, which passed in November 1996 by a margin of 12.8 percent. As a result of that initiative, local governments in California lost the power to tax their citizens. Proposition 218 stipulated that any new tax measure or tax increase for anything (infrastructure improvements included) could not simply be decided by local governments but had to be approved by voters. "If the state had not shifted property tax, Salinas would have approximately $3 million more than it has, based on assessed value [by the 1990s]."[77] Taxes, or rather the lack of tax revenue, drove policy and politics in Salinas and elsewhere throughout the early 2000s, sending the city into a tailspin just as dramatic population increases demanded more and better housing, libraries, parks, infrastructure improvement, and increased transportation systems, often in the poorest neighborhoods. Deteriorating streets, sewers, and sidewalks were all desperately in need of repair, particularly in east Salinas.

Adding to the complexity and difficulty of the moment, environmental regulation and activism was at full strength. Strict environmental guidelines had to be adhered to with every new development in housing, transportation, and infrastructure, and every proposed development plan was met with organized resistance in Salinas by the mostly white middle class who joined forces with some agriculturalists, wanting to preserve farmland (productive or not) at all costs. They were opposed by the less organized and mostly Latino/a working classes and developers who were trying to increase housing and build more shopping centers and businesses, especially on the east side of town.

In 1998 when Anna Caballero took her place as Salinas's first Latina mayor, she faced some of the most serious economic and political challenges in Salinas's history. Nonetheless, she reflected on that period in largely positive terms:

> When I got elected mayor, we ended up with 5 women on the council Gloria De La Rosa, Jan Collins, Jyl Lutes, and Janet Barnes. . . . It was a special time . . . because we got along really well together. We had different views . . . but we could work together on issues [and as a result of that] our decisions were better. . . . We created a friendship that was really supportive of each other. There was so much less ego. The women were more willing to listen to each other and to negotiate towards a position where we all agreed, and it made it lot less contentious. . . . [I]t was really amazing.[78]

In a throwback to the language of comity that Phyllis Meurer and Simón Salinas used previously, much of the spirit of cooperation came from the personalities of the councilmembers rather than from an institutional imperative that demanded mutual support and teamwork.

Despite that hopeful vision and camaraderie, the need for development and housing but lack of revenue to support those projects—coupled with loud objections from environmental activists for any encroachment on precious farmland—split the council and the community between 1998 and the early 2000s. Fiscal crises accelerated in 2004 and led to widely publicized library closures that made negative national headlines for Salinas and created turmoil in the city. It had a shaming effect that persisted even after the crisis ended, with implications that minority-majority cities could not manage fiscally because they were comprised of racially inferior people. It was a damning and grossly unfair portrayal of cities in America that had been systematically impoverished by federal and state policies and practices that were designed to marginalize them.

A new development proposal belied the camaraderie that Anna Caballero described and also encapsulated the collision course that was developing: On one side were Salinas's mostly Latino/a working poor in dire need of housing and infrastructure development, cash-strapped ranchers and farmers needing to make a profit on unproductive land, and developers wanting to build housing, office parks, and shopping centers; on the other side were the mostly white, middle-class Salinas residents who allied with wealthier farmers who believed in preserving all agricultural land and were deeply critical of the development projects that they thought had already laid waste to the downtown.

The Mountain Valley development project came about after over thirty years of dispute over the area north and east of the city, once owned by rancher Jim Bardin and since 1932 by his daughter Marie Sconberg. It was the site of the first incarnation of the local community college, Hartnell, which was established in 1833 as El Colegio de San José (also the first institution of higher learning in California) but damaged beyond repair in the 1906 earthquake. Considered a historic landmark, it attracted a constant stream of visitors. Sconberg complained about the incursions of tourists onto her property as "galling and worrisome" in a 1960 article explaining her decision to tear down the remnants of the college, which was subsequently rebuilt in a new location on West Alisal Street near downtown Salinas.[79]

Fast-forward twenty years to 1988. The Salinas City Council, the Salinas Planning Commission, and residents of east Salinas came together with Shaw Development Company and the Sconberg family to reclaim what had become 200 acres of nonproductive agricultural land and to propose building 102 units of "inclusionary housing" and 751 "homes which will be affordable to working families in Salinas." The development also included a 2-acre park, the largest in the entire east Salinas area, and a childcare center that could accommodate over 100 children "with heated floors to enhance infant care." Shaw developers also planned bike pedestrian pathways and improved roads to allow for better traffic flow. Most importantly, the project included a new 9-acre elementary school, the Mountain Valley Elementary School, under the auspices of the Alisal Union School District, which was at the time suffering from both lack of funding and overcrowding. The project was enthusiastically supported by residents of east Salinas.

Numerous City Councils and Planning Commissions debated the project over the course of fifteen years, which included at least seven public meetings. The environmental impact reports approved the plan, albeit with concerns over transportation, sewage, and water supply, among other infrastructure required to support large-scale development. By 1998, the project appeared to be moving forward. It was desperately sought by residents like Lupe Castillo, who wrote in a poignant letter to the *Californian*, "We have been waiting 15 years for this project to be developed," as she described the great need for schools and housing.[80]

And then, one day in 1998, a "concerned citizen" in Salinas, Amy Pofcher, was on a bike ride, and she stopped to rest and reflect on the project. Pofcher, a teacher, lived in Creekside, one of Salinas's newer developments. She was outraged at the potential loss of wild space but did not perceive that the privilege of home ownership, which she enjoyed, might be extended to Salinas's working poor and mostly Latino/a residents in the Mountain Valley project, something that might go a long way toward offsetting that loss of wild space and agricultural land in the name of socioeconomic justice. She gathered like-minded Salinas residents and formed the anti-development organization, Citizens for Responsible Growth, calling out the Salinas Planning Commission and Salinas City Council for what she considered reckless and haphazard development and a willingness to approve any project that came their way. Her coalition made headlines for years to come as city government attempted to answer the criticism for the Mountain Valley development project (among others). It was a typical response that (willfully or not) overlooked the inequality gap in housing and home ownership between white Americans and people of color in America.[81]

Acknowledging that 3,000 homes had been approved for development projects at Harden Ranch, Creekbridge, and Williams Ranch, one councilmember, Jan Collins, shared the perspective of activists like Pofcher at a city council meeting and worried aloud about environmental impact reports that raised issues over the effects that these new housing developments would have on "traffic, storm water drainage and police services." She argued that infrastructure would be "stressed to the breaking point as none of the fees are sufficient to meet the moneys that we expend." Even though Collins admitted that "in the short term we can cover it," she expressed concern about long-term needs to keep up with infrastructure repair and public services like policing. Salinas Public Works Director John Fair agreed that support for ongoing infrastructure was fundamental to sustain any new building project in years to come: "You don't have any maintenance on new streets for about seven years. Existing streets are the problem," he explained in an interview. "They either have not had the benefit of ongoing maintenance or show the results of underfunded maintenance." Collins voted against the project because of her concerns over the infrastructure that would be needed to support the housing.[82]

Her fellow councilmember, Jyl Lutes, disagreed. Arguing that she was against exactly the kind of helter-skelter approach to development that Collins ascribed to Mountain Valley, she made the case for "well-planned, sustainable, creative, community development projects that conform to the city's General Plan and meet community needs," which she argued, exactly defined Mountain Valley. Furthermore, Mountain Valley would be built on nonproductive farmland on the northeast corridor: "[T]he southwest farmlands will be protected from any and all future growth," she explained, countering the vague environmental argument that all farmland ought to be kept sacrosanct, which overlooked the obvious. Salinas farmland originally taken from Mexican ranchers, and before that from Indigenous People, had been used and reconstituted, modified and reimagined, by human beings over the course of centuries to fit their needs at any given moment. In this moment, the 1990s, there was a pressing need for housing in Salinas to serve the population of working people who made up the agricultural labor force and who deserved to live in the kinds of housing that Pofcher and others in the activist environmental community took for granted in their own lives.

The local version of the environmental movement in the 1990s and early 2000s was myopically focused on challenging all planning decisions regarding development. They mostly ignored the real environmental damage being done in minority, working-poor communities from widespread use of harmful pesticides, however, an issue gaining attention and generating serious concern from policymakers and public health officials beginning in the 1990s.[83]

The disconnect between white, middle-class environmental activists and those victims of environmental degradation who were forced to live next to industrial waste centers and fields polluted by pesticides (especially in agricultural communities such as Salinas) continued through the 2000s. As a result, environmentalists' efforts to stop housing developments in the name of preservation of wild space and farmland weakened their argument on ethical grounds, even if they did not perceive the hypocrisy or contradiction. The battle escalated for years, often pitting the mostly white environmentalists intending to "preserve" wild spaces and agricultural land against social justice activists determined to rectify economic inequality stemming from racist policies and practices.[84]

LIBRARIES IN CRISIS

By 2004, however, housing took a political back seat to libraries. City Manager Dave Mora, Mayor Anna Caballero, and the Salinas City Council faced a budget crisis so acute that even its libraries faced closure. The fact that Salinas was home to one of the great American writers of all time, John Steinbeck, made it all the more alarming and shameful that such a drastic measure happened in this particular municipality.

Salinas was not alone. Throughout California and the nation, other minority-majority urban centers faced similar challenges as they weighed closures of crucial city services and institutions. It was a moment in time when communities of color in California had finally elected minority members to local government but were left stranded economically.[85] African American and Latino/a Californians had suddenly gained political power, at least at local levels, but without the necessary economic support, as white-owned businesses fled, and subsidies from state and federal governments evaporated. Both business and state and federal financing were crucial elements towards re-invigorating communities suffering from decades of inequality.[86] The loss of both devasted these places when it was most needed. In Salinas, however, Mayor Caballero and the city council managed to keep local businesses and agricultural elites engaged and supporting the city, even when financial relief through local tax measures and funding from the state and federal level disappeared. They offered a view of leadership that did not name, much less openly challenge, the devastating effects of structural racism. Instead, theirs was a constant effort to show that they shared American middle-class values and did not present a threat to the status quo as they energetically tried to bring money and support from elites into the city.

"We are in a very tough financial situation," announced the mayor in somewhat of an understatement, after a particularly contentious city council meeting in November 2004 that postponed the decision made in September of that year to close not only the city's three libraries but also its recreation centers, as they faced a $9.2 million budget gap for the upcoming fiscal year.[87] As a last ditch effort to raise revenue, the city proposed a half-cent increase in the sales tax and an increase in the utility tax for larger businesses. Those measures (A and B) would have raised between $8.3 and $10 million a year, meeting the city's deficit and even allowing for some breathing room. Both measures were defeated soundly, however, although measure C (a business licensing tax that would bring in $1.2 million per year) passed. Although all three measures were supported by the Grower-Shipper Association, the Salinas Valley Chamber of Commerce, and other business and community groups, they went down to defeat by a two-thirds margin due to widespread resistance to any measure requiring even incremental tax increases—likely because these would fall most heavily on the Latino/a population who were least able to afford them.

In the same election cycle, however, Anna Caballero and fellow city councilmember Gloria De La Rosa won their respective races by similarly strong majorities, not only with backing from residents in their respective districts, but also drawing solid support from Salinas's conservative business and agricultural communities, indicating that the centrist, pragmatic political climate in Salinas held. Caballero easily defeated Jesse Sanchez ally José Castañada, who represented the more progressive leftwing in the mayor's race. Simón Salinas also won reelection to the state assembly in 2004. Caballero, De La Rosa, and Simón Salinas represented a Latino/a majority that shared a vision of the city that was inclusive and at the same time adhered to traditional American values. They were not disruptors.

Following the disappointing defeat of the tax measures in 2004, and anticipating a crisis in city finances, Mayor Caballero engaged the Salinas Chamber of Commerce, agricultural and business groups, local labor unions, and the general public to raise funds through private means, but their effort did not come close to meeting the city's needs. Some money was raised, but not the $3 million needed to keep the libraries open. City councilmember Jan Barnes conceded, "The bottom line is we don't have the money and we have to make these cuts," which hit the poorest residents, most of whom were Latino/a, the hardest.[88]

On December 14, 2004, the Salinas City Council was forced to close all three branches of its libraries, drawing shock and outrage from as far away as New Zealand; Salinas was ashamed, something shared by places like Compton, Stockton, and other minority-majority communities that similarly faced severe economic crisis, even bankruptcy.[89] Donna Elder, a Salinas high school language teacher, recalled the community outrage that library closures generated, but also Mayor Caballero's powerful leadership role, standing alone and confronting an angry crowd on the library steps with dignity, honesty, and grace. The mayor patiently but firmly explained the dire straits the city found itself in that precipitated such a drastic course of action: "I remember her taking on a crowd when she was mayor. There was a demonstration in front of Steinbeck library. She gave it right back. She took them on. She didn't flinch. I was really impressed with her compassion and her strength."[90] Again, the mayor hardly called for social revolution in the same way Chávez and the UFW had done two decades earlier. She matter-of-factly assessed the situation, critical as it was, and suggested solutions well within the bounds of traditional American structures. She might have been naïve for failing to call out the systemic racism behind the policies that put Salinas in such a vulnerable economic position, but her restrained response meant that she kept the support of the business and agricultural elites whom she still needed politically and economically.

One year later, Communities Organized for Relational Power in Action (COPA), which included churches and business organizations, together with other grassroots groups such as the Citizenship Project, spearheaded a campaign to put Measure M on the November 2005 ballot, and they created compelling advertising to reach everyone in the city. The measure ameliorated the damage done to Salinas by the defeat of Propositions A and B by increasing the sales tax one-half cent, which would raise the city's annual revenue by $11 million for the next ten years. It passed handily with 61 percent of the vote, allowing the libraries and recreation centers to reopen and giving city government room to maintain basic services such as fire and police, even if they could not expand them. It also elevated Caballero's standing as a politician who successfully overcame one of the biggest challenges in Salinas's history without inciting racial or class conflict, something places like Compton or Oakland failed to accomplish.

A RESCUE PLAN: THE NATIONAL STEINBECK CENTER

It was apparent to everyone that Salinas's Main Street had become an eye-sore in the 1990s, and no matter how effectively the city was governed, something had to be done to reinvigorate an area decimated by economic downturns and planning policies that located development and investment elsewhere. Its once-impressive office buildings and hotels had long been ne-glected, and then were badly damaged in the 1989 Loma Prieta earthquake, which destroyed seven vacant buildings on the 100 block of Main Street alone, including the 117-year-old Hotel Cominos, Salinas's pride and joy, but in a sad state of disrepair and dilapidation by the 1980s. In January 1989 the city council appropriated $15,000 to encourage merchants on Main Street to "spruce up their properties," which had fallen into general disrepair, giving the entire downtown a feel of neglect and dilapidation. Property owners on Main Street would be eligible for 10 percent rebates if they improved store-fronts. Ironically, residents and city leaders put their faith in John Steinbeck, the once locally despised but internationally renowned author, whose books they were rumored to have burned on Main Street in the 1940s.

The idea of creating a Steinbeck museum came from a librarian with a tragic past. John Gross was a Hungarian Jew forced by the Nazis into a series of concentration camps. A self-described Anglophile fluent in English, he managed to survive the camps and make his way to the United States work-ing as an interpreter after the war. After earning both bachelor's and master's degrees at the University of Michigan, he became a librarian and lived in Detroit, Chicago, and Fresno, California, before he arrived in Salinas to take the job of library director in 1964. At that time, the local library consisted of only one small storefront building on North Main Street and a house garage in east Salinas. By 1990, under Gross's leadership, the library boasted three new buildings that held over 350,000 volumes and also contained an "internationally recognized collection about native son John Steinbeck."[91] One of Gross's colleagues, a professor of literature and Steinbeck specialist at San Diego State, described him as an "amazing man" to have accomplished what he did "with no money," although Gross always had a library budget to work with as was the case for all department heads in city government.

When Gross first arrived in Salinas, he was shocked that there was so little community interest in Steinbeck, winner of both the Nobel and Pulitzer Prizes and recipient of the Presidential Medal of Freedom. "My

God," Gross remembered thinking at the time. "Nothing is done here. How is it possible?" He soon discovered how unpopular Steinbeck was in Salinas (and throughout Monterey County), both among wealthier residents who believed he had created characters that resembled themselves far too well in his novels, and by working classes who felt caricatured in *Grapes of Wrath*, among other writings: "After all, [Steinbeck] did say things people didn't like. A prophet in his own town is never admired too much," Gross explained. [92] To rectify Salinas's disdain (and disregard) for Steinbeck, Gross utilized funds already budgeted to the library to assemble many of Steinbeck's original manuscripts, first editions of Steinbeck books, and taped interviews with people who had known Steinbeck—which, taken together, made an impressive scholarly archive.

At the same time, Gross collaborated with Salinas community leaders Robert Christiansen, Brian Finegan, and Betty Gheen, who led the campaign to restore Steinbeck's childhood home; they converted it into a restaurant, with the profits benefiting local charities. They and others established the Steinbeck Foundation in 1977.[93] A year later, the Frank E. Gannett Newspaper Foundation donated $5,000 as seed money toward the planning of a "multi-purpose Steinbeck Center," although the details remained vague. The Steinbeck Foundation Board President Donald Wolf estimated that the cost would be around $4 million to $5 million to house the 50,000 pieces that Gross had collected and to display them appropriately for the benefit of the public. However, little was accomplished toward that goal for the first few years. Instead, the foundation mostly focused on funding scholarships, celebrating Steinbeck especially around his birthday, and offering tours of areas of Salinas that related to Steinbeck's novels.

In 1980, Gross received a federal grant that allowed him to create the first Steinbeck Festival. More importantly, the Steinbeck Foundation focused on building the long dreamed of cultural center that would function as equal parts museum, showcase for Steinbeck's work, exhibit hall, and archive for scholars and students. The museum was meant to function as the appealing anchor that would improve the 100 block of Main Street and guarantee that visitors to the Monterey Peninsula would include Salinas in their tours of beaches, golf courses, and the increasingly popular Monterey Bay Aquarium on the former Cannery Row. Equally important, the hope was that the John Steinbeck Museum would also encourage growth of shopping and business investment in downtown Salinas, revitalizing Main Street and the entire downtown. In 1988, fundraising for the National Steinbeck Center (NSC) began in earnest.

The idea was hardly unique to Salinas; it was part and parcel of a nation-wide collaboration between city governments, nonprofits, and public historians to make better use of neglected areas of inner cities by creating important (and more authentic) historical markers that would bring tourists and investment with them. "Build a museum and they will come," became a popular mantra utilized to revive downtowns throughout urban America; these inner-city projects featured genuine representations of their respective histories rather than ignoring the sometimes painful parts of their pasts but rarely achieved the profits and success they aimed for.[94] The Monterey Bay Aquarium, which had revitalized the neglected and dilapidated part of Monterey that once housed fish canneries and industry, was the exception that proved the rule for this line of thinking about utilizing deteriorating urban space and making it profitable and attractive to well-healed tourists and investors.

However, few museums enjoyed the kind of success that the aquarium gave Monterey, nor did they bring economic profit to their cities; most proj-ects usually did not work out as well as public historians, city governments, and developers hoped.[95] Few museum boards, architects, or city planners included the communities of color in their midst in conceptualizing rep-resentations of their respective city cultures, even though they were usually the most affected. Salinas was one of those places. As Salinas transitioned from the majority white community of Steinbeck's imagining to a majority Latino/a city with still substantial (and growing) communities of multiple Asian groups, almost no effort was made to include these groups in the planning for such a cultural center in the heart of their downtown. Latino/as in particular had their own compelling reasons to support city invest-ment elsewhere.

A museum as anchor for redevelopment was a precarious venture at best, even if everyone had a seat at the planning table, which they did not. A de-veloper from San José, Rossi King Enterprises, entered into an agreement to improve Main Street that not only would include the National Steinbeck Center but also "a hotel, office building and outdoor plaza," with an esti-mated $30 million price tag.[96] It all looked promising until the 1989 Loma Prieta earthquake derailed Rossi King's redevelopment plans and led to five years of disputes over what might be done to rescue plans for the National Steinbeck Center and the 100 block of Main Street.

It was not until 1994, twenty years after the original effort by Gross and Steinbeck Foundation organizers, that the city council agreed to a $3.5 million matching grant to build the National Steinbeck Center. They combined the grant with a promise to create an "economic incentive zone" that might encourage business development downtown, an indication of their collective awareness of the shaky economy of the city and need for business growth and employment opportunities for its residents.[97] However, the grant required the Steinbeck Foundation to raise funds to complete the project. A 1995 op-ed piece in the *Salinas Californian* encouraged residents to support the center by arguing that it would enhance downtown by linking Salinas to Monterey Peninsula's tourism industry. According to the editorial, Salinas ought to focus its collective energy on tourism: "A $1 billion industry in Monterey County, employing 16,200 people. Steinbeck Center will give Salinas a handsome piece of that action. Its presence will not only boost the city's economy but diversify it as well," signifying a general worry that Salinas's economy remained too heavily dependent on agriculture and businesses related to agriculture.[98]

Fundraising nonetheless remained stagnant until the David and Lucile Packard Foundation made a substantial grant to support the center. Then Jim Gattis got involved. Gattis, a successful businessman and Salinas booster whose family had come to Salinas as part of the Dust Bowl migration and whose story is documented in earlier chapters, became a central organizing figure in fundraising for the NSC. He admitted to never having read Steinbeck's novels until the board members for the National Steinbeck Center, many of whom had supported his projects, asked for his help. He realized what "an asset this Nobel Prize–winning author is to Salinas." Reading Steinbeck not only gave Gattis a fuller appreciation of the novels, but also the "dual purpose in having his hometown memorialize and honor the body of his work and the realization of what a 'boost' development of the NSC could be to the revitalization of Salinas."[99]

Jim Gattis brought board members Bill Ramsey and Basil Mills with him when he approached the Harden Foundation to ask for grant funding that would match the Packard gift, which he considered "cheeky" ($500,000). To his surprise, they matched the Packard grant and gave him $1 million to build the new center. With that stimulus, Dirk Etienne and Jim Gattis spearheaded a new effort to convince potential donors that the NSC made economic sense for Salinas, but also and equally important, that it might fill a need by "establishing cultural and economic ties with the Monterey Peninsula's bustling tourism industry. . . . [I]n visiting with the top six hotels on the peninsula, there is a real need to take groups places in the evening. . . . People are looking for another place to go [besides the Monterey Bay Aquarium]. . . . [I]f a few key destinations on the Peninsula begin marketing the Steinbeck Center . . . it will help Salinas become a tourist destination," he explained.[100]

The board members sought support and funding from the multibillion-dollar agricultural industry, hoping that Steinbeck's international appeal might extend to the city itself. Etienne and Gattis secured financial commitments from Mann Packing, Tanimura & Antle, Fresh Express, and several other companies to create a special wing of the NSC as a tribute to the agricultural giants of the region.[101] Their collective efforts did not anticipate the reality on the ground as the project was completed.

Community backlash in 1996 and 1997 came from Salinas residents who, oddly, expressed outrage at the contemporary design of the building and threatened to derail construction on that issue alone, even as increases in funding made the NSC a reality at last. Disparaged as sterile and too modern for the downtown, one Salinas teacher described the design as "incongruously like an airport in the Midwest [that] robs the community of its sense of place." The letter writer predicted that the NSC "will no doubt attract some tourists . . . but they will . . . come in and get out as quickly as possible because who wants to spend tourist time in an airport?"[102] Yet, the museum faced challenges unrelated to the design of its building. Like so many other efforts in cities throughout the country, museums simply could not generate enough tourist traffic or investment dollars to support communities beset by serious economic, social, and political problems, especially when they did not represent the very populations that defined city identity.[103] In Salinas's case, the city felt like a Latino/a city, something overlooked completely in the version represented at the NSC.

Many objections for the design had to do with what Steinbeck himself would have thought about the modern representation as opposed to a more traditional one that evoked late nineteenth-century images of Salinas as a majority white place with a sprinkling of Chinese residents and divided along class lines. Steinbeck left a clue, however, in his response to the controversy over the redesign of Cannery Row in Monterey in 1957, after it was sold to the Cannery Row Corporation. In an article written at the time and reprinted in the *Monterey Herald* in 1997, he satirically dismissed "1. The old-old 2. The new-old 3. The pseudo-old," as merely nostalgia for a past that never existed. He came out strongly out in favor of "4. The new."

Young and fearless and creative architects are evolving in America. They are in fact some of our very best artists, in addition to knowing the science and materials of our period. I suggest that these creators . . . are allowed to design something new in the world. . . . Modern materials do not limit design as mud and tile once did . . . then tourists would not come to see a celebration of a history that never happened, an imitation of limitations, but rather a speculation on the future. We never had a Notre Dame or a Chartre. But who knows what future beauty we may create?[104]

Despite all of the controversy over design, the National Steinbeck Center officially opened on June 27, 1998 in a gala called a "night to remember" with over 400 people in attendance. It was "a virtual who's who in the Salinas Valley" that included the author's son Thom Steinbeck and Salinas and Salinas Valley's agricultural elite, most of whom were white Americans with roots reaching back to the late nineteenth century; but it also included the new elites whose families originated from Alisal and Dust Bowl migrations. Salinas Mayor Alan Styles proclaimed enthusiastically that the new center would "put Salinas on the map . . . as a tourist center" rescuing the downtown economy with a projected attendance of hundreds of thousands of visitors a year, a wildly unrealistic figure.

Just as in so many other municipalities, that dream never materialized. At first, the NSC appeared to be the anchor that downtown merchants hoped for. Attendance passed the 100,000 mark the first year of its opening but declined almost immediately thereafter and averaged just a little over 70,000 per year for the next five years, making it impossible for the NSC even to meet its basic needs much less make a profit.[105] Utilizing pledges intended for reserves just to meet day-to-day expenses, the NSC soon found itself operating in the red and indebted to the city, which owned the land it had been built on.

In part the lack of attendance may have been due to reluctance by hotel concierges in the Monterey Peninsula to send groups to Salinas, given the media attention that focused almost exclusively on the city's gang and drug problems. Their fears were largely unfounded, as the gangs avoided Main Street and tourists were not in danger from them. Nonetheless, the expected flow of leisure and corporate tourists from Monterey to Salinas never happened, cutting off the NSC and Salinas from the lucrative tourist industry of the peninsula that they had counted on. However, tourism is a deceptively fragile industry; and, in contrast to agricultural production, it is not a dependable source of city revenue, especially in times of economic downturn or, as recent events have shown, during a pandemic that severely limits travel and social interaction. More importantly, the NSC did not have widespread support within Salinas because the activists and entrepreneurs (from the multiple Asian and Latino/a communities) who formed a solid new business and political cohort had been left out of every part of planning. They had little vested interest or stake in the success of the NSC.

Plagued by ongoing financial woes and attendance that plateaued in the early 2000s, the California Cultural and Historical Endowment, together with local banks, infused the center with enough grant funding to keep it up and running and expand its mission to become more of a conference center than a tourist attraction.[106] But by 2009 in the aftermath of the economic collapse, only 1 percent of the population of approximately 150,000 Salinas residents had joined the membership rolls, and the NSC floundered, inspiring much hand-wringing among residents and city officials alike. Colleen Finegan Bailey, director of the NSC at the time, reflected on the years 2009 and 2010: "Red ink stained the books. Full time staffers dropped from 13 to eight. The city in 2010 covered the center's $180,000 bond payment for a second—and it turned out—final year."[107] Despite the best efforts to expand programs and redefine the mission to be more collaborative, inclusive, and community centered, it was too little too late. The NSC continued to struggle financially, remaining in debt to the city. Yet, it enjoyed a revitalization in the years after 2015 as a conference center and educational facility under the direction of Michele Speich.

The National Steinbeck Center encapsulated all that was important about Salinas in the twenty-first century. Its distinctiveness as an agricultural urban space conflicted at times with its new Latino/a cultural identity, and its status as a minority-majority city challenged its economy and politics on the Central Coast. By the 2000s, it was clear that Salinas had grown apart from the rest of the Central Coast region rather than assumed its center. Although it was still the county seat, a "lettuce curtain" separated Salinas from the wealthier cities of Pebble Beach, Carmel, and even Monterey—formerly working class and industrial, but now a tourist center as well.[108]

FIGURE 9.1   Latino/a dancers performing in Salinas, 2019
COURTESY CITY OF SALINAS.

CHAPTER 9

Agricultural and Urban

Salinas in the Twenty-First Century

BY THE MID-2000S, the Latino/a population, as the majority population in Salinas, became the new normal, but what did that mean going
forward in terms of local politics? The local economy? The city's social and
cultural life? Collectively, Anglo Americans and Salinas's various Asian
communities were afraid of their future. Many also harbored more than a
little resentment over the mixture of fame and notoriety that the Chicano/a
civil rights movement had brought to the city in the 1970s and 80s.

Initially, much had improved beginning in the 1980s. City politics became more inclusive and yet remained moderate (thus acceptable for most
residents). The city continued to be economically stable, with expanding
opportunities for employment in a thriving, innovative agricultural environment that welcomed the new labor force. New arrivals appeared to be
taking their places within the social and cultural fabric of the city, adding
multiple Latino/a cultural events to the city's calendar that already included
representations from various white ethnic, Filipino/a, Chinese, and Japanese
American communities.

The positive changes were not illusory, but they did not last. The new
methods of production and processing that disrupted agriculture throughout the 1990s led to consolidated wealth for some growers and shippers
but to bankruptcy for others; widespread job losses and lower wages for
unskilled workers were common, just when their expanding population

needed employment and when the city needed their tax dollars as it felt the effects of harsh fiscal policies at both state and federal levels. Smaller growers and shippers sold farmland to developers and to the city for badly needed housing, transportation systems, infrastructure, and commercial projects, incurring wrath and renewed activism from environmentalists. Workers, residents, Ag folks, and city government were locked in struggles over land use and water, always in short supply in the region.

The 1989 Loma Prieta earthquake nearly destroyed an already fragile downtown and upended plans for development, just as the political climate became hostile and struggles over representation turned ugly, not only pitting Latino/a activists against whites and Asian Americans, but also dividing the Latino/a community from within. In the wake of the quake and a divided political body, the city struggled to rebuild Main Street, pinning its hopes on the National Steinbeck Center to bring the lucrative tourist industry. However, bad publicity from alarmingly high rates of gang activity doomed that effort. Crime and gang violence reinforced perceptions that Salinas was negatively impacted by the new majority Latino/a population, adding to the already widespread prejudice against them on the peninsula. As a result, developers were reluctant to invest in Salinas, and visitors avoided the city.

The 1990s through the early 2000s saw public schools struggling over funding and issues such as representation and power. The schools in the most heavily populated Latino/a areas, such as Alisal, appointed new leaders from the Latino/a community, some of whom proved to be corrupt, which made for even more damaging headlines and shattered public trust; this led to over a decade of infighting at the school board level as educators partnered with city leaders to combat dropout rates and losing young people to gang life. Meanwhile, the city was facing severe economic crises brought on by demands for services but without a sufficient tax base due to many wealthier residents' exodus to nearby suburbs. In 2004, Salinas even had to close its libraries temporarily, as we saw in the last chapter. Planners, policymakers, and residents alike found themselves frustrated and in almost constant conflict as they struggled for solutions.

Neither the deep cultural and social divides nor the severe economic and political challenges would be healed for over a decade. But they did eventually heal. By the mid-2010s, Salinas appeared to be moving in a more constructive direction. Its school systems, police, and nonprofits rose to the challenge of gang violence and the overpolicing that came with it, which affected every aspect of city life. Charismatic Mayor Dennis Donahue, in partnership with City Manager Ray Corpuz, inaugurated a new era of AgTech that transformed the city, particularly the downtown, and brought positive national attention; by 2017, Steve Forbes was calling Salinas the AgTech epicenter of the nation.[1] The various political and ethno-racial communities within the city combined to create a new, positive identity as a multicultural, multiracial, and culturally rich municipality that more than met the new moment of civil rights activism in 2020. Planning policies for urban renewal focused on inclusivity that gave Salinas's multiple communities a place at the planning table. Latino/a people energetically created a strong political and cultural presence in Salinas and a solid economic one too.

Then the COVID-19 pandemic hit Salinas in the spring of 2020. Salinas had systems in place to cope more effectively than most cities, and certainly better than other cities on the Monterey Peninsula, but the deadly virus nonetheless had a devastating impact on the fieldworkers and service workers who made up most of the population of east Salinas. These Salinas residents could not simply shelter in place or work from home, resulting in enormous community spread. Salinas had 46 percent of all COVID-19 cases in Monterey County, with almost 38 percent of those cases occurring in Alisal (93905 and 93906 zip codes).[2] Besides having high infection rates among workers, Salinas also suffered the economic catastrophe of loss of revenue from the closed restaurants and schools during the pandemic that had fueled agriculture, which had supplied these institutions and businesses with produce.

Still, the city was well managed. It was first and foremost an agricultural town, rather than a tourist destination, and thus was spared the huge economic losses suffered by tourist-based cities on the Monterey Peninsula and throughout the Central Coast region. The city's mantra of cooperation, expansion, inclusion, and mutual understanding may have been more façade than reality, but it also served as a model for a workable new urban ecosystem; it was an urban community of color that embraced rather than defied demographic change in politics and social life and one that understood itself as a proud, innovative agricultural hub forging alliances with the finance and technology centers of Silicon Valley. Former mayor Dennis Donahue described Salinas as "the perfect rural urban lab, the perfect petri dish. Every issue in California plays out here. This is a city of conflict followed by resolution."[3]

POLICING AND POWER

"Salinas doesn't necessarily have a gang problem[;] it has a poverty problem. . . . [I]ndividuals are almost forced to do what they have to do to make their family survive," remarked one observer by way of explaining the high rates of gang activity and crime in Salinas in the 2000s.[4] However, Salinas did have a crime problem, or more precisely, a murder problem, which was directly linked to gang activity. Complex, deeply rooted factors (including poverty) had come together over the course of several decades, giving Salinas one of the highest homicide rates in the country by the early 2000s. "The statistics in Salinas for 2008 and 2009 [were] chilling," reported one analyst; "23 of the 25 homicides in 2008 and all 28 homicides . . . in 2009 [were] classified as gang-related."[5] By way of comparison, Salinas consistently showed double the murder rate of similarly sized Oxnard, California, which also shared a predominantly Latino/a population and high levels of gang activity.

Gangs were blamed both for Salinas's high rates of homicides and for the predominance of murders among young Latino men, although they were not the only victims. One observer recalled, "Growing up I heard of a shooting that occurred in the east side of Salinas, it was a drive-by and a bullet hit a 6-year-old kid who was simply watching television . . . he died," a not uncommon occurrence in Salinas in the 1990s and early 2000s.[6] Yet, out of a total population of well over 160,000, only 3,500 people were active gang members in Salinas at the peak of membership in 2009.[7] Still, although this number comprised a mere 2 percent of Salinas's population, "the rate of gang members in Salinas [was] almost six times the national average [by 2009]. Even using a more robust estimate of a one percent rate of gang members in the United States, Salinas was still double the national average."[8] Salinas gangs were responsible for multiple crimes including auto theft, burglary, identity theft, aggravated assault, homicide, drug trafficking and sales, and robbery. According to an analysis prompted by a series of police shootings in 2014,

> [G]angs have been responsible for the majority of homicides, drive-by shootings, and firearms crimes since 2002. In the same timeframe, gangs committed approximately 25 percent of the total number of violent crimes in Salinas each year. In other words, two percent of the population commits 25 percent of the violent crimes.[9]

Years of attention and investment by local government did not seem to have changed Alisal all that much from its position as the least desirable place to live in Salinas. And the gang problem centered on Alisal, which had the highest rate of homicides in Monterey County. Alisal had fully one-third of the city's record number of homicides.[10] Besides being 95 percent Latino/a by 2015, Alisal had almost triple the rate of housing considered "severely overcrowded" (1.5 occupants per room) and a poverty rate one and a half times that of the city as a whole. It was the most high-density, crime-ridden, and economically distressed area in Salinas.[11]

Although homicides affected much of the community on a day-to-day basis, they disproportionately involved young Latino men who were both the targets and the perpetrators. "Eighteen of Monterey County's forty-nine homicides in 2013 were committed against Hispanic men aged 10 to 24."[12] This high rate of homicides for youth to young adults was an anomaly within the state of California, which reported a 41 percent decrease in homicide rates within that age group from 2006 through 2013.[13]

National data showed the extent that Salinas deviated from the average homicide rate per 100,000 people by the mid-2000s. After a spike in murders per 100,000 people between 1989 and 1991, the homicide rate in America decreased by an average of .25 deaths per 100,000 people a year so that by 2014, the United States dipped to its historic fifty-one year low of 4.5 murders per 100,000.[14] During the same twenty-five years, the homicide rate in Salinas ranged from a record low of 4.69 murders per 100,000 to a record high of 20.5 murders per 100,000.[15]

Crime and gang violence were not merely a law enforcement issue, although they were treated like one. Simón Salinas reflected on the interconnections between gang violence and lack of employment for young people in Alisal. He and other activists strove to break down barriers between those who lived in Alisal and other areas of Salinas:

> I would tell the Northridge merchants you have to help us with this gang issue, this gang violence. You have to help our kids from Alisal to get a job and be part of the community. I would tell them the people on the peninsula don't care that you are in north Salinas. They are going to be afraid to come and shop here because they think the whole city's under siege by gangs. I think they understood. I was trying to make this a better place for all of us but I also need [them] to work with us.[16]

The Salinas Police Department followed the typical (and until recently) unchallenged American practice of overpolicing and underserving in minority communities. The outsized investment of materiel left over from the Vietnam War was granted to police departments everywhere in America in the 1980s and 90s and was utilized to criminalize minority communities solely based on the racial identity of their inhabitants.[17] Salinas came to grips with the problem earlier than most places due to a series of events beginning in 2014.

In 2014, Angel Ruiz died at the hands of Salinas police on March 20, Osmar Hernandez on May 9, Carlos Mejia on May 20, and Frank Alvarado Jr. on July 10. These four officer involved shootings (OIS) in the space of few months proved to be the tipping point that led to a communitywide awakening and overhaul of the police department. In the case of Carlos Mejia, the shooting was captured on cellphone video and immediately received 200,000 hits on YouTube, generating mass protests throughout Monterey County. The other victims of the police shootings were unarmed, and in the case of Mejia, walking away from police rather than confronting them. This weakened officers' claims that Mejia (or the others) posed a significant threat to themselves or to public safety, although Mejia was carrying gardening shears and appeared to be intoxicated. Then, in 2015, Rita Acosta called 911 because her schizophrenic son, José Velasco, ran into the middle of a busy street, and she needed help in restraining him. However, instead of transporting Velasco to a psychiatric facility for treatment, the Salinas police beat him with batons, ostensibly because they witnessed him pushing his mother away. As in the case of Mejia, the incident was recorded on cellphone video by a bystander who was clearly shocked at the overreaction by officers, which also generated communitywide outrage and protests.

To be fair, the police officers were not trained mental health providers and should not have been expected to respond as mental health professionals would. The problem of expecting police officers to handle all varieties of 911 calls and then condemning them for poor outcomes when they are tasked with responding to crises they were never trained to handle was hardly unique to Salinas. It became the wake-up call for the nation grappling with an epidemic of well-publicized police violence, culminating in the murder of George Floyd in 2020. As well, officers could expect very little help from the community when a gang-related homicide did occur. According to one observer, "The shootings that occurred in Salinas are in broad daylight, they occur where people are present; police are always looking for evidence or for the community to help give them clues of the suspects. However, the community is scared; they are afraid that if they tell they will get killed as well."[18]

The officer involved shootings and beatings led to an assessment and overhaul of the Salinas Police Department by the Office of Community Oriented Policing Services (COPS), a team from the U.S. Department of Justice. This team included COPS Office Director Ronald L. Davis, Deputy Director Robert E. Chapman, Senior Social Science Analyst Jessica Mansourian, and Collaborative Reform Specialist George Fachner. The study, which was published in 2016, led to significant changes in the training, operations, and attitudes within the Salinas Police Department, including the hiring of Latina Police Chief Adele Fresé in 2016 and Fire Chief Michele Vaughn. Their hirings signified that the city was serious about changing the racist, sexist culture of these departments, making it more compassionate, responsive, and reflective of Salinas as a minority-majority Latino/a community. The study also led to a collaboration with the Naval Postgraduate School located in nearby Monterey to analyze the roots of crime and violence in Salinas going back to the 1980s. This investigation did not simply blame gang activity for the problem but looked at factors such as high school attendance and dropout rates, employment, extracurricular activities available for young people, and housing density to help explain the attraction of gangs for at-risk youth in the city. The conclusions sometimes surprised researchers. For example, although there was a correlation between truancy, low graduation rates, and lack of extracurricular activity with high gang membership, multifamily housing led to lower rates of gang activity. Extended family and kin living together served as a brake against gangs, which contradicted most assumptions that high-density housing and cramped living conditions brought on by extended family living closely together led to tensions and violence. The opposite was true.[19]

The gang problem in Salinas was all too real, despite the also too real racist response on the part of police targeting Latino/a young people for random stops and searches. Gangs financed their operations with drug sales and used violence to maintain power and control.[20] High crime rates and perceptions of Salinas as a violent municipality upended efforts by city leaders to bring Salinas into the circle of Monterey County communities enjoying the huge economic benefits of a flourishing tourist industry. But when we listen to those whose lives have been most devastated by the gang affiliation of family members or neighbors and friends, and to the police responses that came in their wake, we can appreciate more fully the complexity of the problem of crime and police enforcement. Rather than minimize the damage wrought by gangs or blame overweaponized and undertrained police officers, we need holistic and comprehensive solutions.

I taught a history class at the local California State University, Monterey Bay, in the summer and fall of 2015 with Salinas as a case study because that was where many of my students lived. Although students could choose from a range of paper topics, most of them wanted to focus on crime, violence, and gang activity because it had an outsized impact on their daily lives and family histories. It was a painful process for them to research and write about and, as a result, relive the trauma of watching family members victimized by violence from both gangs and the Salinas police. One student recalled,

> I grew up in the east side of Salinas. In middle school some of my friends were already getting interested in a particular gang. . . . I witnessed how easily others became involved. I had friends who were shot and killed due to their involvement in a particular gang, many of whom were only around 15 or 16 years old. One friend passed away in his sister's arms. He was shot in front of his house and died at the scene.[21]

It made no sense to students that gangs had become such a pervasive part of their lives.

I invited Congressman Jimmy Panetta (a former prosecutor), as well as detectives from the Salinas Police Department, to come to class and share their views and experiences. Students, almost all of whom were Latino/a, challenged both Panetta and the police representatives with what they felt was the pervasive racism in random traffic stops and routine stop and frisks. Many students shared experiences of being stopped by police while walking or biking simply because they were Latino/a. The visiting officers defended those actions as "no harm no foul" when a young person was searched and then released without being arrested. Students thought otherwise and said so in no uncertain terms. One young woman began to cry as she recalled being followed by a police officer as a teenager and feeling terrified. Notwithstanding the opinions of the officers, it harmed students to be followed, stopped, and searched, whether they were subsequently released or not. They shared how frightened and humiliated they felt by the experience. To their credit, the officers apologized to the class.

Still, students understood that gang members lived among them and ought to be stopped. One young woman expressed despair at the interconnected problems of racism and gang violence and crime with their severe impact on individuals, families, and the city itself. She observed that many of Salinas's gang members were mere children who came from its Latino/a community: "The majority of Salinas's [residents] are Mexicans. They do not see that they are killing their own race, at 14–16 years. [D]o they really know what they are defending or what they are claiming?" she asked rhetorically.[22] Worse yet, she believed that young teenagers did not grasp the long-term negative consequences of their criminal behavior:

> Ending up in jail at 14 for attempted murder or murder is basically like getting shot and dying at the scene as well because once someone is a convicted felon what happens to their chances at an education? A job? A life? Young people at risk may not know that by killing someone their opportunities for a successful and productive life might be over, and they are condemned to a life in prison. They are in jail for life.[23]

She blamed the poverty that came from absentee parents who often spent long days doing fieldwork leaving their sometimes very young children at risk:

> I feel that many parents who work in the fields . . . do not give [children] the attention they need which leads them to doing gang related activities. . . . [I]f parents are at work and come home . . . late [children] easily can go in and out of home whenever they wish. . . . [When there are absentee parents] many youths who live in a neighborhood involving violence are at high risk of being the victims or affiliating with a gang.[24]

Even as bystanders, young people in Salinas were traumatized by violence. "A 12-year-old should not be witnessing his friend or family member getting shot and killed." It was painfully obvious to students in my class that kids "need to be focused on what really matters in life such as getting an education, developing life skills, discovering who they are and what their place might be in the world," which was a basic assumption for most white middle-class families in America but seemed out of reach for Alisal children in the 2000s who felt trapped. "A lot of them feel stuck . . . like they will never get out of the bad neighborhood they grew up in." Students argued for prevention. A gang prevention program "can help young kids by being there for them if they need someone to talk to or to give them good advice," according to one student. "They need someone to actually make them feel like they are somebody in life, that they have a purpose to be better than simply a 'gang member.' Young people in Salinas need help, advice, and safe homes without violence."[25]

Most importantly, gang violence was not simply a family issue, but a communitywide problem to solve. "The identity of Salinas is at stake," one student declared. In her view, reducing or even eliminating gang violence meant "changing the identity of the city for the better"—disconnecting Salinas from the inextricable link of gangs and crime. Her solution was not just to offer young people better paths but also to "train teachers and parents to manage disruptive behavior, and to improve community supervision."[26] This young woman, as well as so many others in class, exhibited an impressive faith in the collective power of local government agencies and institutions, in partnership with families, to make positive change.

Another student explained how her father, a gang member who spent years in prison, affected her life and her outlook. Describing herself as "the daughter of an ex-convict who was in and out of prison due to gang-related offenses," she talked about her own trauma-filled childhood as she bore witness to her father "get[ting] arrested, beaten up and jumped."[27] Her narrative showed that police responses to criminals were just as harmful and impactful as the violent behavior of criminal gang members in the lives of children who witnessed parents, siblings, and other adults subjected to arrest.

This young woman described her father's early years in nearby Spreckels as the adopted son of "two loving women, who encouraged his interest in sports, specifically baseball. He grew up to be a joyful, athletic child." As a vulnerable thirteen-year-old, his two mothers separated, however, and abandoned him to extended family members who were affiliated with gangs. "My father began to do drugs, steal, and fight. . . . I see him as a man who had missed opportunities and was surrounded by the wrong people in a time of hardship."[28] She also believed that community support might have made a positive difference for her father when he was most in need. "I sincerely believe if someone had stepped into my father's life before gang members even had a chance to, he would be more than an ex-convict," she emphasized. This student was acutely aware of the deep, long-term consequences of criminal activity, which at least had the effect of deterrence for her. Gang membership "will forever affect him," she explained of her father. "It affects how people perceive him, and it is a defining factor about who he is perceived to be and the opportunities that are denied to him. He cannot vote, for example."[29] Her painful description of her father was palpable: "[He was] an eye sore to the normal citizen and therefore was looked down upon and given few chances."[30]

These narratives showed the profound trauma and fear inflicted upon young children (and the entire community) when they either became victims of violence or bore witness to violence within their families, both by gang members and at the hands of the police who were supposed to protect them. There was little awareness on the part of adults of the pain inflicted on innocents when parents and loved ones were forcibly detained and arrested. Children and adolescents who lost friends or family members experienced severe and lasting trauma that was often misconstrued as simple bad behavior when they acted out at school.

Sometimes dysfunctional family life was blamed, and seemed to have led to gang membership, but not always. Both student narrators and others in this class believed that gang membership might be preempted by the right kind of community intervention and support, suggesting that even those who were the most impacted by the twin assaults of gangs and overzealous police departments still had faith in government and in their community to solve the problem. One student affirmed, "We have the ability to break this cycle, to give children the option and opportunity to change their life significantly."[31]

Without government intervention and widespread community support, gang membership became a powerful replacement for family and unfortunately an attractive alternative to a law-abiding life. Gangs offered vulnerable young people a sense of belonging, economic opportunity, and empowerment that they so desperately needed and actively sought. By 2016, city leaders and community members agreed that this was not a law enforcement issue, but a community call to action.

A coalition of individuals and organizations collectively worked to subvert gangs and lead to a restoration of the public safety—something that was taken for granted in Salinas before the 1960s. Not every policy or practice was effective, but because of forces working to end gang affiliation and the violence that came with it, crime rates decreased significantly after 2016, and young people enjoyed many more opportunities and supports. The effort started at least three decades earlier, as we know from an advertisement that ran in 1986 in the *Salinas Californian:* "Wanted: Police Chief, strong leader. Must be able to fit in and improve the Department's relations with the Latino/a community."[32] City leaders understood the need not only to represent the community better in hiring officers who were Latino/a, but also to train officers who actually lived in the city, preferably in Alisal.

That unsustainable situation changed over the course of the 2000s and certainly by 2016. Programs and policies by city leaders, educators, nonprofits, and community activists all came together to reverse both views of gangs and crime and the policy responses to them. One such effort, conceptualized by Judge John Phillips, offered an alternative means of employment and socioeconomic mobility to Salinas gang members and juvenile offenders. Judge Phillips had grown frustrated with the number of repeat offenders that came before him in juvenile court. The organization that he spearheaded, Rancho Cielo, selected young people who had already become entangled in gangs and taught them culinary, construction, and technical skills. After extensive training, youth were given assistance in finding employment in the mainstream economy that allowed real choice and an escape from the control that gangs wielded so effectively.

Middle schools and high schools offered more options to discourage truancy and to encourage graduation. The local community college, Hartnell, created numerous support programs meant to sustain at-risk youth (both girls and boys) and prepare them for employment, particularly in technology jobs in agriculture. All this policy, planning, and community action worked to significantly reduce gang membership, lower crime rates, and raise expectations even for the most vulnerable young people in Salinas. Although the struggle is ongoing, it is worth emphasizing that interventions at multiple levels can work to ameliorate even the most difficult and complex problems if there is community will at the local level coupled with state and federal support.

Although proximity to Salinas Valley State Prison (22 miles south of the city) and Soledad Prison have been blamed for gang activity, an exhaustive study of the roots of gangs, crime, and violence in Salinas concluded that high school graduations and dropout rates and average daily attendance were more important factors in terms of the predisposition of young people to join gangs. A climate of economic uncertainty that limited job opportunities coupled with the 1990s backlash against bilingual education left many young Latino/a residents out of the educational system and was far more likely to lead to gang activity and high crime rates than the proximity of the prisons.[33]

EDUCATION AS A CHANGE AGENT

The issue of bilingual education took center stage in Salinas as an antidote to the crime problem, which was increasingly understood as a consequence of racism and structural inequality. The origins of bilingual education in Salinas under Virginia Rocca Barton had largely been forgotten, but the issue was revived by the energized California Rural Legal Assistance (CRLA) attorneys in the 1980s in a series of successful lawsuits throughout the state.[34]

Schools routinely used English-language and Anglo American culturally specific intelligence tests (IQ tests) to measure students' intelligence levels and potential for achievement in school and in life and then determined that some students (mostly minorities) would be channeled into classes for the mentally challenged or unfit (educable mentally retarded or EMR classes). Integral to the eugenics movement of the 1930s, those tests had been developed intentionally to sustain race-based hierarchies by offering pseudo-scientific proof of the biological inferiority of people of color in order to set them apart from their white peers and keep them permanently on the margins of Anglo American middle-class life. In the decades after the 1930s, social scientists (particularly from the Chicago School) disputed the basis for the IQ tests—the widespread belief system that race could define (or determine) human intelligence or worth, much less serve as a predictive for future achievement for anyone. In addition, social scientists from the Chicago school used solid quantitative and qualitative evidence to show blatant bias in the standardized testing, especially against non–English-speaking students, who, like their English-speaking African American peers, lived in cultural contexts outside of the Anglo American mainstream and could not hope to answer questions such as "Why is it better to pay by check rather than cash?" especially as third graders. Questions like these obviously did not measure anyone's innate intelligence, but simply showed familiarity with certain Eurocentric, white, middle-class cultural norms.

The use of IQ tests nonetheless persisted in classrooms across the country and were given routinely to all third graders in California through the 1970s to determine their placement in vocational, EMR, or college prep tracks. Students who scored 75 points or higher remained assigned to "normal" classrooms. However, a score of over 60 but below 75 meant that a student was permanently classified as EMR and placed in a classroom for "slow learners," which severely limited their academic (and life) options, as we saw with the Lincoln Elementary policy in Chapter 7. They were not going to college. They were not even going to be able to escape work in the fields or factories. Their parents fought back, with a lot of help from activists and educators.

By the late 1960s, civil rights activists not only joined social scientists, educators, and academics in publicly discrediting the racist ideology behind the eugenics movement, they also began filing lawsuits to stop the testing and tracking entirely. They loudly and effectively challenged both the standardized IQ tests and the policy of the placement system that purposefully, permanently disadvantaged minority students, particularly non-English speakers. They used hard evidence to do so. Thus, when California students in sample districts were retested using Spanish-language IQ tests (although without changing content), their test scores improved dramatically, showing clearly that the students were perfectly intelligent and worthy of college preparatory work; they were just not proficient in English or familiar enough with Anglo American cultural norms to demonstrate their abilities on a single, biased, standardized IQ test.[35]

The attorneys and activists succeeded in changing policy with three important court cases as well as new legislation enacted at state and federal levels.[36] One, particular to Salinas and the Salinas Valley, was brought by CRLA in April 1966. CRLA attorneys set up shop across the street from Salinas High School and immediately dove into the problem of inequality for farmworkers and their families. Deeply influenced by César Chávez and a veritable tidal wave of Chicano/a civil rights successes in labor rights in the 1970s, these young lawyers initiated (successful) legal challenges to the use of the short-handled hoe; but they also challenged the systematic tracking of Mexican American elementary school students into special education programs based on race, programs that ostensibly gave elite growers a steady, compliant workforce and severely limited the chances for second-generation Mexican American children to move from fieldwork to middle-class lives. The CRLA lawsuit, *Diana v. State Board of Education*, led to a discontinuation of the tracking policy, a policy that used obviously flawed and racially biased IQ tests to place Salinas's Spanish-speaking Mexican American students in

EMR classrooms. The case had both state and national repercussions. The main outcome locally was that CRLA succeeded in forcing both Spanish bilingual education and Mexican culture classes in the Salinas schools. The IQ tests continued but were administered in what was supposed to be a more equitable manner, in Spanish for Spanish-speaking students.

Successful civil rights lawsuits and legislation at the state and national levels had given CRLA much needed momentum. In January 1974, the U.S. Supreme Court decided in *Lau v. Nichols* that non-English proficient (NEP) and limited English proficient (LEP) children had a right to bilingual education in public schools.[37] This was followed in 1974 by the passage of the Equal Opportunity Act in Congress, intended to fortify the equal protections clause in the Fourteenth Amendment, on which the *Lau* case was based. *Lau v. Nichols* required change at the state and national levels, and California school districts responded. They scrambled to initiate their own versions of bilingual educational programs. African American parents contested the IQ tests and the tracking of their children into EMR classes too and succeeded in forcing a moratorium on IQ tests and tracking in *Larry P. v. Riles*. Finally, the 1976 *Serrano v. Priest* case challenged the funding discrepancy among public schools in California.

According to California policy and practice, funding for schools depended on property taxes, which in turn were determined by property values. As a result, schools located in wealthier areas enjoyed considerably more funding than those located in places like Alisal, which had depreciating homes and much less revenue to support schools, leading to an enormous gap in the quality of education based on the residence of families. The California Supreme Court supported the students and parents in *Serrano* and determined that the unequal funding model in California was unconstitutional. Instead of linking school funding to local taxes, the court's decision led to a new policy that created a statewide pool of property taxes so that money was shared equally among school districts. Although this new funding system was more equitable, Alisal still bore the brunt of overcrowded classes with an increasing number of students who needed support in language learning and who suffered from the effects of disrupted schooling because of migration when their parents worked as seasonal agricultural laborers and traveled to pick crops. The decision also led to the tax revolt culminating in Proposition 13 two years later, in which parents from wealthier suburbs objected to sharing tax dollars in support of schools in poorer areas.

When Proposition 13 passed by a two-thirds majority in 1978, it led to a significant reduction in property taxes, reducing state revenues by 57 percent, which, in turn, decreased the amount of funding available to fund public schools by a considerable amount.[38] Proposition 13 meant that schools throughout California created their own budgets and revenue sources, which wealthier communities accomplished far more successfully that poorer ones.[39] Because Proposition 13 limited the amount of taxes that could be charged on properties to fund schools throughout the state, elite and even middle-class communities responded by expanding their school budgets to compensate and continued to maintain well-funded schools that allowed their children to thrive educationally. But places like Alisal could not do the same, and students there continued to suffer from neglect and lack of funding, something that led eventually to the conditions that made for fertile recruiting grounds for gang members in places like Salinas.

Funding was not the only issue driving debates over public education by the 1980s. Bilingual education (although not bilingual IQ tests, as discussed earlier) also came under renewed attack—not just from white elites, but also from other minority groups who sided with Anglo Americans in demanding English only in public schools for a wide variety of reasons, not least of which was fear of being overwhelmed by a surging Latino/a majority population in California. Standardized testing itself enjoyed new popularity by the 1990s as elite colleges became increasingly sought after and competitive. Moreover, educators began to question the efficacy of removing students from EMR classes wholesale, mainstreaming underachieving high school students who then dropped out of school at higher and higher rates, presumably because they could not meet the challenges of "normal" schoolwork.[40] In Salinas, increasingly high dropout rates among Latino/a students in the 1990s, although poorly documented, raised serious questions about bilingual education as inhibiting rather than enhancing learning and was connected to concerns over gang membership and criminal activity.

In 1993, Richard Diaz, a demographics consultant for the California Department of Education, found that although dropout rates had fallen statewide, they had risen, sometimes by alarming numbers, in Monterey County schools with the highest numbers of Latino/a non–English-speaking students, even though it was not clear that students had really dropped out. Many students might just have relocated or received high school educations (and their GED degrees) by alternative routes than graduation from public high schools.[41] Nonetheless, critics of bilingual education used that data to support claims that bilingual education programs hurt students more than helped them and ought to be eliminated. They also complained (along with political opponents of immigration at the time) that Mexican American students in bilingual classes did not transition into English-language mainstream classes fast enough and were therefore not assimilating into American culture as quickly as had earlier generations of immigrants who had been forced to learn English in public school. Furthermore, they claimed that minority, non–English-speaking students were being marginalized, segregated, and diminished by being in bilingual education classes, as much or more as when minority students faced discrimination and tracking into EMR classes based on the old IQ tests.[42]

In 1984, Governor George Deukmejian had vetoed a bill passed by the state legislature that would have extended bilingual education in all California schools through 1992. By 1996, California entrepreneur Ron K. Unz promoted Proposition 227, which passed with a 61 percent majority, requiring all California public school instruction to be conducted in English, with some waivers but only if requested by a parent. The proposition required that limited English proficient (LEP) students would be placed in English immersion programs after only a year of bilingual education. The measure also stipulated a commitment by the state for $50 million per year for ten years to support courses for individuals who volunteered to teach or tutor students in English.[43]

Thus, the significant gains of the 1970s and 1980s in achieving equity in the schools for Mexican American Spanish-speaking students—in coalition with advocacy work by Chinese American and African American students, parents, and activists—had all slipped away by the 1990s with the twin impacts of Proposition 13 and sustained attacks on bilingual education for Spanish-speaking students. Increased dropout rates, lower daily attendance, lack of funding for schools generally, and loss of extracurricular and after-school programs all combined to contribute directly to dramatically rising levels of gang-related crime and violence in Salinas, according to multiple sociological studies.[44]

The educational community in Salinas suffered from other woes in the 1990s when decisions that were meant to create equity in school administrations backfired. In 1980, fueled by CRLA's gains in educational access, opportunity, and expanded programs, Mexican American parents in east Salinas demanded (and got) representation at the highest levels of administration in Alisal Union School District, a place once dominated by the formidable Virginia Rocca Barton. But they hired the wrong people.

The most glaring mistake involved the superintendent, Marco Mazzoni, and two co-workers, Paul Carillo Jr. and Raphaelito Tojos. Mazzoni, who was ethnically Italian, was planning a group excursion to Italy, which triggered an investigation of misuse of funds. Carillo and Tojos, who were Mexican American, were similarly caught up in the scandal. Their ethnicity became as much part of the story as their collective corruption and, as a result, not only damaged the school district but also the reputation of the entire Latino/a community for advocating their hiring. The three administrators had spent four years diverting public monies without consequence and were convicted of graft, fraud, and embezzlement of public funds in 1986. One office clerk, Sean McMillan, testified that for several years prior to the hiring of Mazzoni, Tojos, and Carillo, it had been common practice (rather than unique to the three accused) for monies to be siphoned off for personal use in the district offices. The public outcry shook Salinas. The dismissal and conviction of the three administrators followed a wave of dysfunction in the Alisal and Salinas schools. The three individuals were replaced by a succession of Latino/a administrators, many of whom had roots in Alisal but little expertise in school administration. They created a toxic political culture of infighting, backbiting, and turmoil in the ensuing decades, notably under the leadership of Alisal Unified School Board President José Castañeda.[45]

The community as a whole bore the brunt of the scandals and turmoil, which inevitably made the front pages of the local newspapers alongside stories about gang activity and frighteningly high crime rates.[46] Beloved teachers such as Susan Aremas, who had been nurtured in the Alisal schools under the watchful eye of Virginia Rocca Barton, fled to work in other districts. "I have to say it was like teaching in the trenches," recalled Susan about her experience as an elementary schoolteacher in Alisal in this period. She described a chaotic environment for teachers without a stable curriculum. The bilingual education classes that came about in this era differed from the high standards of the Barton years, according to Susan. "The classes were not bilingual because they were only teaching in Spanish and the teachers didn't have the skill. The parents were illiterate. The teachers were not equipped."[47] She became so discouraged by the changes she experienced teaching in Alisal that she moved into a more middle-class school district in north Salinas.

Students suffered from the bad publicity and from the defections of strong teaching staff. By 1999, Monterey County schools, and Salinas school districts in particular, had fallen well below the state average, according to Academic Performance Index (API) results. Ranking schools 1–10 (10 being the highest), six of the nine elementary schools in the Alisal Union School District ranked the lowest with a score of 1. In Salinas, two of the three elementary schools received a 1 and 2 ranking, respectively. Only two of the seven middle and high schools in Salinas (including Alisal) received a 4; the rest were ranked at 1 and 2. It was a dismal outcome. In response, and with echoes of earlier critiques of standardized testing, Assistant Superintendent Nancy Kotowski argued that the API test itself was "flawed."[48]

Parents were also blamed for not "helping out," for not being more involved in their children's academic lives. Language barriers continued to be identified as problems, harkening back to advocacy in the 1970s for fairness in bilingual testing: "In certain districts, language is a barrier," Susan Marquez, a parent from Creekside Elementary School, contended. "The scores are not fair for some people [to be tested only in English]. . . . I mean on the east side there is a different language spoken . . . there is a different world."[49] Collective efforts by nonprofits, agricultural corporations, and philanthropists tried to meet the educational challenges that east Salinas and Alisal presented at the close of the 1990s. Yet, largesse was still largesse and could be withdrawn if philanthropists found better places to invest their resources. Salinas's students needed concerted efforts by state government response rather than philanthropy alone.

Through very specific STEM training programs that prepared students primarily for work in agriculture, the schools channeled Salinas's high school students into the local community colleges (Hartnell and Monterey Peninsula College) and the local California State University campus in nearby Marina (CSUMB). Though well intended and applauded for their success rates, these efforts often had the effect of limiting students—stranding them academically into vocational training and keeping them geographically in the immediate area just when they might have benefited from the challenges and opportunities that full-time college students routinely enjoy when they leave home and are exposed to vastly different people and environments. By leaving the Monterey Peninsula and exploring new worlds beyond vocational training, Salinas's young people might discover careers well outside of STEM and agriculture. To encourage this broader educational and life experience, new programs were introduced in the Salinas schools.

One such program, AVID (Advancement Via Individual Determination), was implemented in Salinas in 1996. Started in San Diego in 1980, AVID's mission was to support and prepare promising students who came from poor and underserved minority-majority communities. The families of these students had little education themselves, so they were not able to guide their children through the byzantine maze of college prep courses, test preparation, and extracurricular activities that made them good candidates for admission into four-year colleges and provided them with the skills they needed to graduate in four years. To level the playing field, AVID students were expected to maintain a rigorous class schedule, which included learning modern foreign languages, as well as engage in demanding coursework in reading, writing, science, math, and critical thinking through tutorials using the Socratic method. They learned note-taking skills, timed writing, how to ask questions in class, collaboration, reading actively, and studying effectively. The program included weekly speakers, trips to college campuses, and parent workshops designed to bring parents into the entire process.

AVID gave Salinas's students the kind of tough academic training along with cultural enrichment that wealthier, whiter communities offered as a matter of course, thereby preparing them to succeed both in the competitive college application process and, as college students, to handle the rigor that most top liberal arts colleges required. One former AVID educator explained:

> We wanted to get them out of the area and expose them to the wider world. We wanted to see them attend colleges and universities that graduate students in four years instead of spending a decade struggling in community college here in Salinas while they tried to balance work and complicated family lives.[50]

Nationwide, AVID boasted a 92 percent rate of enrollment for their students in four-year colleges and universities by 1996, just sixteen years after the program started, an extraordinary success rate.[51] Steven Garza, a twelve-year-old student from El Sausal Middle School, explained that he enjoyed learning how to take notes in class and that AVID "was really fun, and after school, it is a lot better than going into gangs," which was exactly the goal that program organizers hoped for.[52] AVID advocates faced many challenges, however, including a reluctance on the part of many Mexican American families to allow their daughters to leave the area for college. Nonetheless, by 2006, the program was extended to Alisal High School, and the success rate rose to 95 percent.

Despite multiple efforts such as these by educators and others, the culture of the Alisal schools and of East Salinas generally continued to deteriorate well into the 2000s as gang membership only increased, defining the social and cultural world of the city in local and national media.[53] By 2010, the educational system had hit its low point, exemplified by waves of resignations, recalls, and fighting at school board meetings that seemed to be chaotic, with little sense of policy or purpose. "In Alisal there is a culture of intimidation and mistrust. It comes from the board and everyone is subject to it. We found it disturbing," observed California State School Board Member Ted Mitchell in 2010.[54] He had been sent to the district to assume control over the crisis. Sanctioned by the state for failing to meet minimum goals for student achievement, the district was in disarray, suffering a succession of administrators, who although they shared an ethnic identity with residents, appeared ill equipped to do the job of educating children and remained polarized and bitterly political. Police and security guards had to be brought in to keep the peace at board meetings throughout the decade.

In 2012, the nonprofit organization Motivating Individual Leadership for Public Advancement (MILPA) was yet another attempt to disrupt gang activity in east Salinas and Alisal by offering counseling, job training, and educational opportunities to former gang members and felons. MILPA organizers focused their attention on partnerships with east Salinas schools, which had become fertile recruiting grounds for gang members, particularly for the notorious Nuestra Familia group. According to one assessment, "MILPA succeeded in its twin goals of helping ex-felons remain out of gangs and offering at-risk Salinas youth a path out of violence and poverty. Sustained by nearly $2 million in grants and support," MILPA was praised at the national level for offering former felons a chance to redeem lives that had been lost to gang membership. MILPA not only generated support and interest from respected funders such as the California Endowment, but also created important partnerships with the Center on Juvenile and Criminal Justice among other well-known think tanks. Both *The Atlantic* and the *Chronicle of Social Change* applauded MILPA for its work in helping to "direct juvenile justice policy in California." Moreover, several members of MILPA's staff had served on a panel for a California State Assembly subcommittee on public safety and worked in jails and prisons on the East Coast.[55] However, by 2019 prominent leaders from Nuestra Familia had infiltrated this well-respected organization, undermining MILPA's reputation. Court documents and police reports provided local journalists with corroborating evidence of gang infiltration, buttressed as well by multiple unnamed sources "who declined to be named out of fear for their safety or because they are not authorized to speak on the record."[56]

Claudia Meléndez-Salinas, a locally known and well-respected investigative journalist and spokesperson for Alisal Union School District, whose online publication *Voices of Monterey Bay* broke the story, suddenly found herself amid a firestorm at her job site and in the community for daring to disclose the dark side of this organization. Ostracized rather than heralded for her courageous exposé of an organization that purported to support youth, Meléndez-Salinas's experience revealed remaining fissures in the Alisal and Salinas schools that were deeply connected to the city's politics and problems with powerful gangs; these fractures threatened to derail Salinas's best efforts to build an equitable, cohesive, and safe communal city.

Alisal and Salinas schools continued to form partnerships with activist nonprofits. For example, Building Healthy Communities aimed to bring the schools into a vision of the Alisal that celebrated its Latino/a culture and supported students and teachers with significant investments in learning, outreach, and programs designed in coordination with city leaders, all proven methods in dissuading gang membership.[57] These partnerships promised everything that the student narratives advocated. They were hopeful, collective steps that depended on coalition building between the community and local government. The schools faced multiple challenges due to difficulty in maintaining funding and the presence of gangs in the community as MILPA exemplified, but programs such as AVID—combined with programs channeling students through Hartnell Community College, Monterey Peninsula College, and California State University, Monterey Bay—along with the long-term plans initiated by city government to include the schools in planning policies are ameliorating some of those difficulties.

At the state level, some of the inequality produced by attacks on bilingual education programs and Proposition 13 were addressed by the California state legislature in 2013. The Local Control Funding Formula (LCFF) gave all California public schools a base amount of funding, determined that supplementary funds were linked to an individual school's needs rather than its local budget or taxes. The legislation encouraged smaller class sizes by providing a 10.4 percent supplementary grant to schools that could show evidence that they had initiated programs to reduce class sizes in K-3 to twenty-four or fewer students. Schools with student populations including those considered "disadvantaged" (English learners, students on free or reduced-price lunch, or youth in foster care) also received an extra grant consisting of 20 percent of their base grant. Alisal Union School District qualified on both counts (reduced class size and "disadvantaged" students) with 91 percent of its student population meeting the criteria and increasingly showed positive effects from the added investment at the state level.[58]

In 1973, Virginia Rocca Barton wisely noted, "The world is changing and schools have to change with it." Educational outcomes were intertwined with poverty, development, education, and policing in Salinas, as they were elsewhere in urban America. But this city came together in the years after the economic recession of 2008 and 2009 to tackle these issues in a comprehensive manner that proved prescient in light of the COVID-19 epidemic and economic crash of 2020.

CITY PLANNING AND AGTECH

Dennis Donahue, elected mayor in 2006, in partnership with City Manager Ray Corpuz, tackled the interconnected demographic and development challenges of the new century by focusing simultaneously on Main Street and Alisal. Confident, enthusiastic, and always optimistic, Donahue held a variety of positions in sales in agriculture and in the Salinas Chamber of Commerce before successfully running for city council in 2006, and then mayor. The bright vision for the city included a comprehensive plan for development of both the east side and the downtown that might effectively meet the challenges that Salinas faced as an urban center in an agriculturally based rural area. It was a big undertaking.

Corpuz charged the Salinas Planning and Research Corporation (SPARC) with coming up with a new economic development plan for the city, which was largely completed by the time COVID-19 hit in the spring of 2020. SPARC, conceived in 2007, was the brainchild of architect Peter Kasavan, Alfred Diaz-Infante, Gary Tanimura, Lorri Koster, Warren Wayland, and other members of the Salinas Chamber of Commerce who wanted to create a regional and holistic plan for the city that might circumvent the piecemeal planning policies of the 1980s and 90s.[59] SPARC included plans for development of both downtown and Alisal. After Donahue left the mayor's office, he was replaced by former police detective Joe Gunter, who, along with Corpuz and the Salinas Planning Department, kept the often-warring members of the Salinas City Council together to approve two important initiatives. Councilmembers Tony Barrera, José Castañeda, Kimbley Craig, Gloria De La Rosa, Jyl Lutes, and Steve McShane represented divergent constituencies and views that still mostly met in the conservative middle, whatever their respective ethno-racial backgrounds, something that holds true in the current election cycle.

The outcome was the Downtown Vibrancy Plan, which reconstituted the 100 to 300 blocks of Main Street around the revived National Steinbeck Center and the Taylor Building. The Alisal Vibrancy Plan followed.[60] The city also worked with Asian communities to create the Asian Cultural Experience (ACE), focusing on reviving the history of Salinas's Chinatown. The Chinatown Revitalization Area plan rounded out this all-inclusive effort in urban planning in Salinas.

The partnerships with nonprofits, such as Building Healthy Communities and CHISPA, and the multiple community events made the entire planning process cumbersome, but also truly grassroots, community oriented, and ultimately successful; it was a development plan that effectively brought in community members to create equity. The city created a database of over 750 individuals representing about 350 agencies and interests that included both English-speaking and Spanish-speaking city residents, city government committee and board members, local and regional public agencies, businesses and business organizations, development organizations, community organizations, faith-based organizations, educational institutions, and environmental groups.[61] The database documents were all bilingual, and the city widely posted its intentions and progress through both Spanish-language and English local media and on a website. In addition, representatives from city staff presented developments in progress to stakeholders that included business owners, community organizations, educational institutions, environmental groups, and public agencies. Students and faculty at the local California State University (CSUMB) and the community college were invited to provide input.

The city created numerous bilingual events and meetings for additional outreach as a matter of course throughout the planning and implementation processes. Ernesto Lizaola, the community education manager for the Salinas Public Libraries, encapsulated the vision that the city put in place in the early 2000s when the new El Gabilan Library (in Alisal) opened its doors in February 2020:

> Part of the goal of the library and the city is to serve our residents with what they need and not only have their voices heard but be the driving force for change. . . . This is a community driven project.[62]

Lizaola's comment was meant to emphasize inclusiveness for residents of Alisal in the library project as well as in city planning in general.

All the planning would be for naught without jobs. The "Steinbeck Innovation AgTech Summit," first held in downtown Salinas in July 2014, was an effort on the part of city government to bring government and agriculture together with the aim of creating networks that connected startups with innovative ideas to the growers' industry to help develop marketable products. As most California rural communities are also geographically disconnected from any university research hub, they must do so through an industry-based approach to training of applied mechanics. As these places worked to adapt from a network of roads and rail lines, they needed to build comprehensive broadband network to support these efforts. City Manager Ray Corpuz and Economic Development Director Andy Myrick hired consultant SVG Partners from Silicon Valley to help them restore prominence to the downtown through its most important economic driver: agriculture. They also wanted to foster a critical link to the high tech world of Silicon Valley and Stanford University, located barely an hour's drive from Salinas. Praising the effort, Norm Groot, head of the Monterey County Farm Bureau, foresaw "Salinas Valley [as] poised to be the next Silicon Valley for venture capital investment as the global interest in food production for an ever-increasing world population will surely include local advances in traceability, increased yields with less resources consumed, and mechanical harvesting."[63] He predicted that the summit "should raise the profile of the Salinas Valley" to an international level, particularly since the next year's event would be co-sponsored by Forbes, Inc. and renamed "Forbes Reinventing America: The AgTech Summit" (it was later changed again to the "Forbes AgTech Summit"). The AgTech Summit, as it came to be called, raised Salinas's profile in a generally positive way, especially after Steve Forbes pronounced Salinas "The AgTech capital of the world" at the 2016 event.

However, the city's investment in the AgTech Summit came under fire from local critics who were suspicious of spending with little evidence of immediate benefit to the city's coffers. Citing a *Forbes* magazine article that ranked Salinas as one of the worst places to live or do business, critics of the summit argued that Salinas leaders were naïve in investing in such a grandiose event. Critics also deemed the money allocated by the city to Silicon Valley consultants as wasteful, with minimal benefit to Salinas.[64] Their critique was widely disseminated in the local press.

These critics had a point, but their singular focus on expenses and the negative aspects of the AgTech Summit missed the essence of what had always defined Salinas. Exactly like the pragmatic visionaries who created Salinas in the late nineteenth century, Dennis Donahue, Ray Corpuz, and Andy Myrick understood how important it was to construct an image that showcased Salinas as central to food production in the twenty-first century: one that might bring together vast networks of scientific and technological experts with producers, policymakers, and practitioners to make investments that would rescue Salinas from its shaky economic situation and provide year-round, high-level employment for Salinas young people. It was an ambitious undertaking reminiscent of efforts in the late nineteenth and early twentieth centuries to make Salinas into a regional urban center. It required everyone's active participation. It was multiracial, open to both women and men, and, most importantly, cut across class lines. Innovation promised everybody a place at the table. It remains to be seen how this effort plays out in the long term, but clearly Salinas is one of those places—the urban center of a rural, agricultural region—that offers the rest of urban America a model of what a functional, communal city might look like when it embraces diversity rather than recoils from it.

More than anything else, Salinas city councils reflected the interwoven nature of city life and its heterogeneity. The 2020 and 2021 Salinas city councils included Deputy Sheriff Scott Davis, an openly gay Asian American; activist Tony Barrera, a businessman; Steve McShane, a local landscaper and community activist and organizer; Gloria De La Rosa, a former health department nurse who recently retired from politics but served since the 1990s with Anna Caballero; Christie Cromeenes, a businesswoman; and John "Tony" Villegas, a teacher. The newly elected mayor of Salinas in 2021 is businesswoman Kimbley Craig. The historically white, male Grower-Shipper Association showed a similarly novel inclusivity when its members elected Christopher Valadez as president, a Latino man whose grandfather was a Bracero. The membership and staff of the GSA has now included women (Abby Taylor-Silva served as vice president) and minorities in key roles.

By 2020, Americans had faced challenges in everything from public health (COVID-19) to the economy (volatile at best, Depression era at worst) to race relations (tense and explosive), especially for those who lived in urban areas. Unlike many of its counterparts in California and the nation, however, Salinas was not exploding with rage and despair in large part because it was constructed by pragmatists who had a clear and cogent vision of what American life ought to look like. Although Salinas certainly experienced some of the worst racial divisions and class conflicts of the last century, moderate voices have prevailed all along the way, leading to a strong community culture. It aimed to be both inclusive and empowering, even though that inclusivity was more superficial than real for most of its history.

Salinas still often makes the front pages of the local media for its high crime, violence, racial and economic injustice, and severe educational disparities. Yet, just as often, it is a city celebrated for diversity, innovations in education, and new infrastructure. It boasts both a female police chief and female fire chief, and women are at the head of almost all city staff departments, including mayor.

This story shows just how all of this was accomplished—not by one group alone, especially not by white men only, but by a multiracial, gendered community with a shared belief in American ideals of democracy and equality, despite formidable challenges from the nineteenth century on. Salinas people believed in America and all that it stood for, naïvely at times; their profound, unshaken faith in the American model provided the glue for healthy city-building.

In the late nineteenth century when railroad giants and land developers dominated the region (as well as the nation and the state), Chinese and Chinese Americans carved an important niche in the nascent city, demanding and receiving a place in the social, economic, and political order. Women participated fully and actively in city-building throughout Salinas's history too, even when they could not vote or run for office. By the very early twentieth century, the intimacy and fast pace of agricultural development allowed groups who had been marginalized all over California breathing room, both in socioeconomic mobility and in cultural and social inclusion, most notably among Salinas's multiple Asian communities of Chinese, Japanese, and Filipino/a Americans but for Mexican American residents too.

By mid-century, and in the aftermath of the crisis of both the Depression and World War II, the city regrouped quickly but faced its biggest challenge with the advent of the Chicano/a civil rights movement. The United Farm Workers and César Chávez called out racial and class inequality, which split the community racially and politically. Nonetheless, moderate, pragmatic visionaries prevailed as they always had, embracing the new Latino/a majority and facing up to racism.

Salinas fought hard to become the county seat and urban center for Monterey County and for the Central Coast region in the nineteenth century. This came with profound and unexpected challenges but also great opportunities. The crime and violence of the 1990s that tore many minority-majority cities apart also impacted Salinas, which, as the county seat, had two prisons and a jail in close by. But instead of militarizing police, Salinas relied on expert analysis to understand the roots of the problems and made significant changes to its policing strategies, far in advance of other places. As a result of more community-based policing, funding went to build trust and more effective public safety measures rather than to perpetuate the racialized and random targeting of minority male young people. As the county seat and regional urban center, the county public health department is located in Salinas, along with two hospitals (one, Natividad, a trauma center) at the front lines of COVID-19. These institutions wielded considerable power and expertise in handling the devastating pandemic and, as always, worked in partnership with agriculture in managing the virus, which hit Salinas's farmworker communities severely. Even during the crisis, Salinas served as a model of how to cope—with compassion, support, and, most of all, respect and understanding of one another.

Hard-won inclusionary policies and practices came about through activism and through individual and collective effort. Salinas's history illustrated a quintessential American story: a struggle over centuries that showed both cooperation and conflict in a place that blurred the lines between urban and rural. Salinas created a comfortable, pragmatic, modern political and economic structure based on cultural and political inclusions and enough economic opportunity to circumvent real challenges to white privilege—that unfortunately must still be confronted and overturned. Although tested throughout its history, the middle held—based as it was on a hundred years of practical politics: economic and social mobility into the middle classes for enough members of any given group to support the myth that the American dream was truly accessible to all, even when it was not, gilded with superficial cultural inclusions that created a general sense of belonging.

Appendix

I described various population changes and demographic shifts in the narrative of this book; here I include tables to illustrate these shifts in more detail, using census data rather than the anecdotal evidence on which contemporaries and newspaper accounts relied. That said, the total population count for each table does not always conform to the count for individual groups as the census did not always include all racial categories in its population counts (indicated with an asterisk in the tables below). Asian, Indigenous, and Hispanic people were often undercounted, and sometimes they were omitted altogether from total population counts.

Census takers used the category "other races" from 1930 to 1970, which included a variety of nonwhite people (indicated with an asterisk in the tables below). This included Filipino/as, Koreans, South Asians, Pacific Islanders, and anyone who could not be categorized as Black, white, or Hispanic. These more specific categories were available only for cities over 100,000 or more in population. The population of Salinas was below this threshold for these decades.

The category for people of African descent was official labeled "Negro" from 1930 to 1970 on the questionnaires and in the census publications. I have chosen to use "Black" instead in deference to narrators' preference (indicated with an asterisk in the tables below). I've also used the term "American Indian" rather than "Indian," which was used in earlier census publications (indicated with an asterisk in the tables below).

The census collected information differently over the course of the decennial censuses for the category deemed Hispanic or Mexican, which makes it difficult to standardize. Furthermore, anyone deemed Hispanic was identified by ethnic origin rather than by race in federal statistics. For the purpose of these tables, I have labeled the category "Hispanic/Latino" (indicated with an asterisk in tables below), noting that it wasn't until the 1970 census that this category was included on the questionnaire. Previous censuses determined the Hispanic/Latino population through indirect methods. Aggregate totals at the city and county levels vary as well, which is why there are no totals for various years. The first table below shows how information for this category was collected and labeled between 1930 and 2000.

1930	Mexican was included as a category for race.
1940	Mexican was eliminated as a category for race; white population of Spanish "mother tongue" was included as a category.
1950	"Persons of Spanish surname" was included as a category in five southwestern states.
1960	"Persons of Spanish surname" was included as a category in five southwestern states.
1970	Self-identification question was included, asking if origin or descent was Mexican, Puerto Rican, Cuban, Central or South American, or other Spanish.
1980	Self-identification question was included, asking about Spanish/Hispanic origin.
1990	Self-identification question was included, asking about Spanish/Hispanic origin.
2000	Self-identification question was included, asking about Spanish/Hispanic/Latino origin.

**TOTAL POPULATION OF CALIFORNIA, MONTEREY COUNTY,
AND SALINAS FROM 1930 TO 2000**

	1930	1940	1950	1960	1970	1980	1990	2000
California	5,677,251	6,907,387	10,586,223	15,717,204	19,957,715	23,667,902	29,670,021	33,871,648
Monterey County	53,705	73,032	130,498	198,351	250,071	290,444	355,660	401,762
Salinas	10,263	11,586	13,917	28,957	58,896	80,479	108,777	151,060

DEMOGRAPHICS OF CALIFORNIA FROM 1930 TO 2000

	1930	1940	1950	1960	1970	1980	1990	2000
Total*	5,677,251	6,907,387	10,586,223	15,717,204	19,953,134	23,667,902	29,670,021	33,871,648
White	5,040,247	6,596,763	9,915,173	14,455,230	17,761,032	18,030,893	20,524,327	20,170,059
Black*	81,048	124,306	462,172	883,861	1,400,143	1,819,281	2,208,801	2,263,882
American Indian*	19,212	18,675	19,947	39,014	91,018	201,369	242,164	333,346
Japanese	97,456	93,717	84,956	157,317	213,277	261,822	312,989	288,854
Chinese	37,361	39,556	58,342	95,600	170,419	322,309	704,850	918,325
Filipino	30,470	Included in other races	40,242	65,459	135,248	357,492	731,685	918,678
Hispanic/ Latino*	368,013	Included in white	758,400	1,426,538	3,101,589	4,544,331	7,687,938	8,455,926
Other races*	3,444	34,370	5,227	20,723	178,671	N/A	N/A	N/A

DEMOGRAPHICS OF MONTEREY COUNTY FROM 1930 TO 2000

	1930	1940	1950	1960
Total*	53,705	73,032	130,498	198,351
White	44,368	66,162	122,421	180,567
Black*	269	435	2,721	7,918
American Indian*	32	89	128	695
Japanese	613	589	1,564	3,173
Chinese	2,271	2,247	713	1,080
Filipino	Included in other races	Included in other races	Included in other races	4,223
Hispanic/ Latino*	N/A	N/A	N/A	N/A
Other races*	9,074	6,435	5,356	695

	1970	1980	1990	2000
Total*	250,071	290,444	355,660	401,762
White	223,924	200,035	227,008	224,682
Black*	12,031	18,825	22,849	15,050
American Indian*	1,139	2,927	3,017	4,202
Japanese	3,246	3,828	4,196	3,363
Chinese	1,345	1,590	2,165	2,193
Filipino	6,699	8,568	11,421	11,449
Hispanic/ Latino*	52,715	75,129	119,570	187,969

DEMOGRAPHICS OF SALINAS FROM 1930 TO 2000

	1930	1940	1950	1960
Total*	10,263	11,586	13,917	28,957
White	8,949	10,385	12,747	27,269
Black*	55	99	312	377
American Indian*	N/A	16	8	35
Japanese	385	418	162	296
Chinese	197	328	338	347
Filipino	Included in other races	Included in other races	Included in other races	582
Hispanic/ Latino*	N/A	N/A	N/A	N/A
Other races*	1,259	1,102	858	172

	1970	1980	1990	2000
Total*	58,896	80,479	108,777	151,060
White	53,157	50,478	59,343	68,218
Black*	873	1,443	3,276	4,943
American Indian*	285	969	1,031	1,903
Japanese	463	750	970	787
Chinese	670	675	894	856
Filipino	2,245	3,514	5,190	5,863
Hispanic/ Latino*	15,941	33,892	55,084	96,880

TABLE SOURCES
All the following volumes are available digitally:

U.S. Census Bureau. "Census of Population and Housing." https://www.cen-sus.gov/prod/www/decennial.html

U.S. Census Bureau. "Fifteenth Census of the United States: 1930." Washington, DC: GPO, 1933.

"Population: Volume III, Part 1, Table 2: Color, Nativity, and Sex for the State, Urban, Rural: 1930, 1920, 1910" (p. 233).

"Population: Volume III, Part 1, Table 13: Composition of the Population, by Counties" (p. 252).

"Population: Volume III, Part 1, Table 15: Composition of the Population, for Cities, 10,000 or More" (p. 261).

"Census of Population and Housing: 1930. Vol. 6 (Supplement): Special Report on Foreign-Born White Families by Country of Birth of Head, with an Appendix Giving Statistics for Mexican, Indian, Chinese, and Japanese Families" (tables p. 217). Washington, DC: GPO, 1933.

U.S. Census Bureau. "Sixteenth Census of the United States: 1940. Population: Volume II, Part 1: United States Summary and Alabama—District of Columbia." Washington, DC: GPO.

"Table 6: Minor Races by Nativity, and Sex, for the State, Urban, Rural: 1910 to 1940" (p. 518).

"Table 21: Composition of the Population, by Counties: 1940" (p. 541).

"Table 24: Foreign Born White, by Country of Birth by Counties, by and for Cities, 10,000 to 100,000: 1940" (pp. 564 and 566).

"Table 25: Indians, Chinese, and Japanese by Sex, for Counties, and for Cities of 10,000 to 100,000: 1940 and 1930" (p. 567).

"Table 31: Composition of the Population, for Cities, 10,000 to 100,000: 1940" (p. 601).

U.S. Bureau of the Census. "U.S. Census of Population, 1950: Volume II, Part 5. California: Characteristics of the Population." Washington, DC: Census Bureau.

"Table 14: Race by Sex, for the State, Urban and Rural" (pp. 5–57).

"Table 34: General Characteristics of the Population for Standard Metropolitan Areas, Urbanized Areas, and Urban Places of 10,000 or More" (pp. 5–102).

"Table 42: General Characteristics of the Population for Counties" (pp. 5–163).

"Table 47: Indians, Japanese, and Chinese, by Sex, for Selected Counties and Cities: 1950" (pp. 5–179).

U.S. Bureau of the Census. "U.S. Census of Population, 1960: Volume 1, Part 6. California: Characteristics of the Population." Washington, DC: GPO, 1963.

"Table 15: Race by Sex, for the State, by Size of Place, 1960" (pp. 6–58).

"Table 21: Characteristics of the Population for Standard Metropolitan Statistical Areas, Urbanized Areas, and Urban Places of 10,000 or More" (pp. 6–140).

"Table 28: Characteristics of the Population for Counties" (pp. 6–197).

U.S. Bureau of the Census. "U.S. Census of Population: 1960. Subject Reports, Persons of Spanish Surname." Final Report PC(2)-1B. Washington, DC: GPO, 1963.

"Table A: Spanish-American, Mexican-American Population of Five Southwestern States as Variously Identified in Censuses 1930–1960."

Social Explorer (SE) Tables, Census 1980. U.S. Census Bureau and Social Explorer. "Table STF1:T7—Race" and "Table STF1:T8—Spanish Origin."

Social Explorer (SE) Tables, Census 1990. U.S. Census Bureau and Social Explorer. "Table STF1:P7— Detailed Race" and "Table STF1:P8—Persons of Hispanic Origin."

Social Explorer (SE) Tables, Census 2000. U.S. Census Bureau and Social Explorer. "Table SF1:P7—Race"; "Table SF1:P4—Hispanic or Latino, and Not Hispanic or Latino, by Race"; "Table SF1:PCT5—Asian Alone with One Asian Category for Selected Groups."

Campbell Gibson and Kay Jung. "Historical Census Statistics on Population Totals by Race, 1790 to 1990, and by Hispanic Origin, 1970 to 1990, for the United States, Regions, Divisions, and States." Working Paper No. 56. Washington, DC: U.S. Census Bureau, 2002. https://purl.fdlp.gov/GPO/LPS33172

U.S. Census Bureau. "The Hispanic Population: 2000." Washington DC: U.S. Census Bureau, 2001. https://www.census.gov/library/publications/2001/dec/c2kbr01-03.html:

Since the 1980 census, the Hispanic population has been counted through self-identification with a direct question on Hispanic/Spanish/Latino origin or descent. Prior to the emergence of this concept, various combinations of immigrants' place of birth, parental birthplace, Spanish language usage, racial identification, and individual surnames were used to construct estimates of a population group similar to today's notion of the "Hispanic" population.

Margo J. Anderson, Constance F. Citro, and Joseph J. Salvo, eds. "Hispanic/Latino Ethnicity and Identifiers." In *Encyclopedia of the U.S. Census*, 2nd ed. (pp. 264–266). Washington, DC: CQ Press, 2012. http://dx.doi.org.stanford.idm.oclc.org/10.4135/9781452225272.n84

Notes

INTRODUCTION

1. For an analysis of the rapid socioeconomic rise of Depression era immigrants from the Southwest to California, see James N. Gregory, "Dust Bowl Legacies: The Okie Impact on California, 1939–1989," *California History*, 68 (3) (Fall 1989): 74–85.

2. Shirley Ann Wilson Moore, *To Place Our Deeds: The African American Community in Richmond, California, 1910–1963* (Berkeley: University of California Press, 1999); Alex Schafran, *The Road to Resegregation: Northern California and the Failure of Politics* (Berkeley: University of California Press, 2018); Robert O. Self, *American Babylon: Race and the Struggle for Postwar Oakland* (Princeton: Princeton University Press, 2003); Emily E. Straus, *Death of a Suburban Dream: Race and Schools in Compton, California* (Philadelphia: University of Pennsylvania Press, 2014).

3. Lori A. Flores, *Grounds for Dreaming: Mexican Americans, Mexican Immigrants, and the California Farmworker Movement* (New Haven and London: Yale University Press, 2016).

4. Resistors did protest this racism throughout the city's history; Salinas maintained a very American structure of white privilege.

CHAPTER 1

1. See Lisbeth Haas, *Conquests and Historical Identities in California, 1769–1936* (Berkeley: University of California Press, 1995); Lisbeth Haas, *Saints and Citizens: Indigenous Histories of Colonial Missions and Mexican California* (Berkeley: University of California Press, 2014); Kelly Lytle-Hernandez, *City of Inmates: Conquest, Rebellion, and the Rise of Human Caging in Los Angeles 1771–1965* (Chapel Hill: University of North Carolina Press, 2017); Malcolm Margolin, *The Ohlone Way: Indian Life in the San Francisco-Monterey Bay Area* (Berkeley: Heyday Press, 2014).

2. Anne B. Fisher, *The Salinas: Upside Down River* (Fresno: Fresno Valley Publishers, 1977), 195.

3. Carl Abbott, *How Cities Won the West: Four Centuries of Urban Change in Western North America* (Albuquerque: University of New Mexico Press, 2008), 4.

4. Carol Lynn McKibben, *Racial Beachhead: Diversity and Democracy in a Military Town* (Stanford: Stanford University Press, 2012).

5. Margolin, *The Ohlone Way.*

6. Tomás Almaguer, "Interpreting Chicano History: The World Systems Approach to Nineteenth Century California," *Review* (Fernand Braudel Center), 4 (3) (Winter 1981): 459–507; Haas, *Conquests and Historical Identities;* Haas, *Saints and Citizens.*

7. Anne F. Hyde, *Empires, Nations, and Families: A New History of the North American West, 1800–1860* (Lincoln: University of Nebraska Press, 2011), 5, 11–13.

8. Ibid.

9. Major Rolin C. Watkins, ed., *History of Monterey and Santa Cruz Counties, California: Cradle of California's History and Romance* (Chicago: S. J. Clarke Publishing Co., 1925), 27.

10. Paul Parker, "Alisal Was Almost County Seat," *Salinas Independent* (March 19, 1937), 1.

11. Lori A. Flores, *Grounds for Dreaming: Mexican Americans, Mexican Immigrants and the California Farmworker Movement* (New Haven and London: Yale University Press, 2016).

12. Mrs. Johnson, "Schools in Monterey County, Compiled from Old Records," unpublished manuscript, Monterey County Historical Society, 1. According to Mrs. Johnson, in 1863 the Monterey County Board of Supervisors divided the district in half, making one "Natividad" (100 students assigned) and the other "Alisal" (158 students). In 1867 the district was divided again, and the new district was named "Spring." It was not until 1868 that "Salinas City School District" was created out of sections of Natividad, Spring, and Alisal. In 1870, the Oak Grove district was established, and in 1877 the rest of Alisal was renamed "Blanco."

13. For a theoretical analysis of the settler colonialism and its impact on the American West, see James Belich, *Replenishing the Earth: The Settler Revolution and the Rise of the Anglo-World, 1783–1939* (New York: Oxford University Press, 2009); Penelope Edmonds, *Urbanizing Frontiers: Indigenous Peoples and Settlers in 19th-Century Pacific Rim Cities* (Vancouver: University of British Columbia Press, 2010); Walter L. Hixson, *American Settler Colonialism: A History* (New York: Palgrave Macmillan, 2013); Aziz Rana, *The Two Faces of American Freedom* (Cambridge, MA: Harvard University Press, 2010).

14. Parker, "Alisal Was Almost County Seat."

15. Ibid. All quotes in this paragraph are from Parker, "Alisal Was Almost County Seat."

16. Ibid.

17. See Belich, *Replenishing the Earth;* Edmonds, *Urbanizing Frontiers;* Hixson, *American Settler Colonialism;* Rana, *The Two Faces.*

18. *Salinas City Index* (May 8, 1873), Leach Family Collection.

19. Haas, *Conquests and Historical Identities*; Margolin, *The Ohlone Way*.

20. For an excellent discussion of how early boosters used racial language to attract white settlement, papering over the already apparent diversity of California's nineteenth-century population, see David M. Wrobel, *Promised Lands: Promotion, Memory, and the Creation of the American West* (Lawrence: University of Kansas Press, 2002).

21. Sandy Lydon, *Chinese Gold: The Chinese in the Monterey Bay Region* (Capitola, CA: Capitola Book Company,1985).

22. See Albert M. Camarillo, *Chicanos in a Changing Society: From Mexican Pueblos to American Barrios, 1848-1930 (Dallas: Southern Methodist University Press, 1979)*; George J. Sánchez, *Becoming Mexican American, Ethnicity, Culture and Identity in Chicano Los Angeles, 1900–1945* (Oxford: Oxford University Press, 1993).

23. Stephen J. Pitti, *The Devil in Silicon Valley: Northern California, Race, and Mexican Americans* (Princeton: Princeton University Press, 2003).

24. Ibid. See also Beth Lew-Williams, "'Chinamen' and 'Delinquent Girls': Intimacy, Exclusion, and a Search for California's Color Line," *Journal of American History*, 104 (3) (2017): 632–655; Elliott Young, *Alien Nation: Chinese Migration in the Americas from the Coolie Era Through World War II* (Chapel Hill: University of North Carolina Press, 2014). The histories of Salinas that were usually published in the local newspaper, the *Salinas Californian*, never mentioned nonwhite or female city-builders.

25. The strategy of settlement and city-building to support California's new statehood and also to reinforce San Francisco's growing population and economic development led to a proliferation of towns established and incorporated between 1850–1900. See https://calafco.org/resources/incorporated-cities/california-cities-incorporation-date for a complete list; see also David Vaught, *Cultivating California: Growers, Specialty Crops, and Labor, 1875–1920* (Baltimore and London: Johns Hopkins University Press, 1999).

26. See Abbott, *How Cities Won the West*. The following is an example of many articles published by the San Francisco newspapers documenting urban development throughout the Northern California region: "Monterey County," *San Francisco Chronicle (1869–Current File)* (June 8, 1890). https://search-proquest-com.stanford.idm.oclc.org/docview/572215626?accountid=14026

27. See Gray Brechin, *Imperial San Francisco: Urban Power, Earthly Ruin* (Berkeley and Los Angeles: University of California Press, 2006).

28. Ibid.

29. Belle Yang, *Baba: A Return to China upon My Father's Shoulders* (New York: Harcourt Brace, 1994), 32.

30. Speech by William Henry Leach (August 23, 1888), courtesy Anne Leach,

Salinas. See Erika Lee, *At America's Gates: Chinese Immigration During the Exclusion Era, 1882–1943* (Chapel Hill: University of North Carolina Press, 2003).

31. Yang, *Baba*, 32.

32. See Andrew Needham and Allen Dieterich-Ward, "Beyond the Metropolis: Metropolitan Growth and Regional Transformation in Postwar America," *Journal of Urban History*, 35 (7) (2009): 943–969; Alex Schafran, *The Road to Resegregation: Northern California and the Failure of Politics* (Berkeley: University of California Press, 2018).

33. Wrobel, *Promised Lands*.

34. For a thorough analysis of the proliferation of sometimes short-lived railroad settlements in the West, see Caroline Fraser, *Prairie Fires: The American Dreams of Laura Ingalls Wilder* (New York: Henry Holt, 2017): Richard White, *"It's Your Misfortune and None of My Own": A New History of the American West* (Norman: University of Oklahoma Press, 1991); Richard White, *The Transcontinentals and the Making of Modern America* (New York: Norton, 2011). For an analysis of longer-lasting settlements in Northern California, see Schafran, *The Road to Resegregation*; Cecilia M. Tsu, *Garden of the World: Asian Immigrants and the Making of Agriculture in California's Santa Clara Valley* (Oxford: Oxford University Press, 2013).

35. Salinas Local History packet, official census data, 1880. Population numbers varied due to conflicting anecdotal evidence from newspapers and from observers with different agendas. Boosters minimized nonwhite populations and exaggerated white settlement numbers.

36. Lydon, *Chinese Gold*.

37. Rutillus Harrison Allen, "Economic History of Agriculture in Monterey County, California, During the American Period," unpublished doctoral dissertation, University of California, 1953, 3.

38. Annual report for Monterey County assessor, 1865. Cited in Allen, "Economic History of Agriculture in Monterey County," 12.

39. Ibid., 14.

40. See Lawrence J. Jelinek, *Harvest Empire: A History of California Agriculture* (San Francisco: Boyd & Fraser, 1979); Michael Magliari, "Populism, Steamboats and the Octopus: Transportation Rates and Monopoly in California's Wheat Regions, 1890–1896," *Pacific Historical Review*, 58 (4) (1989): 449–469; Michael Magliari, "California Populism, A Case Study: The Farmers' Alliance and People's Party in San Luis Obispo County, 1885–1903," unpublished doctoral dissertation, University of California, Davis, 1992; and Rodman W. Paul, "The Wheat Trade Between California and the United Kingdom," *Mississippi Valley Historical Review*, 45 (3) (1958): 391–412, on the organization of wheat farming in nineteenth-century California.

41. Watkins, *History of Monterey and Santa Cruz Counties*, 379.

42. Ibid.

43. Allen, "Economic History of Agriculture in Monterey County," 25.

44. Ibid.

45. Ibid., 23.

46. Schafran, *The Road to Resegregation*.

47. See William F. Deverell, *Whitewashed Adobe: The Rise of Los Angeles and the Remaking of Its Mexican Past* (Berkeley: University of California Press, 2004); Nayan Shah, *Contagious Divides: Epidemics and Race in San Francisco's Chinatown* (Berkeley: University of California Press, 2001); Michel-Rolph Trouillot, *Silencing the Past: Power and the Production of History* (Boston: Beacon Press, 1995); Wrobel, *Promised Lands*.

48. See Roland De Wolk, *American Disruptor: The Scandalous Life of Leland Stanford* (Berkeley: University of California Press, 2018), 75.

49. William Cronon, *Nature's Metropolis: Chicago and the Great West* (New York and London: Norton, 1991), 97. For an excellent analysis of railroad building in California, see De Wolk, *American Disruptor*.

50. Cronon, *Nature's Metropolis*; Jonathan Levy, *Freaks of Fortune: The Emerging World of Capitalism and Risk in America* (Cambridge, MA: Harvard University Press, 2012), 156.

51. See Richard White, *Railroaded: The Transcontinentals and the Making of Modern America* (New York and London: Norton, 2011). Local newspapers reported the web of interconnecting smaller railroad lines that linked farming regions with port towns. For example, the *Santa Cruz Weekly Sentinel* announced a new line in 1873 that connected Watsonville and the Pajaro Valley with Santa Cruz with the headline "Santa Cruz Railroad Co." (June 28, 1873), 1.

52. Vaught, *Cultivating California*, 10.

53. Tsu, *Garden of the World*; Vaught, *Cultivating California*.

54. See De Wolk, *American Disruptor*; White, *Railroaded*.

55. Charles Crocker, Collis Huntington, Leland Stanford, and Mark Hopkins are considered "the big four" railroad giants of nineteenth-century California. See De Wolk, *American Disruptor*; and White, *Railroaded*. The term "instant city" was coined by Gunther Barth in his book of the same name, *Instant Cities: Urbanization and the Rise of San Francisco and Denver* (New York: Oxford University Press, 1975).

56. See White, *Railroaded*.

57. Thom Taft, Salinas Chamber of Commerce (June 25, 2017); Dorothy Vera, "Salinas: From Halfway House to Bustling City," *Salinas Californian* (July 1968), scrapbook collection, Local History, 70117, n.p.

58. See Tsu, *Garden of the World*; Young, *Alien Nation*.

59. See Lydon, *Chinese Gold*, for an examination of Chinese experiences in Monterey and Pacific Grove, which included several incidents of mob violence and eventually the burning of Chinatown in 1888, 1889, and finally its complete destruction in 1902; see also Wellington Lee, "Salinas Chinatown Memories," unpublished, John Steinbeck Library, Salinas.

60. See Fraser, *Prairie Fires*, for a detailed account of the catastrophic impact of the collective settlement and farming strategies of the West.

61. Dorothy Vera, "Story of Salinas: Luck and a Lot More," *Salinas Californian* (June 25, 1991), 2.

62. See Mike Davis, *Late Victorian Holocausts: El Nino Famines and the Making of the Third World* (New York: Verso Press, 2001).

63. See De Wolk, *American Disruptor.*

64. Eugene Sherwood, "Salinas City," *Petaluma Weekly Argus* (September 3, 1868), 3.

65. *San Francisco Chronicle* (June 22, 1873), 3. If this were true then that means that the same 5,000-square-foot lot was now selling for $500,000, which cannot be accurate, even if the *Chronicle* reported it to be so.

66. *Santa Cruz Weekly Sentinel* (December 6, 1873), 3.

67. See Wrobel, *Promised Land.*

68. https://calafco.org/resources/incorporated-cities/california-cities-incorporation-date

69. David Freund, *Colored Property: State Policy and White Racial Politics in Suburban America* (Chicago: University of Chicago Press, 2007), 47.

70. See Darnell Hunt and Ana-Christina, Ramon, eds., *Black Los Angeles: American Dreams and Racial Realities* (New York: New York University Press, 2010); Mark Wild, *Street Meeting: Multiethnic Neighborhoods in Early 20th Century Los Angeles* (Berkeley and Los Angeles: University of California Press, 2005).

71. See Patricia Nelson Limerick, *The Legacy of Conquest: The Unbroken Past of the American West* (New York and London: Norton, 1987); White, *"It's Your Misfortune and None of My Own."*

72. Watkins, *History of Monterey and Santa Cruz Counties*, 379.

73. Parker, "Alisal Was Almost County Seat."

74. Vera, "Salinas: From Halfway House to Bustling City"; Watkins, *History of Monterey and Santa Cruz Counties*, 379.

75. See Abbott, *How Cities Won the West.*

76. See Shirley Ann Wilson Moore, *Sweet Freedom's Plains: African Americans on the Overland Trails, 1841–1869* (Norman: University of Oklahoma Press, 2016) for examples of African American migrant stories; see also Camarillo, *Chicanos in a Changing Society*; Deverell, *Whitewashed Adobe*; Pitti, *The Devil in Silicon Valley*; Sánchez, *Becoming Mexican American*; Tsu, *Garden of the World.*

77. Robert B. Johnston, "Salinas 1875–1950: From Village to City," pamphlet published by Fidelity Savings and Loan Association, 1980, 1.

78. See biographical sketches of individuals deemed prominent circa 1880s in *Monterey County*, pamphlet published by Salinas Board of Trade, n.d., Salinas Public Library, Local History, Pamphlets, vertical file, 50–88.

79. Salinas Board of Trade publication (1888), *Monterey County*, archives, Salinas Public Library, 24, 52–54; see also De Wolk, *American Disruptor*, 136–138.

80. See Abbott, *How Cities Won the West.*

81. See Edward E. Baptist, *The Half Has Never Been Told: Slavery and the Making of American Capitalism* (New York: Basic Books, 2014), 337.

82. Robert Johnston, unpublished manuscript (March 7, 1976), Monterey County Historical Society, Johnston Papers, 4.

83. Hubert Howe Bancroft, *History of California*, 1890, IV, 741, cited in manuscript notes 94.501C170, Robert Johnston Papers, Monterey County Historical Society.

84. *San Francisco Wasp*, clipping file, Monterey County Historical Society.

85. Vaught, *Cultivating California.*

86. Ibid.; Sarah D. Wald, *The Nature of California: Race, Citizenship, and Farming Since the Dust Bowl* (Seattle: University of Washington Press, 2016).

87. See Lew-Williams, "'Chinamen' and 'Delinquent Girls'"; Peggy Pascoe, *What Comes Naturally: Miscegenation Law and the Making of Race in America* (Oxford: Oxford University Press, 2010); Nayan Shah, *Stranger Intimacy: Contesting Race, Sexuality, and the Law in the North American West* (Berkeley: University of California Press, 2011).

88. See Pascoe, *What Comes Naturally*; Shah, *Stranger Intimacy.*

89. Minutes of the Salinas City Council meetings reflected these concerns. For Progressive era legislation governing morality, see Rebecca Edwards, "Politics, Social Movements, and the Periodization of U.S. History," *Journal of the Gilded Age and Progressive Era*, 8 (4) (2009): 463–473.

90. See William Deverell and Tom Sitton, eds., *California Progressivism Revisited* (Berkeley, Los Angeles, and London: University of California Press, 1994).

91. Camarillo, *Chicanos in a Changing Society.*

92. "Mrs. P. W. Gydison Enters into Rest: Was Widow of Founder of Danish Lutheran Church," *Salinas Daily Index* (October 21, 1914), 1.

93. Harrison's Series of Pacific Coast pamphlets, Monterey County, n.d., 54.

94. Since the publication of Mary P. Ryan's famous study, *Cradle of the Middle Class: The Family in Oneida County New York, 1790–1865* (Cambridge, UK: Cambridge University Press, 1981), scholars have routinely integrated and emphasized the work of middle-class women in building modern cities and infrastructure.

95. *San Francisco Bulletin*, 1870, n.p., taken from manuscript notes 94.501C170, Robert Johnston, Monterey County Historical Society. See also Deverell, *Whitewashed Adobe*; Trouillot, *Silencing the Past*; Wrobel, *Promised Lands.*

96. *Salinas Standard* (February 1870), n.p., taken from manuscript notes 94.501C170, Robert Johnston, Monterey County Historical Society.

97. Harrison's Series of Pacific Coast pamphlets, Monterey County, 1889.

98. See Deverell, *Whitewashed Adobe.*

99. Minutes, Salinas City Council (April 7, 1873), 48; see also Deverell, *Whitewashed Adobe;* Trouillot, *Silencing the Past.*

100. See Lew-Williams "'Chinamen' and 'Delinquent Girls'"; Pascoe, *What Comes Naturally;* Shah, *Stranger Intimacy.*

101. See *East of Eden, Of Mice and Men,* and *The Red Pony* for examples of interracial intimacy.

102. Minutes, Salinas City Council (May 7, 1873), 58.

103. Minutes, Salinas City Council (July 17, 1873), 79.

104. Minutes, Salinas City Council (July 22, 1873), 80.

105. Minutes, Salinas City Council (April 20, 1874), 141.

106. Minutes, Salinas City Council (October 9 & 20, 1873), 85–101.

107. See Johnston, "Salinas 1875–1950"; Laura Barraclough described a similar mythical West in the San Fernando Valley, *Making the San Fernando Valley: Rural Landscapes, Urban Development, and White Privilege* (Athens: University of Georgia Press, 2011). See also Deverell, *Whitewashed Adobe;* and Wrobel, *Promised Lands.*

108. Minutes, Salinas City Council (February 2, 1874), 109.

109. Minutes, Salinas City Council (March 4, 1874), 111.

110. Minutes, Salinas City Council (February 2, 1874), 122.

111. Minutes, Salinas City Council (July and August 1874), 182–188.

112. Minutes, Salinas City Council (August 10, 1874), 188. The nineteenth-century city council meeting minutes showed a paper trail of funding for Salinas from banks in San Francisco with explanations such as the following: "The mayor sign (sic) the bonds . . . and give them to the city-treasurer [who] . . . Bankers in San Francisco and there to collect said bonds upon delivering to Woods and Freeborn the bonds ($14,137.50) and to return the same to Salinas City and that the Salinas City Bank be allowed for so collecting and delivering the said money and to keep back said amount ($21.21)."

113. Ibid., 189–190.

114. See Diana L. Ahmad, *The Opium Debate and Chinese Exclusion Laws in the Nineteenth Century American West* (Reno: University of Nevada Press, 2007); Saxton Alexander, *The Indispensable Enemy: Labor and the Anti-Chinese Movement in California* (Berkeley: University of California Press, 1971); Charlotte Brooks, *Alien Neighbors Foreign Friends: Asian Americans, Housing and the Transformation of Urban California* (Chicago: University of Chicago Press, 2013); Erika Lee, *At America's Gates;* Charles J. McClain, *In Search of Equality: The Chinese Struggle Against Discrimination in Nineteenth Century America* (Berkeley: University of California Press, 1994); Jean Pfaelzer, *Driven Out: The Forgotten War Against Chinese Americans* (New York: Random House, 2007); Elmer Sandmeyer, *The Anti-Chinese Movement in California* (Urbana: University of Illinois Press, 1939); Shah, *Contagious Divides.*

115. Frances Dinkelspiel, *Towers of Gold: How One Jewish Immigrant Named Isaias Hellman Created California* (New York: St. Martin's Press, 2008), 72–74.

116. See Shah, *Contagious Divides*.

117. "The Ravages of a Terrible Disease Described," *San Francisco Examiner* (September 3, 1882), 1.

118. Kent Seavey, "A Short History of Salinas," unpublished guide. http://www.mchsmuseum.com/salinasbrief.html

119. Lew-Williams, "'Chinamen' and 'Delinquent Girls.'"

120. The following samples from the minutes of the Salinas City Council showed Women's Christian Temperance Union petitions to control space and behavior in the 1880s:

> April 6, 1886: Petition of J. R. Leese and others asking for an Ordinance removing washhouses outside of city limits was received and referred to the Ordinance Committee with instructions to report at next regular meeting (660) . . . Ordinance #134 prohibiting wash houses within certain limits was passed . . . ordinance no 135 regulating the issuance of liquor licenses was passed . . . Ordinance no. 136 prohibiting houses of ill game was passed (662); Petition from Women's Temperance Union asking Council to pass an ordinance prohibiting the use of tobacco by minors and prohibiting the sale of tobacco to minors was received and action postponed (676). Requests for liquor licenses were routinely denied: Petition by China Lamorra for a liquor license and denied (706); and every request for establishment of entertainment oriented businesses were carefully scrutinized: J. D. Carr petitioned for regulating theatrical license and referred to Ordinance committee. April 5, 1888: Mayors report city assessment $1,045,940. Biggest expense: school fund 24 cents . . . city collector fired for inability to collect license taxes. By Dec 1887 it was $25,000. Not $15,000 and also passed by a two thirds margin (744). July 8, 1887: The proposition to incur a municipal indebtedness of $15,000. For public improvements within the corporate limits of Salinas City having received more than two-thirds votes . . . adopted as Ordinance 152 held July 5, 1887: Hughes, Tynan, Smith, Tolman Trimmer . . . It was moved and carried that the mayor be authorized to procure the necessary bank bonds for the proposed indebtedness. (715). July 25: The clerk was instructed to advertise sale of city bonds. [This last was added in different ink.] (716)

121. See Lew-Williams, "'Chinamen' and 'Delinquent Girls,'" 632–655; see also Wellington Lee, "Salinas Chinatown Memories," unpublished manuscript, Salinas Public Library.

122. Dorothy Viera, "Old Slides Recall Early Chinatown Fire," *Salinas Californian*, n.d. Vertical clipping file, Steinbeck Library, Salinas.

123. Dorothy Viera, "Tempers Flared Hotly in Salinas in 1896 over Fire Department," *Salinas Californian*, n.d. Vertical clipping file, John Steinbeck Library, Salinas.

124. Minutes, Salinas City Council (June 23, 1893), vol. 2 1889–1896, 211.

125. Minutes, Salinas City Council (July 3, 1893), vol. 2 1889–1896, 212.

126. Lydon, *Chinese Gold*.

127. Ahmad, *The Opium Debate and Chinese Exclusion Laws*; Alexander, *The Indispensable Enemy*; Brooks, *Alien Neighbors*, 11–38; Erika Lee, *At America's Gates*; McClain, *In Search of Equality*; Pfaelzer, *Driven Out*; Sandmeyer, *The Anti-Chinese Movement in California*; Shah, *Contagious Divides*.

128. See Lydon, *Chinese Gold*, for an examination of Chinese experiences in Monterey and Pacific Grove, which included several incidents of mob violence and eventually the burning of Chinatown in 1888, 1889 and finally its complete destruction in 1902; Wellington Lee, "Salinas Chinatown Memories," unpublished, John Steinbeck Library, Salinas; Blanche Chin Ah Tye, *Full of Gold: Growing Up in Salinas Chinatown Living in Post War America* (North Charleston, SC: CreateSpace Independent Publishing Platform, 2015).

129. Ryan, *Cradle of the Middle Class*; Shah, *Contagious Divides*.

130. See Paul Boyer, *Urban Masses and Moral Order in America, 1820–1920* (Cambridge, MA: Harvard University Press, 1978); "The Movement in Sacramento, San José, Salinas, etc. (1874, Jun 22)," *San Francisco Chronicle (1869)*; Ryan, *Cradle of the Middle Class*.

131. Minutes, Salinas City Council (August 10, 1874), 189–190.

132. See Ryan, *Cradle of the Middle Class*.

133. Minutes, Salinas City Council (1872–1889), vol. 1.

134. Minutes, Salinas City Council (March 14, 1876), 299.

135. Ryan, *Cradle of the Middle Class*.

136. See Boyer, *Urban Masses and Moral Order in America*; Ryan, *Cradle of the Middle Class*; Sánchez, *Becoming Mexican American*.

137. Boyer, *Urban Masses and Moral Order in America*.

138. See Minutes, Salinas Civic Women's Club, Monterey County Historical Society.

139. It was suggested by the sanitary commission that the Salinas City Council look into the Chinese people as a health threat in the wake of smallpox epidemic that the commission believed "been brought here from abroad," meaning from Chinese immigrants moving from San Francisco, which had experienced a similar epidemic. See Shah, *Contagious Divides*.

140. Minutes, Salinas City Council (June 12, 1876), 314.

141. Minutes, Salinas City Council (August 7, 1876), 323; Minutes, Salinas City Council (September 3, 1877), 376.

142. See Einhorn, *Property Rules*.

143. Minutes, Salinas City Council Meetings (April 4 & 16, 1887), 698, 702.

144. Robert Johnston, unpublished manuscript (March 7, 1976), Monterey County Historical Society, Johnston Papers, 9.

145. *Salinas Daily Index* (March 30, 1902), n.p., Jim and Jeri Gattis Collection.

146. Vaught, *Cultivating California.*

CHAPTER 2

1. Blanche Chin Ah Tye, *Full of Gold: Growing Up in Salinas Chinatown, Living in Post War America* (North Charleston, SC: CreateSpace Independent Publishing, 2015). Ah Tye was the first Chinese woman born in Salinas.

2. See Stephen Pitti, *The Devil in Silicon Valley: Northern California, Race, and Mexican Americans* (Princeton: Princeton University Press, 2003) for a comparison with east San José.

3. Ah Tye, *Full of Gold,* 17.

4. See Linda Ivey, "Ethnicity in the Land: Lost Stories in California Agriculture," *Agricultural History,* 81 (1) (Winter 2007); Beth Lew-Williams, "'Chinamen' and 'Delinquent Girls': Intimacy, Exclusion, and a Search for California's Color Line," *Journal of American History,* 104 (3) (2017): 632–655; Cecilia M. Tsu, *Garden of the World: Asian Immigrants and the Making of Agriculture in California's Santa Clara Valley* (Oxford: Oxford University Press, 2013).

5. Ah Tye, *Full of Gold,* 20. By contrast, in large municipalities in California Chinese people were completely excluded from city life. See Diana L. Ahmad, *The Opium Debate and Chinese Exclusion Laws in the Nineteenth Century American West* (Reno: University of Nevada Press, 2007); Charlotte Brooks, *Alien Neighbors, Foreign Friends: Asian Americans, Housing, and the Transformation of Urban California* (Chicago and London: University of Chicago Press, 2009), 11–38; Erika Lee, *At America's Gates: Chinese Immigration During the Exclusion Era, 1882–1943* (Chapel Hill: University of North Carolina Press, 2003); Charles J. McClain, *In Search of Equality: The Chinese Struggle Against Discrimination in Nineteenth Century America* (Berkeley: University of California Press, 1994); Jean Pfaelzer, *Driven Out: The Forgotten War Against Chinese Americans* (New York: Random House, 2007); Elmer Sandmeyer, *The Anti-Chinese Movement in California* (Urbana: University of Illinois Press, 1939); Alexander Saxton, *The Indispensable Enemy: Labor and the Anti-Chinese Movement in California* (Berkeley: University of California Press, 1971); Nayan Shah, *Contagious Divides: Epidemics and Race in San Francisco's Chinatown* (Berkeley: University of California Press, 2001).

6. Ah Tye, *Full of Gold,* 19.

7. Ibid., 20–21.

8. For comparisons between Asian's experiences living in Salinas and living in Silicon Valley, see Ivey, "Ethnicity in the Land"; and Tsu, *Garden of the World.*

9. Ah Tye, *Full of Gold,* 20.

10. Ivey, "Ethnicity in the Land"; Tsu, *Garden of the World.*

11. Ah Tye, *Full of Gold,* frontispiece.

12. For various experiences of Chinese people in California cities, see Ahmad, *The Opium Debate and Chinese Exclusion Laws*; Brooks, *Alien Neighbors, Foreign Friends,* 11–38; Erika Lee, *At America's Gates*; McClain, *In Search of Equality*; Pfaelzer, *Driven Out*; Sandmeyer, *The Anti-Chinese Movement in California*; Saxton, *The Indispensable Enemy*; Shah, *Contagious Divides.* For the multiple ways in which Chinese people integrated in agricultural towns, see Ivey, "Ethnicity in the Land"; and Tsu, *Garden of the World.*

13. Mary P. Ryan, *Cradle of the Middle Class: The Family in Oneida County New York, 1790–1865* (Cambridge, UK: Cambridge University Press, 1981).

14. See Richard White, *The Transcontinentals and the Making of Modern America* (New York: Norton, 2011); Roland De Wolk, *American Disruptor: The Scandalous Life of Leland Stanford* (Berkeley: University of California Press, 2018).

15. Ahmad, *The Opium Debate and Chinese Exclusion Laws*; Brooks, *Alien Neighbors,* 11–38; Erika Lee, *At America's Gates*; McClain, *In Search of Equality*; Pfaelzer, *Driven Out*; Sandmeyer, *The Anti-Chinese Movement in California*; Saxton, *The Indispensable Enemy*; Shah, *Contagious Divides.*

16. For analyses of Chinatowns in smaller towns around San Francisco and Los Angeles, see Timothy Fong, *The First Suburban Chinatown: The Remaking of Monterey Park, California* (Philadelphia: Temple University Press, 1994); Michael Andrew Goldstein, "Truckee's Chinese Community: From Coexistence to Disintegration, 1870–1890," unpublished master's thesis, University of California, Los Angeles, 1988; Ivey, "Ethnicity in the Land":); Barbara Pricer, *The Chinese in Northern California* (Quincy, CA: Barbara Pricer, 1996); Brian Tom, *Images of America: Marysville's Chinatown* (Charleston, SC: Arcadia Publishing, 2008); Tsu, *Garden of the World*; Connie Young Yu, *Chinatown, San José, USA* (San José: San José Historical Museum Association, 1994).

17. Ah Tye, *Full of Gold*; Ivey, "Ethnicity in the Land"; Tsu, *Garden of the World.*

18. Chinatown was burned, rebuilt, and burned down in nearby Pacific Grove in 1889, 1898, 1902, and 1906. Buffalo Soldiers stationed nearby helped Chinese people put out the fires in 1902 and 1906. See Carol Lynn McKibben, *Racial Beachhead: Diversity and Democracy in a Military Town* (Stanford: Stanford University Press, 2012), 35.

19. See the *Salinas Daily Index,* which published articles from time to time in the 1910s on Italian and other southern European immigrant laborers brought in to build brick walls or work in manual labor.

20. See Sucheng Chan, *This Bittersweet Soil: The Chinese in California Agriculture, 1860–1910* (Berkeley: University of California Press, 1986); and Tsu, *Garden of the World.*

21. See Sandy Lydon, *Chinese Gold: The Chinese in the Monterey Bay Region* (Capitola, CA: Capitola Book Company, 1985).

22. Matthew Jacquez, bachelor of arts candidate, Stanford University, Public Policy and Data Science, expected graduation 2023.

23. McKibben, *Racial Beachhead*, 34–36.

24. Ivey, "Ethnicity in the Land"; Lydon, *Chinese Gold*.

25. Brooks, *Alien Neighbors, Foreign Friends*; Pitti, *The Devil in Silicon Valley*.

26. For an analysis of population characteristics in Monterey County, see Carol Lynn McKibben, *Beyond Cannery Row: Sicilian Women, Immigration, and Community in Monterey, 1915–99* (Urbana and Chicago: University of Illinois Press, 2006); McKibben, *Racial Beachhead*.

27. See Ivey, "Ethnicity in the Land"; Lew-Williams, "'Chinamen' and 'Delinquent Girls'"; Tsu, *Garden of the World*.

28. Chapter 3 focuses on this new wave of migration from the Depression era, which includes refugees from the Dust Bowl.

29. See Wellington Lee, "Salinas Chinatown Memories," unpublished manuscript, Salinas Public Library, 6.

30. See Erika Lee and Judy Yung, *Angel Island: Immigrant Gateway to America* (Oxford and New York: Oxford University Press, 2010).

31. Brooks, *Alien Neighbors, Foreign Friends*; Erika Lee, *At America's Gates*; Wellington Lee, "Salinas Chinatown Memories"; Lydon, *Chinese Gold*; Shah, *Contagious Divides*.

32. Wellington Lee, "Salinas Chinatown Memories"; Lydon, *Chinese Gold*.

33. Wellington Lee, "Salinas Chinatown Memories."

34. Ibid.

35. Email from Wellington Lee to Carol McKibben (June 10, 2017).

36. See Ivey, "Ethnicity in the Land"; Tsu, *Garden of the World*.

37. See Brooks, *Alien Neighbors, Foreign Friends*; Scott Kurashige, *The Shifting Grounds of Race: Black and Japanese Americans in the Making of Multiethnic Los Angeles* (Princeton: Princeton University Press, 2008); Dawn Bohulano Mabalon, *Little Manila Is in the Heart: The Making of the Filipina/o Community in Stockton, California* (Durham and London: Duke University Press, 2013); Pitti, *The Devil in Silicon Valle*; George J. Sánchez, *Becoming Mexican American: Ethnicity, Culture, and Identity in Chicano Los Angeles, 1900–1945* (Oxford and New York: Oxford University Press, 1993).

38. Robert O. Self famously described the strategy behind Oakland's post–World War II regional development as an "industrial garden." Oakland's city leaders believed in placing their city at the center of a carefully constructed mosaic of business development and industry that would, in turn, support (and be supported by) suburbs made up of white single-family homeowners. In this scenario, Oakland would become a thriving commercial, industrial, and cultural center for the region. Things did not work out that way, however, as Self made clear. Instead of supporting a thriving Oakland, industries such as Ford and General Motors abandoned the city along with businesspeople, professionals, and the white middle class.

Industrial investment created flourishing suburbs instead. African Americans and other minority groups became the majority population in Oakland by the 1970s. The mostly white residents in towns surrounding Oakland such as San Leandro, Fremont, and Milpitas did not rely on Oakland as a center for either employment or social life. Instead of an increasing tax base and a thriving center of business and culture, Oakland lost investment and became marginalized as a minority-majority community and was impoverished as a result, even as those suburbs prospered at its expense. San Francisco rather than Oakland became the destination for finance and culture in the region. Silicon Valley suburbs became the foundation for the innovation economy that flourished by the end of the century.

39. Minutes, Salinas Chamber of Commerce (February 23, 1926).

40. David M. Wrobel, *Promised Lands: Promotion, Memory, and the Creation of the American West* (Lawrence: University of Kansas Press, 2002).

41. David Vaught, *Cultivating California: Growers, Specialty Crops, and Labor, 1875–1920* (Baltimore and London: Johns Hopkins University Press, 1999).

42. See Dorothy Vera, "Salinas Banking 90 Years Old," *Salinas Californian* (October 1963), n.p.

43. Salinas's early settlers fell somewhere between the horticultural ideal Vaught described in *Cultivating California* and the colonial settler mentality described by Belich: James Belich, *Replenishing the Earth: The Settler Revolution and the Rise of the Anglo World, 1783–1939* (New York: Oxford University Press, 2009).

44. Minutes, Salinas Chamber of Commerce (March 23, 1926).

45. See Michael Magliari, "Populism, Steamboats and the Octopus: Transportation Rates and Monopoly in California's Wheat Regions, 1890–1896," *Pacific Historical Review*, 58 (4) (1989): 449–469.

46. See Ivey, "Ethnicity in the Land," 112.

47. *Salinas Daily Index* (July 22, 1916), 1.

48. Ibid.

49. For an analysis of internal migrations see Elliott Barkan, *From All Points: America's Immigrant West, 1870s–1952* (Bloomington: University of Indiana Press, 2007).

50. Ibid. See also Becky Nicolaides, *My Blue Heaven: Life and Politics in the Working-Class Suburbs of Los Angeles, 1920–1965* (Chicago: University of Chicago Press, 2002).

51. See Barkan, *From All Points*; Brooks, *Alien Neighbors, Foreign Friends*; William Deverell and Tom Sitton, eds., *California Progressivism Revisited* (Berkeley: University of California Press, 1994); Kevin Starr, *Inventing the Dream: California Through the Progressive Era* (Oxford: Oxford University Press, 1985).

52. Ivey, "Ethnicity in the Land"; Tsu, *Garden of the World*.

53. Leonard J. Arrington, "Science, Government, and Enterprise in Economic Development: The Western Beet Sugar Industry," *Agricultural History*, 41 (1) (1967): 2.

54. The two most important protections for the development of this industry at the turn of the last century were the McKinley Tariff (1890) and the Dingley Tariff (1897), which allowed American sugar beet manufacturers to remain competitive with their European counterparts in spite of higher labor costs.

55. Arrington, "Science, Government, and Enterprise in Economic Development," 6–7.

56. *Monterey County*, pamphlet published by the Salinas Board of Trade, n.d., Salinas Public Library, Local History, Pamphlets, vertical file, 24, 52–54.

57. De Wolk, *American Disruptor*.

58. Robert B. Johnston, "Salinas 1875–1950: From Village to City," pamphlet published by Fidelity Savings and Loan Association, 1980, 1.

59. *Pacific Rural Press*, 94 (7) (August 18, 1917): "90 to 95 per cent of beet growers are either American citizens or capable of becoming so. Orientals do most of the hand labor, white folks the rest. About 10,000 acres in the Salinas district are operated by the company or leased to tenants. Another official of the company estimates that about 200 private outside growers are producing the rest."

60. See Jimmie Don Conway, "Spreckels Sugar Company: The First Fifty Years," unpublished master's thesis, San José State University, Department of History, 1999, 85. According to Conway, "white European immigrants found work inside the factory. European immigrants were employed both as skilled and unskilled laborers. Factory wages were better than field worker wages, working conditions were better and living conditions were much improved for those who worked in the factory operations."

61. *Salinas Daily Index* (March 30, 1902), n.p., Jim and Jeri Gattis Collection.

62. Interview with Ron Cacas by Carol Lynn McKibben (August 20, 2019), Salinas.

63. Ibid.

64. Ibid.

65. Ibid.

66. Ibid.

67. Ibid.

68. See Edwin B. Almirol, *Ethnic Identity and Social Negotiation: A Study of a Filipino Community in California* (New York: AMS Press, 1985); Rick Baldoz, *The Third Asiatic Invasion: Empire and Migration in Filipino America, 1898–1946* (New York and London: New York University Press, 2011); Mabalan, *Little Manila Is in the Heart*; Dioscoro R. Recio, "Filipino Community Remembers Immigrants," *The Californian* (June 12, 1993), 1A; Rick Rodriguez, "Filipino Community Recognition Grows," *Salinas Californian* (September 30, 1974), 11.

69. None of the collections in various Spreckels archives (University of California Davis, Special Collections) contain evidence that Spreckels considered the city

of Salinas as a place of interest, much less for investment. *Salinas Daily Index* (January 4, 1898), n.p., Jim and Jeri Gattis Collection.

70. *Salinas Daily Index* (September 26, 1899), 1, Jim and Jeri Gattis Collection.

71. Juan Villa, "Remembering the Spreckels Sugar Factory," *Salinas Californian* (March 19, 2015). http://www.thecalifornian.com/story/news/education/2015/03/19/remembering-spreckels-sugar-factory/25056149/

72. Ibid.

73. See David Vaught, "Factories in the Field Revisited," *Pacific Historical Review*, 66 (2) (1997): 149–184. See also Ivey, "Ethnicity in the Land"; and Tsu, *Garden of the World*.

74. *Salinas Daily Index* (May 17, 1911), 1, Jim and Jeri Gattis Collection.

75. *Salinas Daily Index* (November 25, 1903), 2, Jim and Jeri Gattis Collection.

76. *Salinas Daily Index* (April 27, 1899), cited in Conway, "Spreckels Sugar Company," 30.

77. Conway, "Spreckels Sugar Company," 120.

78. Ibid., 118.

79. Ibid., 124.

80. Ibid., 130.

81. Ibid.

82. *The Issei of the Salinas Valley: Japanese Pioneer Families, Family Stories, and Photos from the Late 1800s to 1942* (Salinas Valley Japanese American Citizens League 2010).

83. See Arrington, "Science, Government, and Enterprise in Economic Development."

84. See Daniel Cornford, ed., *Working People of California* (Berkeley: University of California Press, 1995); Cletus E. Daniel, *Bitter Harvest: A History of California Farmworkers, 1870–1941* (Berkeley: University of California Press, 1981). Carey McWilliams, *Factories in the Field: The Story of Migratory Farm Labor in California* (Santa Barbara and Salt Lake City: Peregrine Publishers, 1971); Richard Steven Street, *Beasts of the Field: A Narrative History of California Farmworkers, 1769–1913* (Stanford: Stanford University Press, 2004).

85. Rick Baldoz, *The Third Asiatic Invasion: Empire and Migration in Filipino America, 1898–1946* (New York and London: New York University Press, 2011), 32–33.

86. For an analysis of immigration in California and the West during this period of stringent anti-immigration legislation and sentiment, see Barkan, *From All Points*.

87. Annual Report, Commission on Immigration and Housing in California, 1914, cited in McWilliams, *Factories in the Field*, 163; Barkan, *From All Points*, parts II and III.

88. *Salinas Daily Index* (March 1904), 3, Jim and Jeri Gattis Collection.

89. See Eiichiro Azuma, *Between Two Empires: Race, History, and Transnationalism in Japanese America* (Oxford: Oxford University Press, 2005); Brooks, *Alien Neighbors*,

Foreign Friends; Dolores Hayden, *The Power of Place: Urban Landscapes as Public History* (Cambridge, MA: MIT Press, 1995), 210–225; Kurashige, *The Shifting Grounds of Race*.

90. McWilliams, *Factories in the Field*.

91. Vaught, *Cultivating California*, 77–78.

92. See Tomás Almaguer, *Racial Fault Lines: Historical Origins of White Supremacy in California* (Berkeley: University of California Press, 1994), 157–158; Ronald Takaki, *Strangers from a Different Shore: A History of Asian Americans* (New York: Penguin Books, 1989), 81.

93. The circuitous routes from sending countries to various places in California were commonplace among all groups. See Barkan, *From All Points*; and *The Issei of the Salinas Valley*.

94. McWilliams, *Factories in the Field*, 105–106: "In 1882 there were 132,300 Chinese in California but only 86 Japanese resided in the state . . . the importation of the Japanese [was due to] the development of sugar beet production. Here was a new farm industry, requiring an extremely arduous variety of hand labor, in connection with which the Japanese could be quietly and unobtrusively imported. . . . Japanese farm laborers appeared in Fresno in 1890, Pajaro Valley in 1893 (in the sugar beet fields) . . . by 1904 they were to be found in every part of the state. There were 2,039 Japanese in California in 1890; by 1900 this figure had increased to 24,326, and by 1910 when the Chinese and Japanese populations were approximately equal, there were 72,156 Japanese in the state."

95. See Tsu, *Garden of the World*; Vaught, "Factories in the Field Revisited."

96. *The Issei of the Salinas Valley*.

97. For a sampling of scholarly literature on gender and migration, see Caroline Brettell and James H. Hollifield, eds., *Migration Theory: Talking Across Disciplines* (New York: Routledge, 2000); Pierrette Hondagneu-Sotelo, *Gender and U.S. Immigration: Contemporary Trends* (Berkeley: University of California Press, 1999); Jan Lucassen and Leo Lucassen, eds., *Migration, Migration History, History: Old Paradigms and New Perspectives* (New York and Berlin: Peter Lang, 1997); McKibben, *Beyond Cannery Row*; Mai Ngai and Jon Gjerde, *Major Problems in American Immigration History* (Boston: Cengage Learning, 2013).

98. *The Issei of the Salinas Valley*.

99. Interview with Henry and Kent Hibino by Carol Lynn McKibben (March 6, 2018), Salinas.

100. Ivey, "Ethnicity in the Land."

101. See Brooks, *Alien Neighbors, Foreign Friends*; Kurashige, *The Shifting Grounds of Race*.

102. *Salinas Daily Journal* (March 1, 1921), front page, John Steinbeck Library Collection.

103. *Salinas Daily Index* (July 1911), Jim and Jeri Gattis Collection.

104. See Brooks, *Alien Neighbors, Foreign Friends*; Kurashige, *The Shifting Grounds of Race*; Mabalon, *Little Manila Is in the Heart*; Pitti, *The Devil in Silicon Valley*.

CHAPTER 3

1. "Beet Sugar," *Pacific Rural Press,* 59 (13) (March 31, 1900): 196.

2. A. A. Tavernetti, "Summary of Agricultural Crops of Monterey County," Salinas, California, Monterey County Agricultural Commissioners Office, 1929–1940.

3. Ibid.; also see William Orville Jones, "The Salinas Valley: Its Agricultural Development, 1920–1940," unpublished doctoral dissertation, Stanford University, 1947, 312.

4. Tavernetti, "Summary of Agricultural Crops of Monterey County." 1932.

5. Ibid.; also see Rutillus Harrison Allen, "Economic History of Agriculture in Monterey County, California During the American Period," unpublished doctoral dissertation, University of California, 1953, 78–84; Jones, "The Salinas Valley," 314; Helen Boyden Lamb, "Industrial Relations in the Western Lettuce Industry," unpublished doctoral dissertation, Radcliffe College, 1942, 55.

6. Allen, "Economic History of Agriculture in Monterey Count"; Lamb, "Industrial Relations in the Western Lettuce Industry."

7. Interview with Linda Wong Gin by Carol Lynn McKibben (August 30, 2019), Chinese Community Center, Salinas.

8. For a thorough analysis of profit, loss, and power in the lettuce industry in the 1930s, see Francis James Smith Jr., "The Impact of Technological Change on the Marketing of Salinas Lettuce," unpublished doctoral dissertation, University of California, 1961, 241.

9. Minutes, Salinas-Watsonville Lettuce Men's Association (August 19, 1930), Salinas Western Growers Association. All the following notes for the Salinas-Watsonville Lettuce Men's Association are from the Salinas Western Growers Association, as shown here. For simplicity, these notes are referred to hereafter as minutes from the Grower-Shipper Association.

10. *Salinas Index-Journal* (January 10, 1930), 1, 5.

11. Ibid., 1.

12. *Salinas Index-Journal* (January 3, 1936), 1.

13. *Salinas Independent* (January 4, 1935), 1.

14. Lamb, "Industrial Relations in the Western Lettuce Industry."

15. Raymond Clapper, "Town's Lettuce Boom Revives Days of '29," *Washington Post* (July 27, 1934), n.p., Grower-Shipper Association archive.

16. Ibid.

17. See Linda Ivey, "Ethnicity in the Land: Lost Stories in California Agriculture," *Agricultural History,* 81 (1) (Winter 2007); Cecilia M. Tsu, *Garden of the World: Asian Immigrants and the Making of Agriculture in California's Santa Clara Valley* (Oxford: Oxford University Press, 2013).

18. Kaufman cited in Ivey, "Ethnicity in the Land." See also Edwin B. Almirol, *Ethnic Identity and Social Negotiation: A Study of a Filipino Community in California* (New

York: AMS Press, 1985); Lori Flores, *Grounds for Dreaming: Mexican Americans, Mexican Immigrants, and the California Farmworker Movement* (New Haven and London: Yale University Press, 2016); *The Issei of the Salinas Valley: Japanese Pioneer Families, Family Stories, and Photos from the Late 1800s to 1942* (Salinas Valley Japanese American Citizens League, 2010); Sandy Lydon, *Chinese Gold: The Chinese in the Monterey Bay Region* (Capitola, CA: Capitola Book Company,1985); David T. Yamada, *The Japanese of the Monterey Peninsula: Their History and Legacy, 1895–1995* (Monterey: Japanese American Citizens League, 1995).

19. *Salinas Daily Index* (January 9, 1930), 1.

20. Editorial, *Salinas Index-Journal* (January 9, 1930), 2, Monterey County Historical Society.

21. Lydon, *Chinese Gold.*

22. Burton Anderson, *From Valley to Sea: 25 Years with the Coastal Grower* (Salinas: Monterey County Historical Society, 2015), 8.

23. *Salinas Index-Journal* (April 22, 1933), n.p., Grower-Shipper Association, clipping file, folder: "Newspaper Clippings, 1933."

24. Ibid.

25. Ibid. See also Smith, "The Impact of Technological Change on the Marketing of Salinas Lettuce."

26. Minutes, Grower-Shipper Association (August 12, 1932).

27. Pink sheet (August 6, 1932), Grower-Shipper Association, clipping file, folder: "Newspaper Clippings, 1933."

28. *Salinas Index-Journal* (April 22, 1933), n.p., Grower-Shipper Association, clipping file, folder: "Newspaper Clippings, 1933."

29. Minutes, Grower-Shipper Association (April 30, 1934):

Beard . . . complained bitterly about the lack of support both in cars and financial matters he was receiving from the Shippers . . . unless the Shippers got behind him he was ready to close out the whole effort . . . after Mr. Beard withdrew from the meeting the situation was discussed fully and it was decided to appoint a committee to investigate and to decide . . . advisability of hiring Mr. Beard at his stipulated salary of $15,000.000 per year as an employee of the Association . . . all shippers would be assessed about $3.00 per car out of . . . the matter should be presented to Attorney Gardner of Watsonville.

30. Minutes, Grower-Shipper Association (May 8, 1934).

31. Clapper, "Town's Lettuce Boom Revives Days of '29."

32. Minutes, Grower-Shipper Association (May 8, 1934):

The GSA at last agreed to pay Beard 1 cent per crate of lettuce (whether it sold or not), and in exchange, Beard monitored Department of Agriculture market reports every morning to ascertain just how much lettuce "173 consuming markets throughout the country" might already have at their disposal and "how much [these consumers] are likely to eat in a week." The Growers Exchange circumvented the earlier system when "a city which could consume only two cars of lettuce in a week would have five or six cars in the yards."

33. Ibid.

34. Ibid.

35. Minutes, Grower-Shipper Association (May 10, 1932). The *Index-Journal* gave a brief history of the FMNS's significance for Salinas's farmers.

36. Minutes, Grower-Shipper Association (June 7, 1932):

H. A. Hunt, County Agricultural Commission . . . distributed a paper on lettuce pests and their control . . . increasing . . . as the same crops are grown from year to year on the same land. . . . A letter from Mr. O. D. Miller was read suggesting action on reducing rents and further reducing wages of field labor. . . . The Secretary read a wage scale agreed on at Stockton between laborers shippers.

37. Minutes, Grower-Shipper Association (December 6, 1932):

It was the sense of the meeting that next year's markets may very well be as poor as this year's and that it is quite possible they may get to the 85 cent and 90 cent level of the present market on lettuce from the Southern sections. . . . It was the sense of this meeting that Mr. Knowlton and Mr. Tracy should review the relations between this Association and the Western Growers in either one or both of their meetings in an effort to secure from them more cooperation and greater assistance than has been accorded in the past.

"Notes," San Francisco California Office California Growers & Shippers Protective League, in Minutes, Salinas-Watsonville Lettuce Men's Association (December 14, 1932). In this way, the Salinas GSA maintained connections and cooperation from other California associations and nationally. "General discussion developed . . . it was agreed to have the Vegetable, Deciduous and Citrous interests prepare briefs of statistics demonstrating the percentage of gross returns paid in freight charged from 1918 to 1932; the increasing volume industry cannot continue to pay the present fixed charges from the standpoint of either the grower or shipper."

38. Minutes, Grower-Shipper Association (May 22, 1933):

In August 1928 the fight for reduced and otherwise revised refrigeration rates was started. . . . On motion of H. L. Strobel . . . this committee was unanimously empowered to represent this District and make the best deal possible. . . . The Salinas-Watsonville Lettuce Clearing House hereby formed as a non-profit association to control the operations . . . in harvesting, packing, grading, inspecting and shipping lettuce grown in the counties of Monterey, Santa Cruz, and San Benito . . . in order to prevent a possible disaster to the industry.

39. Minutes, Grower-Shipper Association (June 25, 1933).

40. Clapper, "Town's Lettuce Boom Revives Days of '29."

41. *Salinas Index-Journal* (June 1, 1933), n.p., Grower-Shipper Association, clipping file, folder: "Newspaper Clippings, 1933."

42. Clapper, "Town's Lettuce Boom Revives Days of '29."

43. Major Rolin C. Watkins, ed., *Monterey and Santa Cruz Counties, California: Cradle of California's History and Romance* (Chicago: S. J. Clarke Publishing Co., 1925), 379.

44. *Salinas Index-Journal* (December 30, 1925), evidenced by the number of money orders (22,500) and letters posted (60,000) in three days every year that consistently gave the city "a first-class rating" by the United States government.

45. Lamb, "Industrial Relations in the Western Lettuce Industry," 60.

46. *Salinas Index-Journal* (January 16, 1930), 2.

47. Watkins, *Monterey and Santa Cruz Counties*, 380, 384.

48. See Anderson, *From Valley to Sea*; William Orville Jones, "The Salinas Valley: Its Agricultural Development, 1920–1940," unpublished doctoral dissertation, Stanford University, 1947; Lamb, "Industrial Relations in the Western Lettuce Industry." For migration patterns within the state, see Elliott Robert Barkan, *From All Points: America's Immigrant West, 1870s–1952* (Bloomington: University of Indiana Press, 2007).

49. *Salinas Independent* (November 16, 1929), 1.

50. Minutes, Grower-Shipper Association (1930–1938).

51. Every year the local papers listed all rodeo participants, which included representation from each ethnic organization, business group, women's group, GSA, and labor unions. See, for example, the *Salinas Morning Post*, which listed on its front page on July 18, 1930 twenty-six floats representing the Japanese Society, Catholic Organizations, the Bing Kong Society (Chinese), Mexican F. Morales Float, Business and Professional Women, Sui Sing Society, Rizal Lodge No. 3 (Filipino/a), Labor Council, Rotary Cub, Kiwanis, Chambers of Commerce from San José and other nearby towns, among others.

52. Minutes, Grower-Shipper Association (1930–1938).

53. Minutes, Grower-Shipper Association (September 16, 1930).

54. *Salinas Independent* (November 16, 1929), 3.

55. See Paul Boyer, *Urban Masses and Moral Order in America, 1820–1920* (Cambridge, MA: Harvard University Press, 1978); Robin L. Einhorn, *Property Rules: Political Economy in Chicago, 1833–1872* (Chicago: University of Chicago Press, 2001); Jon C. Teaford, *The Unheralded Triumph: City Government in America, 1870–1900* (Baltimore: Johns Hopkins University Press, 1984); David Vaught, *Cultivating California: Growers,*

Specialty Crops, and Labor, 1875–1920 (Baltimore and London: Johns Hopkins University Press, 1999).

56. *Salinas Index-Journal* (October 17, 1929), 2.

57. *Salinas Index-Journal* (November 1, 1929), 1.

58. Ibid.

59. Minutes, Salinas Women's Civic Club (1909–1940), Monterey County Historical Society.

60. See Almirol, *Ethnic Identity and Social Negotiation*; interview with Ron Cacas by Carol Lynn McKibben (August 20, 2019), Salinas.

61. There are too many examples to cite here but suffice it to say that almost every issue of the *Salinas Morning Post* and the *Salinas Index-Journal* (later renamed *The Californian*) during the 1930s contained mention of the Filipina Women's Club as strong civic-minded activists. For example, the *Salinas Index-Journal* (October 29, 1934, p. 2) featured a large photograph of the new "Miss Philippines" Anne Avila with a one-column write-up about the celebration of Flag Day sponsored by the Filipina Women's Club that drew thousands of visitors from all over the state.

62. *Salinas Index-Journal* (January 17, 1930), 1.

63. *Salinas Index-Journal* (June 14, 1930), 1.

64. *Salinas Index-Journal* (August 8, 1933).

65. See Blanche Chin Ah Tye, *Full of Gold: Growing Up in Salinas Chinatown, Living in Post War America* (North Charleston, SC: CreateSpace Independent Publishing, 2015); Almirol, *Ethnic Identity and Social Negotiation*; *The Issei of the Salinas Valley*; Lydon, *Chinese Gold*; Yamada, *The Japanese of the Monterey Peninsula.*

66. *Salinas Index-Journal* (February 15, 1930), 2; see also *Salinas Index-Journal* (March 4, 1930), 1: "[Furthermore,] [w]ith 38 building permits listed in Salinas last month calling for structures approximating $364,000.00 in value this city established a record here for all time. . . . [The city council gave] approval for a new subdivision in the Spring district; [and passed] resolutions directing the opening of a new alley and a new street."

67. *Salinas Index-Journal* (January 2, 1933),1. The Salinas National Bank's 1932 business report showed "the most successful year since its organization in 1929. It opens the year 1933 with a very large cash and secondary reserve. . . . The Salinas National Bank starting from scratch October 21st 1929 has enjoyed a most phenomenal growth. Closing its books for the year 1932, it shows resources of over $2,100,000.00."

68. *Salinas Index-Journal* (January 2, 1933), 1.

69. *Salinas Independent* (January 4, 1935), 1.

70. Ibid.

71. Clapper, "Town's Lettuce Boom Revives the Days of '29."

72. Ibid.

73. Interview with Ben Lopez by George Robinson (December 1, 1976), Salinas; Salinas History Conference Roundtable, 2012; interview with Ron Cacas by Carol Lynn McKibben (August 20, 2019), Salinas; "History of the Japanese-Americans in the Salinas Valley," unpublished paper, n.d., given to author by Hibino family; "The Orchid King," in Po Bronson, *Why Do I Love These People: Honest and Amazing Stories of Real Families* (New York: Random House, 2005), 229–244.

74. Clapper, "Town's Lettuce Boom Revives the Days of '29."

CHAPTER 4

1. See Rick Baldoz, *The Third Asiatic Invasion: Empire and Migration in Filipino/a America, 1898–1946* (New York and London: New York University Press, 2011); Dawn Bohulano Mabalon, *Little Manila Is in the Heart: The Making of the Filipina/o Community in Stockton, California* (Durham and London: Duke University Press, 2013).

2. Unnamed Filipino/a spokesman, *Salinas Independent* (July 1, 1933), 1

3. The two main newspapers in town, *Salinas Daily Index-Journal* and the *Salinas Independent*, featured this event on their front page every year in great detail.

4. See Reynaldo C. Ileto, "Rizal and the Underside of Philippine History," in *Filipinos and their Revolution: Event, Discourse and Historiography* (Quezon City: Ateneo de Manila University Press, 1998). Jean Ventua, president of Salinas's Asian Cultural Center, summarized Ileto's analysis of Rizal and his place in Filipino/a lore as follows:

> Ileto described Rizal as a charismatic figure. Aside from the fact that he was handsome, an intellectual, a novelist and polymath, he was also viewed as something of a seer and healer. [Rizal] was a European-educated ophthalmologist, a vocation mostly unknown in the Philippines at the time, which, when he returned to the Philippines and set up a practice seemed to confer almost miraculous healing powers upon him. [See Ileto, "Rizal and the Underside," 308–311]. He also (according to Ileto) made use of the Philippine obsession with Christ's passion, or passion play (the *Pasyon*) by playing up his role as a self-sacrificing Christ-like figure during his imprisonment and execution: "When Rizal was brought back to Manila and thrown into prison on November 1896, one of the first things he did was to design and send to his family a little sketch of 'The Agony in the Garden,' beneath which he wrote, 'This is but the first Station.' More significant than his feelings about his impending death is the fact that by sending to his family the biblically-inspired sketch and note, which would later come to the attention of more and more people, Rizal was shedding signs of an impending reenactment of the *Pasyon*" [Ileto, 317]. In fact, when he was taken to his place of execution, he insisted on walking, rather than being taken in a wagon, as was the usual procedure, and was heard to say "I forgive everyone from the bottom of my heart," and

"consummatum est!" before being shot (also recounted in Ileto). Whether or not all this was true, it has remained in the popular view of him as a Philippine hero. I think this Christ-like feeling about Rizal was still present among Filipinos of the 1930s, and may have accounted for some of the tone of reverence and emotion surrounding that play, which, in way, was also a *Pasyon*.

5. "Merchants Display National Flags in Honor of Filipinos," *Salinas Daily Index* (December 30, 1925).

6. Ibid.

7. *Salinas Daily Index* (December 29, 1925), 1.

8. Ibid.

9. Ibid.

10. *Salinas Daily Index* (December 31, 1925), 1, 5.

11. *Salinas Independent* (January 5, 1934), 3.

12. Ibid.

13. See Mabalon, *Little Manila Is in the Heart*.

14. *Salinas Daily Index* (July 9, 1930), 2.

15. See Linda Ivey, "Ethnicity in the Land: Lost Stories in California Agriculture," *Agricultural History*, 81 (1) (Winter 2007); Cecilia M. Tsu, *Garden of the World: Asian Immigrants and the Making of Agriculture in California's Santa Clara Valley* (Oxford: Oxford University Press, 2013).

16. Ibid.

17. Editorial, *Salinas Index-Journal* (January 10, 1930), 2.

18. *Salinas Daily Index* (July 7, 1930), 2.

19. This specific quotation came from an interview with Edward F. Moncrief by Carol Lynn McKibben (May 17, 2018), Salinas. Montcrief's book, *Raising the Blackbirds: A Story of an Immigrant Farmworker and His Community* (Salinas: Singwillow Publishing, 2016), documented the housing crisis among farmworkers in the 1970s. However, it has been echoed in conversations with a variety of Salinas's residents from all walks of life. For evidence of this in other agricultural towns in California, see Ivey, "Ethnicity in the Land."

20. *Salinas Index-Journal* (January 16, 1930), 2.

21. After the passage of the North American Free Trade Agreement in 1994, manufacturers moved plants from California and throughout the United States to Mexico and to Southeast Asia countries and justified the oppressive, even horrific, wages and working conditions—especially for teenage girls—as appropriate for them based on age, gender, and race. See Aiwha Ong, *Spirits of Resistance and Capitalist Discipline: Factory Women in Malaysia* (Albany: SUNY Press, 2010).

22. Minutes, Salinas Chamber of Commerce (May 4, 1926).

23. For an excellent overview of Filipino/a experience in the United States in this era, see Baldoz, *The Third Asiatic Invasion*; and Mabalan, *Little Manila Is in the*

Heart. For thorough analyses of Mexican and Mexican American experiences in the United States and California during the 1930s, see Lori A. Flores, *Grounds for Dreaming: Mexican Americans, Mexican Immigrants, and the California Farmworker Movement* (New Haven: Yale University Press, 2016); Stephen J. Pitti, *The Devil in Silicon Valley: Northern California, Race, and Mexican Americans* (Princeton: Princeton University Press, 2003); George J. Sánchez, *Becoming Mexican American: Ethnicity, Culture and Identity in Chicano Los Angeles, 1900–1945* (Oxford: Oxford University Press, 1993).

24. See Edwin B. Almirol, *Ethnic Identity and Social Negotiation: A Study of a Filipino/a Community in California* (New York: AMS Press, 1985), 54.

25. *Salinas Index-Journal* (January 22, 1930), 2.

26. Ibid.

27. *Salinas Index-Journal* (January 23, 1930), 1, 3.

28. *Salinas Index-Journal* (January 24, 1930), 2.

29. *Salinas Independent* (January 25, 1935), 4.

30. See Almirol, *Ethnic Identity and Social Negotiation*.

31. Ibid. Interview with Ruth Andresen by Carol Lynn McKibben (May 18, 2018), Salinas; interview with Jen Ventua by Carol Lynn McKibben (May 28, 2018).

32. *Salinas Index-Journal* (February 1, 1930), 2.

33. Cited in Dioscoro R. Recio, "Filipino/a Community Remembers Immigrants," *Californian* (June 12, 1993), 1A.

34. For a deep analysis of Filipino/a American experience in Salinas, see Almirol, *Ethnic Identity and Social Negotiation*.

35. Recio, "Filipino/a Community Remembers Immigrants."

36. Ibid.

37. Cited in Rick Rodriguez, "Filipino/a Community Recognition Grows," *Salinas Californian* (September 30, 1974), 11.

38. Ibid.

39. Beginning in 1850, California prohibited marriages between whites and persons deemed nonwhite. In 1880, this prohibition was amended to include Asians: "Negro, mulatto, or Mongolian." The prohibition was amended again in 1901 and 1909 to include prohibiting whites from marrying "persons of Japanese descent." This was amended again in 1931 to generally "prohibit marriages between persons of the Caucasian and Asian races." In 1933 the statute specifically targeted Filipinos/as, echoing the hysterical reaction of the *Salinas Index-Journal*'s editorial outlawing marriages between "whites and Malays."

40. See Flores, *Grounds for Dreaming*, 39.

41. Interview with Bill Ramsey by Carol Lynn McKibben (October 15, 2018), Salinas.

42. See Almirol, *Ethnic Identity and Social Negotiation*.

43. Rodriguez, "Filipino/a Community Recognition Grows."

44. Ibid.

45. Ibid.

46. Almirol, *Ethnic Identity and Social Negotiation.*

47. Rodriguez, "Filipino/a Community Recognition Grows."

48. Ibid.

49. *Salinas Independent* (February 9, 1934), 1.

50. Ibid.

51. Ibid.

52. Ibid.

53. Editorial, *Salinas Index-Journal* (January 13, 1934), 2.

54. Business licenses were issued to Sam Ah Tye for a cigar and soda shop, to the Fuji Drug Store and Pharmacy, to Kotick's furniture store and to Feldman's menswear (Jewish), among many others (Monterey County Historical Society). Also, the minutes of the Salinas Chamber of Commerce reflected diversity of ethnicity in the surnames of its members to include anyone who wished to join this booster organization without discrimination as to race or ethnicity; city directories showed both mixed-race neighborhoods and business ownership.

55. Editorial, *Salinas Index-Journal* (August 3, 1933), 4.

56. Ibid.

57. *Salinas Daily Index* (January 13, 1930), 4.

58. *Salinas Independent* (March 30, 1934), 1.

59. A glance through the society pages of the *Salinas Independent, the Salinas Morning Post,* and the *Salinas Index-Journal (Californian)* from the late 1920s into the present contains numerous references to meetings, events, and commemorations of important milestones for Jewish life and for this organization in Salinas.

60. *Salinas Index-Journal* (November 1, 1929), 3.

61. *Salinas Index-Journal* (July 1, 1933), 2.

62. See Eiichiro Azuma, *Between Two Empires: Race, History, and Transnationalism in Japanese America* (Oxford: Oxford University Press, 2005); Charlotte Brooks, *Alien Neighbors, Foreign Friends: Housing and the Transformation of Urban California* (Chicago: University of Chicago Press, 2009); Scott Kurashige, *The Shifting Grounds of Race: Black and Japanese Americans in the Making of Multiethnic Los Angeles* (Princeton: Princeton University Press, 2008).

63. *Salinas Index-Journal* (October 31, 1929), 1.

64. *Monterey County Post* (July 25, 1933), 1.

65. *Salinas Index-Journal* (January 5, 1934), 1.

66. See Elliott Robert Barkan, *From All Points: America's Immigrant West, 1870s–1925* (Bloomington and Indianapolis: Indiana University Press, 2007), 163.

67. *Salinas Independent* (January 5, 1934), 1.

68. Minutes, Grower-Shipper Association (September 27, 1932).

69. *Salinas Daily Journal* (March 1, 1921), front page, John Steinbeck Library Collection.

70. Ibid.

71. "Description of Courses," Salinas Evening School, 1938–1939, Monterey County Historical Society.

72. *Salinas Index-Journal* (January 8, 1934), 3.

73. *Salinas Index-Journal* (July 8, 1933), 1.

74. *Salinas Index-Journal* (May 11, 1934), 1.

75. Ibid.

76. See Daniel Martinez HoSang, *Racial Propositions: Ballot Initiatives and the Making of Postwar California* (University of California Press, 2010); Kurashige, *The Shifting Grounds of Race*, 1–35; Shirley Ann Wilson Moore, *To Place Our Deeds: The African American Community in Richmond, California, 1910–1963* (Berkeley: University of California Press, 1999); Sánchez, *Becoming Mexican American*; Robert O. Self, *American Babylon: Race and the Struggle for Postwar Oakland* (Princeton and Oxford: Princeton University Press, 2003), 135–149.

77. See Brooks, *Alien Neighbors, Foreign Friends*; Kurashige, *The Shifting Grounds of Race*; Carol Lynn McKibben, *Racial Beachhead: Diversity and Democracy in a Military Town* (Stanford: Stanford University Press, 2012); Pitti, *The Devil in Silicon Valley*.

78. *Salinas Daily Index* (January 13, 1930), 4.

CHAPTER 5

1. Raymond Clapper, "Town's Lettuce Boom Revives Days of '29," *Washington Post* (July 27, 1934), 10, Grower-Shipper Association archive.

2. John Steinbeck, *Harvest Gypsies*, originally published by the *San Francisco News* (1936) (Berkeley: HeyDay, 2019), 23.

3. The communal burning of Steinbeck's books on Main Street cannot be documented, but it is a commonly shared story among Salinas residents to illustrate their reaction to what they perceived was a terrible betrayal by a native son. A white Salinas native whose family was part of the elite, Steinbeck was expected to portray the city and its people positively rather than critically.

4. For an insightful analysis of the impact Dust Bowlers had on California and their quick ascendancy to middle class and even great wealth, see James N. Gregory, "Dust Bowl Legacies: The Okie Impact on California, 1939–1989," *California History*, 68 (3) (Fall 1989): 74–85.

5. See Dorothea Lange, *An American Exodus: A Record of Human Erosion* (New York: Reynal & Hitchcock, 1939); Carey McWilliams, *Factories in the Field: The Story of Migrant Farm Labor in California* (Boston: Little Brown, 1939); John Steinbeck, *East of Eden*

(New York: Viking Press, 1952); John Steinbeck, *The Grapes of Wrath* (New York: Viking Press, 1939).

6. See Steinbeck, *Harvest Gypsies*, 26–31.

7. See Linda Ivey, "Ethnicity in the Land: Lost Stories in California Agriculture," *Agricultural History*, 81 (1) (Winter 2007); Cecilia M. Tsu, *Garden of the World: Asian Immigrants and the Making of Agriculture in California's Santa Clara Valley* (Oxford: Oxford University Press, 2013); David Vaught, "Factories in the Field Revisited," *Pacific Historical Review*, 66 (2) (1997): 149–184.

8. Mary Martha Ramsey Day, "All of These Things Happened Before I Was 12 Years Old," written in 1982. Courtesy of Bill Ramsey, Salinas, 2018.

9. Ibid.

10. Ibid.

11. Ibid.

12. Interview with Bill Ramsey by Carol Lynn McKibben (April 12, 2017), offices of Mann Packing, Salinas.

13. Ibid.

14. Editorial, *Salinas Index-Journal* (May 4, 1935).

15. *Monterey County Post* (March 21, 1933), 1.

16. Ibid.

17. Ibid.

18. Ibid.

19. Steinbeck, *Harvest Gypsies*, 23–24.

20. *Salinas Index-Journal* (April 13, 1934), 1.

21. Ibid.

22. Ibid., 2.

23. Ibid., 1.

24. Ibid., 4.

25. Ibid.

26. *Salinas Index-Journal* (April 12, 1934), 2.

27. Bill Ramsey interview (April 12, 2017).

28. For a thorough analysis of the experiences of Dust Bowl refugees in California, see James N. Gregory, *American Exodus: The Dust Bowl Migration and Okie Culture in California* (New York and Oxford: Oxford University Press, 1989).

29. Interview with Joanne Adcock Schmidt by Carol Lynn McKibben (August 28, 2017), Salinas.

30. *Salinas Independent* (June 14, 1935), 2.

31. Interview with Joanne Adcock Schmidt.

32. Minutes, Grower-Shipper Association (August 16, 1934).

33. Minutes, Grower-Shipper Association (March 13, 1934). The representatives from the Central Labor Council argued that "it was pointed out that there are

several advantages to the Shippers employing as much local help as possible among them being the reduction of strike likelihood, the discouragement of migrants whose presence in the community is a potential social menace and aggravates the relief problem which may be thrown back on localities at any time."

34. Helen Boyden Lamb, "Industrial Relations in the Western Lettuce Industry," unpublished doctoral dissertation, Radcliffe College, 1942, 300.

35. Interview with Joanne Adcock Schmidt.

36. "The 'Oakies' Make Good, Too!" *Daily Oklahoman* (February 25, 1940), 12.

37. Ibid.

38. Ibid.

39. Ibid.

40. Ibid.

41. Ibid.

42. Hebbron quoted in ibid.

43. Ibid. For a thorough analysis of 1920s and 1930s settlement patterns in California, see Becky Nicolaides, *My Blue Heaven: Life and Politics in the Working-Class Suburbs of Los Angeles, 1920–1965* (Chicago and London: University of Chicago Press, 2002).

44. *Salinas Index-Journal* (May 9, 1934), 1.

45. Ibid.

46. *Salinas Independent* (January 11, 1934), 2.

47. Ibid.

48. Numerous editorials emphasized the value of labor and of unions and sided with them in the multiple strikes of the era. According to an editorial in the *Monterey Peninsula Herald* in 1935, "The most important agricultural union in this section of California is the Fruit and Vegetable Workers Union. . . . It is neither red nor pink, but is normal and American. Its leaders are not 'outside agitators' or racketeers . . . but respected citizens of Salinas. That . . . is the American Way." Cited in Lamb, "Industrial Relations in the Western Lettuce Industry," 307.

49. "The success of California agriculture requires that we create and maintain a peon class," quoted in John Steinbeck, *Harvest Gypsies*, 23.

50. "Doss Tells of Membership in This Area," *Salinas Morning Post* (May 16, 1937).

51. Minutes, Grower-Shipper Association (October 16, 1933).

52. Ibid.

53. Minutes, Grower-Shipper Association (August 4, 1930).

54. Ibid.; "A.S. Doss Questioned at Labor Board Hearing at Pre-Strike Negotiations," *Salinas Morning Post* (April 15, 1937).

55. "Lettuce Field Hands Talk of 'Blacklist,'" *San Francisco Chronicle* (May 5, 1937).

56. Minutes, Grower-Shipper Association (April 10, 1934).

57. Minutes, Grower-Shipper Association (August 12, 1930), Jeffrey Hotel, Salinas.

58. Minutes, Grower-Shipper Association (August 19, 1930).

59. Minutes, Grower-Shipper Association (September 23, 1930).

60. Ibid.

61. Ibid.

62. The Grower-Shipper Association has a scrapbook of newspaper clippings from the era clearly documenting alliances between the Salinas Sheriff's Department, city government, and growers and shippers allied against union organizers and workers from 1933–1941.

63. Minutes, Grower-Shipper Association (September 23, 1930).

64. Minutes, Grower-Shipper Association (March 13, 1934).

65. Minutes, Grower-Shipper Association (September 23, 1930).

66. Ibid.

67. Minutes, Grower-Shipper Association (February 28, 1933).

68. Minutes, Grower-Shipper Association (April 3, 1933).

69. Minutes, Directors Meeting, Grower-Shipper Association (October 23, 1934), Grower-Shipper Association archive, Salinas.

70. Minutes, Grower-Shipper Association (February 7, 1935).

71. Minutes, Grower-Shipper Association (July 17, 1933).

72. The National Labor Relations Act (NLRA) of 1935 was part of New Deal legislation that banned company unions, guaranteeing workers in the private sector the right to organize into unions and take collective action, such as going on strike if their demands for higher wages and better working conditions were not met. Some of these protections were overturned twelve years later with the passage of the Taft-Hartley Act of 1947. However, agricultural workers as well as domestic workers were excluded from these protections until the passage of the California Agricultural Labor Relations Act of 1975 (ALRA).

73. Minutes, Grower-Shipper Association (August 8, 1933).

74. *Monterey County Post* (February 10, 1933), 1.

75. Ibid.

76. Ibid.

77. Ibid.

78. Minutes, Grower-Shipper Association (October 10, 1933):

[The] walkout of lettuce workers . . . occurred in the Salinas Valley at 2:00pm yesterday the 9th, and was slated to take place in the Pajaro Valley at the same hour on the same day. . . . Mr. Moody [George Moody, labor commissioner] gave a general outline of the general labor conditions in the country with particular reference to labor. He said that his Department of the State Government was interested in keeping people at work but that he had no arbitrary authority to make any settlement of disputes but that he hoped to act as a mediator and help effect a settlement of the differences between the employer and the employed. . . . Mr. Moody had no criticism to offer of the wages now but thought the wide range between the amounts earned being paid by the packers on piece work and the trimmers was a bad condition and should be changed.

79. Ibid.

80. Ibid.: "[T]he harm caused by a layoff of a few days would be negligible but that the situation would probably become very serious if allowed to run on for any length of time. . . . That the field workers were already being drawn into the trouble and that continuance with the strike would involve all labor connected with the industry."

81. Minutes, Grower-Shipper Association (October 12, 1933).

82. Ibid.

83. Minutes, Grower-Shipper Association (October 13, 1933).

84. Ibid.

85. Ibid.

86. Ibid.:

The strikers had been very self-confident and had decided to stand pat for their demands but that at an afternoon meeting with Mr. Creel . . . both shippers and the labor [agreed] to return to their respective orgs and to sell the proposition not as arbitration but as a compromise agreement. . . . All workers to return to their jobs with the assurance that they would not be discriminated against except as was necessary for shippers to protect their present workers. . . . That all reference to a closed shop was dropped.

87. Minutes, Grower-Shipper Association (October 16, 1933).

88. Minutes, Grower-Shipper Association (October 25, 1933).

89. Minutes, Grower-Shipper Association (March 13, 1934):

Wm Murray, chairman of the National Employment Commission of Monterey County . . . to classify the unemployed, especially those with dependents and to place them in employment. . . . [H]e requested that the vegetable people give his commission as much co-operation as possible to the end that the local people be given preference and thereby reduce the demand for local relief. . . . [T]he Government money the Board of Supervisors have been expending for relief is about gone and that no other source of funds has been found to take its place.

90. Ibid.

91. Minutes, Grower-Shipper Association (August 22, 1934).

92. Ibid.

93. Minutes, Grower-Shipper Association (April 24, 1934).

94. Ibid.

95. Minutes, Grower-Shipper Association (May 21, 1934).

96. Minutes, Grower-Shipper Association (August 28, 1934).

97. Ibid.

98. Minutes, Grower-Shipper Association (August 30, 1934).

99. Ibid.

100. Ibid.

101. *Salinas Independent* (June 14, 1935), 2. The article continued:

The vow taken by Communists which includes the destruction of government, the spreading of discontent and their methods of ingratiating themselves into organized groups in order to "wreck the machinery" has been known for a long time.

To erase their effort the workers have . . . become direct actionists. More than one person with wild soviet ideas found himself the target of a well-directed fist. . . . These skunks advocate violence . . . some of these radicals were pitched bodily down the labor temple stairs after they "shot off" in meeting.

For the past few years the Reds have looked upon labor camps as ideal places in which to sow the seeds of warped minds.

102. *Salinas Independent* (January 4, 1935), 1.

103. Central Labor Council Minutes, cited in *Salinas Independent* (June 7, 1935), 5.

104. Minutes, Grower-Shipper Association (September 1, 1936).

105. Ibid.

106. Minutes, Grower-Shipper Association (August 12, 1936).

107. Minutes, Grower-Shipper Association (September 1, 1936).

108. Minutes, Grower-Shipper Association (September 3, 1936).

109. Ibid.

110. Minutes, Grower-Shipper Association (September 4, 1936).

111. Ibid.

112. Ibid.

113. Ibid.

114. Editorial, *Salinas Independent* (September 11, 1936). 1.

115. Ibid.

116. *Salinas Independent* (September 18, 1936), 1.

117. Ibid.

118. Minutes, Grower-Shipper Association (September 9, 1936).

119. Ibid.

120. Minutes, Grower-Shipper Association (September 20, 1936).

121. Minutes, Grower-Shipper Association (September 29, 1936).

122. Minutes, Grower-Shipper Association (September 13, 1936).

123. Ibid.

124. *Salinas Independent* (September 26, 1936), 1:

Cannot be gone into in a brief statement. . . . As an example of some of the wild rumors which have been developed . . . was the story that Salinas was in the possession of a group of vigilantes, who were using gas bombs from which babies had died, and that men were beaten, left lying in the streets and were blinded by the gas . . . and that the strikers had violated the truce and cut the ropes on a lettuce truck, dumping same. On investigation it was proven that the rope broke . . . and the lettuce unloaded of its own accord.

125. *Salinas Independent* (September 18, 1936), 1.

126. Ibid.

127. *Salinas Independent* (October 9, 1936), 1.

128. Minutes, Grower-Shipper Association (October 5, 1936).

129. *Salinas Independent* (September 23, 1936), 1.

130. *Western Worker* (March 27, 1937), Scrapbook, "Clippings, National Labor Relations Board Meeting," Grower-Shipper Association archive, Salinas.

131. Editorial, *Salinas Independent* (March 25, 1937).

132. Ibid.

133. Ibid.

134. Ibid.

135. Ibid.

136. Ibid.

137. *East Salinas Pioneer* (May 9, 1940), 1.

CHAPTER 6

1. Salinas, California General Plan for Future Development, 1950, John Steinbeck Library, Historic File 25115, Planning and Zoning.

2. Ibid.

3. *Salinas: City in a Hurry*, 1940, Local History, Economic Conditions, folder 1, John Steinbeck Library, 1.

4. Interview with Jim Gattis by Carol Lynn McKibben (September 18, 2017), Salinas.

5. Interview with Albert Fong by Carol Lynn McKibben (March 7, 2019), Salinas.

6. Phone interview with Everett Alvarez Jr. by Carol Lynn McKibben (August 24, 2018).

7. Interview with Bill Ramsey by Carol Lynn McKibben (October 15, 2018), Salinas.

8. Yasuo W. Abuko, "Henry Hibino . . . Mayor of Salinas," *Nichi Bei Times* (January 1, 1974), Henry Hibino collection. After the war, James Abe returned from incarceration to become harvesting chief for Bud Antle, a large shipper and important member of the GSA.

9. The term "Issei" is used to describe the first generation of Japanese immigrants. Due to racial restrictions in immigration policy, Issei were deemed ineligible for naturalization and citizenship. See Mae Ngai, *Impossible Subjects: Illegal Aliens and the Making of Modern America* (Princeton: Princeton University Press, 2004), 37.

10. Interview with Mas and Marcia Hashimoto by Carol Lynn McKibben (March 27, 2019), Watsonville.

11. "SUHS Graduation," *Salinas Californian* (June 5, 1942), n.p., clipping file, Local History, John Steinbeck Library.

12. Interview with Ruth Andresen by Carol Lynn McKibben (June 28, 2019), Salinas; "SUHS Graduation."

13. 1930. −1940 city directories for Salinas.

14. Interview with Dr. Byron Chong and Alfred Fong (March 19, 2019), Chinese Christian Church, Salinas; see also Jean Vengua, https://voicesofmontereybay.org/2019/05/02/stories-of-chinatown/, for an overview of the ways Asian communities in Salinas interacted personally and professionally over time.

15. Interview with Kay Endo Masatani by Larry Hirahara (March 3, 2019), Salinas.

16. Interview with Mas and Marcia Hashimoto.

17. Ibid.

18. Ibid.

19. Ibid.

20. The march began on April 9, 1942 and was characterized by extreme abuse and deprivation of Filipino/a and American captives on the part of Japanese soldiers. After the war, the march was judged a war crime by the Allied military commission.

21. Colleen Finegan, "Incarceration for Profit: The Role of Central California Farmers in the Incarceration of the Japanese" (August 1, 1986), unpublished paper, private collection, Finegan family, 4.

22. Abuko, "Henry Hibino": "The fact that a federalized California National Guard artillery unit was stationed in the Philippines when World War II broke out and many of the men were captured on Bataan didn't help the feeling back home against Japanese Americans."

23. Carol Lynn McKibben, *Racial Beachhead: Diversity and Democracy in a Military Town* (Stanford: Stanford University Press, 2012), 56–57.

24. Interviews with Kay Masatani, Sus Ikeda, and Mae Sakasegawa by Larry Hirahara (March 3, 2019), Salinas.

25. Mas and Marica Hashimoto interview (March 27, 2019). For an excellent analysis of the conflicts within the camps among incarcerated Japanese and Japanese Americans, see Ngai, *Impossible Subjects*, 169–201.

26. Mas and Marica Hashimoto interview (March 27, 2019).

27. For an analysis of conflicts among Japanese internees within the camps, see Ngai, *Impossible Subjects*,175–201.

28. Mas and Marica Hashimoto interview (March 27, 2019). Although most survivors did not join actively in the civil rights movement on the Monterey Peninsula, championed largely by African Americans from nearby Fort Ord and Seaside, many sympathized with its aims. They expressed less sympathy with the Chicano/a civil rights movement in the 1970s under César Chávez, however, focused as it was on labor rights. For Japanese Americans in Salinas, most of whom were on the other side of the bargaining table from the farmworkers, the United Farm Workers appeared to be a threat to the social and economic order of the city, whereas the African American version of civil rights struck closer to home, singularly based as it was on race and racism rather than on labor issues. For an analysis of African American civil rights on the Monterey Peninsula, see McKibben, *Racial Beachhead*.

29. Minutes, Grower-Shippers Association (June 22, 1943), 1943–1949, Grower-Shippers Association archive, Salinas.

30. Bill Ramsey interview (October 15, 2018).

31. The center was constructed on the rodeo grounds at the north end of Salinas. It is a California Registered Historical Landmark, No. 934.

32. Mas and Marica Hashimoto interview (March 27, 2019).

33. Interview with Mas and Marcia Hashimoto by Carol Lynn McKibben (April 16, 2019), Palo Alto.

34. Mas and Marica Hashimoto interview (March 27, 2019).

35. Email interview with Larry Hirahara by Carol Lynn McKibben (March 3, 2019).

36. "Survey of Attitudes of Salinas Citizens Toward Japanese-Americans" (Salinas: Salinas Chamber of Commerce, 1943).

37. Ibid. See also Lori A. Flores, *Grounds for Dreaming: Mexican Americans, Mexican Immigrants, and the California Farmworker Movement* (New Haven: Yale University Press, 2016), 41.

38. "Democratic Life for All," *Monterey Peninsula Herald* (May 11, 1945), 9.

39. Abuko, "Henry Hibino."

40. Ibid.

41. Sus Ikeda interview (March 3, 2019).

42. McKibben, *Racial Beachhead*.

43. See Carol Lynn McKibben, *Beyond Cannery Row; Sicilian Women, Immigration, and Community in Monterey, 1915–1999* (Urbana and Chicago: University of Illinois Press,

2006), 75–97; David T. Yamada, *The Japanese of the Monterey Peninsula: Their History and Legacy, 1895–1995* (Monterey: Japanese American Citizens League, 1995).

44. McKibben, *Racial Beachhead;* Sherie Mershon and Steven Schlossman, *Foxholes and Color Lines: Desegregating the U.S. Armed Forces* (Baltimore and London: Johns Hopkins University Press, 1998).

45. McKibben, *Racial Beachhead,* 59–61.

46. Kay Masatani interview (March 3, 2019).

47. Everett Alvarez Jr. phone interview (August 24, 2018); phone interview with Casey Sakasegawa Wong by Carol Lynn McKibben (September 17, 2018); Salinas city directories, 1940–1950. Japanese Americans worked to overturn the law that kept them as tenant farmers rather than landowners according to the Alien Land Law, which was challenged in the postwar era but not overturned until the California Supreme Court did so in *Fujii v. California* (1952). See McKibben, *Racial Beachhead.*

48. This facility was called the Clubhouse and was the first government-constructed permanent USO center in the United States.

49. Robert B. Johnston, "Salinas 1875–1950: From Village to City," pamphlet published by Fidelity Savings and Loan Association, 1980, 23.

50. Interview with Ruth Andresen by Carol Lynn McKibben (June 28, 2019), Salinas.

51. Ibid.

52. "USO Council Enters Fourth Year in Salinas, Making Bigger Plan for Future," *Salinas Californian* (January 26, 1944), 2.

53. See Cynthia Enloe, *Bananas, Beaches, and Bases: Making Feminist Sense of International Politics* (Berkeley: University of California Press, 1990); McKibben, *Racial Beachhead.*

54. Interview with Jim Gattis by Carol Lynn McKibben (September 25, 2017), Salinas.

55. Bill Ramsey interview (October 15, 2018).

56. Everett Alvarez Jr. phone interview (August 24, 2018).

57. Ibid.

58. Ibid.

59. Ibid.

60. Jim Gattis interview (September 25, 2017).

61. Carey McWilliams report to Tolan Committee, San Francisco (September 24, 1940), the Alisal, folder 1, John Steinbeck Library.

62. "Bravo Salinas!" *Salinas Index-Journal* (March 16, 1940), 6.

63. GSA usually referred to itself as an "association" but not always. Concerning the membership dues, Bruce Church announced the following: "If dues for the first quarter of 1943 have not been paid, the member is not in good standing to maintain his membership in the union [meaning GSA]" (July 14, 1943).

64. Minutes, Grower-Shipper Association (June 12, 1946).

65. Minutes, Grower-Shipper Association (June 25, 1954).

66. Christopher R. Henke, *Cultivating Science, Harvesting Power: Science and Industrial Agriculture in California* (Cambridge, MA: MIT Press, 2008), 54–65.

67. See Deborah Cohen, *Braceros: Migrant Citizens and Transnational Subjects in the Postwar United States and Mexico* (Chapel Hill: University of North Carolina Press, 2011).

68. For an analysis of the ways government agencies and the GSA worked together to ensure a steady supply of workers from Mexico, see Cohen, *Braceros*, 28–29; Flores, *Grounds for Dreaming*, 80; David G. Gutiérrez, *Walls and Mirrors: Mexican Americans, Mexican Immigrants, and the Politics of Ethnicity* (Berkeley: University of California Press, 1995), 133–138.

69. Minutes, Grower-Shipper Association (June 12, 1946).

70. The minutes of meeting from the GSA consistently referred to Mexican temporary workers as "Mexican nationals." The term "Bracero" is never used.

71. Minutes, Grower-Shipper Association (October 7, 1943).

72. Minutes, Grower-Shipper Association (December 7, 1944).

73. Minutes, Grower-Shipper Association (May 16, 1944).

74. Minutes, Grower-Shipper Association (February 15, 1944; September 5, 1944; & September 13, 1944).

75. Ibid.

76. Minutes, Grower-Shipper Association (May 10, 1945).

77. Minutes, Grower-Shipper Association (August 24, 1945).

78. Henke, *Cultivating Science, Harvesting Power*, 106.

79. Minutes, Grower-Shipper Association (August 21, 1952).

80. See Cohen, *Braceros*; Flores, *Grounds for Dreaming*, 53; Ngai, *Impossible Subjects*, 127–166.

81. Minutes, Grower-Shipper Association (March 15, 1951). See Ngai, *Impossible Subjects*, 127–166.

82. See Flores, *Grounds for Dreaming*, 39–107.

83. Cohen, *Braceros*; Ngai, *Impossible Subjects*, 127–166.

84. For a thorough analysis of this program, see Cohen, *Braceros*; Flores, *Grounds for Dreaming*, 39–107; Ngai, *Impossible Subjects*, 127–166.

85. Diana Lizbeth Soria, "Impact of the Bracero Program in Salinas," California State University, Monterey Bay (May 16, 2016).

86. Interview with Herminia Alvarez by Diego Ruiz (July 18, 2016), Salinas.

87. Interview with Eugenio Martinez by Diego Ruiz (July 15, 2016); Diego Ruiz, "The Exploitation of Our Guests," July 2016 family oral history paper prepared for Salinas History Project.

88. Interview with Eugenio Martinez and Herminia Alvarez by Diego Ruiz (July 18, 2016 & July 19, 2017), Salinas.

89. Minutes, Grower-Shipper Association (June 26, 1958). Public Law 78 was a measure that had been passed in 1951. The GSA minutes are incorrect in attributing the passage of this measure to the bus accident in 1958.

90. Flores, *Grounds for Dreaming*, 135–162.

91. Minutes, Grower-Shipper Association (August 21, 1952).

92. Minutes, Grower-Shipper Association October 16, 1952).

93. Cohen, *Braceros*, 30. See also James D. Cockcroft, *Outlaws in the Promised land: Mexican American Workers and America's Future* (New York: Grove Press, 1986), 74.

94. Minutes, Grower-Shipper Association (August 21, 1952).

95. Minutes, Grower-Shipper Association (September 25, 1952).

96. In multiple news reports throughout the 1950s and 1960s, the CSO represented workers in coalition with other labor organizations. For example, "Field-worker Drive Approved," *Salinas Californian* (May 12, 1965), 2.

97. "Salinas CSO Represented at Area Meet," *Salinas Californian* (November 2, 1957), 6; for a thorough discussion of the Community Service Organization in Salinas, see Flores, *Grounds for Dreaming*, 75–107.

98. Ibid.

99. Minutes, Grower-Shipper Association (February 8, 1951).

100. Ibid.

101. Minutes, Grower-Shipper Association (October 15, 1951).

102. Minutes, Grower-Shipper Association (February 7, 1952).

103. Minutes, Grower-Shipper Association (May 23, 1951).

104. Minutes, Grower-Shipper Association (October 16, 1952).

105. Minutes, Board of Supervisors (March 22, 1945), Alisal, folder 1, John Steinbeck Library.

106. Ibid.

107. Minutes, Grower-Shipper Association (August-October 1952).

108. Minutes, Grower-Shipper Association (July 24, 1952).

109. Bill Ramsey interview (October 15, 2018).

110. See Gutiérrez, *Walls and Mirrors*, 152–178; Ngai, *Impossible Subjects*, 230.

111. For a thorough examination of the long-standing flow of population on the southern border, see Michael Dear, *Why Walls Won't Work: Repairing the U.S.- Mexico Divide* (Oxford: Oxford University Press, 2013); Gutiérrez, *Walls and Mirrors*. For an analysis of the impact of the 1965 Immigration Act on the Mexican border, see Ngai, *Impossible Subjects*, 127–166.

112. Charles Gordon, "The Amiable Fiction," *Case Western Reserve Journal of International Law*, 1 (2) (1969): 124–130. See also Douglas S. Massey, "America's Immigration Policy Fiasco: Learning from Past Mistakes," *Daedalus*, 142 (3) (Summer 2013): 5–15.

113. *San Jose Mercury News* (May 2, 1979), clipping file, GSA box.

114. Interview with Ron Cacas by Carol Lynn McKibben (August 20, 2019), Salinas.

115. See Marilynn S. Johnson, *The Second Gold Rush: Oakland and the East Bay in World War II* (Berkeley and Los Angeles: University of California Press, 1993); Roger W. Lotchin, *The Bad City in the Good War: San Francisco, Los Angeles, Oakland, and San Diego* (Bloomington: Indiana University Press, 2003); Shirley Ann Wilson Moore, *To Place Our Deeds: The African American Community of Richmond, California, 1910–1963* (Berkeley: University of California Press, 2000); Robert O. Self, *American Babylon: Race and the Struggle for Postwar Oakland* (Princeton: Princeton University Press, 2003); Josh Sides, *L.A. City Limits: African American Los Angeles from the Great Depression to the Present* (Berkeley: University of California Press, 2006).

116. See Elaine D. Johnson, "Sociological Study of the Monterey Area," prepared for the City Planning Commission, Monterey, California, October 1968. According to the report, "Monterey County not only has a higher percentage of negro residents than the state as a whole, it also has a much higher percentage of residents of foreign stock (25.7% for Monterey county and 19% in the U.S.) . . . the heavy concentration of Mexican residents is in the Salinas area." Johnson used school enrollments to count ethnic Mexican people and trace their origins more precisely than census data, which counted all Hispanic people as white. See also Flores, *Grounds for Dreaming*, for an in-depth analysis of the Mexican American community experience in Salinas during these decades.

117. U.S. Census and City of Salinas Department of Finance records.

118. Charlotte Brooks, *Alien Neighbors, Foreign Friends: Housing and the Transformation of Urban California* (Chicago: University of Chicago Press, 2009), 239.

119. See Eiichiro Azuma, *Between Two Empires: Race, History, and Transnationalism in Japanese America* (Oxford: Oxford University Press, 2005).

120. See "History of the Japanese-Americans in the Salinas Valley," unpublished paper, n.d., given to author by Hibino family.

121. Ibid. For an analysis of Japanese farmers in San Mateo, see Paul G. Nauert, "'The Proudest of All Flowers,' Chrysanthemum Cultivation, Japanese American Community, and Suburban Boosterism in Redwood City California, 1906–1942," unpublished paper, 2018.

122. Interview with Henry and Kent Hibino by Carol Lynn McKibben (March 6, 2018), Salinas. He was referring to the Nunes family who were prominent members of Salinas's agricultural community.

123. *Salinas Californian* (December 31, 1971), 2.

124. See Flores, *Grounds for Dreaming.*

125. For an excellent analysis of postwar Asian inclusion in American society, see Brooks, *Alien Neighbors, Foreign Friends.*

126. City census records.

127. Their fears came true with the upsurge of anti-Asian rhetoric surrounding the recent COVID-19 pandemic in which China and Chinese people were blamed for spreading the virus to Americans by former President Donald Trump.

128. See Gordon H. Chang, *Friends and Enemies: The United States, China, and the Soviet Union, 1948–1972* (Stanford: Stanford University Press, 1990), 282–287. According to Chang, U.S. strategy under Nixon and Kissinger meant pitting China against the Soviet Union to benefit U.S. interests. Chinese Americans in Salinas appreciated this overture even as they saw how fragile the new relationship was, attuned as they were to Chinese issues and China–United States relations.

129. Minutes, Salinas City Council (July 19, 1971 & September 20, 1971).

130. For the ways in which the interests of minority groups diverged in California following World War II, see Mark Brilliant, *The Color of America Has Changed: How Racial Diversity Shaped Civil Rights Reform in California* (Oxford: Oxford University Press, 2012), ch. 5; Brooks, *Alien Neighbors, Foreign Friends;* Scott Kurashige, *The Shifting Grounds of Race: Black and Japanese Americans in the Making of Multiethnic Los Angeles* (Princeton: Princeton University Press, 2008).

131. Linda Wong Gin interview (August 30, 2019).

132. See *Diana v. California State Board of Education*, Civ. No. C-70, 37 RFP (N.D. Cal., 1970, 1973); McKibben, *Racial Beachhead*, 156.

133. Ibid., 182.

134. Linda Wong Gin interview (August 30, 2019).

135. Ibid.

136. Ibid.

137. Ibid.

138. See J. Morgan Kousser, "Racial Justice and the Abolition of Justice Courts in Monterey County" (September 9, 2000), unpublished: http://resolver.caltech.edu/CaltechAUTHORS:20130913-160303883

139. Interview with Dr. Byron Chong by Carol Lynn McKibben (March 26, 2019), Salinas.

140. Ibid.

141. Ibid.

142. "Two-fold Celebration in Chinatown Draws Crowd," *Salinas Californian* (April 17, 1961), n.p., clipping file, Monterey County Historical Society.

143. Ibid.

144. Dr. Byron Chong interview (March 26, 2019).

145. "Two-fold Celebration in Chinatown Draws Crowd."

146. "Filipino Session Scheduled Sunday on Group Needs," *Salinas Californian* (July 21, 1970), 10.

147. Edwin B. Almirol, *Ethnic Identity and Social Negotiation: A Study of a Filipino Community in California* (New York: AMS Press, 1985).

148. Ibid., 183.

149. Ibid., 191–205, 207–208.

150. Ibid., 217.

151. Ibid.

152. Ibid., 216.

153. Interview with Ron Cacas by Carol Lynn McKibben (September 3, 2019), Salinas.

154. Ron Cacas interview (August 20, 2019).

155. Interview with Ron Cacas by Carol Lynn McKibben (September 3, 2019), Salinas.

156. Ibid.

157. Ibid.

158. See Dawn Bohulano Mabalon, *Little Manila Is in the Heart: The Making of the Filipina/o Community in Stockton, California* (Durham and London: Duke University Press, 2013), 172.

159. Susan Aremas interview (September 19, 2019).

160. Ibid. See David Freund, *Colored Property: State Property and White Racial Politics in Suburban America* (Chicago and London: University of Chicago Press, 2007); Richard Rothstein, *The Color of Law: A Forgotten History of How Our Government Segregated America* (New York and London: Liveright Publishing, 2017).

161. Susan Aremas interview (September 19, 2019).

162. Ibid.

163. Ibid.

164. Ibid.

165. Ibid.

166. Ibid.

167. Ibid.

CHAPTER 7

1. Interview with Ruth Andresen by Carol Lynn McKibben (November 6, 2018), Salinas.

2. Ibid.

3. Ibid.

4. "Salinas Expanded 1/8 in Size by Two Annexations," *Salinas Californian* (January 30, 1947), 1.

5. "Mayor Warns of Attempts to 'Confuse,'" *Salinas Californian* (May 15, 1950), 1

6. *Salinas: City in a Hurry*, 1940, Local History, Economic Conditions, folder 1, John Steinbeck Library, 2.

7. Salinas, California General Plan for Future Development, 1950, John Steinbeck Library, Historic File 25115, Planning and Zoning.

8. "Help Salinas Grow—Vote Yes! Zoning Is Not a Tool to Be Employed in Economic Conflict!" Monterey County Historical Society.

9. J. Morgan Kousser, "Racial Justice and the Abolition of Justice Courts in Monterey County" (September 9, 2000), unpublished: http://resolver.caltech.edu/CaltechAUTHORS:20130913-160303883

10. Ibid.

11. Ibid.

12. Carol Lynn McKibben, *Racial Beachhead: Diversity and Democracy in a Military Town* (Stanford: Stanford University Press, 2012), 147–154.

13. Kousser, "Racial Justice and the Abolition of Justice Courts in Monterey County," 45–46.

14. Ibid.

15. Interview with Dr. Byron Chong by Carol Lynn McKibben (March 26, 2019), Salinas; interview with Linda Wong Gin by Carol McKibben (August 30, 2019), Chinese Community Center, Salinas. For an in-depth analysis of the ways Anglo Americans made room for Asian Americans in segregated neighborhoods in California, see Charlotte Brooks, *Alien Neighbors, Foreign Friends: Asian Americans, Housing and the Transformation of Urban California* (Chicago: University of Chicago Press, 2009); McKibben, *Racial Beachhead*, chs. 3 and 4; Kousser, "Racial Justice and the Abolition of Justice Courts in Monterey County," 46.

16. *Salinas Californian* (September 26, 1946), 5, cited in Kousser, "Racial Justice and the Abolition of Justice Courts in Monterey County."

17. *Salinas Californian* (August 11, 1947), 2.

18. "City of Salinas Report: Alisal Annexation" (November 23, 1962), 1. John Steinbeck Library, Local History.

19. "Unite—And Fast," *Salinas Californian* (October 8, 1950), 8.

20. Ibid.

21. "Bravo Salinas!" *Salinas Index-Journal* (March 16, 1940), 6.

22. Ibid.

23. "Many Improvements—The Alisal—18 Years Old," *Salinas Californian* (June 1947 & October 1947), n.p., Local History, the Alisal, folder 2, John Steinbeck Library.

24. "Tenure Assured for Alisal Teachers in Event of Annexation," *Salinas Californian* (October 5, 1950), 20.

25. Ibid.

26. Eric C. Brazil, "A Class of Their Own: 75-Year Anniversary Reveal Effects of System That Tracked Students by Race," *San Francisco Examiner* (November 21, 1999), 1, 12.

27. Ibid.

28. Interview with Virginia Rocca Barton by Carol Lynn McKibben (September 27, 2017), Salinas.

29. Ibid.

30. Ibid.; Teresa Douglass, "Children First," *Salinas Life* (April 25, 2015), 1C, 8C; Mildred Ramos, "Español with Ease," *California Teachers Association Journal*, 54 (8) (1958): 23–38.

31. See Natalia Mehlman Petrzela, *Classroom Wars: Language, Sex, and the Making of a Modern Political Culture* (New York: Oxford University Press, 2015).

32. Ramos, "Español with Ease."

33. Ibid.

34. Ibid., 38. Ramos wrote in glowing terms about the successes of the bilingual program:

> Every year the number of teachers wishing to teach Spanish increases. From a pilot program in one elementary school the idea has taken such fire that a majority of the teachers in all schools of the district are teaching Spanish Language experiences resulting from such a program equip pupils for more rapid progress in high school. They possess a language readiness denied others who do not study a second language at the elementary level. There are advantages in teaching another language at an age when the student has a natural ability to absorb it. This natural ability is at its peak in the early years and wanes with the approach of adolescence. With the feeling that a longer learning period is vital to the acquisition of another language, children who are introduced to the delights of speaking a foreign tongue at an early age will be able to take their place at the conference tables of the future and converse with the family of nations in each one's respective language.

35. Brazil, "A Class of Their Own."

36. "Complaint for Injunction and Declaratory Relief" (January 7, 1970), 2, *Diana v. California State Board of Education*, Civ. No. C-70, 37 RFP (N.D. Cal., 1970, 1973).

37. Phone interview with Everett Alvarez Jr. by Carol Lynn McKibben (August 24, 2018).

38. Ibid. Although Dockers were not introduced by Levi Strauss & Co. until much later, Everett Alvarez referred to the slacks worn by Salinas boys as "Dockers."

39. Interview with Albert Fong by Carol Lynn McKibben (March 7, 2019), Salinas.

40. Everett Alvarez Jr. phone interview (August 24, 2018).

41. "State Grants," *Salinas Californian* (October 5, 1950).

42. "Alisal Joins Salinas," *Salinas Californian* (June 12, 1963), 12.

43. Rodeo edition, *Salinas Californian* (July 1963), 48.

44. The minutes of Salinas City Council for the era show that almost every single meeting included debate about how the city could fund improvement projects for Alisal.

45. *Salinas: City in a Hurry*; see Robert O. Self, *American Babylon: Race and the Struggle for Postwar Oakland* (Princeton and Oxford: Princeton University Press, 2003), 23–61. Robert Self famously described the ideology behind Oakland's regional development as an "industrial garden," in which city leaders believed a carefully constructed mosaic of commercial, retail, and industrial development surrounded by suburban living would support a thriving city center. In a similar way, Salinas's city leaders conceived of a clear and determined strategy of urban development based on agricultural productivity, commerce, and industry that added population and provided a solid tax base, which in turn supported the development of the town itself, its schools, parks, recreation centers, and transportation systems. Like Oakland's city-builders, Salinas's leaders expected federal and state support as well in everything from urban development to the construction of highways.

46. Most industries left the area with the economic downturns of the 1970s and 1980s. The Bardin ranch provided a good example of rethinking uses for agricultural land. See Eric C. Brazil, "Old Hartnell Destroyed to Save Land," *Salinas Californian* (December 19, 1960), 1.

47. "Drug Concern to Locate here," *Salinas Californian* (October 26, 1950), 1.

48. "Firm Leases Building on Sanborn Road," *Salinas Californian* (October 26, 1950).

49. Email interview with Olga Reyna Garcia to Carol Lynn McKibben (July 6, 2020).

50. Ruth Andresen interview (November 6, 2018).

51. For a contextual analysis of environmentalism, both nationally and on the peninsula, see Connie Y. Chiang, *Shaping the Shoreline: Fisheries and Tourism on the Monterey Coast* (Seattle: University of Washington Press, 2008); Carol Lynn McKibben, *Beyond Cannery Row: Sicilian Women, Immigration, and Community in Monterey, California, 1915–99* (Urbana and Chicago: University of Illinois Press, 2006).

52. Ruth Andresen interview (November 6, 2018).

53. Ibid.

54. Ibid.

55. Ibid.

56. Ibid.

57. The environmental justice movement did not emerge until the 1990s, and intersected as it was with anti-racism, was off the radar for the mostly white liberal environmentalists of the 1970s.

58. See Mark Brilliant, *The Color of America Has Changed: How Racial Diversity Shaped*

Civil Rights Reform in California (Oxford: Oxford University Press, 2012), for an examination of how specific goals shaped the views and strategies of different minority communities in California in the postwar era.

59. "Top 10 Stories," *Salinas Californian* (December 31, 1970), 1.

60. There is an enormous scholarship on César Chávez and the rise of the United Farm Workers beginning with Ernesto Galarza, *Farmworkers and Agribusiness in California, 1947–1960* (Notre Dame: University of Notre Dame Press, 1977). See Frank Bardacke, *Trampling out the Vintage: César Chávez and the Two Souls of the United Farm Workers Movement* (London and New York: Verso, 2011); Matt Garcia, *From the Jaws of Victory: The Triumph and Tragedy of the United Farm Workers Movement* (Berkeley and Los Angeles: University of California Press, 2012); Miriam Pawel, *The Union of Their Dreams: Power, Hope, and Struggle in César Chávez's Farm Worker Movement* (New York: Bloomsbury Press, 2009). For Salinas, see Lori A. Flores, *Grounds for Dreaming: Mexican Americans, Mexican Immigrants, and the California Farmworker Movement* (New Haven: Yale University Press, 2016).

61. Interview with Bill Ramsey by Carol Lynn McKibben (April 12, 2017), offices of Mann Packing, Salinas.

62. See Flores, *Grounds for Dreaming*, 208.

63. Interview with Ruth Andresen by Carol Lynn McKibben (June 28, 2019), Salinas.

64. Olga Reyna Garcia email (July 6, 2020).

65. Ibid.

66. Ibid.

67. Eric C. Brazil, "Recognition Sought by Chávez's Union," *Salinas Californian* (July 25, 1970), 1.

68. Olga Reyna Garcia email (July 6, 2020).

69. Interview with Lucy Pizarro by Carol Lynn McKibben (August 24, 2019), Salinas.

70. Interview with Phyllis Meurer by Carol Lynn McKibben (June 5, 2019), Salinas.

71. Interview with Jack Armstrong by Carol Lynn McKibben (August 21, 2019), Salinas.

72. Ruth Andresen interview (June 28, 2019).

73. Ibid.

74. Ibid.

75. Olga Reyna Garcia email (July 6, 2020).

76. Ibid.

77. Ruth Andresen interview (June 28, 2019).

78. "Pic n Pac, Union Agree," *Salinas Californian* (October 9, 1970), 1.

79. Eric C. Brazil, "Chávez Furious: 30 Growers Sign Teamster Contract," *Salinas*

Californian (July 28, 1970), 1; numerous interviews with members of the Grower-Shipper Association who negotiated with Chávez and with Dolores Huerta reinforced the general critique of the UFW as fomenting a social revolution.

80. Eric C. Brazil wrote a number of articles on the topic: "Recognition Sought by Chavez's Union," *Salinas Californian* (July 25, 1970), 1; "Lettuce Boycott Called; Growers Stay Confident," *Salinas Californian* (September 17, 1970), 1; "Judge Enjoins Boycott of Antle's Produce," *Salinas Californian* (October 9, 1970); "State Court Lets Chávez out of Jail," *Salinas Californian* (December 24, 1970), 1. See also interviews with Ann Lisk, Simón Salinas, Susan Aremas, Philip Tabera, Phyllis Meurer, Linda Wong Gin, Ruth Andresen, Jack Armstrong, and Tom Nunes, among many other Salinas residents who experienced the era firsthand, by Carol Lynn McKibben (2018–2019), Salinas.

81. Ruth Andresen interview (June 28, 2019).

82. Flores, *Grounds for Dreaming*, 208.

83. Garcia, *From the Jaws of Victory*; Philip Martin, "Labor Relations in California Agriculture," University of California, Berkeley, 2001. https://escholarship.org/uc/item/6pd3x07d

84. See Bardacke, *Trampling out the Vintage*; Garcia, *From the Jaws of Victory*; Pawel, *The Union of Their Dreams*.

85. In fact, according to current GSA President Christopher Valdez, the decision by the Antle Company to sign with the Teamsters was complicated

by their own financial hardships and challenges at the time. Unionization may not have been an outcome of pressure resulting from changing social climate or limited to management and employee relations but may have been affected by other economic factors that were affecting the health of the business, and industry at that time. Hence, there may be more to the story here to influence the company's decision to sign with the Teamsters.

86. Tom Nunes, agricultural history of the Salinas Valley, courtesy to author (November 29, 2019).

87. F. Robert Nunes, *Foxy: The Creation of a Brand* (F. Robert Nunes, 2005), 55.

88. Garcia, *From the Jaws of Victory*; Nunes, *Foxy*.

89. Tom Nunes, agricultural history agricultural history of the Salinas Valley (November 29, 2019).

90. Ibid.

91. Minutes, Grower-Shipper Association (June 23, 1969), Grower-Shipper Association archive (February 6, 1969–December 18, 1970). The growers would supplement their workforce with students on their summer break.

92. See Charles Gordon, "The Amiable Fiction," *Case Western Reserve Journal of International Law*, 1 (2) (1969): 124–130; minutes, Grower-Shipper

Association (September 10, 1969), Grower-Shipper Association archive (February 6, 1969–December 18, 1970).

93. Ibid.

94. Minutes, Grower-Shipper Association (February 6, 1969), Grower-Shipper Association archive (February 6, 1969–December 18, 1970).

95. See Carey McWilliams, *California: The Great Exception* (Berkeley: University of California Press, 1974), 150–170.

96. Minutes, Grower-Shipper Association (June 6, 1969), Grower-Shipper Association archive (February 6, 1969–December 18, 1970).

97. See Edward Moncrief, *Raising the Blackbirds* (Salinas: Singwillow Publishing, 2016).

98. Sixto Torres quoting Moncrief's *Raising the Blackbirds*.

99. Minutes, Grower-Shipper Association (March 4, 1969), 4, Grower-Shipper Association archive (February 6, 1969–December 18, 1970).

100. Minutes, Grower-Shipper Association (June 23, 1969), Grower-Shipper Association archive (February 6, 1969–December 18, 1970).

101. Olga Reyna Garcia email (July 6, 2020); Claudia Meléndez Salinas, "New Rules on Pesticide Use Near Schools Take Effect," *Monterey Herald* (January 2, 2018); Lauren J. Stein, Robert B. Gunier, Kim Harley, Katherine Kogut, Asa Bradman, and Brenda Eskenazi, "Early Childhood Adversity Potentiates the Adverse Association Between Prenatal Organophosphate Pesticide Exposure and Child IQ: The CHAMACOS Cohort," *NeuroToxicology*, 56: https://doi.org/10.1016/j.neuro.2016.07.010

102. Ron Strochlic, et al., "The Agricultural Worker Health Study: Case Study No. 5 Salinas Valley," California Institute for Rural Studies (June 2003).

103. Christopher R. Henke, *Cultivating Science, Harvesting Power: Science and Industrial Agriculture in California* (Cambridge, MA: MIT Press, 2008).

104. Minutes, Grower-Shipper Association (July 14, 1970).

105. Phone interview with Terrence O'Connor by Azucena Marquez (February 23, 2018).

106. Richard Chávez, Negotiation Division, memo to César Chávez, Dolores Huerta, et al., "RE: What Is Happening in Negotiations?" (August 2, 1980).

107. See Brilliant, *The Color of America Has Changed*, for an examination of how specific goals shaped the views and strategies of different minority communities in California in the postwar era.

108. Edwin B. Almirol, *Ethnic Identity and Social Negotiation: A Study of a Filipino Community in California* (New York: AMS Press, 1985), 111.

109. Ibid.

110. Ibid., 111–112. For an analysis of the history of the short-handled hoe and the relationship with the UFW, see Taylor Cozzens, "Defeating the Devil's Arm:

The Victory over the Short-Handled Hoe in California Agriculture," *Agricultural History*, 89 (4) (Fall 2015): 494–512.

111. Almirol, *Ethnic Identity and Social Negotiation*, 112.

112. Interview with Susan Aremas by Carol Lynn McKibben (September 19, 2019), Salinas.

113. Ibid.

114. Ibid.

115. Letter to Grower-Shipper Association in author's possession, found in box of newspaper clippings at Salinas GSA office in basement. For their part, the association denied any role in coordinating any effort associated with soliciting or supporting goon squads, according to Christopher Valdez, current GSA president.

116. Ibid.

117. James D. Cockcroft, *Outlaws in the Promised Land: Mexican American Workers and America's Future* (New York: Grove Press, 1986).

118. *Englund v. Chávez*, 8 Cal.3d 572, Azucena Marquez, "Unintended consequences: Labor and Law in Salinas, California, 1970-1980," unpublished paper, 2018.

119. See Daniel Martinez HoSang, *Racial Propositions: Ballot Initiatives and the Making of Postwar California* (Berkeley: University of California Press, 2010).

120. César Chávez, "Farm Workers Initiative Is Needed to Guard Abuses, 1976," *Los Angeles Times* (April 8, 1976).

121. Interview with Maria Belen Loredo by Savannah Delgadillo (February 17, 2018), Salinas, Azucena Marquez, "Unintended consequences: Labor and Law in Salinas, California, 1970-1980," unpublished paper, 2018.

122. Interview with Miguel A. Delgadillo Lomeli by Savannah Delgadillo (February 17, 2018), Salinas, Azucena Marquez, "Unintended consequences: Labor and Law in Salinas, California, 1970-1980," unpublished paper, 2018.

123. Martin, "Labor Relations in California Agriculture"; see also Garcia, *From the Jaws of Victory*; Pawel, *The Union of Their Dreams*.

124. Zoom interview with Tom Nunes by Carol Lynn McKibben and Matt Garcia (May 28, 2020).

125. Ibid.

126. Ibid.

127. Ibid.

128. Ibid.

129. The following narrative came from F. Robert Nunes, *Foxy: The Creation of a Brand* (F. Robert Nunes, 2005), 25; interview with Nunes family by Carol Lynn McKibben (July 10, 2019), Salinas; Tom Nunes Zoom interview (May 28, 2020).

130. Ibid.

131. Nunes, *Foxy*.

132. Ibid.; Nunes family interview (July 10, 2019; Tom Nunes Zoom interview (May 28, 2020).

133. Ibid.

134. The packaging was invented by Edward H. "Ted" Taylor, son-in-law to one of Salinas's earliest and most successful shippers, Bruce Church. Taylor's label was Fresh Express.

135. Interview with James Lugg by Carol Lynn McKibben (March 19, 2018), Salinas.

136. Ibid.

137. Ibid.

138. Nunes, *Foxy*, 25; interview with Nunes family by Carol Lynn McKibben (July 10, 2019), Salinas; Tom Nunes Zoom interview (May 28, 2020).

139. Ibid.

140. Tom Nunes Zoom interview (May 28, 2020).

141. Ibid.

142. Ibid.

143. Bruce Church was one of the original founders of Salinas Valley Memorial Hospital and its first board president. His daughter and son-in-law, JoAnne and Ted Taylor, followed his example, not only supporting the hospital and other Salinas-based institutions through numerous fundraising activities, but also sponsoring communitywide events such as the annual Cherries Jubilee Car Show in August that raised funds for the hospital and other nonprofits in the city.

CHAPTER 8

1. Interview with Jack Armstrong by Carol Lynn McKibben (August 21, 2019).

2. Interview with Ruth Andresen by Carol Lynn McKibben (July 23, 2015), Salinas.

3. See Alex Schafran, *The Road to Resegregation: Northern California and the Failure of Politics* (Berkeley and Los Angeles: University of California Press, 2018); Robert O. Self, *American Babylon: Race and the Struggle for Postwar Oakland* (Princeton: Princeton University Press, 2003).

4. Interview with Lucy Pizarro by Carol Lynn McKibben (August 24, 2019), Salinas.

5. Interview with Simón Salinas by Carol Lynn McKibben (June 5, 2019), Salinas.

6. Tom Nunes, agricultural history of the Salinas Valley, courtesy to author (November 29, 2019).

7. Interview with Simón Salinas by Carol Lynn McKibben (March 12, 2020), Carmel.

8. See Daniel Martinez HoSang, *Racial Propositions: Ballot Initiatives and the Making of Postwar California* (Berkeley: University of California Press, 2010).

9. Proposition 13 decimated city coffers by removing the power of local municipalities to raise property taxes that funded infrastructure, libraries, and schools. The towns and cities like Salinas with increasingly large minority populations and poor people were the hardest hit by the loss of funding that Prop 13 created. See interview with former Salinas City Manager Dave Mora by Carol Lynn McKibben (March 14, 2019), Salinas; Schafran, *The Road to Resegregation*; Self, *American Babylon*.

10. See City of Salinas, Community Economic Profile, 1970–1978, City of Salinas and Salinas Chamber of Commerce (November 1978), Local History, John Steinbeck Library. According to this document, the population of the city increased from 13,917 in 1950 to 28,957 by 1960 and by 1978 reached 78,402. Taxable retail sales (no information available for 1950) in 1960 was $78,471,000, but by 1978 had increased dramatically to $413,167,000. The total number of dwellings in the city grew from 4,371 in 1950 to 8,550 in 1960 to 25,326 in 1978, showing continued efforts by the city to support increases in housing development as the population increased. These figures are supported by numerous firsthand accounts of stability and economic growth, despite labor conflicts, the national recession, and Reagan's spending cuts in California. Interview with Vern Horton by Carol Lynn McKibben (October 1, 2019), Salinas. Horton was born and raised in Alisal to working-class parents but rose to prominence in the banking industry in Salinas and Monterey County. As of this writing, he was retired maintained a presence as president and CEO, Capital One Bank, Salinas.

11. See City of Salinas, Community Economic Profile, 1970–1978. Interview with Vern Horton by Carol Lynn McKibben (October 1, 2019).

12. Minutes, Salinas City Council (November 3, 1969).

13. Minutes, Salinas City Council (January 12, 1970).

14. Minutes, Salinas City Council (July 26, 1971).

15. Minutes, Salinas City Council (August 2, 1971).

16. *Salinas Californian* (December 31, 1975), 1.

17. "Salinas: Some Noses Were up in the Air and Others Were out of Joint," *Salinas Californian* (December 31, 1977), 5.

18. California Action Desk, "Questions on Anti-Poverty Council," *Salinas Californian* (February 5, 1968), 1.

19. *Salinas Californian* (December 31, 1969), 1–2.

20. Minutes, Salinas City Council (December 8, 1969). Information about the War Lords in this paragraph and next comes from this city council meeting.

21. Ibid.; *Salinas Californian* (December 31, 1969), 1–2.

22. "Principal Expresses Need for Better Communication," *Salinas Californian* (October 29, 1971), 1.

23. Minutes, Salinas City Council (October 6, 1969).

24. *Salinas Californian* (December 31, 1974), 1.

25. See Schafran, *The Road to Resegregation.*

26. Ibid.; Self, *American Babylon.*

27. "Annexation Approved for Emporium Proposal," *Salinas Californian* (July 23, 1968), 1.

28. By contrast, the Vibrancy plans for both Main Street and Alisal, which happened simultaneously under City Manager Ray Corpuz in 2014–2019, were arduous processes, but they gave Salinas residents from every interest group and ethnic community a place at the planning table. Interview with Lisa Britton and Jonathan Moore, city planners, and with Andy Myrick, economic development manager, by Carol Lynn McKibben (March 23, 2017), Salinas.

29. "Reagan Bares 5.7 Billion Budget," *Salinas Californian* (February 5, 1968), 1.

30. Minutes, Salinas City Council (October 6, 1969).

31. Dave Mora interview (March 14, 2019).

32. Michelle Alexander, *The New Jim Crow: Mass Incarceration in the Age of Colorblindness* (New York: New Press, 2011), inspired a new scholarly analysis of the impact of mass incarceration on minorities in the United States beginning in the 1970s.

33. "Prison Farm Purchase Near Soledad OK'D," *Santa Cruz Sentinel* (March 8, 1946), 1.

34. "State Medium Security Prison at Soledad," *Salinas Californian* (February 4, 1950), 17.

35. Ibid.

36. "Buffet Nine Has Practice Set Sunday," *Salinas Californian* (February 21, 1950), 11.

37. "Inmates Give Blood Bank Best Day Yet," *Salinas Californian* (October 9, 1950), 2.

38. "Employment Picture in Area Bright," *Salinas Californian* (January 5, 1950), 3.

39. "Prison 'Gang' Attacks and Kill Soledad Felon," *Salinas Californian* (February 22, 1965).

40. Eric C. Brazil, "Black Muslim Petitions Federal Court . . . Soledad Inmate Files $1 Million Civil Rights Suit," *Salinas Californian* (August 10, 1966), 1.

41. "Top Ten Stories," *Salinas Californian* (December 31, 1970), 2.

42. Eve Pell, "The Soledad Brothers: How a Prison Picks Its Victims," *Ramparts Magazine* (August 31, 1970), 48–52.

43. For a thorough analysis of the history of gang activity associated with the prison, see Julia Reynolds, *Blood in the Fields: Ten Years Inside California's Nuestra Familia Gang* (Chicago: Chicago Review Press, 2014).

44. Lucy Pizarro interview (August 24, 2019).

45. Walter Neary, "New Districts Change City's Politics," *Salinas Californian* (October 14, 1991), 1B.

46. Interview with Anna Caballero by Mariela Pizarro (September 15, 2019), Salinas.

47. Ibid.

48. Ibid.

49. Ibid.

50. Interview with Simón Salinas and Phyllis Meurer by Carol Lynn McKibben (June 5, 2019), Salinas.

51. Ibid.

52. Ibid.

53. Interview with Simón Salinas by Carol Lynn McKibben (June 5, 2019), Salinas.

54. Ibid.

55. Ralph Portuondo, who was of Cuban descent, was the first Latino/a elected to the Salinas City Council in 1985.

56. Simón Salinas and Phyllis Meurer interview (June 5, 2019).

57. Ibid.

58. Ibid..

59. Ibid.

60. Ibid.

61. Simón Salinas interview (June 5, 2019).

62. Simón Salinas and Phyllis Meurer interview (June 5, 2019).

63. Walter Neary, "Interview with Jess Sanchez: North Salinas Council Race Heats Up," *Salinas Californian* (January 25, 1991), 3C.

64. Walter Neary, "Interview with Anna Caballero: North Salinas Council Race Heats Up," *Salinas Californian* (January 25, 1991), 3C.

65. State of the Cities Data Systems, SOCDS, "Census Data: Salinas, CA": https://www.huduser.gov/portal/datasets/socds.html

66. Ibid.

67. Walter Neary, "New Districts Change City's Politics," *Salinas Californian* (October 14, 1991), 1B.

68. Anna Caballero interview (September 15, 2019).

69. Phone interview with Gloria De La Rosa by Carol Lynn McKibben (August 5, 2020).

70. Anna Caballero interview (September 15, 2019).

71. See McKibben, *Racial Beachhead*.

72. Dave Mora interview (March 27, 2019).

73. Ibid.

74. In August 2014, city council members Tony Barrera, Kimbley Craig, and Steve McShane had grilled Elizabeth Martinez over her inability to raise private funding to repay $125,000 to the city's general fund that Mayor Donohue wanted to

be used to renovate a sculpture in Sherwood Park. The exchange between Martinez and the city council members became so heated that Martinez resigned and won a $400,000 harassment lawsuit with the city.

75. Dave Mora interview (March 27, 2019).

76. Joe Szydlowski, "Housing Focus of New State Budget," *Salinas Californian* (January 12, 2019), 2A.

77. Barbara Paris, "Interview with Dave Mora: Officials Say Improvements in Salinas' Infrastructure Are Strangled by Lack of Funds and Planning," *Monterey County Weekly* (February 25, 1999).

78. Anna Caballero interview (September 15, 2019).

79. Eric C. Brazil, "Old Hartnell Destroyed to Save Land," *Salinas Californian* (December 19, 1960), 1.

80. Lupe Castillo, Letters, *Salinas Californian* (March 10, 1999), 1.

81. See Richard Rothstein, *The Color of Law: A Forgotten History of How Our Government Segregated America* (New York: Norton, 2017).

82. See minutes, Salinas City Council (February 2, 1999). Collins asked rhetorically at the meeting:

> Will we have the infrastructure to support this growth? No, not at this time. This is a good development. There is no question that good development is needed on the east side, but we have to look at what is good for the whole city. If you look at the big picture that encompasses cumulative effects, it adds to various systems that exceed capacity. . . . My arguments came right out of the environmental impact report.

83. See multiple works by Robert D. Bullard on the impact of racism and racist policies on minority communities, beginning with Robert D. Bullard ed., *Unequal Protection: Environmental Justice and Communities of Color* (San Francisco: Sierra Club, 1994).

84. See Laura R. Barraclough, *Making the San Fernando Valley: Rural Landscapes, Urban Development, and White Privilege* (Athens: University of Georgia Press, 2011).

85. Self, *American Babylon*; Straus, *Death of a Suburban Dream*.

86. See Self, *American Babylon*, 177–255, and Thomas J. Sugrue, *The Origins of the Urban Crisis: Race and Inequality in Postwar Detroit* (Princeton: Princeton University Press, 1996). For a good analysis of the impact on Compton, see Straus, *Death of a Suburban Dream*. For the impact in a minority-majority community near Salinas, see McKibben, *Racial Beachhead*.

87. Zachary Stahl, "Council Will Hold off Cuts," *Salinas Californian* (November 17, 2004), 1.

88. Ibid.

89. Associated Press, "Closures Catch Eye of Library Group: Issue Puts City in Unwanted Spotlight," *Salinas Californian* (December 27, 2004).

90. Phone interview with Donna Elder by Carol Lynn McKibben (April 26, 2020).

91. "Library Director Moves On: John Gross Leaves Legacy of Literature," *Salinas Californian* (August 31, 1990), 1C.

92. Ibid., 3C.

93. Betty Farrell Doty, "Steinbeck Foundation Forms to Honor Author," *Salinas Californian* (February 26, 1977), 28.

94. See Erika Lee Doss, *Memorial Mania: Public Feeling in America* (Chicago: University of Chicago Press, 2010); Andrew Hurley, *Beyond Preservation: Using Public History to Revitalize Inner Cities* (Philadelphia: Temple University Press, 2010); Johanna Miller Lewis, "Build a Museum and They Will Come: The Creation of the Central High Museum and Visitor Center," *Public Historian*, 22 (4) (Autumn 2000): 29–45.

95. See Doss, *Memorial Mania*; Dolores Hayden, *The Power of Place: Urban landscapes as Public History* (Cambridge, MA: MIT Press,1995); Hurley, *Beyond Preservation*; Lewis, "Build a Museum and They Will Come"; Edward T. Linenthal, "Committing History in Public," *Journal of American History*, 81 (1994): 986–991.

96. Lynn Christensen, "Timeline of the Redevelopment Efforts in Oldtown Salinas," *Salinas Californian* (January 27, 1996), 8A.

97. Ibid.

98. "Support Plans to Build the New Steinbeck Center," *Salinas Californian* (January 14, 1995), 4A.

99. Jim Gattis email to Carol Lynn McKibben (March 11, 2020).

100. J. Kyle Henley, "Officials Hoping to Boost Tourism," *Salinas Californian* (October 2, 1997), 1.

101. Jim Gattis email (March 11, 2020).

102. David Legare, "Critic: Steinbeck Center a Misfit in Oldtown," *Salinas Californian* (February 22, 1997), 6A.

103. Doss, *Memorial Mania*.

104. John Steinbeck, "Steinbeck View of Row Less Than Romantic," *Monterey Peninsula Herald*,1957 (reprinted June 1, 1997), n.p., courtesy of Peter Kasavan.

105. J. Michael Rivera, "Steinbeck Center an Anchor of Oldtown Attractions," *Salinas Californian* (April 26, 2001), 39.

106. Zachary Stahl, "Museum Grows: Attendance Slips Since '98 Opening," *Salinas Californian* (March 25–26, 2006), 1A.

107. Mike Hornick, "Steinbeck Center's Colleen Bailey Newsmaker of the Year," *Salinas Californian* (January 1–2 2011), 5A.

108. See Connie Y. Chiang, *Shaping the Shoreline: Fisheries and Tourism on the Monterey*

Coast (Seattle: University of Washington Press, 2008); Carol Lynn McKibben, *Beyond Cannery Row: Sicilian Women, Immigration, and Community in Monterey, California, 1915–99* (Urbana and Chicago: University of Illinois Press, 2006).

CHAPTER 9

1. Keynote address at opening of Forbes AgTech Summit (June 29, 2017), Salinas.

2. See the County of Monterey Health Department: https://www.co.monterey.ca.us/government/departments-a-h/health/diseases/2019-novel-coronavirus-covid-19/2019-novel-coronavirus-2019-ncov-local-data-10219#sumaryreport

3. Interview with Dennis Donahue by Carol Lynn McKibben (February 18, 2017), Salinas.

4. Alison Gatlin, "Interview with Raul Damien Tapia: Not a Gang Problem, a Poverty Problem," *Salinas Californian* (November 15, 2014), 14.

5. Although the national and state average for homicides per 100,000 people decreased from 1990 to 2020, Salinas's crime rate increased; there was some decline in 2005–2006 but it rose again beginning in 2008. Salinas's homicide rate in 2013 was 31 percent higher than in the rest of Monterey County. See Tracy L. Onufer, "Understanding Environmental Factors That Affect Violence in Salinas, California" (2009): https://calhoun.nps.edu/handle/10945/4466

6. Ashley D. Macias, "Gangs in Salinas: A Decade of Failure? A Decade of Success?" California State University, Monterey Bay (September 2016).

7. Louis Fetherolf, "90-Day Report to the Community" (July 21, 2009): https://www.cityofsalinas.org/sites/default/files/services/police/pdf/90-DayReport-071909.pdf, 6.

8. Onufer, "Environmental Factors That Affect Violence in Salinas," 5.

9. Ibid., 6.

10. City of Salinas, "Alisal Neighborhood Revitalization Strategy Area, 2015": https://www.cityofsalinas.org/sites/default/files/departments_files/community_development_files/housing_division_files/alisal_neighborhood_revitalization_strategy_area_2015.pdf, 4.

11. Ibid., 8.

12. "Lost Youth: A County-by-County Analysis of 2013 California Homicide Victims Ages 10 to 24" (Washington, DC: Violence Policy Center, 2015), 23.

13. "Lost Youth," 2.

14. U.S. Department of Justice, Bureau of Justice Statistics, "Crime Reported by Salinas Police Department, California": https://www.salinaspd.org/

15. Ibid.

16. Interview with Simón Salinas by Carol Lynn McKibben (June 5, 2019), Salinas.

17. See Lawrence D. Bobo and Victor Thompson, "Unfair by Design: The War on Drugs, Race, and the Legitimacy of the Criminal Justice System," *Social Research: An International Quarterly*, 73 (2) (2006): 445–472; Malcolm D. Holmes, Brad W. Smith, Adrienne B. Freng, and Ed A. Muñoz, "Minority Threat, Crime Control, and Police Resource Allocation in the Southwestern United States," *Crime and Delinquency*, 54 (2008): 128–152.

18. Elva Martinez, "Gangs in Salinas: What Motivates Young People into Joining Gangs?" California State University, Monterey Bay (September 2015).

19. Onufer, "Environmental Factors That Affect Violence in Salinas."

20. See Julia Reynolds, *Blood in the Fields: Ten Years Inside California's Nuestra Familia Gang* (Chicago: Chicago Review Press, 2014).

21. Martinez, "Gangs in Salinas."

22. Ibid.

23. Ibid.

24. Ibid.

25. Ibid.

26. Ibid.

27. Macias, "Gangs in Salinas."

28. Ibid.

29. Ibid.

30. Ibid.

31. Ibid.

32. See Lisa Eiseman, *The First Policewoman: A History of the Salinas Police Department* (Trafford Press, 2005), 245.

33. Onufer, "Environmental Factors That Affect Violence in Salinas."

34. See Natalia Mehlman Petrzela, *Classroom Wars: Language, Sex, and the Making of a Modern Political Culture* (New York: Oxford University Press, 2015).

35. "Sharp IQ Increases Shown by Mexican-American Students," *Los Angeles Times* (May 9, 1969); "Wrong Results from IQ Tests," *San Francisco Chronicle* (January 27, 1970).

36. *Diana v. State Board of Education, Lau v. Nichols,* and *Larry P v. Riles.*

37. In *Lau,* non–English-speaking Chinese students brought a class action suit in which they argued that the San Francisco Unified School District's failure to provide equal educational opportunities for children who did not speak English amounted to a violation of the Fourteenth Amendment. In his deciding opinion on January 21, 1974, Justice Douglas ordered that "the district must take affirmative steps to rectify the language deficiency in order to open its instructional program to these students." See Petrzela, *Classroom Wars*, 75–76.

38. See www.californiataxdata.com

39. See Gloria Penner, G., Megan Burke, and Natalie Walsh, "Prop 13's Impact on Schools": https://www.kpbs.org/news/2010/mar/26/prop-13s-impact-schools/

40. See Donald L. McMillan, Irving G. Hendrick, and Alice V. Watkins, "Impact of *Diana, Larry P.,* and PL 94–142 on Minority Students," *Exceptional Children*: https://journals.sagepub.com/doi/10.1177/001440298805400505

41. "Dropout: Monterey County Rate Climbs," *Salinas Californian* (May 26, 1994), 2C

42. "Bilingual Education," *Salinas Californian* (November 22, 1997), 6A; see Petrzela, *Classroom Wars.*

43. See Daniel Martinez HoSang, *Racial Propositions: Ballot Initiatives and the Making of Postwar California* (Berkeley: University of California Press, 2010), ch. 7; "Local Views: Unz Initiative Hits Home," *Salinas Californian* (May 23, 1998).

44. See Onufer, "Environmental Factors That Affect Violence in Salinas."

45. "State Steps in at 2 Local Schools," *Salinas Californian* (March 12, 2010), 1, 8.

46. Onufer, "Environmental Factors That Affect Violence in Salinas."

47. Interview with Susan Aremas by Carol Lynn McKibben (September 19, 2019), Salinas.

48. "Local Schools Score Below Stat," *Salinas Californian* (January 26, 2000), 1.

49. Ibid., 1, 8.

50. Phone interview with Corliss Kelly, AVID educator, by Carol Lynn McKibben (February 27, 2020).

51. Jeremiah Armstrong, "El Sausal Students Take Part in College Prep Program," *Salinas Californian* (December 10, 1996), 13.

52. Ibid.

53. Onufer, "Environmental Factors That Affect Violence in Salinas."

54. "State Steps in at 2 Local Schools."

55. Israel Villa, "How a Community Organization Took Control of a Nonprofit Community Group in Salinas," *Voices of Monterey Bay* (October 24, 2019).

56. Ibid.

57. Onufer, "Environmental Factors That Affect Violence in Salinas."

58. See Delia Gomez, Alisal Union School District Local Control Accountability Plan, https://www.alisal.org/cms/lib/CA02215153/Centricity/Domain/213/2017-20-LCAPDRAFT.6.28.171.pdf

59. Email interview with Peter Kasavan by Carol Lynn McKibben (March 14, 2020).

60. Interview with Lisa Brinton and Jonathon Moore by Carol Lynn McKibben (March 23, 2017), Salinas.

61. City of Salinas, Economic Development Element: http://www.emcplanning.com/about_us/1_Salinas_EDE_Vol_I_040214_sm.pdf

62. "Salinas Spoke, Library Listened," *Salinas Californian* (February 21, 2020).

Index